IN SICKNESS AND IN HEALTH

To Our Mothers

IN SICKNESS AND IN HEALTH

The British Experience 1650–1850

Roy Porter

and

Dorothy Porter

Fourth Estate · London

First published in Great Britain in 1988 by
Fourth Estate Ltd
113 Westbourne Grove
London W2 4UP

British Library Cataloguing in Publication Data

Porter, Roy, 1946–
   In Sickness and In Health: The British experience
   1650–1850.
   1. England. Man. Health 1650–1850. Social
   aspects
   I. Title II. Porter, Dorothy
   362.1′042′0942

   ISBN 0-947795-77-4

Typeset in Plantin by York House Typographic, London
Printed and bound in Great Britain by The Bath Press, Avon

C O N T E N T S

ACKNOWLEDGEMENTS

This book has been several years in the making, and the authors have benefited during this time from conversations with, and pre-publication access to the writings of, scholars far too numerous to name here. We offer them our hearty collective thanks. We would, however, like to single out for mention Mary Fissell, Marie Roberts, Sylvana Tomaselli and Andrew Wear, who have made extremely helpful comments on earlier drafts. At various stages our researches have been greatly helped by Ben Barkow, Anne Darlington and Jenny Wood, and in the final stages Sally Bragg has worked wonders on the word-processor. As always the Wellcome Institute has provided the ideal milieu for research; we would particularly like to thank the library staff for so efficiently obtaining books on Inter-Library Loan and Andy Foley for his hours on the photocopier.

We are furthermore greatly indebted to all who have helped to put this book so speedily, so efficiently, and so pleasurably into production. Jean Runciman proved, as ever, an excellent critic as well as copy-editor, and we are most grateful to Mrs Judy Batchelor for spotting errors while making her first-rate index. Not least, we wish to express our gratitude to all at Fourth Estate, Michael Mason, Jane Charteris and Vicky Barnsley in particular, for their unflagging encouragement and enthusiasm with this project.

Chapter 1:
Introduction

In June 1714, Mr Spectator invited his readers to imagine a convocation of all the 'Misfortunes of Mankind'. Alongside those that were self-inflicted (for instance, the 'Bundles of Calamities' smiting 'Multitudes of Lovers'), and those too trivial to justify complaint (the 'Wrinkles' of 'Old Women', with their 'red Noses', 'large Lips, and rusty Teeth'), there were genuine maladies aplenty. Not least 'among this Collection of humane Miseries', 'the greatest Part of the Mountain [was] made up of bodily Deformities', and 'there were likewise Distempers of all Sorts'.[1]

This Spectatorial vision of universal sickness, suffering and woe contained, of course, nothing novel. The ubiquity of disease and death in this lapsarian vale of tears had, after all, been a favourite theme of popular piety right through medieval times, reinforced in seventeenth-century England by Puritan ideas of original sin and the humanist conceit of *mundus senescens*, which saw Creation itself undergoing the physical dissolution of old age. Melancholy, mutability and mortality, deformation and decay, sin and sorrow defined the sublunary condition of man, according to playwrights, poets, and preachers from Shakespeare through Swift to Sterne:

> The weariness, the fever, and the fret
> Here where men sit and hear each other groan;
> Where palsy shakes a few sad last grey hairs
> Where youth grows pale, and spectre-thin and dies;

added Romantic exactitude to the tradition.[2]

But to acknowledge that it was a cultural commonplace to portray man as a diseased being groaning in an expiring world is not to say it was merely a topos or to belittle the awesomeness of sickness for individual sufferers. The findings of historical demographers and epidemiologists, of medical and social historians alike, have converged to create a Boschian panorama spanning the whole of the seventeenth century, and the first half, at least, of the eighteenth, as an epoch when populations proved exceptionally susceptible to wave upon wave of deadly epidemics. Most fearsome, of course, under the early Stuarts, was bubonic plague. In terms of aggregate long-term incidence, deaths, and disturbance, however, smallpox proved a far more daunting foe. 'The small pox has been very much here', wrote Elizabeth Purefoy from darkest Buckinghamshire in 1737, 'and all who have had it (but one) died'.[3]

In the eighteenth century in particular, deadly fevers – contemporaries called them 'spotted', 'miliary', 'hectic', 'malignant', etc. – struck down hundreds of thousands, young and old alike,[4] while the so-called 'new' diseases gained ground – some crippling, such as rickets; some fatal, such as tuberculosis. Today's minor nuisance, like 'flu, was yesterday's killer.[5] 'The Hooping Cough is yet with us', wrote George Crabbe in 1829, '& many children die of it.'[6] And all this against a background of endemic maladies, such as malaria and infantile diarrhoea, and a Pandora's box of other infections (dysentery, scarlatina, measles, etc.) that commonly proved fatal, above all to infants, to say nothing of a hundred and one other pains, eruptions, swellings, ulcers, scrofula, and wasting conditions, not least the agonizing stone and the proverbial gout, which threatened livings and livelihoods, and all too often life itself.[7]

Resistance to infection was evidently weak. This is hardly surprising. Precipitate demographic rise under the Tudors, followed by climatic reverses and economic crises under the Stuarts, had swollen the ranks of the malnourished poor.[8] New and virulent strains of disease possibly emerged. England's good communications network and high job and geographical mobility – it was a land of 'movers' rather than 'stayers' – proved favourable to disease spread: the market society meant free trade in maladies. Few settlements were far enough off the beaten track to escape epidemic visitations travelling along the trade routes (out-of-the-way places could, however, have impressively high life expectancies).[9] And yet the regionality of what was still largely a rural society also meant that disease spread erratically and patchily, with the consequence that there was always a large reservoir of susceptibles, not yet immune, especially amongst the young, ready sacrificial victims to smallpox or scarlet fever.

Above all, pre-modern medicine had few effective weapons against the infections from which people died like flies. Once smallpox, enteric fever, or pneumonia struck, doctors fought a losing battle. In the generation after 1720, the population of England and Wales actually *declined*, primarily because of the ravages of epidemic disease.[10]

Our understanding of the biology of man in history has vastly improved. As yet, however, little attention has been paid to what this ceaseless Darwinian war between disease and populations meant to the individual, considering disease neither as a black block on a histogram nor just as a trope about the human condition betwixt womb and tomb, but as experienced torment and terror. Every soul lived in the shadow of death; indeed, being in the land of the living was itself the survivor's privilege, for so many of one's peers – one's brothers and sisters – had already fallen by the wayside, having died at birth, in infancy or childhood. Life's fine thread was ever precarious,[11] and every statistic hides a personal tragedy. The historical record abounds with sad tales of those who ate a hearty breakfast in the pink of health, only to be dead of apoplexy or convulsions, plague or, later, cholera, before the week was out. Elizabeth Iremonger told her friend Miss Heber the sad tale of her nephew's wife, Eleanor Iremonger, whose delivery of a boy was followed a week later by a 'fever that baffled all art and, on the ninth morning, she sunk finally to this World!'[12]

'Many dyed sudden deaths lately', lamented the late-Stuart Nonconformist minister, Oliver Heywood, ever alert to the workings of Providence:[13]

> 1, Nathan Crosly buryed Octob 25 1674, 2, Timothy Wadsworth, dyed Octob 23 suddenly in his chair without sickness, 3, Edw Brooks wife dyed under the cow as she was milking, 4, a woman at great Horton wel, had a tooth drawn, cryed oh my head laid her hand on, dyed immediately, 5, one Richard Hodgsons wife at Bradford on munday Nov. 2, dyed on tuesday the day after, &c.

Over a century later, the Somerset parson, William Holland, marked the bitter fate of a father buried on the day his child was christened.[14] Amidst the bumper harvest of the Great Reaper recorded in the *Gentleman's Magazine* obituary columns, many expired when apparently in the prime of health – cut off by mad-dog bites, by sudden strokes, or through travelling accidents ('I shall begin to think from my frequent overturns', quipped Elizabeth Montagu, 'a bone-setter a necessary part of my equipage for country visiting').[15] Accidents are not unique to modern technology and urbanism. A Norwich newspaper noted in 1790 how:[16]

> On Thursday last (March) a fine boy, about five years of age, fell thro' the seat of the necessary belonging to Mr. Mapes, in the Hay-market, the reservoir to which is not less than 40 feet deep; in this shocking situation he remained from a quarter past ten till three o'clock in the afternoon, before he was discovered by his cries. A person immediately went down to his relief, and when he had raised him halfway up, the bucket in which the child was, striking against a timber that had not been perceived, he was again precipitated to the bottom head forward.

This child survived, so did others, for instance James Clegg, the Derbyshire minister-cum-doctor, who reported 'a very merciful deliverance when mounting [his] mare'.[17] Many, however, fared worse, such as Thomas Day, leading light of the Lunar Society, who died after being thrown from a half-broken-in horse. Visitations came out of the blue, and some deaths were particularly cruel. A Mrs Fitzgerald went to the theatre, and laughed so much she laughed herself to death. Or take the exemplary exit of the Rev. Mr M'Kill, pastor of Bankend in Scotland, so 'remarkable' that it 'made an impression upon the minds of his parishioners':[18]

He mounted the pulpit in good health, lectured as usual, and it being the last sabbath of the year, chose for his text these words, 'we spend our years as a tale that is told'. He was representing, in a very pathetic manner, the fleeting nature of human life, and of all earthly things, when, on a sudden, he dropped down in the pulpit and expired instantly.

'He looks much better than you would imagine', Lady Jane Coke assured a friend about her husband's convalescence on 26 February 1750: 'sleeps well, and I think I may assure you that he is better to-day than he has been for some time, so that I hope the worst is over'. She tempted fate: before sunset, he was dead.[19]

Disease was matched by other dangers, even oncoming thunderstorms. 'William Church', writes the pious Isabella Tindal, 'was speaking to my son John at the time, and saying "The Lord cometh in his chariot, in the clouds to gather his people to himself" . . . he was struck by the lightning . . . and fell down dead.'[20] Falls, drownings, fires, firearm explosions, mishaps with tools, knives and poisons, and traffic accidents were perpetual hazards, not least because without ambulance and casualty services, trauma or blood-loss readily proved fatal before effectual medical aid was forthcoming.[21] William III, of course, died after his horse stumbled on a mole-hill (Jacobites toasted the little gentleman in velvet), and the third Cambridge Professor of History met his end tumbling off his horse while drunk. The Rev. Ralph Josselin recorded scores of such mishaps, or as he saw them, 'Providences':[22]

I heard that Major Cletheroe, September 21, coming homewards at Redgewell his Horse, stumbled and fell downe upon him and brake his bowells, he was taken up and spake but he dyed about 4 or 5 hours later, Lord in how many dangerous falls and stumbles hast thou preserved mee . . . .

Most ironically of all, William Stout, the Lancaster Quaker who distrusted doctors and championed self-care, received his first blow in years – a broken leg – when he was run down by the local surgeon's horse.[23]

Some mortifications of the flesh had their black comedy: 'Up, and to the office,' wrote Pepys, '(having a mighty pain in my forefinger of my left hand, from a strain that it received last night in struggling avec la femme que je mentioned yesterday).'[24] Yet serious injuries and often death followed from apparent trifles. Erasmus Darwin's son, Charles, a promising medical student, died of septicaemia following a trivial dissecting-room cut.[25] Unable to take life's pains, multitudes of English people took their lives instead.[26] More philosophical minds reflected on their chances. 'The present is a fleeting moment', mused Gibbon, just turned fifty,[27]

the past is no more; and our prospect of futurity is dark and doubtful.

This day may *possibly* be my last: but the laws of probability, so true in general, so fallacious in particular, still allow me about fifteen years; and I shall soon enter into the period, which, as the most agreable of his long life, was selected by the judgement and experience of the sage Fontenelle.

He never did; probability, or, perhaps, Providence, was unkind, and the historian of the Roman Empire declined and fell shortly afterwards through post-operative sepsis following surgery on a hydrocele as big as a football.

Yet Gibbon was lucky: all six of his siblings died in infancy. Samuel Pepys was one of eleven children born to his parents. Only one brother and a sister survived into adulthood. A single measles epidemic massacred nine members of Cotton Mather's fifteen-strong household in early eighteenth-century colonial Boston.[28] Half a century later, Dr Johnson's friend, Hester Thrale, produced twelve children: seven of them did not reach their teens.[29] Out of William Godwin's twelve brothers and sisters, only half survived to adult life. His contemporary, William Holland, had four children die within a fortnight of scarlet fever.[30] Francis Place's résumé of the brief lives of his own children conveys the appalling arbitrariness of existence:[31]

1. Ann – born 1792. Died aged 2 years of the small pox
2. Elizabeth – April 1794. Died in Chile – Mrs Adams
3. Annie – 27 Jan 1796 – . . . Mrs Miers
4. Francis – 22 June 1798
5. Jane – died an infant
6. Henry – d . . . . d
7. Mary – 6 Jany. 1804
8. Frederick Wm. – 14 Oct 1805
9. Jane – 29 Oct 1807
10. Alfred – died an infant
11. John – 1 Jany 1811
12. Thomas – 4 Augst. 1812. Died at Calcutta 16 Sept 1847. Widow and 5 children
13. Caroline – 29 July 1814. Died 1830
14. William ⎱ Twins 6 Feb. 1817 ⎰ died – 1829
    Henry ⎰   ⎱ died an infant

The radical tailor himself outlived almost all his offspring.[32]

Thus English people during the 'long eighteenth century'[33] were overshadowed by the facts and fears of sickness and by death itself. He had only three complaints, Byron bantered to his friend, Henry Drury, in 1811:[34]

viz. a Gonorrhea, a Tertian fever, & the Hemorrhoides, all of which I literally had at once, though [the surgeon] assured me the morbid action of only one of these distempers could act at a time, which was a great comfort, though they relieved one another as regularly as Sentinels.

When John Locke's father wrote to him in 1659, assuring him of his 'health and quiet', the son – then training to be a doctor – responded that this was 'a blessing this tumbling world is very spareing of'.[35] For sickness was all too often the unwelcome, omnipresent guest, and households doubled as hospitals. A letter from Lady Caroline Fox to her sister, the Countess of Kildare, sending for medicines, reads like a dispatch from the front:[36]

> . . . as yet there is no amendment in my dearest child [Stephen]; he will be better for some hours almost a whole day sometimes then be as bad as ever again. I wonder I keep my spirits so well as I do, but my trust in Providence is great. My poor Charles was restored to me when there were no hopes left, and I will hope for the same blessing again with regard to my dear Ste. Louisa is perhaps set out by this time; seeing her will be a pleasure to me, but I fear she will find a melancholy house . . . Poor William has had a little fever, but was well again when I heard of him . . . .

'Every body is ill', exclaimed Keats to his brother in 1820.[37] This was neither a metaphysical paradox nor a piece of poetic licence, but merely an update on his friends and family.

Not surprisingly, therefore, health was on everybody's mind and filled their conversations. Sickness challenges the stomach (the two are not unconnected) for pride of place in Parson Woodforde's diaries. 'I was very nervous today. My Cow a great deal better this morning', he chronicled on 17 January 1796. The next day:[38]

> Poor Mr Bodham much altered for the worse. It is thought that he cannot long survive, fallen away amazingly, takes but very, very little notice of anything. Laudanum and Bark his chief Medicine. Dr. Lubbock & Dr. Donne from Norwich have both been there lately, and they say that he is out of the reach of any Medicine, he might live some little time, but is beyond recovery.

Some things improved. The day after, his cow-doctor visited her and pronounced 'her to be . . . out of all danger.'

Thus, in the world we have lost, sickness was a constant menace. 'One's very body', suggested Tobias Smollett – himself, of course, a doctor as well as a novelist – should be seen as a 'hospital'. Just as prudence dictated that every man should be his own lawyer, so every man should be his own physician, for he, if anyone, was expert in his own 'case' (contemporary idiom for both 'body' and 'corpse').[39] So it is hardly surprising that the everyday lives of ordinary people in earlier centuries reverberate with their own ailments, and those of their kith and kin. William Holland wearily recorded how his acquaintances made health their hobbyhorse, tiring him with talk of boluses and bandages. Worst of all was a certain Tom Poole, who 'fancys he understands Physick because his brother who is now dead was brought up an Apothecary'. Not so: 'he is in fact an Universal Pretender, not an Universal Genius as he wishes to be thought.' Holland wilted under other great medicine bores amongst his neighbours, like his fellow-clergyman, Mr Wollen, who 'talked a good deal of his complaints and produced many boxes of Pills as good for one thing or other.'[40] How fine the line dividing health care from hypochondria.

Themes
Our aim in this book is to explore the cultures of health, sickness, and suffering produced by the high levels of morbidity and mortality experienced in Georgian England. We make no claim to contribute to historical epidemiology or demography, or to medico-historical geography. Others have researched, and are researching, the wider causes and consequences of diseases in early modern England.[41] Their findings form an indispensable background and basis for our studies, and we do not intend to replicate or restate their work here.

Nor is it our plan to survey medical provision in pre-modern England. We will say almost nothing about medical practitioners and practice. There will be no discussion of the medical profession, its distribution, skills, and therapies; its grasp, or want, of scientific knowledge, clinical experience, or curative powers. We do not judge how successfully doctors battled with disease. These are, of course, crucial topics; Georgian medicine remains neglected: till very recently the only book devoted to Georgian medicine was well over fifty years old.[42] Fortunately, valuable new research is appearing. Charles Webster, Margaret Pelling, and Lucinda Beier have recently given us a much clearer idea of both the scatter of practitioners in early modern England and of their abilities; similar researches, above all by Geoffrey Holmes, Joan Lane, and Irvine Loudon, have shed light on the eighteenth and early nineteenth centuries.[43]

The subject of this book, in other words, is not medicine and doctors in society, but sick people.[44] This is not to imply that it is our intention to write about lay healing, or folk traditions, regarded as techniques ('alternative medicine') in contradistinction to professional medicine. Far from it. For one thing, drawing such hard-and-fast distinctions risks anachronism: serious lay/professional divisions postdate our period.[45] For another, our focus is not upon *healing* at all, even in the forms of lay or community action. Rather, we are concerned with perceptions of health and experiences of sickness. We are interested in people's awareness of their own bodies, their organs and functions, the interplay of the mental and physical, of body and soul. We shall investigate what people did – or failed to do – to preserve their health, and subsequently, how they responded to pain and disability. We aim to recreate their sense of the stages of life, and their responses when illness threatened foreclosure. We shall investigate how people identified, named and interpreted the ailments that afflicted them, how they explained their causes and meanings, and how they projected their courses – in many cases, of course, foreseeing and resigning themselves to inevitable death.

Thus, it is an inquiry first and foremost into beliefs. Many attitudes were, of course, platitudes – ancestral wisdom about the necessity of temperance, the danger of cold, or damp, or surfeit, or the ominous import of crows gathering on the chimney-pots; and we shall draw heavily upon such commonplaces, discussing how they were perpetuated by word of mouth and through 'do-it-yourself' health guides written for lay consumption. But our aim is not solely to reiterate such 'natural beliefs' within a composite *mentalité* of health and sickness, the lay medical mind.[46] Rather, where sources permit, we have tried to align individuals' responses when sick to their own wider projects in life – to their sense of identity, family duties, social status, cosmic hopes and fears.[47] Sickness did not merely make sense within the wider social fabric, but was often crucial in shaping the self.

If we emphasize *attitudes*, however, that is not because we believe that lay *actions* were any the less important. They clearly were. For it was a society in which primary care chiefly meant self-care, and patients were rarely passive in the face of doctors' orders. It is simply that we cannot examine such activities here. We have attempted elsewhere to plot the practical steps people took to combat sickness, both through self-help and through summoning the services of medical professionals.[48]

Orientation

If it is a truism, it is nonetheless true, that until recently, the history of medicine typically had doctors as its heroes. In today's social history and historical sociology, the commercial, professional, and institutional dimensions of organized medicine have instead been brought centre-stage, and the scholarly tone has increasingly been critical of, or even hostile to, the profession. These more radical approaches commonly read back into the past critiques of the power structure and hegemonic functions of today's medicine as developed by Marxists, by Foucault, by Illich, by anti-psychiatrists, and not least by feminists.[49]

Radical critics are right to insist that historically there has been far more to 'medicine' than the life-saving heroics of great doctors. We part company, however, from their assumptions (sometimes explicit, sometimes implied), in that it does not seem illuminating to construe the relations between medical practitioners and the laity during the long eighteenth century in terms of the consolidation of professional dominance, of social control, or of 'deviance' and 'labelling' theory.[50] Nor are we, unlike many critics, *primarily* concerned in this book with the ideological undercurrents of health and sickness beliefs, and the class and professional interest these encoded, though we do not for a moment deny their importance. We principally hope to explore not the manipulative potential but the manifest personal *meanings* such concepts conveyed within the *Lebenswelt* of those espousing them.

Not that we intend our approach to be exclusively, still less, naïvely, individualistic. Far from it, for even lexicons of so private a thing as pain clearly obey the Wittgensteinian dictum that there are no private languages. It was often a matter of life and death to translate personal pain into communication. Yet we shall argue that illness experience formed a long, dark night of the soul which was commonly crucial to individualization; sickness shaped the self. Personal experiences thus form our texts; our approach is primarily hermeneutic; and we shall show how identical micro-organisms provoked very distinctive responses amidst different individuals.

Two analogues may prove fruitful. One lies in the parallel problem of interpreting personal religious faith, as, for example, the autobiographical writings of John Bunyan.[51] In such cases, the historian's business is not to sit in judgement, but rather to identify the genres of narrative, the languages of piety, through which the believer finds expression. In the light of these public conventions, the personal nuances that make each witness special can be interpreted. Merely because they purport to be inspired from Above and nursed in the soul does not lead the historian – interested, as Gibbon put it, in the 'second causes' of faith – to despair of making sense of transcendental transports.

What applies to crises of faith must surely hold good for crises of health. Since William James's *The Varieties of Religious Experience*, we have had admirable models for the interpretation of the archetypes of inner experience. Surely we can approach the varieties of sickness experience in comparable ways. We need not believe that because sickness is inner, it must be ineffable and beyond inquiry, nor that it must automatically be rendered reductionistically into categories alien to its own. Sociology has boldly viewed sickness as a strategy of the actor or a 'role' legitimized by society; and psychoanalysis has decoded it as the somatized symptom of the wiles and conflicts of the psyche.[52] We wish to deny neither; but here we aim primarily to interpret sickness experience on its own terms. The common ground between religious and sickness experience in our culture has been surprisingly little studied, though this theme has been rewardingly explored by medical anthropologists.[53]

Another parallel may be drawn, this time with literature and the interpretative dilemmas it poses. The historian of sickness must learn the elementary lesson from the literary critic that texts are not simply facts, possessed of a single fixed meaning, the surface one. Understanding requires imaginative, sympathetic and polysemic reading. After all, the languages of the body and sickness bear special emotional charges; constantly conveying metaphorical as well as literal meanings, their messages are spiritual no less than somatic. Indeed, authors have themselves commonly depicted the toils of writing through the idiom of sickness (fever, constipation); composing a book, Sterne suggested, was like composing a cough, and writing itself is the author's disease, the *cacoethes scribendi*.[54] A number of writers have themselves traced the inner odyssey of being sick.[55]

Thus, literary scholarship demands of us a sensitivity to the complexities of

texts.[56] Nevertheless, dangers lurk in modern literary theory's tendency to
prioritize the self-standing text and its exegesis, and its dismissal of the naïve
notion that there is extratextual life, a reality outside. It would be well-nigh
obscene to deny the 'author' when the authors of the texts discussed below
were undergoing heroic surgery or suffering dissolution on the sickbed.
Certain recent works examining the history of healthy and sick bodies through
the use of such deconstructionist textual methods – for example, Francis
Barker's *The Tremulous Private Body* and Elaine Scarry's *The Body in Pain* –
combine narcissistic absorption in semiotic scenarios with cavalier indifference to historical context and questions of authorial intention and agency.[57]
We must respect texts, but surely we must also respect those people whose
biographies they register. Just these questions have fortunately been central to
students of the history of autobiography, with their explorations of the
dynamics of the construction of the 'self'; and they are grist to the mill of the
excellent biographer.[58]

Does history-writing itself afford us insights and models? Neither the
orthodox history of medicine, we have argued, nor some of its radical
alternatives, sets much store by evaluating personal experience. The mould,
however, is now being broken, as for example in the work of Lucinda Beier
and Andrew Wear, Jonathan Barry and Johanna Geyer-Kordesch upon sick
people in the seventeenth and eighteenth centuries respectively.[59] Moreover,
one sector of medical history has pioneered a more experience-oriented
approach: the history of insanity. Here, spurred by anti-psychiatric critiques
of the 1960s, researchers have fruitfully explored insane people's histories of
their madness. To arrive at the histories of the sick via the stories of the insane
may seem a circuitous detour indeed, but it has perhaps been a necessary and
fruitful one.[60]

Then again, recent developments in 'people's history' open tempting vistas.
The histories of politics, crime, education, and so forth were long written from
an official point of view, from 'above', through the eyes of legislators,
reformers, pedagogues, authority-figures, and the like. Alternative histories
have now been advanced, exploring the view 'from below', as seen from the
grassroots, by the common people, indeed the 'victims'. Peasant cosmologies
and proletarian cultures – traditionally familiar only when labelled as 'superstitious' or 'irrational' by the censoring, distorting, uncomprehending gaze of
authority – have been reconstructed. Thanks to scholars such as Le Roy
Ladurie, Carlo Ginzburg, and Peter Burke, we see how society comprised
many subcultures, some complimentary, some competing – involving gender-
defined no less than class-oriented world-views. We also see traditions of
popular and often lower-class self-help, 'moral economy', and co-operative
community-support systems, quite distinct from the individualist, market-
oriented values sanctioned by élite circles. These new histories have stressed
the centrality of ideological struggle, the tussles of different groups to defend
or impose their own renderings of reality, deploying rival systems of rationa-
lity and legitimacy (the law, magic, the appeal to the past, to science, and so
forth). We are not, of course, suggesting that the terms of 'people's history'

can automatically be applied to the study of lay health and sickness cultures: patients from polite society were hardly under the doctors in the same way as peasants were under their masters. Nevertheless, it offers suggestive leads for the reconstitution of discourses too long 'hidden from history'.[61]

Such 'people's history' further meshes with traditions of French scholarship (stimulated by the *Annales*, by Foucaultian structuralism, and by ethnography), which have pioneered histories of the body.[62] In particular, they have emphasized how the language of the body perhaps forms the supremely highly-charged and value-laden symbolic representational system, the junction between self and society. They have shown how the body is an object of thought and communication, at the heart of a comprehensive politics of power.

Christianity crucified the body, yet promised its resurrection.[63] Peasant society revelled in the magical anarchy of the flesh, which authorities, in turn, attempted to repress.[64] The law systematically punished the body, through what we tellingly call corporal and capital punishment.[65] The civilizing process sought to hide the shame of the flesh in clothes, manners, and morals,[66] and education aimed to train and discipline it.[67] And not least, public health and personal hygiene movements attempted to clean it up,[68] domesticate it, and tame its sexuality.[69]

This book is not about such battles over the body. But it is fundamentally concerned with the role played by such value-laden bodies of discourse in structuring discussion of health and sickness, cleanliness and dirt, discipline and disorder, inner and outer, virginity and violation. Not least, such discourses about the body personal and the body politic moralized and politicized the experiences of sickness. Who was to blame for illness? What stigmas did particular diseases carry? How did right living go with healthiness, and health with holiness, but vice find its due punishment in sickness? Powerful public prejudices – about nakedness, decency, order, bearing, and so forth – coloured the sense individuals made of being sick.

Sources
Oceans of evidence could be trawled for this study of minds in sickness and in health. Not least, abundant official records survive – Poor Law disbursements, hospital admission registers and patient case-books, and court and military records, for instance – sufficiently rich to hold out hopes of systematic and even statistical analyses. We have, in the event, chosen not to draw upon these, because the mediation of experience in them posed grave interpretative problems.[70] How does one disentangle authentic first-person experience from the language of the recording agency, be he a clerk or a hospital doctor?[71]

Hence the bulk of the testimony examined here is first-hand: the letters, journals, diaries, autobiographies, commonplace books, and table-talk of sufferers themselves, alongside the comments of those immediately surrounding them. These materials are subjective, and we have studied only a fragment of all such surviving records. Our work is therefore necessarily impressionistic.[72]

In the nineteenth century, Charles Darwin devoted a copious journal exclusively to his illnesses.[73] No equally revealing document seems to have survived from the eighteenth century. Augustans would perhaps have found such chronicles mawkish and unmanly – Swift sardonically told Stella that 'a journal, while I was sick, would have been a noble thing, made up of pain and physic'.[74] Stoicism, vanity, or propriety precluded excessive parade of one's infirmities. Gibbon told readers of his *Memoirs*:[75]

> I will not follow the vain example of Cardinal Quirini who has filled half a volume of his memoirs with medical consultations on his particular case; nor shall I imitate the naked frankness of Montaigne, who exposes all the symptoms of his malady, and the operation of each dose of physic on his nerves and bowels.

Nevertheless, the sources are gratifyingly – if impossibly! – full; it was a golden age of diaries and letter-writing, and health is prominent in both. Indeed, some kept diaries specifically, as William Lucas of Hitchin put it, as an 'antidote to illness',[76] though equally, of course, illness could put a stop to diarizing, most famously with Pepys:[77]

> And thus ends [he recorded in his final entry, on 31 May 1669] all that I doubt I shall ever be able to do with my own eyes in the keeping of my journall, I being not able to do it any longer, having done now so long as to undo my eyes almost every time that I take a pen in my hand; . . . And so I betake that course which is almost as much as to see myself go into my grave – for which, and all the discomforts that will accompany my being blind, the good God prepare me.

If authors such as Gibbon were themselves sometimes reticent, their editors have wielded the censoring pen more freely, thinking sickness incidental, unedifying, and even distasteful. Such matters were excised, for example, from early printed versions of Ralph Josselin's diary, now fortunately restored in the latest, complete text.[78] Parson Woodforde's painstaking accounts of inoculation procedures were cut by an editor who included every dinner he ate. Only by systematically going back to the manuscripts could this potential source of misapprehension be overcome.[79]

Journals and letters from this period are often gloriously full. Relying upon them, however, creates its own problems, as it means that, for the pre-modern centuries, one is habitually eavesdropping on protagonists principally from the higher ranks. Hence our sick parade cannot be assumed to be 'representative' of society as a whole; at best, it is representative of a particular literate élite. Diarists are definitionally self-absorbed, and disproportionately come from Protestant Dissent, just as those members of the lower orders who left personal documentation are exceptional people, and hence perhaps misleading guides to the consciousness of their fellows.

Thus, we must be humble in generalizing from the testimony of those relatively few people who recorded their experience of sickness – or whose records have at least survived. It may be with sickness as it was with sex. Take Pepys and Boswell: their sex lives may have been quite atypical, and one aspect of their exceptionality may have been precisely the fact that they wrote the details down. Was it, in the same way, mainly the morbidly introspective, the hypochondriacal even, who bothered to leave posterity the stories of their stools, spots, and sciaticas? Overall, even if we have interpreted the mounds of evidence we have sifted over the last five years with reasonable sensitivity, we must stress that we have merely sampled what survives; we would not wish to attribute to the evidence undue coherence or homogeneity. A corps of doctors, educated by common teachers and textbooks, might well come to interpret sicknesses in more or less identical and predictable ways: that is how professions work.[80] But maybe the reverse was true of the sick themselves. Did the private and dreadful experience of having one's very existence threatened accentuate the lonely diversity of experience? Perhaps the sick person is always singular.

In these circumstances, we have chosen to press individual identity to the fore of our discussion, and have often juxtaposed contradictory voices, without attempt at resolution. Yet the fact that the same individuals recur in chapter after chapter should at least lend some coherence to the discussion, some sense that a John Locke, a Parson Woodforde, or an Emily, Countess of Leinster, held not a mish-mash of one-off views but voiced something like a coherent *Weltanschauung*. To provide context, we have also drawn upon wider sources of ideas and opinion, such as magazines, and not least the growing body of popular medical works targeted at the laity; the views of such books surely square in some way, however obliquely, with the mind of their readers.[81]

So diversity is one keynote. The other is meaning. We are not here dealing with the absolute and objective facts of sickness – viruses and vital statistics – but with people's responses to the misfortunes heaped upon them by those secret microbes. In the *Spectator* paper mentioned at the beginning of this chapter, Addison conjured up the calamities of life – disease, deformity, decay, depression. He went on to propose a game: everyone could disburden himself of his own particular misery, by exchanging it for another's. His sufferers jumped at the opportunity. The diseased man swapped sickness for family strife; the galley-slave traded in his servitude for the gout; and so forth. Each quickly discovered himself to be worse off than before. Of course, Addison's message was the folly of crying out against fate; but it was also his way of saying that every man got the pains in life he deserved and which were appropriate to him. It is our aim, above all, in this book to analyse such alignments between sickness and the self.

Will this be good for your worship's eyes?[82]

Notes

[1]   Bond (ed.), *The Spectator*, IV, 506-8 (23 June 1714, no.558) and 509-11 (25 June 1714, no.559). For discussion see Garrison, 'Medicine in *The Tatler, Spectator* and *Guardian*'.

[2]   Williamson, 'Mutability, Decay and Seventeenth Century Melancholy'; Delumeau, *La Peur en Occident*; Ariès, *Hour of our Death*. For Keats see Goellnicht, *The Poet-Physician*.

[3]   Mitchell (ed.), *Purefoy Letters*, 99.

[4]   Bynum and Nutton (eds), *Theories of Fever from Antiquity to the Enlightenment*.

[5]   Stevenson, 'New Diseases'.

[6]   Faulkner (ed.), *Selected Letters of George Crabbe*, 352.

[7]   Dobson, 'Population, Disease and Mortality in Southeast England, 1600-1800'; *idem*, *Chronology of Epidemic Disease and Mortality in Southeast England*; *idem*, *From Old England*; Howe, *Man, Environment and Disease in Britain*; Clarkson, *Death, Disease and Famine in Pre-Industrial England*; Chambers, *Population, Economy, and Society in Pre-Industrial England*; Wrigley and Schofield, *Population History of England*; Flinn, 'Stabilization of Mortality in Pre-Industrial Western Europe'.

[8]   Famine itself, however, ceased to be a mass killer in England, and, unlike on the Continent, mortality crises do not seem to have been sparked off by starvation. See Appleby, *Famine in Tudor and Stuart England*.

[9]   Wrigley, 'No Death Without Birth'.

[10] Wrigley and Schofield, *Population History of England*.

[11] Imhof, 'Methodological Problems in Modern Urban History Writing'.

[12] Bamford (ed.), *Dear Miss Heber*, 221.

[13] Turner (ed.), *Rev. Oliver Heywood*, III, 207.

[14] Ayres (ed.), *Paupers and Pig Killers*, 44.

[15] Climenson (ed.), *Elizabeth Montagu*, I, 33.

[16] Goodwyn (ed.), *Selections from Norwich Newspapers*, 28.

[17] Doe (ed.), *Diary of James Clegg*, II, 341.

[18] Quoted in Porter, 'Lay Medical Knowledge in the Eighteenth Century', 157.

[19] Rathborne (ed.), *Letters of Lady Jane Coke*, 45.

[20] Harris (ed.), *Family Memorials*, 32

[21] See Hair, 'Deaths from Violence in Britain'.

[22] Macfarlane (ed.), *Diary of Ralph Josselin*, 21.

[23] Marshall (ed.), *Autobiography of William Stout*, 236-7.

[24] Latham and Matthews (eds), *Diary of Samuel Pepys*, V, 40.

[25] King-Hele, *Doctor of Revolution*, 123.

[26] MacDonald, 'Inner Side of Wisdom'; *idem*, 'Madness, Suicide, and the Computer'; Anderson, *Suicide in Victorian and Edwardian England*.

[27] Bonnard (ed.), *Edward Gibbon. Memoirs*, 188.

[28] Silverman, *Life and Times of Cotton Mather*, 268-9.

[29] Schwartz, *Daily Life in Johnson's London*, 143.

[30] Ayres (ed.), *Paupers and Pig Killers*, 25.

[31] Thale (ed.), *Autobiography of Francis Place*, 298. More generally for childhood deaths see Pollock, *Forgotten Children*, 124f.; *idem*, *Lasting Relationship*, 93f.

[32] Thale (ed.), *Autobiography of Francis Place*, 274.

[33] This book covers a timespan of roughly between 1650 and 1850, though concentrating on eighteenth-century material. There is no recognized shorthand label for this period. To avoid repetition of longwinded strings of words, we refer to it with phrases such as 'long eighteenth century', 'Georgian', or simply 'pre-modern'.

[34] Marchand (ed.), *Byron's Letters and Journals*, II, 58.

35 De Beer (ed.), *Correspondence of John Locke*, I, 82.

36 Fitzgerald (ed.), *Correspondence of Emily, Duchess of Leinster*, I, 199; another letter
    from Caroline Fox to Emily of 24 April of the same year was equally crammed with
    medical news: I, 214. She noted that year (I, 243) that being thus 'tedious' was a great
    fault of friends who were often sick.

37 Gittings (ed.), *Letters of John Keats*, 354.

38 Beresford (ed.), *Diary of a Country Parson*, IV, 258-9.

39 Smollett, *Life and Adventures of Sir Launcelot Greaves*, quoted in Skultans, *English
    Madness*, 50.

40 Ayres (ed.), *Paupers and Pig Killers*, 96, 207.

41 See above ref. 7.

42 Chaplin, *Medicine in England During the Reign of George III*. See Bynum, 'Health,
    Disease and Medical Care'; Lester King's excellent works have little to say about sick
    people: see *Medical World of the Eighteenth Century*; *idem*, *Road to Medical Enlighten-
    ment*; *idem*, *Philosophy of Medicine: The Early Eighteenth Century*.

43 Webster (ed.), *Health, Medicine and Mortality*; *idem*, 'Medicine as Social History';
    Pelling, 'Apothecaries and Other Medical Practitioners in Norwich Around 1600';
    idem, 'Appearance and Reality: Barber-Surgeons, the Body and Disease'; *idem*,
    'Medical Practice in Early Modern England'; Holmes, *Augustan England*; Lane
    ' "The Doctor Scolds Me" '; *idem*, 'The Medical Practitioners of Provincial England
    in 1783'; Beier, *Sufferers and Healers*; Loudon, 'Nature of Provincial Medical Practice
    in Eighteenth-Century England'; *idem*, *Medical Care and the General Practitioner*.

44 Little research has been done on sick people in the past, though see Guthrie, 'The
    Patient'; Mullett, 'Lay Outlook'; and Porter, 'Patient's View'; *idem* (ed.), *Patients
    and Practitioners*. For today's concerns see Illich, *Limits to Medicine*; and for
    contemporary perspectives, see Ann Cartwright, *Patients and Their Doctors*; Brody,
    Stories of Sickness, 171f.

45 Bynum and Porter (eds), *Medical Fringe*, 'Introduction'.

46 For work along these lines see Herzlich and Pierret, *Illness and Self*.

47 Illuminating is Brody, *Stories of Sickness*.

48 See Porter and Porter, *Patient's Progress*.

49 For discussions, see Figlio, 'Sinister Medicine?'; Woodward and Richards, 'Towards
    a Social History of Medicine'; Wright and Treacher (eds), *Problem of Medical
    Knowledge*, 'Introduction'.

50 We are, of course, here referring to the literate and articulate laity upon whose
    evidence we have drawn in this study. For these matters see Jewson, 'Medical
    Knowledge and the Patronage System'; *idem*, 'Disappearance of the Sick Man from
    Medical Cosmology'. Whether we should see the medical profession policing and
    controlling the poor in this period is another issue: see Goubert (ed.), *Médicalisation*.

51 Bottrall, *Every Man a Phoenix*.

52 Cf. Turner, *Medical Power*, 39f; Groddeck, *Meaning of Illness*.

53 Though see Sheils (ed.), *Church and Healing*. For medical anthropology see Blac-
    king, *Anthropology of the Body*; Kleinman, *Patients and Healers*; Loudon (ed.), *Social
    Anthropology*; Helman, *Culture, Health and Illness*; MacDonald, 'Anthropological
    Perspectives on the History of Science and Medicine'. Kleinman's work is particu-
    larly helpful in examining the relative costs and benefits of the somatizing and
    psychologizing of sickness in different cultures.
        It will be seen that our present approach is no more interested in the retrospective
    psychoanalytical attempt to divine the 'true' psychodynamic cause of the supposedly
    psychosomatic disorders of great people than in the traditional medical history
    parlour game of retrospective diagnosis.

54 Sontag, *Illness as Metaphor*; Rousseau, 'Literature and Medicine'. We trust this book

is not indigestible.

55 See Virginia Woolf's splendid essay, 'On Being Ill'; Cousins, *Physician and Litera-ture*; Sacks, *A Leg to Stand On*; Brody, *Stories of Sickness*. Woolf, in fact, notes how rarely writers have captured the extraordinary imaginative and emotional worlds of the sick, chiefly because sickness is considered vulgar and disgusting.

56 In this book, space limitations for the most part preclude formal analyses of alternative readings of texts of the kind that Jean Starobinski has undertaken so admirably for Montaigne in his 'The Body's Moment'.

57 Barker, *Tremulous Private Body*; Scarry, *Body in Pain*. For a fuller criticism of the approaches used in these works, see Porter, 'Body Politics'.

58 Spacks, *Imagining a Self*; Cox, *Stranger Within Thee*; Lyons, *Invention of the Self*; Cockshutt, *Art of Autobiography*; Delaney, *British Autobiography*; Martin, *Tennyson: The Unquiet Heart*.

59 Beier, 'In Sickness and in Health'; Wear, 'Puritan Perceptions of Illness'; Barry, 'Piety and the Patient'; Geyer-Kordesch, 'Cultural Habits of Illness'.

60 Showalter, *Female Malady*; Peterson, *Literature of Madness*; Porter, *Mind Forg'd Manacles*; idem, *Social History of Madness*.

61 See the discussion in Porter, 'Patient's View'; and idem, 'Introduction' to *Patients and Practitioners*, and the references there cited. An admirable instance of the reconstitu-tion of past health and sickness experiences of a subordinate group is offered in Duden, *Geschichte unter der Haut*, a study of the attitudes to their bodies of a sizeable cohort of women in eighteenth-century Germany. One problem with this study is that these experiences are known essentially only through the records of their physician.

62 For discussion see Loux, 'Popular Culture and Knowledge of the Body'; Goubert, 'Twenty Years On'; Gelfand, 'The *Annales* and Medical Historiography'; Burke, 'Revolution in Popular Culture'; MacDonald, 'Anthropological Perspectives on the History of Science and Medicine'.

63 Camporesi, *Incorruptible Flesh*; idem, *Bread of Dreams*.

64 Muchembled, *Popular Culture*.

65 Foucault, *Discipline and Punish*; Ignatieff, *Just Measure of Pain*.

66 Elias, *Civilizing Process*.

67 Childs, 'Prescriptions for Manners'.

68 Vigarello, *Le Corps Redressé*; Ginnie Smith, 'Prescribing the Rules of Health'; Watkins, 'English Revolution in Social Medicine'.

69 Foucault, *History of Sexuality*; Mort, *Dangerous Sexualities*; Bristow, *Vice and Vigilance*.

70 Lack of expertise, and/or lack of space, has led us to omit other sorts of evidence, such as the visual. That this is a bad thing is argued in Porter, 'Seeing the Past'.

71 See Risse, 'Hospital History'; Thomas, 'Old Poor Law and Medicine'.

72 For an introduction see Matthews (ed.), *British Diaries*; idem (ed.), *British Autobiographies*.

73 Colp, *To Be an Invalid*, 43f.

74 The Rev. William Jones kept a sickness journal but it seems not to have survived. See Christie (ed.), *Diary of the Rev'd William Jones*. Samuel Johnson kept one, in Latin, during the last few months of his life. For Swift's comment see Williams (ed.) *Swift, Journal to Stella*, 366.

75 Bonnard (ed.), *Edward Gibbon. Memoirs*, 29.

76 Bryant and Baker (eds), *Quaker Journal*, I, 17.

77 Latham and Matthews (eds), *Diary of Samuel Pepys*, IX, 564 (31 May 1669).

78 Macfarlane (ed.), *Diary of Ralph Josselin*, xxvi.

79 Beresford (ed.), *Diary of a Country Parson*, I, 40-1, 190-2.

80 Freidson, *Profession of Medicine*. Even that is only partly true, as we show in chapter 6 of Porter and Porter, *Patient's Progress*.
81 Smith, 'Prescribing the Rules of Health'; Porter, 'Lay Medical Knowledge in the Eighteenth Century'.
82 Sterne, *Life and Opinions of Tristram Shandy*, 265.

SECTION I

Health

Chapter 2:
Keeping Well

> The greatest pleasure of life is love, the greatest treasure contentment, the greatest possession health, the greatest ease is sleep, the greatest medicine is a true friend.[1]

Eighteenth-century platitudes about the good life are revealing in their very banality. The way of the Cross seems to have receded to a degree that Christians of earlier centuries would have found shocking. Good health moves in to take its place.

'Health is the basis of all happiness this world gives', judged Samuel Johnson in 1782, sinking towards the grave.[2] Health – Sir Walter Scott called it 'the mainspring of the microcosm' – was a theme susceptible of myriad variations.[3] 'What are the gifts of fortune in comparison to the enjoyment of health!' exclaimed Lady Elizabeth Holland around the same time – and who knew better than she about fortune's gifts?[4]

> Grant that it may continue, and that I may, whilst life lasts, feel no other anguish than what is incidental to the gradual decay of mortality. Let it be gradual, for I am too happy to bear with equanimity the thought of being torn from the felicity of a life replete with every blessing human nature is capable of relishing.

Thus, in the age's tremulous prose, a *grande dame* offered her paean to Hygeia, deity of health.

Proverbs, too, told the same edifying tale: money could no more buy health than love. 'Better in health than in good conditions', ran the old saw – a view reformulated by that arch dictum-monger Walter Shandy: 'O blessed health . . . thou art above all gold and treasure'.[5] Health was commended, apostrophized, beseeched and, in its absence, lamented, throughout the correspondence, literature, and popular piety of the day. The accomplished poet, Elizabeth Carter, for example, penned an 'Ode to Health', entreating its guardian spirit:[6]

And come, Hygeia, bland and fair,
Flush'd with the glow of morning air;
With coral lip and sparkling eye,
Complexion of ensanguin'd dye.

The poet personified health as the *sine qua non* of all earthly blessings:

Health I intreat; whose jocund throng
Wantons each laughing grace among;
With Health the dancing minutes crown'd
The field of all my wishes bound.

But if Miss Carter offered hosannas to health, often the tone was more
didactic. 'Count your blessings' was the unmistakable subtext of a hymn to
well-being spliced into *The Conduct of Servants in Great Families*, designed to
instruct domestics to keep themselves fit, show gratitude, and forsake envy of
their betters:[7]

Health is a Blessing from above,
    Which Riches cannot buy;
The Life of Life, the Bodies Peace,
    And pleasing Harmony,
To Him, whose kind Support upholds
    This sinking House of Clay,
Of chearful Hallelujah's I'll
    The grateful Tribute pay.

Because whilst others tortur'd lye
    Bound with Afflictions Chain,
I walk at large Secure and Free
    From Sickness and from Pain.
Their Life is Death, their Language Groans,
    Their Meat is Juice of Galls;
Their Friends as Strangers, Wealth as Want,
    Their Houses Prison Walls.

Above all, domestic medicine texts hammered the health message home.
'Little apology is necessary', apologized Hugh Smythson in the 'Introduction'
to his massive home-medicine guide, the *Family Physician* (1781),[8]

for introducing to the world a work calculated to promote the happiness
of mankind; and the *preservation* and *restoration* of HEALTH, the first
grand article in the enumeration of earthly blessings, are subjects of a
nature so very agreeable and interesting, that few arguments will be
required, to persuade the world to receive with regard, and treat with

attention, every attempt to facilitate objects of such universal importance.

Required or not, Smythson did indeed enumerate such arguments, building upon the Biblical notion that the human body was *'fearfully and wonderfully made'*, and so endowed with extremely 'nice and delicate organs of sense'. These were, of course, perilously vulnerable to the 'great variety of dangers and maladies *which flesh is heir to'*, and hence needed special prophylactic care.

Above all, everyone agreed prevention was better than cure. Back in the sixteenth century, it had been one of Montaigne's maxims that 'Tis no time to bath and clean a man's self when he is seized on by a violent fever'. Hence, he continued, 'I am more solicitous to improve my health when I am well, than to restore it when I am sick'.[9] Such sentiments were ten-a-penny: 'It is most certain', reiterated the fashionable Bath physician, George Cheyne, 'that 'tis easier to *preserve* Health, than to *recover* it; and to *prevent* Diseases, than to *cure* them.'[10] Cheyne set down these views in his popular health guide, the *Essay on Health and Long Life* (1724), which went through some ten editions in twenty years; but they were already extremely familiar in print, appearing, for instance, some half a century earlier in John Archer's *Every Man His Own Doctor* (1671), which asserted, opening its first chapter ('On The Preservation of Health') that its brief was to cover the 'Hygienial Part of Physick', that is, 'Rules how present health may be preserved, and how to beware not to fall into a Disease'. Every man, Archer stated, citing the old adage, must be either a physician or a fool by the age of forty. To be a home physician, the reader was assured, no expertise was needed in anatomy and pharmacy; in fact, these might prove positively misleading in treading health's highway.[11]

But it was not merely specialist medical writings that catechized the creed of health. The literary periodicals of the day also bombarded readers with health propaganda. Subscribers to the *Gentleman's Magazine* for 1767 thus found themselves confronted with an 'ODE TO HEALTH', sent in by a grateful convalescent, which gushed:[12]

> Hail rosy Health, celestial, blooming Fair,
> Offspring of Temperance, Virtue's sweetest child,
> And soft Content, that smooths the brow of Care,
> Parent of Joy and Pleasure ever Mild.
> I feel thy influence, life-bestowing pow'r
> While the warm tide glides swiftly through my
>   veins;
> And while reclin'd in blooming Hebe's bow'r
> I consecrate to thee the living strains.

What, then, are we to make of such effusions, so popular throughout the century? Were they nothing but vapid pieties and literary fillers, modes of 'musak', so clichéd that people grew deaf to them? Probably not. For if we listen carefully, we detect a growing concern for health from the late seventeenth century onwards. Historians of the Enlightenment tell us that the idiom of reason and criticism, of freedom and humanity, was ever on the lips of progressive society. Thanks to the work of Peter Gay, however, we can now see how health, too, served as a barometer of improvement for the *philosophes*. For those chanting the war-cries of *sapere aude* and *écrasez l'infame*, physical well-being was high on the political agenda, replacing the mysterious will-o'-the-wisp of holiness. Public health became crucial to programmes of political reform, alongside the elimination of physical torture and famine. And their commitment to progress encouraged the 'party of humanity' to portray themselves as physicians to society itself. It is no accident that Gay titled one of his chapters with a medical metaphor: 'the recovery of nerve'.[13]

Since Gay wrote, the affinities between the Enlightenment and a rising health culture have been explored from various viewpoints. Jaundiced about modernity, Ivan Illich exposed the *Aufklärer* as fantasists, nursing promethean pipe-dreams of the medical conquests of suffering and even death, and superseding sanctity with sanitation, and above all, a new pagan cult of the body beautiful, youthful and sexy. Utilitarianism promised the victory of pleasure over pain, and utopians, such as Godwin and Condorcet, pointed to a promised land not merely of longevity but of this-worldly immortality itself. *Frankenstein* was just over the horizon.[14]

For Michel Foucault, the Enlightenment valorization of health had different meanings; it embodied the values of the aspiring third estate. The magic of *ancien régime* aristocratic hegemony lay in blood, a mystical commodity, rationed and transfused by strict laws of inheritance. By contrast, robust physical health was an egalitarian ideal, open to all who pursued an appropriate *nouveau régime* of emancipatory self-help and self-culture. Good health thus encapsulated a more democratic, more individualistic, yet also, in its way, more elusive *summum bonum*.[15]

There is no need here to chart the precise pathways between Enlightenment ideals and the quest for health.[16] It is, however, worth noting just how many of its champions in Britain were either doctors themselves or were positively engaged with promoting health, from Locke and Mandeville through to Erasmus Darwin and Thomas Beddoes.[17] And that new optimism which marked the *siècle des lumières* manifested itself in the positive conviction that health, like knowledge, could be a reality not a chimera, accessible through praxis. To indicate the percolation of such attitudes, let us revert to Lady Holland's apostrophe to Hygeia. Having, as we have seen, prized the 'enjoyment of health' over the 'gifts of fortune', she went on to express a touching zest for the prolongation of earthly delights.[18]

> Formerly in the bitterness of sorrow I prayed for death; I looked to it as a relief to a broken spirit, and when I viewed its approach with indifference I imputed to philosophy that resignation and contempt, which despair alone had caused. Now I am a coward indeed; a spasm terrifies

me, and every memento of the fragile tenure of my bliss strikes a panic through my frame.

Here, in cameo form, we see the traditions of Christian mortification and Stoic apathy in the face of death displaced in favour of aspirations towards, albeit not quite expectation of, the bounty of health.

We may perhaps detect the same allegiances voiced more frivolously some years earlier within the same aristocratic circle, in a series of flirtatious letters playing upon medical themes exchanged between Lady Caroline Lamb and her cousin, Lord Hartington. The old tropes of love as a disease, of the body as worm-food, the world as a hospital, and Christ as physician, no longer surface. Here passion is not a malady, but physic, and health, love, and vitality are intimately associated:[19]

> My most sanative elixir of Julep [Lady Caroline addresses him], my most precious cordial confection, my most dilutable sal polychrist and marsh mallow paste, truly comfortable spirit of hartshorn, tincture of rhubarb and purgative senna tea! It is impossible, my most exquisite medicine chest, for me to describe the delightful effect the potion you sent me this morning had upon me. Prescribe such powders to all the EPHEMRA [*sic*] who die for love of your Lordship's tricoloured eyes, and remember, cousin my heart and heart of my cousin, that your all faithful gallipot was only waiting for a line to dose you with letters every day . . . .

In matters of health, the Georgians neither presumed nor despaired; they were neither so fatalistic as to think its quest mere moonshine, nor so sanguine as to take its blessings for granted. Man's fate was mixed. Even the ultra-sardonic Byron could state: 'I am tolerably well in Health, that is to say, instead of an Ague, & Clap, and the Piles, all at once, I have only the two last.'[20] True, some boasted of their rude good health. A seasoned campaigner against the evils of Bacchus, Dr Erasmus Darwin, was wont to brag, 'I drink water *only*, and am always well' (abstaining had indeed cured him of gout); and, of course, homespun radicals such as William Cobbett, champion of sturdy independence and flail of the parasitical professions had a stake in parading their own well-being.[21]

Indeed, some people genuinely enjoyed the pink of health. 'She never knew a day's sickness', wrote Parson Woodforde of 'poor Mrs Peachman', a parishioner just deceased. Francis Place claimed never to have been ill until he was in his sixties (the secret, he believed, lay in hard work and in maintaining a free perspiration, so that the body did not stew in its own toxins).[22]

But more typically, the bloom of health was experienced not as normal but as an unexpected bonus. John Baker scribbled on 19 June 1778: 'remarkably well all this day', and the reader sympathizes with his astonishment, for his diaries read overall as chronicles of wasted flesh, and only two days previously he had been dosing himself for chronic arthritis.[23] The blue-stocking, Elizabeth Montagu, obviously experienced the same pleasant shock on the *dies praeclaris* she wrote down, 'I am so well in health that I scarce know myself'.[24] Sometimes, of course, such professions must be taken with a pinch of salt, as when the young buck, Edward Fitzgerald, effusively reassures his mother that he is 'perfectly well. I never was so well in the beginning of any winter almost. I have no cold, no bowels, not even a cold in the head'; no man is on oath to his mother about his health.[25] Poignantly, the most positive paeans to health came from those who enjoyed it least. 'Banish money – Banish sofas – Banish wine – Banish music – But right Jack Health, – Honest Jack Health, true Jack Health – banish Health and banish all the world', sang John Keats, surely aware even then how numbered were his days.[26]

The Healthy Constitution

Health maintenance counted, if life were to be bearable. Diseases were agonizing, medicine disgusting and commonly useless anyway. And without a certain robust physicality, Georgian daily life was hard to sustain, except for the ultra-pampered few. After all, most power was still muscle power. Riding horseback – or, for the poor, going Shanks pony – was often the only way of travelling; long childbearing careers were the curse men inflicted upon women (many, of course, could not take the strain and died); damp, cold, overwork, and poor diet all racked the system.[27] Health was crucial but a rare prize.

On one point all were agreed: good health did not grow on trees. Like wealth, it needed to be earned. The sober Quaker, Mrs Galton, argued that cultivating health was every individual's prime duty.[28] This is an interesting opinion, coming from one who was deeply pious. For Christian theology had long regarded as vanity undue concern for the welfare of the *body* as distinct from the soul. Remember the lilies of the field; take no concern for the morrow; God would provide, and life's thread depended upon Grace and the mysteries of Providence.[29]

Yet Christians of all denominations were disencumbering themselves of these vestiges of medieval mortification and asceticism. In the eighteenth century, the Anglican upper clergy were prominent in founding hospitals and promoting smallpox inoculation, while John Wesley himself wrote the century's most popular medical self-help text, *Primitive Physick*.[30] Dissenters also moved with the times. 'Lord teach me to prize health', beseeched the Presbyterian, Richard Kay, in the 1730s, then just beginning his medical career.[31] A century later, the Unitarian-turned-Positivist, Harriet Martineau, denounced Christians' temptation to wallow in spiritual suffering, which left them sorely neglectful of their duties to promote well-being. The charge was echoed by her Anglican contemporary, Charles Kingsley, who averred that there was 'something impious' in that 'neglect of personal health' which the 'effeminate ascetics' of the Oxford Movement liked to affect to suggest holy abstraction.[32]

If people then had a duty to foster health, how precisely was it to be safeguarded and improved? Advice about the rules of keeping well filled the air. Scores of proverbs identified health hazards and offered preservatives against pains ('air slays sooner than the sword'; 'where the sun enters, the doctor does not', etc.). And for those so minded, masses of home-care books, targeted at lay readers of all levels of literacy flooded the market. While warning that serious illness should be left strictly to medical practitioners, such books set out rules of health for all to follow to forestall such a necessity. Works such as John Burton's *Treatise on the Non-Naturals* (1738) or John Arbuthnot's *An Essay Concerning the Nature of Aliments* (1731) explained the thinking behind health care to the educated, whereas Wesley's *Primitive Physick* simply told the barely literate how to look after themselves with little more than a pot of honey, a string of onions, a pitcher of cold water, and a prayer.[33]

Pepys serenaded his good fortune at the close of 1664:[34]

So ends the old year, I bless God with great joy to me; not only from my having made so good a year of profit, as having spent 420l. and laid up 540l. and upward.

But if he purred over his profits, his health mattered still more:[35]

But I bless God, I never have been in so good plight as to my health in so very cold weather as this is, nor indeed in any hot weather these ten years, as I am at this day and have been these four or five months.

People were often mystified as to precisely what tipped the balance between being well or ill. Yet this did not stop Pepys – like many others – from prescribing to himself 'Rules for my health', as he had set down in the previous year, when suffering from his bowels:[36]

1. To begin to keep warm as I can. 2. Strain as little as ever I can backwards, remembering that my pain will come by and by, though in the very straining I do not feel it. 3. Either by physic forward or by clyster backward, or both ways, to get an easy and plentiful going to stool and breaking of wind. 4. To begin to suspect my health immediately when I begin to become costive and bound, and by all means to keep my body loose.

Pepys here records only the fine print of his regimen. He had no need, of course to tabulate all the home truths with which he was utterly familiar. Amongst these, the *sine qua non* for positive health, everybody understood, lay first and foremost in building up a robust constitution (a state of 'crasis'), as an investment in well-being and a security against future illness.[37] By contrast, a corrupt constitution was as disastrous for the individual as for the state. Specific attacks of disease were alarming, but nothing boded worse than the erosion of one's very system. 'I wish I could speak more favourably of poor

Clarke', wrote Gibbon to his friend John Holroyd,[38]

> but I much fear . . . whether his complaint is bilious, that is a very *soft*
> word; but his situation is as bad as you conceive. Dr Addington (whose
> skill is I believe equal to his humanity) as well as his very sensible
> Apothecary, seems only determined between the fear of a short fit or a
> *long* palsy.

Gibbon concluded with what was tantamount to a death sentence: 'His
Constitution is broke up'. The vitiation of one's very system was a terrible,
probably irremediable, blow. 'My constitution will no longer allow me to toil
as formerly', complained the asthmatic Tobias Smollett to Dr Moore in 1762.
What did this mean? 'I am now so thin you would hardly know me. My face is
shriveled up by the asthma like an ill-dried pippin, and my legs are as thick at
the ankle as at the calf'.[39] Reporting on her father's sickness, Lady Palmerston
looked to the silver lining of this belief – a strong constitution might pull
someone through even dangerous sickness:[40]

> Papa is a little better for the change of air, but not much. He is certainly
> weak and ill and in very low spirits. He is broken within the last few
> months, there is no concealing from oneself, yet he had so strong a
> constitution that one hopes he may pick up again.

So the constitution was the inner stock of vitality and strength, the vigour
that flowed when all one's organs worked effectively together, without the
artificial crutches of medicines. If life were a flame, hot and bright, then one's
constitution was the wax, the oil, and the wick.[41] If one lacked a good
constitution in the first place, or if it fell into decay, medicines would not avail
when infection struck or some local disorder erupted. Contemporary therapeutics cast physic in the role of auxiliary, useful by dint of its capacity to
reinforce spontaneous, internal powers of resistance.

Thus the constitution was the very foundation of well-being. The analogy
with the British Constitution rang loud and true. Thus Isabella Duke,
suffering from some form of 'scurvy', told her physician, John Locke, that she
had no hope of recovery from her specific ailment, 'unless it be by mending the
Habit of my Body in general, and sweetning my Blood'.[42]

To enjoy a good constitution, it was vital to lay sound foundations in infancy
and consolidate them in youth. The plan for establishing a sturdy constitution
spelt out by John Locke in his *Some Thoughts Concerning Education* (1693), and
by many like-minded authors besides, became extremely popular.[43] As a
psychologist, Locke saw beliefs and morals as the products of education; and
in much the same way, as a physician he regarded physique as the outcome of
initial physical training.

This Lockian outlook stressed the positive value, indeed the necessity, of
early hardening. Nothing could be worse than to spoil the new-born infant

with cosseting. An over-heated birth-room was positively harmful, swaddling (whose rationale was to 'support' the limbs) was counter-productive (it would enfeeble rather than strengthen), and the automatic, ritualistic dosing of the new-born baby with medicines, and even alcoholic cordials, typically practised by the granny midwife, would equally weaken by inducing dependency. Overall, too much 'cockering and tenderness'[44] would first create and then confirm delicacy, thereby entailing dependence upon artificially maintained environments, spawning spindly, hothouse creatures, lifelong valetudinarians habituated to stimulants and medicines.

Instead, from their earliest days, babies needed a cool environment, loose clothes, freedom of movement, and simple nourishment (initially the mother's breast). In time, they should be systematically exposed to a more bracing regime, including unheated bedrooms, going barefoot, cold-water bathings, and even – Locke's fiendishly ingenious suggestion – wearing shoes that would 'leak water' when it rained. (His follower, James Nelson, judged this was a bit much.)[45] In other words, the real protection for that fragile bundle of humanity lay not in defeating disease through medicines, but in the attempt by prophylaxis to strengthen its inner, intrinsic vital powers. Indeed, Juliana-Susannah Seymour took this thinking to its logical conclusion. The very presence of the doctor was a menace to the child; introduce the physician into the nursery, and his medicines would prove a time-bomb.[46] Sometimes, Hygeia and Aesculapius seemed to the Georgians less like allies than antagonists.

This 'hardening' regime had powerful emotional and ideological resonances, not least with fashionable primitivism and the romantic myth that the lower orders, forced to live hard, must be healthier and more resilient than the rich. It agreed with models of manliness that prized nonchalance towards pain.[47] It seemed of a piece with the new 'cooling' treatments for fevers successfully urged by Thomas Sydenham in the late Stuart age. Its faith in fresh air and cold water squared with a new accent upon cleanliness ('one of the half virtues', according to the *Spectator*) and personal hygiene.[48] And, finally, psycho-historians would have us believe that such hardening procedures provided handy medical legitimation for parents eager to act out repressed hatred of their offspring.[49]

Be that as it may, this strategy of constitutional 'hardening' enjoyed an enduring vogue as the best way of 'immunizing' the body against disease. As Seymour's *On the Management of Children* warned, 'Delicacy is the Parent of a thousand Mischiefs'.[50] In his widely-read early nineteenth-century manuals on conduct, William Cobbett likewise insisted that children should grow up 'naturally' in the fresh air, getting abundant exercise; nurses' cordials and doctors' powders would implant debilitating dependency.[51] Cobbett regarded his own robust frame as the proof of the pudding. Thomas Bewick, the Newcastle engraver and nature lover, agreed, praising, and identifying himself with, the 'hardy inhabitants of the fells' of Northumberland, who, 'notwithstanding their apparent poverty', were able to 'enjoy health and happiness in a degree surpassing that of most other men'. Bewick also valued the advice of the Venetian writer, Cornaro, and others who had urged temperance as the secret of longevity.[52] Poorer folk, of course, got hardened not by design but willy-nilly. As William Stout wrote about his teenage apprenticeship in late Stuart Lancaster:[53]

> I attended the shop in winter with the windows open, without [any] sash or screen till nine in the evning, and with the windows shut and the dore open till ten a'clock without coming into the house except to our victuals or to the fire, having our bed in the shop; and had my health well all the time. Which . . . made me so hardy that at any time I could endure the couldest season if dry.

Safeguarding Health
Thus people believed in avoiding mollycoddling children, but rather trusting to nature: thereby a stout constitution could be established as a reservoir of health. But how could such 'stamina' be safeguarded throughout adult life? As attitudes and actions alike show, many believed the answer lay in faithfully following a regime of health. In other words, it was vital to order each department of life – clothing, environment, the ensemble of activities making up the day, and so on – in the light of their health implications, so that each element should be beneficial, and the whole would provide a balanced and varied economy of living. Everything mattered; each individual had the power in myriad minor ways to further healthy living – or equally to jeopardize it. 'I'm a great friend to Air', recorded Lady Mary Coke, delighted to get back into her own home, 'where I might have as many windows op'ned as I pleased'. Visiting Lady Lucy Howard of Stoke, she reported:[54]

> I was of infinite use both to her & her House by opening all the windows, which were as closely shut as if it had been the coldest day in Winter, but I suppose you know She has always a fire in her Bed Chamber the hottest day in summer; how can She have her health with such management?

But was Lady Lucy herself following a rival health-care regime of her own based upon toasting? If so, it was in defiance of best – or, at least, fashionable – opinion, medical and lay.

From the Greeks onwards, doctors had systematized all these items of vital importance to healthy living, dubbing them collectively the 'non-naturals'. There were said to be six in all, as George Cheyne listed them:[55]

> 1. The Air we breathe in. 2. Our Meat and Drink. 3. Our Sleep and Watching. 4. Our Exercise and Rest. 5. Our Evacuations and their Obstructions. 6. The Passions of our Minds.

Lay writers sometimes made merry with the technical term, 'non-naturals'. Cowper joked about the term with his friend Mrs King, 'Physicians call them

Non-Naturals. I suppose to deter their patients from the use of them'. But through the implied contrast with the 'naturals', i.e., with the *intrinsic* constitutional health produced by its 'humours', people understood very well how inner well-being hinged upon observing these more external 'non-natural' dicta. All those serious about their health applied themselves to such items as getting adequate sleep, taking exercise, and keeping the bowels open.[56]

Diaries themselves bear abundant witness to this fact. Indeed, one of the prime reasons why people maintained diaries so religiously was precisely to keep track of physical routines, with a view, if necessary – as all too often it was! – to shaming themselves into mending their ways, for the sake of their health, their self-esteem, and even their soul. Many Georgian diarists weighed themselves regularly, even using proper Sanctorius chairs, and recorded their avoirdupois – though this frequently makes sorry reading, for it is commonly, as with Sir Joseph Banks and his sister, Sophia, a tale of gravitation from plumpness to porcine obesity (by 1794, Sophia weighed fourteen and a half stone). When John Baker depressed the scales in 1772, he admitted, 'I was then extremely fat and weighed above 15 stone, I think, 10 pounds'. Even so, he was still under half the weight of George Cheyne at his grossest.[57] It was possibly also with an eye to health that a few diarists – Robert Hooke, for example – also recorded their orgasms, often by a cryptic symbol. Best theory had it that too much and too little sex were equally debilitating, though ideas about the ideal frequency differed.[58]

Many journals thus served as logs of health, not least other people's. For diarists such as Joseph Farington were positively nosey about their friends' regimens and habits. He had a conversation with the watchmaker, Johnson:[59]

> I asked him how he preserved his health being so constantly employed in a sedentary business. He said by abstemiousness. That He never eats so much as He could, and when He finds himself a little indisposed He reduces the quantity of his usual allowance. He never takes Physick. He eats water gruel for breakfast – drinks half a pint at night. He scarcely knows what it is now to feel very hungry. Sometimes He is low and faint with a sinking of the stomach: but rest from business for a day restores him. He drinks a glass of cold water every morning when He gets up. Dr Fothergill of Bath told him that would carry off accumulating bile.

Farington was impressed. But what made his friend the critic George Stevens so healthy? Farington obviously gave him a grilling:[60]

> Stevens told me that he usually rises at 6 oClock or sooner and immediately after dressing drinks 2 or 3 dishes of Chocolate, in a short time; after which He walks to London though at this time of the year it is dark at that hour. [He then spent the day in town.] He usually, when alone, drinks about a pint of wine; and in about an hour and half or two hours after sitting down to dinner, drinks two or three dishes of very

strong Coffee. He takes no other refreshment throughout the evening, and devotes the whole time till eleven oClock, when He goes to bed, to reading etc. At Dinner he eats of only one plain dish; mutton or beef; and a bit of pudding. He neither eats soup or fish.

Who but someone with a rare faith in the value of attention to the non-naturals – rise at six, walk to work, eat no soup, etc. – would bother to record all that? Only those preoccupied with the healthy life would then go around advising others how to protect it. 'My deare Ned', wrote Lady Brilliana Harley to her son, 'be carefull of yourself, and forget not. Doo exercise; for health can no more be had without it, then without a good diet.'[61] 'Be temperate in all things in your diet', the Polonian William Penn admonished his children, 'for that is physic by prevention; it keeps, nay it makes people healthy and their generation sound.'[62] 'Exercise and application', Thomas Jefferson explained to his daughter, 'produce order in our affairs, health of body and cheerfulness of mind',[63] echoing David Hume's advice to his nephew: 'use some exercise. Relaxation . . . for health is absolutely necessary'.[64]

The positive pursuit of health thus required eternal vigilance. The mid-eighteenth-century Sussex grocer, Thomas Turner, pondered his health a lot – indeed, was a bit of a hypochondriac. Yet he often got blotto in village binges, which punished him with positively Boswellian hangovers.[65] These he duly, and shamefacedly confessed in the privacy of his journal, making promises to mend which remind one that within a decade James Boswell himself would become the grand journalist of debauch.[66]

Boswell was mainly concerned to reform his social demeanour and his inner self, leaving his physical health prey to the depredations of claret, whores, surgeons, and quacks; he died with his constitution broken.[67] A model of petty-bourgeois caution by contrast, Turner set about safeguarding his constitution. He boned up on medical books, and culled recipes and advice from magazines. And not least, he dictated a minutely detailed regimen for living:[68]

I think it therefore [right] (as it's a matter of so great importance to my health etc.) to draw up rules of proper regimen, which I do in manner and form following, and which, at all times when I am in health, I hope I shall always have the strictest regard to follow, as I think they are not inconsistent with either religion or morality: First, be it either in the summer or winter, to rise as early as I possibly can; that is, always to allow myself between 7 and 8 hours' sleep, or full 8, unless prevented on any particular or emergent occasion. 2ndly, to go to breakfast between the hours of 7 and 8 from Lady Day to St. Michael, and from St Michael to Lady Day between the hours of 8 and 9. 3rdly, my breakfast to be always tea or coffee and never to exceed 4 dishes. If neither of those, half a pint of water or water gruel; and for eatables, bread and cheese, bread and butter, light biscuit, buttered toast, or dry bread, and one morn in every week, dry bread only. 4thly, nothing more before dinner, and always to dine between the hours of 12 and 1 o'clock if at home. 5thly, my dinner to be meat, pudding, or any other thing of the like nature, but always to have regard, if there is nothing but salt provision, to eat sparingly; and to eat plenty of any sort of garden stuff there is at table, together with plenty of bread and acids, if any, at table; and always to have the greatest regard to give white or fresh meats and pudding the preference before any sort of highly seasoned, salt, or very strong meat; and always one day in every respective week to eat no meat. 6thly, my drink at dinner to be always boiled water with a toast in it, or small beer, but water if I can have it, and never to drink anything stronger until after dinner. 7thly, if I drink tea at home or abroad, to be small, green tea and not more than 4 dishes; and if I eat anything, not more than two ounces. 8thly, my supper never to be meat but weak broth, water gruel, milk pottage, bread and cheese, bread and butter, apple-pie or some other sort of fruit pie, or some such light diet; my drink, water or small beer, and one night at the least in every week to go to bed without any supper. 9thly, never to drink any sort of drams or spiritous liquors of what name or kind soever. 10thly, if I am at home, in company, or abroad, if there is nothing but strong beer, never to drink more than 4 glasses, one to toast the king's health, the 2nd to the royal family, the 3rd to all friends and the 4th to the pleasure of the company; if there is either wine or punch etc., never, upon any terms or persuasions whatever, to drink more than 8 glasses, nor each glass to hold or contain more than half a quarter of a pint, nor even so much if possibly to be avoided. 11thly, if I am constrained by extreme drought to drink between meals, that to be toast and water, small beer, or very small wine and water; to wit, 1/4 pint of red or white wine to one pint of water. 12thly, never to drink any small or strong beer, winter or summer, without being warmed if possible. And lastly always to go to bed at before ten o'clock when it can be done.

Perhaps the fact that his young wife was at that time sinking under – even visibly dying from – an agonizing gynaecological disorder helped to impress upon him the precariousness of health.

As Turner's blueprint for health shows, keeping well was regarded as an art demanding time, attention, and self-discipline. Yet it hardly required heroic self-denial (' . . . not more than eight glasses . . . '). And its core was simplicity itself. As the Northerner, Humphrey Senhouse, boasted in old age:[69]

Many years have elapsed since I have been confined by indisposition or have taken a single drug from the shop of an apothecary. The prescription which I recommend to all my patients is Air, Exercise, Temperance.

Above all, the watchword was moderation. 'The temperate', wrote the youthful Erasmus Darwin,[70] 'enjoy an ever-blooming Health free from all

Infections and disorders luxurious mortals are subject to.' If temperance
triumphed, he concluded, 'the whimsical Tribe of Phisicians' would go
without their fees, and:[71]

> We should not meet those pale thin and haggard countenances which
> every day present themselves to us. No doubt men would still live their
> Hundred, and Methusalem would lose his Character; fever banished
> from our Streets, limping Gout would fly the land, and Sedentary Stone
> would vanish into oblivion and death himself be slain.

Not till the nineteenth century did 'temperance' acquire its overtones of total
abstinence.[72] In the Georgian period, the temperate man was rather he who
followed the *via media*. This was the message laid out – at immoderate length!
– in some doggerel printed in the *Gentleman's Magazine*:[73]

> *The Economy of Life*
> Be cautious of extremes in all you do,
> And still through life a middle course pursue;
> Avoid repletion, Mammon's baneful curse,
> But Inanition more – for that's still worse;
> The first by nature or by art is cur'd,
> The last a longer time must be endur'd.
> 'Tis easier to deplete the loaded frame,
> Than, when exhausted, to recruit the same . . . .

And so it droned on. In sum, the author claimed,[74]

> Extremes in both by prudent men are shunn'd
> Who squander not in early life that fund
> Of health – on which in future they rely,
> The blest resource of late infirmity.

For the learned, temperance evoked the Greek notion of the 'golden mean',
but most needed to look no further than to commonsense and experience in
following due measure and avoiding extremes. Thus exercise was recommended, yet most Georgians would have judged today's exhausting aerobic
work-outs as not merely unnecessary but positively foolish (Byron's boxing
and Hellespontine swimming were exceptional, perhaps in compensation for
his lameness).[75]

Riding was recommended – nothing better for toning up the muscles and
invigorating the digestion, not to mention rousing the mind and spirits; and
pedestrianism enjoyed a vogue late in the century. For those too old or frail to
ride, driving in a carriage was suggested; mechanical rocking-horses at home,
for adults and children alike, had their fans, and garden swings were believed
ideal for airing the fair. Yet everyone warned against excessive exertion,

especially if it brought on sweats and thirst, followed by sudden coolings and exhaustion.[76] Endurance sports – running, rowing, mountaineering, etc. – did not find favour until they became part, alongside team games, of the 'muscular Christian' ethos of the Victorians.[77]

If the norms for exercise aimed at moderation, so too did recommendations for diet. Medical opinion typically suggested mixed and balanced eating, a blend of animal and vegetable food, to be taken in controlled quantities. Unusual diets, of course, had their enthusiasts. There were a few dozen noted vegetarians, including medical men such as the quack hygienist-cum-sex-doctor, James Graham, and, occasionally, George Cheyne, famed for his seed and milk diet and his advocacy of fasting.[78] As a young man, Benjamin Franklin followed the Baptist health writer, Thomas Tyron, into a vegetarian diet – doing which, he said, 'occasioned an inconveniency' amongst his friends. Georgian vegetarians were less concerned about animal rights than about poisoning the gut with rotting flesh.[79]

But many thought such measures extreme, faddish, and even harmful. William Cobbett, abominator of tea but extoller of 'good and plentiful plain food', argued that fasting, far from being healthsome, was a conspiracy invented by the fat friars of the Catholic Church to enfeeble the people and make them docile.[80] Most commentators did not believe healthy living required such heroics. Even Cheyne mainly condemned the dangers of indigestible dishes (those that were rich, salted, pickled, smoked, or highly-seasoned), and distilled liquors, and inveighed against gluttony. 'The great *Rule*', he stressed, 'of Eating and Drinking for *Health*, is to adjust the *Quality* and *Quantity* of our Food to our *digestive* Powers', concluding that 'Nothing conduces more to *Health* and *Long Life*, than *Abstinence* and *plain* Food, with due *Labour*'.[81]

Georgian notions of 'moderation' were hardly Lenten. Deploring excessive quaffing of alcohol, Cheyne advised his readers not to sink more than a couple of pints of wine a day; two chicken legs and a wing were sufficient flesh for a meal.[82] And many argued that while excess was, of course, harmful, so also was too little, since it would erode one's stamina.[83] Valuing the warming, stimulant and strengthening effects of nourishment, many had grave doubts about living low as a route to health. In the Georgian pudding-time, opinion valued the 'healthy' appetite as a mark of a 'healthy' constitution.[84]

One other desideratum increasingly commanded a place alongside the non-naturals and temperance as part of the trinity of positive health: cleanliness. Dirt, disease, and disorder began to be conflated in the Georgian mind, while hygiene linked the management of body appearance with the pursuit of health. Be clean and you will be healthy, was the message of health-care books such as Buchan's *Domestic Medicine*. Of course, perceptions of dirt and pollution are utterly culture-bound, as are the priorities of hygiene; and the Georgians were habituated to facets of filth that seem intolerable now – bedbugs, hair nits, chamber-pots slopping over in the sideboard. Plumbed-in baths remained almost exotic, and basic aspirations low: Samuel Johnson was not ashamed to be no lover of clean linen.[85]

Nevertheless, much evidence suggests that cleanliness was increasingly perceived as propaedeutic to healthiness – indeed, in John Wesley's astounding phrase, was 'next to godliness'. After all, filth, medical theory suggested, bred the miasmas that produced infections.[86] And individuals developed elaborate cleaning and grooming rituals for their health's sake – washing the skin with soap, scrubbing the nails, brushing the teeth and hair, using the flesh brush to stimulate the circulation, applying astringents, and so forth. Hygienic procedures had specific rationales. For example, washing would unclog the pores and thus promote 'invisible perspiration' – then believed a crucial channel for the expulsion of toxins.[87] But should we not also view this rising concern with personal hygiene as a mark of a wider movement to assert control over, and sanitize, the body?

Dirt disturbed the health-conscious. It mattered dearly to Pepys. At one point, he remarks of his wife, Elizabeth, 'she is busy going with her woman to the hot house to bathe herself'. Yet he remained sceptical: 'she now pretends to a resolution of being hereafter very clean. How long it will hold I can guess'.[88] Many Georgians were assiduous over personal cleanliness. William Cowper was a stickler for dental hygiene. Living deep in rural Buckinghamshire, he found he had to send to London for toothbrushes: 'People do not brush their teeth at Olney'.[89]

Health thus required attention to life-style, temperance, and hygiene. Each lay partly within the individual's power. What had to be done could be tabulated in simple rules. Having expounded his system of childrearing, John Locke concluded:[90]

> And thus I have done with what concerns the body and health, which reduces itself to these few and easily observable rules. Plenty of open air, exercise and sleep; plain diet, no wine or strong drink, and very little or no physic; not too warm and strait clothing; especially the head and feet kept cold, and the feet often used to cold water, and exposed to wet.

Far better to heed these positive rules of health than to use 'the ladies' diet-drinks or apothecaries' medicines'.[91]

But did the Georgians practise what they preached? Often enough. They energetically travelled for their health, sometimes to the South, sometimes by sea, sometimes to spas to take the waters, sometimes to the coast to try sea bathing. Of course, people rode simply for pleasure too, and descended upon Bath for the gambling or to fleece a rich widow.[92] But it would be misleading to minimize the pains taken to strengthen the system and corroborate health. Not least, many put themselves to the trouble of regular courses of self-physicking – diet-drinks, vomits, purges, bitters, cordials, all frequently attended with unpleasant side-effects – in hopes of fortifying the constitution.[93] People looked ahead to keep illness at bay. During one of his rare bouts of wellness, William Cowper chatted the matter over with his physician: 'Air and Exercise are his theme, them he recommends as the best physic for me', he tells his cousin Lady Hesketh, following it up with a modest proposal:[94]

> Come therefore my Dear, and take a little of this good physic with me, for you will find it beneficial as well as I; Come and assist Mrs U[nwin] in the reestablishment of your Cousin's health. Air and exercise and She and You together will make me a perfect Samson.

If the axioms of health were to be heeded, they had to be simple, practical, and commensurable with social etiquette. There was not, of course, wholehearted agreement on what they were. Many, as we have stressed, advocated the hardening regime, and lauded the virtues of perspiration. But some dissented, as did Elizabeth, Lady Pembroke, who had her own favourite ways of protecting her health:[95]

> People of a thin habit should keep themselves warm & guarded against moist, sharp, & cold air, but they should be as carefull to avoid also too free a perspiration. The custom of wearing flannell next the skin, particularly in bed, is allmost as bad as a Diabetes. It enfeebles, drains, & ematiates.

Farington likewise had a friend sceptical of the 'cool' regime:[96]

> Sharpe spoke much of warmth being the great preservation of life, & of the mistaken notion that people should harden themselves by severe exposure. He observed that the masses of people who are necessitated to it prove the fallacy of the principle. – Warm clothing is of the utmost consequence to preserve health, & in this unsteady climate should be little varied.

We should thus not expect unanimity; what we do see, however, is lively interest and practical inquisitiveness. 'The desire of life and health' is implanted in man's nature, exclaims Laurence Sterne's hero, Tristram Shandy. What a delicious irony, then, that it is his wise old fool of a father, 'phthisical' and racked with sciatica, ever vexing himself with musty old tomes and intricate arguments, who perverts the pursuit of health into a hobbyhorse, and worries himself sick over it.[97] Maintaining health should be simplicity itself, as George Cheyne emphasized in the 'Conclusion' to his *Essay of Health*:[98]

> If Men would but observe the *golden Mean* in all their *Passions, Appetites* and *Desires*; if in all their *Thoughts, Words and Actions*, they would but mind, I will not say the *End* of their *Being* and *Existence* here, but the *End* to which their *Thoughts, Words* and *Actions* naturally tend in their last *Resort*; And, *Lastly*, If in the *Gratifications* of their *Appetites, Passions* and *Desires*, they follow'd the uncorrupted *Dictates* of *Nature*, and

neither spurred her on beyond her *Craving*, nor too violently restrained
her in her *innocent Biass*; they would enjoy a greater Measure of *Health*
than they do; have their *Sensations* more *delicate*, and their *Pleasures*
more *exquisite*; live with less *Pain*, and die with less *Horror*.

The historian must take notice of such formulations precisely because they
were widely read and sometimes followed. When, in 1781, Lady Pembroke
wanted to give some health advice to her son – it concerned that evergreen
subject, wearing flannel – she laboriously transcribed a page from Cheyne,
rounding off her letter with: 'So says Doctor Cheyne, from whose Book the
above is copied (*so you see what a wise woman I am*)'.[99] Thus Cheyne, by then
dead some forty years, was still being consulted by a lady, and his name was
assumed familiar to the next generation.

Health remained a prized commodity in Georgian England. 'I have never
possessed or abused the insolence of health', reflected Gibbon.[100] Its presence
was worthy of remark, even rather perturbing – at one point Byron
complained that Lady Milbanke was 'dangerously well'.[101] Because health
was threatened from all sides, and because medicine lacked magic bullets,
prevention was paramount. No wonder the likes of Mr Woodhouse began to
loom so large. People had to take care:[102]

– Bonjour! – a good morrow! – so you have got your cloak on betimes! –
but 'tis a cold morning, and you judge the matter rightly – 'tis better to
be well mounted, than go o'foot – and obstructions in the glands are
dangerous – And how goes it with thy concubine – thy wife – and thy
little ones o' both sides? and when did you hear from the old gentleman
and lady – your sister, aunt, uncles and cousins – I hope they have got
better of their colds, coughs, claps, toothaches, fevers, stranguries,
sciaticas, swellings, and sore eyes.

NOTES

[1]   Thomson (ed.), *Letters of a Grandmother*, 138. The sentiments are those of Sarah,
      Duchess of Marlborough.
[2]   Chapman (ed.), *Letters of Samuel Johnson*, II, 507 (letter 806). For Johnson see
      Mulhallan and Wright, 'Samuel Johnson'; Porter, 'Hunger of Imagination'.
[3]   Quoted in Brett (ed.), *Faber Book of Diaries*, 12.
[4]   Ilchester (ed.), *Lady Holland's Journal*, I, 182-3.
[5]   Tilley (ed.), *Dictionary of Proverbs*, 299. See also 'Health is better than wealth'; more
      hard-bitten is 'health without money is half an ague'. For Walter Shandy, see Porter,
      'Against the Spleen', 86; Bloom and Bloom, 'This Fragment of Life'; Furst, 'Sterne
      and Physick'; Walter believed he had the answer: 'The whole secret of health'
      depends upon the equipoise of 'radical heat' and 'radical moisture'. Sterne, *Life and
      Opinions of Tristram Shandy*, 388.
[6]   Dodsley, *Collection*, II, 310-12.
[7]   Seaton, *Conduct of Servants*, 297.

8   Smythson, *Compleat Family Physician*, v.

9   Taylor, *Montaigne and Medicine*, 85. Cf. Starobinski, 'Body's Moment'.

10   Cheyne, *Essay on Health and Long Life*, 2.

11   Archer, *Every Man His Own Doctor*, 3. Cf. Everard, *Method and Means of Enjoying Health*; Faust, *Catechism of Health*.

12   *Gentleman's Magazine*, 37 (1767), 517, as quoted in Porter, 'Lay Medical Knowledge in the Eighteenth Century', 146; see also Porter, 'Laymen, Doctors and Medical Knowledge'; and Garrison, 'Medicine in the *Tatler*'.

13   Gay, *Enlightenment*, vol. II; *idem*, 'Enlightenment as Medicine and as Cure'.

14   Illich, *Limits to Medicine*, 141f.; Passmore, *Perfectibility of Man*, 171f.; for ideas of longevity, see Trimmer, *Rejuvenation*.

15   Foucault, *History of Sexuality*, I. For discussion see Rousseau and Porter (eds), *Sexual Underworlds*, 'Introduction'. For the democratic, egalitarian potential of health, sec Buchan, *Domestic Medicine*. For the magic of blood, see Wintrobe, *Blood*.

16   Porter, 'Was there a Medical Enlightenment?'

17   Dewhurst, *John Locke*; McNeil, *Under the Banner of Science*; Stansfield, *Thomas Beddoes*.

18   Ilchester (ed.), *Lady Holland's Journal*, I, 183.

19   Bessborough and Aspinall (eds), *Correspondence of Lady Bessborough*, 206.

20   Marchand (ed.), *Byron's Letters and Journals*, II, 56.

21   King-Hele (eds), *Letters of Erasmus Darwin*, 179; Porter, 'Drinking Man's Disease'; Cobbett, *Advice to Young Men*.

22   Beresford (ed.), *Diary of a Country Parson*, II, 7; Thale (ed.), *Autobiography of Francis Place*, 277.

23   Yorke (ed.), *Diary of John Baker*, 455.

24   Climenson (ed.), *Elizabeth Montagu*, I, 293.

25   Fitzgerald (ed.), *Correspondence of Emily, Duchess of Leinster*, II, 61.

26   Gittings (ed.), *Letters of John Keats*, 3, discussed in Porter, 'Patient's View', 192. Keats's sentiment is, of course, a parody of Falstaff in I Henry IV, act 2 scene 4.

27   Cf. Porter, *English Society*, chs. 1 and 7.

28   Hankin (ed.), *Life of Mary Anne Schimmelpenninck*, II, 28.

29   Bottomley, *Attitudes to the Body*; Wear, 'Puritan Perceptions of Illness'; Camporesi, *Incorruptible Flesh*.

30   Woodward, *To Do the Sick no Harm*; Porter, 'Gift Relation'; *idem*, 'Medicine and Religion'; Farr, 'Medical Developments and Religious Belief'; Wesley, *Primitive Physick*; Rousseau, 'John Wesley's *Primitive Physick*'.

31   Brockbank and Kenworthy (eds), *Diary of Richard Kay*, 18; Barry, 'Piety and the Patient'; see also Doe (ed.), *Diary of James Clegg*, I, 10: after developing a swollen throat which was so painful it was difficult 'even to breath', Clegg thought he was on the 'brink of the grave', but as he tottered on eternity he reflected that:

> I desired to live to do God more and better service than ever I had done and evidence the truth of my repentance by a real reformation. Many fervent prayers were (I believe) put up for mee by my hearers who expressed then more affection to mee than ever they had done before, and it pleased God who is longsuffering and abundant in goodness to answer them by calling mee back to life and restoring mee to health.

32   Martineau, *Autobiography*, II, 47; Webb, *Martineau*; Kingsley (ed.), *Charles Kingsley*, I, 58-59. On Kingsley see Haley, *Healthy Body and Victorian Culture*, 255ff.

33   Arbuthnot, *Essay Concerning the Nature of Aliments*; *idem*, *Essay Concerning the Effects of Air*; Burton, *Treatise on the Non-Naturals*; Cheyne, *Essay on the True Nature and Due Method of Treating the Gout*; *idem*, *English Malady*; *idem*, *Essay on Regimen*; *idem*, *Natural Method of Cureing*; *idem*, *Rules and Observations for the Enjoyment of*

Health and Long Life; Grosvenor, *Health, an Essay*; Maynwaring, *Method and Means of Enjoying Health*. For discussion see G. Smith, 'Prescribing the Rules of Health'.

34 Latham and Matthews (eds), *Diary of Samuel Pepys*, IV, 177.

35 Ibid.

36 Ibid., 333.

37 See Risse, 'Health and Disease'; Temkin, 'Health and Disease'; Engelhardt, 'Concepts of Health and Disease'; Riesse, *Conception of Disease*.

38 Norton (ed.), *Letters of Edward Gibbon*, II, 44.

39 Knapp, *Tobias Smollett*, 246; cf. Rousseau, *Tobias Smollett*.

40 Lever (ed.), *Letters of Lady Palmerston*, 80.

41 Niebyl, 'Old Age, Fever, and the Lamp Metaphor'.

42 De Beer (ed.), *Correspondence of John Locke*, III, 645.

43 Axtell (ed.), *Educational Writings of John Locke*; Romanell, *John Locke and Medicine*; Dewhurst, *John Locke*; Nelson, *Essay on the Government of Children* – Nelson divided his subject up into three heads: 'Health', 'Manners', and 'Education'; see also 'Juliana-Susannah Seymour' [i.e. John Hill], *On the Management and Education of Children*, a work eloquent as to how health was often found in the cottage though not in the palace nursery: p.29. Pollock, *Forgotten Children*; Ariès, *Centuries of Childhood*; Fildes, *Breasts, Bottles and Babies*, 79f.

44 Locke, *Some Thoughts Concerning Education*, 61.

45 Nelson, *Essay on the Government of Children*, 127. Locke, *Some Thoughts Concerning Education*, 64.

46 Seymour, *On the Management and Education of Children*.

47 Childs, 'Prescriptions for Manners'.

48 See Bond (ed.), *Spectator*, V, 157. G. Smith, 'Cleanliness'; *idem*, 'Physical Puritanism and Sanitary Science'; *idem*, 'Thomas Tryon's Regimen'; Turner, *Taking the Cure*, ch. 6: 'The Strange Power of Cold Water'. Wright, *Clean and Decent*. Childs, 'Prescriptions for Manners', discusses cleanliness, 203ff.

49 DeMause, *History of Childhood*. The use of cold baths on children was certainly taken to extremes on occasion. See the case of Elizabeth Grant discussed in Pollock, *Forgotten Children*, 130, 133, 169.

50 Seymour, *On the Management and Education of Children*, 57. 'Seymour' was the *nom de plume* of Sir John Hill.

51 Cobbett, *Advice to Young Men*, 264. In the upbringing of his children 'the first thing of all was health': 274.

52 Weekley (ed.), *Memoir of Thomas Bewick*, 34-5, 57.

53 Marshall (ed.), *Autobiography of William Stout*, 80.

54 Home (ed.), *Letters and Journals of Lady Mary Coke*, III, 104, 121.

55 Cheyne, *Essay on Health and Long Life*, 3.

56 Niebyl, 'The Non-Naturals'; Rather, 'Six Things Non-Natural'; Miller, 'Airs, Waters, and Places in History'.

57 Yorke (ed.), *Diary of John Baker*, 231. For Banks, see O'Brian, *Joseph Banks*, 197; Viets, 'George Cheyne'.

58 One health-obsessed diarist who itemized sexual intercourse was Robert Hooke, who charted it alongside the state of his stomach, and the quantity and quality of his sleep. He was probably anxious about the effects of sex upon his metabolism. See Robinson and Adams (eds), *Diary of Robert Hooke*; Beier, *Sufferers and Healers*, 147ff. On the question of optimal frequency of intercourse see Porter, 'Spreading Carnal Knowledge'; *idem*, 'Sex and the Singular Man'.

59 Garlick and Macintyre (eds), *Diary of Joseph Farington*, III, 675-6.

60 Ibid., II, 475.

61 Lewis (ed.), *Letters of The Lady Brilliana Harley*, 24.

62 Penn, *Letter to His Wife and Children*, 11.
63 Randolph, *Domestic Life of Thomas Jefferson*, 115.
64 Greig (ed.), *Letters of David Hume*, II, 305.
65 Vaisey (ed.), *Diary of Thomas Turner*, 139-42.
66 Ibid. 147-8.
67 Ober, *'Boswell's Clap'*; Brady, *James Boswell. The Later Years*, 489ff.
68 Vaisey (ed.), *Diary of Thomas Turner*, 26.
69 Hughes, *North Country Life*, II, 86.
70 King-Hele (ed.), *Letters of Erasmus Darwin*, 3.
71 Ibid.
72 Harrison, *Drink and the Victorians*.
73 *Gentleman's Magazine*, 65 (1795), 948.
74 Ibid.
75 Raphael, *Byron*, 31-2. Cf. Fuller, *Medicina Gymnastica*. In Peacock's *Gryll Grange*, Mr Macborrowdale urged skating to bring about 'a healthy mind in a healthy body'. Garnett (ed.), *Novels of Thomas Love Peacock*, 893.
76 Buchan, *Domestic Medicine*, 99.
77 Haley, *Healthy Body*, 123.
78 For vegetarianism, see G. Smith, 'Thomas Tryon's Regimen for Women'; Thomas, *Man and the Natural World*, 288f.
79 Franklin, *Autobiography*, 19-20.
80 Cobbett, *Advice to Young Men*, 262.
81 Cheyne, *Essay on Health and Long Life*, 74.
82 Ibid., 40.
83 In sex likewise. Lady Byron believed she was ill partly because 'of the frustration of *one* of the purposes of my existence'; Stein, *Ada*, 27.
84 Cf. Jarrett, *England in the Age of Hogarth*, 20, 23, 24, 41.
85 Buchan, *Domestic Medicine*, ch. 8; G. Smith, 'Cleanliness'; Douglas, *Purity and Danger*; Wright, *Clean and Decent*.
86 Riley, *Eighteenth Century Campaign to Avoid Disease*, 19f.
87 In peasant culture, a counter-argument urged the protective value of dirt. See Loux, 'Popular Culture and Knowledge of the Body'. Latham and Matthews (eds), *Diary of Samuel Pepys*, VI, 40.
88 Discussed in Broadhurst, 'Peeps with Pepys at Hygiene and Medicine', 165-72.
89 King and Ryskamp (eds), *Letters and Prose Writings of William Cowper*, II, 513. Cf. Raymond (ed.), *Reminiscences of Captain Gronow*, 350:

During Lord Byron's sojourn at Lisbon, he was much amused with Dan Mackinnon's various funny stories. Upon one occasion Dan's time was entirely taken up by presenting women with tooth-brushes, a supply of which he had received by the packet from London. Opposite his quarters there lived two very pretty Portuguese ladies, who, unmindful of Dan's proximity, and of the fact that his windows commanded a view of their chamber, dressed, undressed, and went through their morning ablutions and toilet. Dan's astonishment was great when he perceived that the fair ones never brushed their teeth; and he lost no time in sending his servant with two toothbrushes in paper, well perfumed and sealed up. The ladies opened the packet, and appeared delighted with the present; but judge of Mackinnon's horror in beholding those dainty creatures perseveringly brushing their raven locks with the tiny brushes!

90 Locke, *Some Thoughts Concerning Education*, 94.
91 Ibid., 94.
92 Neale, *Bath 1680-1850*; Barbeau (ed.), *Life and Letters at Bath*; Schnorrenberg,

'Medical Men of Bath'; Turner, *Taking the Cure*, 72f., 82f.

[93] See, for instance, Fitzgerald (ed.), *Correspondence of Emily, Duchess of Leinster*, I, 330.

[94] King and Ryskamp (eds), *Letters and Prose Writings of William Cowper*, II, 537.

[95] Herbert (ed.), *Pembroke Papers*, 83.

[96] Garlick and Macintyre (eds), *Diaries of Joseph Farington*, VI, 2397.

[97] Discussed in Porter, 'Against the Spleen', 85.

[98] Cheyne, *Essay of Health and Long Life*, 231.

[99] Her letter concluded with a health PS: 'Don't forget your bathing'. Herbert (ed.), *Pembroke Papers*, II, 84.

[100] Bonnard (ed.), *Edward Gibbon: Memoirs*, 40.

[101] Marchand (ed.), *Byron's Letters and Journals*, VIII, 101.

[102] Sterne, *Life and Opinions of Tristram Shandy*, 517.

Chapter 3:
Embodiment

Georgians could never take it for granted that they would wake up well, or, when they fell sick, that medicine would restore them. Health was truly a prize. *Mens sana in corpore sano* – a healthy mind in a healthy body – was the great desideratum. It was necessary to keep the constitution in good repair; general rules – heeding the non-naturals, moderation, and hygiene – would provide a basis.

But the human frame was more than just a machine to keep in good shape. It was also a lived body; each person's experience of flesh and blood existence was unique; and sensations of sickness unsettled the secure sense of self – people complained they were 'not themselves'. Hence it was vital to know one's own body. But there was the rub.

For the body was such a complicated, devious and unpredictable entity to understand and keep in trim. Georgians were pleased to admire the body beautiful, the perfect proportions of the nude as depicted by the anatomy-minded artists who founded the Royal Academy.[1] In their devotions they celebrated the human form as the pinnacle of Creation, man made in God's image, the supreme evidence of natural theology, echoing William Perkins, the seventeenth-century Puritan who contended that 'our bodies are God's workmanship, we must glorify him in our bodies . . . yea, we must not hurt or abuse our body, but present them as holy and living sacrifices unto God'.[2]

But there was another side. All too frequently, bodies were strange or monstrous, bizarre rather than beautiful. The Georgians flocked to raree-shows to gawp at the freaks – a mocking Gulliver world of limbless midgets, Siamese twins, and giants, including the Irishman, Byrne, all 7ft. 2½ in. of him, whose corpse was 'snatched' after his death by 'resurrectionists' acting for the surgeon William Hunter, who conducted the final indignity of dissection.[3] Society displayed an unquenchable fascination – prurient though not yet guilt-ridden – over those who seemed to defy nature – freaks who claimed to fast for years, or to expire and revive at will; hermaphrodites; or Mary Tofts, the Godalming peasant who claimed to give birth to litters of rabbits.[4] The macabre mystery of dying – and the possibility of resuscitation –

drew crowds to executions, some trusting in the miraculous property of the hanged corpse, when touched, to heal.[5] It made news when, in 1796, a cricket match was fought at Greenwich Hospital, between a one-armed team and a one-legged team. The body, that most immediate and familiar object of existence, was yet the most unfathomable – truly the glory, jest, and riddle of the world.[6]

And indeed in practical terms, managing the body and keeping it healthy posed grave problems. How was one to know, for example, what was really going on inside – inside oneself, or others, such as one's children? Of course, one could scrutinize the external organs and facies for reassurances of health and marks of malady. How far, and how skilfully, this was done poses some puzzles. Hygiene and cleanliness tracts recommended thorough body-washing, grooming, and attention.[7] But toilet facilities – especially for whole-body bathing at home – remained rudimentary even for the affluent.[8] The Georgians, moreover, seem to have made love semi-clad and slept in night-attire. Hence, it may have been the exceptional person who routinely stripped naked, and so could give the body a thorough inspection.[9] Many, of course, were so corpulent as to be physically incapable of inspecting their nether parts at all (did Gibbon ignore his hydrocele because he couldn't actually see it?). Fatness may account for the fact that some women seem to have given birth without even being aware they were with child; corseting and ample clothing allowed others to conceal pregnancy.[10] Swaddling new-born babies presumably also hid even surface body changes – though that practice was, of course, rapidly falling from favour. The lower-class custom of sewing infants into their clothes for winter warmth would have had the same effect.[11] Thus, etiquette and material culture may have combined to limit people's familiarity even with their own 'two yards of skin'.[12]

It is noteworthy, for instance, that Queen Caroline, George II's wife, resisted surgical examination because it must then have come to light that she was suffering from a hernia; were this discovered by the King, she feared he would lose sexual interest in her, thus destroying her sway at court.[13] It may say much about habits of body covering, love-making, and medical reticence that her own husband and the court physicians alike seem to have been unaware of the Queen's condition.[14]

Understanding One's Insides
If there were various obstacles to familiarity even with body surfaces, gauging subcutaneous processes – getting a window on to the constitution itself – was doubly difficult. When pain was felt, how should this be indexed to a particular organ, process, or malady? How was one to tell if it was to be a fleeting twinge or chronic, trivial or serious? Pain itself defies verbalization and analysis.[15] And the Georgians had to manage such problems in the absence of diagnostic procedures taken for granted today. Was one just 'hot' or did one really have a fever? There were no thermometers to pop into the mouth to test one's 'temperature'. Lay people had a subjective awareness of

the pulse – whether it was racing or weak, regular or erratic – but almost none left record of trying to count it. In that respect their practice was much as that of doctors, who themselves did not get far beyond talk of 'hard' and 'languid' pulses.[16]

One clue to the body's internal condition lay in meanings of visible symptoms. After all, doctrines about the legibility of visible emblems and signatures had been prominent in Renaissance humanism and in popular lore alike. The cosmos was so constituted (stated the theory of correspondences) that the outer mirrored the inner and thus could be 'read' as evidence of it. Everybody knew obvious instances of how surface physiological changes indicated both disease – the yellow skin of jaundice – and emotional states – the goose-flesh or cold perspiration of fear, the blush of shame, and so forth. Traditional humoral theory saw these as instances of a comprehensive semiotics in which a person's visible 'complexion' (roughly, physical appearance and bearing) interlinked with 'temperament' (disposition) and 'humour' – that is, the unique balance of the four 'humours', or vital body fluids, within. Thus, visible signs were markers of integral constitutional attributes. Swarthy skin colour went with the 'black looks' of the melancholy man, determined by a superfluity of black bile in his abdomen. Melancholy itself was no disease, but a build-up of physical symptoms could indicate the onset of 'melancholy' as a truly pathological condition. Likewise, the red face and the prominent, pulsating arteries of the sanguine man characterized an abundance of blood. These would be normal in a person of sanguine humour. But if present in excess, they would be read as the physical symptoms of a distemper of the blood. Phlebotomy was indicated to prevent seizure or stroke.[17]

The same epistemology provided the foundations for another traditional body of knowledge that read the outer to understand the inner: physiognomy. One of the Renaissance sciences, physiognomy, scrutinized structures of the cranium and expressions of the countenance as windows on to character; the physical was an index of the spiritual, moral, and personal. The discipline perhaps fell under a cloud early in the eighteenth century, when the deceptive and physiognomy-defying figure of the 'hypocrite' seized the public imagination; but the immense prestige of Lavater in the late Enlightenment commanded many converts, such as William Cowper and the Rev. William Holland.[18] The astrological 'zodiac man' also remained popular, a heuristic anatomical diagram in which each body region was keyed to its retrospective astrological sign, supposedly crucial – in the light of an individual's horoscope – in determining his health prognosis.[19]

Humoral theory, physiognomy, and astrology alike waned during the Hanoverian century.[20] Yet people had to continue to rely heavily on reading external signs as tokens of the invisible beneath the skin. Common sense taught that bearing and mien reflected their general robustness – a truth only confirmed when people confused the issue by applying cosmetics and creating a look. The trusted clinician such as William Heberden was precisely the doctor who, merely by his expert gaze, would be able to reach a differential diagnosis.[21]

Yet, of course, outward appearances could tell only so much. Some more precise soundings of inner events were essential. Did this mean, then, that people boned up on anatomy and physiology, to understand the fibres of cartilage, the mechanics of muscles and arteries? A few perhaps. In mid-Georgian Sussex, Thomas Turner pored over Richard Wiseman's renowned surgical texts, and Edward Gibbon and Adam Smith were two of many literati who attended William Hunter's famous anatomy lectures. On the whole, however, the production of 'physiologies for the people' was mainly a nineteenth-century innovation.[22]

The Georgians did not aim for exact knowledge of their own inner parts. Maybe this is revealed by the language used for their insides, which was charged and polysemic, but often anatomically imprecise. People spoke of 'sympathies' between organs, of 'obstructions', or of want of 'spirits', and so forth. Their terms were allusive, applying metaphors from the world at large, and not least from emotional processes.[23] Recourse to this kind of terminology – whose unsatisfactoriness contemporaries themselves deplored – suggests the sheer difficulty of finding objective speech forms to label the inner operations. Outer organs all possessed clear, monosyllabic, vernacular names – arm, back, breast, ear, hair, hand, head, neck, skull, skin, tongue, etc.[24] But the lexicon of inner anatomy was vaguer. People often complained, for example, of having pains in their 'reins' – a term absent from contemporary medical dictionaries. Could they point to them? What were they – a region, an organ, or a function? 'Reins' seems sometimes to have been a synonym for 'kidneys' – though that merely raises the question of how the 'kidneys' were conceptualized. But sometimes the term referred more broadly to the general area of the lower back, with hints of euphemistic reference to the sexual organs. Likewise, people commonly spoke of their spleen being disordered – producing the disorder known as the 'spleen' – irritability, depression, etc.: how many such people even knew where their spleen was?[25]

Moreover, the unfamiliar was familiarized within an anatomy which was emotional and symbolic rather than scientific, like Gray's. Bodily parts acquired meaning as the objective correlatives of experience. The liver was supposed to be the seat of the passions; the kidneys controlled temperament; the heart was the centre of the emotions. Thus, talk of a weak heart, or a stout, feeble or strong heart – or indeed of being 'hearty' or 'big-hearted' – traded upon rich metaphors, and projected imaginative pictures of the invisible workings within. By contrast, specific heart disease was rarely spoken of. Strokes and seizures were attributed to the blood, and dropsy was a failure of urinary discharge, without the recognition that it was the side-effect of a failing heart.[26] Satirists, however, from Swift to Sterne treated this twining of soma with simile as little more than a tendentious semantic sleight of hand.[27]

Georgian body language cared less for soberly 'naming the parts' than for creating a system of inner and organic referents for feelings. People commonly somatized their experiences through a vocabulary trading in pairs of localized binary opposites. They said they were 'up' or 'down', 'high' or 'low', 'in' or 'out' of spirits. Thus, when George Cheyne spoke of constitutions being either highly-strung or flat, he was imagining the nerves as like strings. If nerves lost their tension, through overlading with food, for example, they would fail to convey signals sharply throughout the body, and the person would become 'flat', dulled in sensation. Likewise, 'acrimonious' people were thought to have over-acid stomachs, perhaps through gorging on unripe fruit.[28]

Overall, our analysis of letters and diaries suggests that the Georgians took only a limited interest in the anatomy of their bodies for its own sake. Organs meant much less than functions, and functions were monitored via ease and 'dis-ease'. When the Georgians conceptualized their bodies, their concern was with essential health-preserving systems. These involved visible changes and palpable feeling – above all, of course, pain. Thus, if one had a hearty appetite, ate, felt comfortable after a meal, and developed a good appetite again some hours later, it seemed proof positive of that capital blessing, a 'good stomach'.[29] Often, however, such 'tangibility' was mediated through a complicated network of symbolic meanings. Thus, all agreed that the blood should be sweet. Scores of remedies existed for 'cleansing' or 'purifying' the blood, to restore such purity. But one could not experience the quality of one's blood directly, as one could feel hunger or 'wind'. That could, of course, be experienced only through a learnt system of coded response – feelings of 'blood pressure' or weakness – keyed to beliefs about that particular humour.[30]

Fuelling the System

So which organic processes did the health-conscious person believe paramount? Above all, those most intimately associated with the paradigm of the body as a through-put system, especially the absorption of food and the expulsion of waste. The active body obviously needed nourishment to provide strength and warmth: analogies with furnaces, lamps, and steam-pumps readily came to mind: all needed their fuel. Hence, health consciousness fixed upon the stomach, dubbed by Edward Jenner the 'grand Monarque of the Constitution'[31] – or, as the proverb put it, 'the belly carries the legs and not the legs the belly'. 'The great Wisdom and Happiness of Man', adjudged the early Georgian physician, John Woodward, 'consists in a due Care of the Stomach and Digestion'[32] – an apothegm echoed in Samuel Johnson's remark that 'he that does not mind his belly will hardly mind anything else'.[33]

The rational-utilitarian mind of the Enlightenment endorsed a work ethic that treated man as a producer. To produce he had first to consume. The vision of man as an active consumer, whose vitality constantly needed replenishing, chimed with the emergent 'consumer society'. The stomach symbolized the material reality of man. Mary Anne Schimmelpenninck reported the gross Erasmus Darwin as characteristically saying that 'man is an eating animal, a drinking animal, and a sleeping animal, and one placed in a material world, which alone furnishes all the human animal can desire'. Darwin was a philosophical materialist, who believed that enthusiastic trenchermanship made one hale and hearty.[34]

Thus, the stomach itself needed to be energetic and in good tone, to digest food in substantial quantities, and process it into blood and spirits. Hence, the best foods were rich and strong ('body building'). The diet of the rich, biased towards meat and wine, was typically thought more invigorating than the gruel and water of the poor. For was not meat more nourishing than vegetable food? and red meat better than white, because richer in blood?[35] Hence, the Englishman's devotion to roast beef was not mere patriotic gloating, gluttony or fantasizing, but, according to the folklore of good health, positively therapeutic. 'My Stomach brave today', purred Parson Woodforde in 1795, 'relished my dinner'.[36] Even when debilitated, he still looked forward to his roast beef, believing it would restore his spirits. The final entry in his diary includes a last supper of beef:[37]

> Very weak this Morning, scarce able to put on my Cloaths and with great difficulty, get down Stairs with help. Mr. Dade read Prayers & Preached this Morning at Weston Church – Nancy at Church. Mr. & Mrs. Custance & Lady Bacon at Church. Dinner to day, Rost Beef etc.

One of Locke's correspondents informed him that his wife, 'in order to her health . . . is entered into a course of gluttony, for she is never well but when she is eating'.[38] The aptly named William Stout likewise had a touching faith in the restorative power of wholesome food and a good stomach. Having suffered for a month with a 'sore distemper', during which time he was let blood, and thus weakened by his doctor, he finally rebelled. 'I got some apatite for nurishment':[39]

> The doctor said I was feverish and must take weak meat and drinke, but I coveted better. My neighbour John Bryer visited me often and once merrily told me I must take better meat and drink, and toud where there was very good ail, and sent for some, and I drank one or two glassess of it, which very much refreshed me. And my apatite increasing, I easily recovered.

'Appetizing' dishes – e.g., those with strong aromas and piquant sauces and pickles – would best tickle the digestion; and if these failed, medicinal drinks such as tonics and bitters might succeed in rousing digestive juices. Thus, the best stomach was that which spontaneously produced hunger pangs, perhaps after air and exercise.

This philosophy, linking the healthy body to a 'healthy appetite', did not, however, go unchallenged. A counter-current warned that serious eating would wear the stomach out.[40] Rich food and drink were indigestible, and so would bloat the gut, depress the spirits, and clog the channels of the nerves. Excess was poison. Forcing the intestines into heroic activity gutted life's candle; light eating would preserve it.[41]

So an alternative 'low diet' regime was proposed as the best preservative.

This won numerous advocates, not least amongst critics of 'luxury'. What is interesting, however, is that this counter-gastronomy arose at all. For it signals how fundamentally entrenched was the belief that good health – indeed life at all – depended upon stoking up the stomach. When Jane Austen wanted to mock valetudinarianism, she showed Mr Woodhouse picking over his food ('an egg boiled very soft is not unwholesome').[42]

The body was thus a vital system, but one dependent upon copious replenishment of stimulus. A good stomach animated the system as a whole, but in particular, it replaced and nourished the blood. If today's medical folklore sees the heart and lungs as the crucial organs, the Georgian equivalent championed the primacy of the stomach and liver in maintaining the blood, still commonly seen as the very source of vitality (so many cultural resonances identified blood with life itself, as in 'lifeblood', bloodshed, or in the symbolism of the Eucharist). Maintaining the proper quality and quantity of the blood-supply was essential to health. Lack of blood – if, for example, it failed to flow in phlebotomy – was ominous. Excesses could be equally dangerous, in threatening apoplexy. Moreover, blood readily became tainted, corrupt, too thin (serous) or thick (viscid). Hence, the popular faith in bloodletting, regarded not just as a specific against particular maladies (e.g., the overheating produced by a fever) but generally as a healthy prophylactic, designed to evacuate stale, and stimulate the manufacture of fresh blood.[43] Above all, blood had to flow, for bright, vibrant, pulsing blood was the best index of that animation and circulation the Georgians associated with living well. As George Cheyne insisted,[44]

> The Grand Secret, and Sole Mean of Long Life, is, To keep the Blood and Juices in a due State of Thinness and Fluidity, whereby they may be able to make those Rounds and Circulations through the animal Fibres, wherein Life and Health consist, with the fewest Rubs, and least Resistance, that may be.

Another internal agent whose ebullient flow was equally vital was the animal or vital spirits, whose office was to mediate between the corporeal organs and the mind, will, inner senses, and consciousness.[45] Blood was tangible; these spirits, by contrast, were aetherial – entities whose existence was chiefly recognized by their effects. When in fine fettle – thanks to good nourishment – they produced 'fine', 'elastic', or 'high' spirits; if depleted or 'clogged', they begat that baleful low spiritedness known as the 'English malady'. For, as Anne Bradstreet had versified it in the seventeenth century:[46]

> The vital spirits they're call'd, and well they may
> For when they fail, man turns unto his clay.

The animal spirits were intermediaries between the somatic and the psychic, the material and the merely metaphorical. They led a kind of double life, as states of feeling and as real entities, of which mental states were the symptoms. Can one be sure, for instance, which terms are literal, and which figurative, when Lady Louisa Conolly informs her sister, 'I am rejoiced to hear you are better . . . and that your spirits are so good, though your blood is so *foul*'?[47]

Cleansing the System

So the body comprised a flow system needing constant refuelling. It was no less important, however, that waste be efficiently expelled. The first consumer society was eager to appropriate nature in the form of food; but the Georgians also feared being poisoned by what they took in. Hence, popular physiology paid no less attention to the bowels than to the stomach; together they formed a single, continuous operation, ever active, awake or asleep.[48]

Pre-modern letters or journals teem with references to the discharge of bodily waste, and to the vital importance of efficient bowels to a happy and healthy existence. Diarists constantly bewail their constipation, and dwell on their bowel motions, and the number, size, shape, hue, odour, and texture of the stools they produced. A late seventeenth-century child, Mary Nelthorpe, thus informed her mother:[49]

> This is to lett my Mother know
> Her Worme is well from top to toe
> Except my Bumps, they so exceed,
> They make we scratch untill I Bleed;

> But now I think ont, It is fitt,
> To lett you know how oft I shitt;
> Two stooles a day, but sometimes none
> Take one time with another one;
> And that I may not one thing miss;
> Bout twice as oft I goe to piss.

Urine was inspected, to judge its colour (dark spelt melancholy, blood was dangerous) and taste (sweet urine indicated diabetes), and to search out sediment;[50] and the old art of uroscopy, though repudiated by the faculty, retained its hold on the popular imagination as a diagnostic tool.[51] A health folklore enabled people to read their discharges: turds that swam around in the pot, for example, were meant to be ominous, denoting internal windiness.[52]

It is obvious why urine and faeces assumed such diagnostic significance.[53] With so little direct access to internal processes, evacuations offered the best first-hand evidence of inner health or decay. There is, in any case, reason to think that these natural functions were often terrible sources of discomfort and disease. 'Gravel' – sediment in the urine – was common, as were bladder stones; both produced sharp, often excruciating, pains in urination, as, of course, did gonorrhoea. Retention of urine and 'strangury' – pains in passing it, or worse still, a stoppage – were frequent.[54] Constipation was also a scourge for the well-off, with their heavy meat and pastry diets and lack of fibre. Opiate dosing also blocked the bowels.[55] George II died of a heart attack after straining too much while on the close-stool. It is thus hardly surprising that the Georgians were avid consumers not just of dinners but of 'laxatives' (mild) and 'purgatives' (strong). Senna and rhubarb form part of the standard bill of fare, clysters of soap, tobacco, etc., were widely tried, and the brave submitted to mercury and calomel. Purging was a panacea. For contemporaries were terrified of auto-poisoning. Gastric processes raised ferments that produced putrid matter (flatulence, bile, indurated faeces). But all the body fluids formed health threats; unless regularly purged, they would grow stale and fetid, or, as with dropsy, would flood the system. Sweating was advocated, to carry off rank moisture through the pores. If natural perspiration failed, sweats could be induced artificially, through medicines ('diaphoretics' or 'sudorifics'), by applying hot cloths, etc., or even by a visit to the bagnio or the hummum. A cold signalled the closing of the pores; one consequently almost drowned in phlegm.[56]

Also popular was the idea of aiding nature by purging and cleansing the stomach, through inducing artificial vomits. Cheyne regarded vomiting as the key to good health. People used emetics widely in practice.[57]

The fluids associated with the reproductive system likewise had to be discharged regularly – not too often, but certainly not too little. Copious menstrual flow was thought desirable for women, purging bad blood. When the 'courses' failed in teenage girls in particular, it was seen as symptomatic of a more profound malady, often called the 'green sickness'. Marriage was widely prescribed, as the best way of purging this stoppage.[58] Georgian sexual folklore thus believed excessive continence had its dangers, for it allowed rank matter to accumulate. When Samuel Johnson caught his friend, Dr Robert James, with a whore, James explained it was only for his health's sake: without regular discharges, he fell sick.[59] Of course, potential cures could prove worse than the disease: Georgian opinion regarded masturbation as a perilous means of procuring discharge because it excited excessive imagination.[60]

The healthy body was thus a system whose well-being depended upon generous input and easy outflow. The woman who readily became pregnant, produced numerous babies, delivered them easily, and had a good breast of milk, fulfilled the criteria of health.[61] This conveyor-belt body could obviously be seen as analogous to a machine: 'the play of the animal machine continues to be easy and regular', noted Gibbon.[62] Or, as Sara Coleridge depicted it early in the nineteenth century, 'Life is the steam of the corporeal engine; the soul is the engineer who makes use of the steam-quickened engine'.[63] Yet if there was something 'modern' about the machine metaphor, theirs remained a conception of the body broadly consonant with the traditional humoral theory as first codified by the Greeks, standardized in humanist medicine, and widely deployed by pre-modern practitioners.[64] Humoral medicine stressed the cardinal importance of the body fluids, pre-eminently blood, phlegm, yellow bile (choler), and black bile (melancholy). Each needed to be present in the right balance and quantity – neither too much nor too little

– for good health. This, however, was tailored to the individual in question. The health of different people hinged upon different levels of the key fluids, producing those differences in appearance, life habit, complexion, and temperament characteristic of human diversity. Yet the dividing line between difference and pathology was fine. A mild superfluity (or deficiency) of a particular humour could easily turn into the excess (or lack) which spelt disease. Physical health thus depended upon a delicate equilibrium.

Georgian medics gradually abandoned humoralism, while (as Rosenberg has stressed) continuing to underwrite its implicit holism. Lay people likewise. In the early Stuart age, Anne Bradstreet wrote a poem entitled 'Of the Four Humours in Mans Constitution'.[65] Such doctrinal commitments seem to disappear, and when Sterne showed Walter Shandy bandying such terms around, it was to guy him as an anachronism. Yet humoralism left two enduring legacies: a concern with fluids and their through-put, and the notion that pains were symptomatic of systemic disorders. Holism dominated thinking about the body.

The Body as a Sign System

The healthy body was thus one performing its natural functions easily and (Locke insisted) regularly.. 'Piss and fart, a sound heart', ran the proverb. Sometimes, there was an arresting openness about bodily needs and the calls of nature. Carousing after dinner, gentlemen would relieve themselves in pots stationed in the sideboard. One day, Pepys opened a door to find Lady Sandwich 'doing something upon the pot'.[66] But Pepys was a man of the world, we might say, living in easy-going Restoration times. We may be mildly surprised, however, to find, at the beginning of the nineteenth century, the teenage Elizabeth Wynne calmly recording in her journal, without a blush, that in Switzerland the ladies prefer to undergo medical treatments by means of enemas.[67] Are we thus studying a century which was unusually uninhibited and 'enlightened' about the body?

Reality proves more complex. What was taboo, and where lines were drawn between openness and secrecy, the frank, the decent, and the obscene, seems to have depended on the individuals or circles concerned. To discredit his Yahoos, Swift shows them shitting down from the trees upon Gulliver (such copious evacuations may have struck a doctor as rather healthy!), and he suggests that the knowledge that 'Celia shits' is enough to make one lose one's 'wits'. Writing to Stella, Swift chooses to spell 'ur–e' in place of 'urine'.[68] But his disgust at body processes seems untypical. The perfectly proper Lady Mary Coke retailed an anecdote in her journal of one maid of honour at a masquerade, who, being called short, dashed into a room of ease, and finding no vessel there but the hat of a reveller masquerading as a Turk, pissed into it.[69] Miss Wynne seems to feel totally unabashed about recording that her father had got piles[70] – though the coy William Cowper found that complaint unmentionable, writing to Lady Hesketh, 'I have been ill, but nobody must ask what I have ail'd'. He did, however, give her a generous clue by saying it was the 'excruciating disorder' God had visited upon the Philistines while the Ark was captive with them.[71] Contemporary letters often refer to menstruation, though commonly through such euphemisms as 'the French lady', or a 'certain time'.[72]

What made certain natural functions – and indeed the flesh in general – shameful, was much debated by the Georgians (not least obliquely in their vast output of erotica, which, of course, traded upon obscenity).[73] Explorers were discovering the immense variety of sexual habits and notions of decency amongst the nations of mankind. Enlightenment outlooks discarded moral universalism, hinting that all was in the eye of the beholder. Why, then, should perfectly natural acts such as defecation be objectionable? asked Samuel Rolleston, Archdeacon of Salisbury, in his anonymous *Philosophical Dialogue concerning Decency* (1751). What could be improper about such vital and healthful actions?[74]

Standards regulating body exposure, he noted, were matters of social convention. Some civilizations copulated in public. Moreover, '*nature* no more requires that a woman's legs should be cover'd than a man's; and therefore it can be no dictate of *nature* that a lady should be asham'd, if she discovers as high as her calf.'[75] What offended was relative from culture to culture. Indeed, the very *idea* of offensiveness was culture-bound (though, he argued, given that it was so powerful, it was decent to uphold decency).

The good archdeacon thereby echoed the teasing equivocations of Bernard Mandeville on the sense of *pudor*. The rules of bodily propriety were, as Mandeville insisted, both arbitrary and hypocritical: it was more titillating to conceal erogenous zones than to expose them.[76] As champions of liberty and individualism, the Georgians were permissive in allowing display of the torso and in discussing what was taboo.[77] As advocates of civilization, they saw virtue in the progress of decency and delicacy.[78] As Gibbon put it, 'the pains and pleasures of the body how important soever to ourselves are an indelicate topic of conversation.'[79]

The body certainly had its own sanctity. The Rev. William Jones deplored what he found an unreasonable delicacy about corpses amongst the sensitive:[80]

Feby 13th. 1815. Fine gemmen & ladies shudder at the very idea of viewing a corpse! After all the anxious care that they bestow to pamper, adorn, perfume, etc, their own frail bodies, how mortifying it must be to them to think of the havoc of death, how soon they will become *loathsome*, & a prey to *worms*!

Hence, few were willing to have their corpse dismembered on death, for postmortem purposes. One was Lady Caroline Holland,[81] another was the eccentric physician, Messenger Monsey, who required that he be anatomized before his body was slung in the Thames.[82]

The very mixed reactions to the emergence of the man-midwife, replacing the traditional women-only birthing ceremony, capture some of the dilemmas posed by ambivalence towards the body. Polite and educated women seem happily to have accepted the male accoucheur, overcoming in the name of medical progress what they saw as the false delicacy of hiding their 'privities' from doctors. By contrast, critics male and female could see only scandal in this development. One reason why physicians did not routinely give their patients 'hands-on' physical examinations may lie in taboos against exposing one's flesh to the outside gaze.[83] Sexual matters produced similar equivoca-tions. In general, the Georgian age endorsed the relatively free expression of erotic desires. Yet it simultaneously bred phobias over the 'evils' of masturba-tion, which, according to *Onania*, amounted to 'self-pollution'.[84]

How then did people overall relate to their bodies? One set of injunctions, of course, supported by Calvinistic Christianity, taught people to despise carna-lity, and to envisage themselves as wormy corpses, rotting by the day: 'all flesh is grass.' Walter Shandy thus spoke of his 'ass' to refer to all that was unregenerate;[85] Richard Kay rather more politely implored God to remind him 'that I am dust'.[86] Plenty of Georgians, in particular Dissenters, believed that *contemptus mundi* required contempt for the body.

Yet in an overtly worldly age, quite different attitudes came into their own. There was a certain pride in the flesh. It was right to be comely, and fat – within limits – was in fashion.[87] Daring *décolletages* exposed great expanses of bosom – a token not just of beauty, but also of fecundity.[88] Conversely, men were expected to possess a good *embonpoint*. John Bull was always fat, hale, and hearty, quite distinct from *maigre* Johnny Crappo.[89] Not until the Regency dandies did bucks aspire to be trim and slim, dieting like Byron on dry biscuits and soda-water.[90]

Pride in the flesh manifested itself in the increasing attention paid to handsomeness, beauty, and feminine sex appeal. Ideally, beauty was health, health beauty: but all too often, beauty was the product of art not nature, and was purchased through the use of health-damaging garments (tight-laced corsets) and cosmetics (typically lead-based).[91]

Particular parts of the body assumed special importance. For example, fine, white teeth were a prerequisite for a pleasing face, and a good set was prized, for tooth decay was common. Still in his mid-twenties, Richard Kay had dreadful toothache; his father yanked out the offender. He noted, 'this is the seventh Tooth I've lost in a few years Time . . . O Tooth-Ach, O cruel Pain.'[92] The fear of exposing rotting or missing molars was one reason, presumably, why Lord Chesterfield instructed the polite never to laugh in public. Lady Mary Coke was shocked to see the Duchess of Portland all gums: 'the loss of her teeth makes a great alteration; She looks very old'.[93] Such ravages were commonly repaired by dentures; Georgian dentistry was primarily cosmetic.[94] For bad looks were assumed to betray bad health. Lady Gower had a distemper that left her with a 'red face'; she was recommended the Tunbridge waters; she refused, being unwilling to face company.[95]

Eyes likewise were attractive when they functioned well. But many people suffered from squints and irregularities – Aubrey was struck by Birkenhead's 'great goggli eies', and Johnson hated the idea of being known as 'blinking Sam'.[96] Smallpox often damaged the sight, as did poor light, burning the midnight oil, and so forth. Strained eyes gave great pain – Pepys, of course, abandoned his diary because of eyestrain. Many wore glasses, not least Lemuel Gulliver.[97]

Hair was a further index of health, though the fashion for wigs disguised hair loss. Shelley was self-conscious of his own thinning, greying locks, fearful it was a symptom of venereal infection. There was a good trade in hair restorers, patent and home-brewed. Georgy Capel concluded a letter to her grandmother in 1815:[98]

> P. S. I should be more obliged to you than I can express if you would send me a Bottle of 'Mather's Ointment' to keep the Hair on, for mine has fallen off to such a degree that it is quite thin and no remedy that I have yet had has had any effect.

Skin condition was crucial. Youthful skin was expected to possess a bloom, though its fading could be compensated by ornamentation and cosmetics. Patches, powder, wigs, lace, gauze, perfumes, etc., were used in vast profusion by women and men alike, to repair the ravages of time and, in particular, the disfigurements of smallpox.[99] Of course, deploying such aids to beauty – the very need to 'put on a face' – was itself an admission that natural beauty had faded.

Beauty in life, people increasingly thought, should be perpetuated by beauty in death. From the Black Death through to the Puritans, grisly tomb decoration had taught the horrors of mortality, the putrefaction of the flesh, serving as a *memento mori*. Eighteenth-century funeral monuments, by contrast, dwell upon the attractiveness of the dead, even endowing the corpse, Ariès suggests, with a morbid eroticism.[100]

Overall, it was a culture possessing an articulate body language. There were hierarchies of value and worth. Right was superior to left, tall to short, young to old, fat to thin.[101] The buttocks were objects of sport and humiliation; the genitals, too, sometimes, but they could also be called 'the more noble parts' – Gibbon's habitual self-ironical phrase.[102] The heart symbolized strength, love and loyalty; and the 'bowels' carried similar connotations, being the metaphorical site of decency, conscience, or 'guts'. Thus, Alexander Carlyle roundly condemned a certain 'Webster, who had no bowels, and could do mischief with the joy of an ape'; and Gibbon, deploring his aunt's shabby treatment by her family, remarked in mock exoneration that 'her more wealthy relations were not *absolutely* without bowels'.[103] Moreover, the classification of the organs mirrored status hierarchy. Mary Anne Schimmelpenninck noted:[104]

> every class of society has its own glory. The poor, his physical strength; the middle, the power of mental research; the elevated, the charm of

manner, the amalgam which fits them as keystones to solidify the arch of society. Then let us rejoice in our own, and rejoice in our neighbours' gifts, but not expect to find all united in one.

If the body was thus 'classed', no less was it 'gendered':[105]

> when in ordinary Discourse [Addison wrote in the *Spectator*] we say a man has a fine Head, a long Head, or a good Head, we express ourselves metaphorically and speak in relation to his Understanding; whereas when we say of a Woman, she has a fine, or a long, or a good Head, we speak only in relation to her Commode.

Above all else, the nose was the pinnacle of breeding.[106] When, in *Tristram Shandy*, the hero loses his nose at birth, it is a loss ominous of all his future losses. Pamphagus, by contrast, claims *'nihil me paenitet hujus nasi'* ('my nose has been the making of me').[107]

The body was thus far more than a mere carcass. It was an instrument of communication, a weapon of war, an expressive medium of the self, the prime symbol of class, status, and gender in the face-to-face atmosphere of the world we have lost; and an eternal puzzle.

NOTES

1   Bynum and Porter (eds), *William Hunter and the Eighteenth-Century Medical World*, 11, 13, 29; Darlington, 'The Teaching of Anatomy'.
2   Quoted in Wear, 'Puritan Perceptions of Illness', 63.
3   For visiting freaks, see De Beer (ed.), *Diary of John Evelyn*, III, 197-8. For dwarfs, see Yorke (ed.), *Diary of John Baker*, 291. Park and Daston, 'Unnatural Conceptions'; Altick, *Shows of London*; Morley, *Memoirs of Bartholomew Fair*; Friedli, 'Passing Women'; Fiedler, *Freaks*; Porter, 'Monsters and Madmen'.
4   Rousseau, *Tobias Smollett*, 164-8.
5   Linebaugh, 'Tyburn Riot'.
6   Boucé, 'Imagination, Pregnant Women and Monsters'.
7   G. Smith, 'Prescribing the Rules of Health'.
8   Wright, *Clean and Decent*.
9   Cf. Mitchell and Penrose (eds), *Letters from Bath*, 181, where Penrose complained that ladies' hair was full of lice.
10 For one such anecdote, about Lady Effingham, see Sorlien (ed.), *Diary of John Manningham*, 189.
11 Cf. Ariès, *Centuries of Childhood*; Stone, *Family, Sex and Marriage*, 161, 424.
12 Elias, *Civilizing Process*; Broadbent, 'Image of God'.
13 See Sedgwick (ed.), *Lord Hervey's Memoirs*, 326-8.
14 It is possible that prudery plays a part here. The important point, however, is that even the surface of bodies could be 'invisible'. For Boswell debating whether a married woman who would undress before her husband was modest see Weis and Pottle (eds), *Boswell in Extremes*, 141.
15 Wear, 'Historical and Cultural Aspects of Pain'; Keele, *Anatomies of Pain*; Scarry, *Body in Pain*; Bakan, *Disease, Pain and Sacrifice*; De Moulin, 'Historical-Phenom-

enological Study of Bodily Pain'.

[16] Lawrence, 'Educating the Senses'.

[17] Baker, *Dignity of Man*; Bambrough, *Little World of Man*; Barkan, *Nature's Work of Art*, 8f.

[18] Porter, 'Making Faces'; Shortland, 'Skin Deep'; Tytler, *Physiognomy in the European Novel*; King and Ryskamp (eds), *Letters and Prose Writings of William Cowper*, III, 367: Cowper speaks of his skill in '*phyznomy*'; Ayres (ed.), *Paupers and Pig Killers*, 25. Viscount Torrington, another addict, spoke of his 'lavaterisms': Andrews (ed.), *Torrington Diaries*, IV, 44. For Mary Anne Schimmelpenninck's fascination with Lavater, see Hankin (ed.), *Life of Mary Anne Schimmelpenninck*, I, 171.

[19] Capp, *Astrology and the Popular Press*, 180f.

[20] Lewenthal, *In the Shadow of the Enlightenment*, 13f.

[21] Before the nineteenth century, medicine saw no gains in minute hands-on physical examination. See Reiser, *Medicine and the Reign of Technology*, 1f.; Bynum and Porter (eds), *Medicine and the Five Senses*.

[22] Vaisey (ed.), *Diary of Thomas Turner*, 167. Cooter, 'Power of the Body'.

[23] O'Neill, *Five Bodies*.

[24] Dirckx, *Language of Medicine*, 16f.

[25] Porter, 'Against the Spleen'.

[26] However, people did actually examine their blood, when it was spilt in injuries or in phlebotomy, to test its colour, density, and 'serousness' (i.e., its semi-clear 'serum'). Each of these features had its import. See Wintrobe, *Blood*; Shorter, *Bedside Manners*, chs. 1 and 2.

[27] Furst, 'Sterne and Physick'; Miller (ed.), *Memoirs of Martin Scriblerus*.

[28] Cheyne, *English Malady*, 47f.

[29] Arbuthnot, *Essay Concerning the Nature of Aliments*.

[30] Wintrobe, *Blood*.

[31] Miller (ed.), *Letters of Edward Jenner*, 7; cf. Squirrell, *Maxims of Health*; Arbuthnot, *Essay Concerning the Nature of Aliments*.

[32] Levine, *Dr Woodward's Shield*, 12.

[33] Boswell, *Life of Johnson*, I, 467.

[34] Hankin (ed.), *Life of Mary Anne Schimmelpenninck*, I, 241.

[35] Mennell, *All Manner of Foods*, 182f.

[36] Beresford (ed.), *Diary of a Country Parson*, IV, 213.

[37] Ibid., V, 412.

[38] De Beer (ed.), *Correspondence of John Locke*, I, 341.

[39] Marshall (ed.), *Autobiography of William Stout*, 91.

[40] The theme of Trotter, *View of the Nervous Temperament*. See Porter (ed.), 'Introduction' to Trotter, *Essay on Drunkenness*.

[41] Cheyne, *Essay on Health*; Willich, *Lectures on Diet and Regimen*. See G. Smith, 'Prescribing the Rules of Health'.

[42] Austen, *Emma*, 55.

[43] Wintrobe, *Blood*.

[44] Cheyne, *Essay on Health and Long Life*, 220.

[45] See Myer, 'Tristram and the Animal Spirits', and the references there cited.

[46] Ellis (ed.), *Works of Anne Bradstreet*, 126.

[47] Fitzgerald (ed.), *Correspondence of Emily, Duchess of Leinster*, III, 253.

[48] See Beier, *Sufferers and Healers*, 133f; Buchan, *Domestic Medicine*, 151.

[49] Hertford Record Office. We owe this quotation to the kindness of Dr Linda Pollock.

[50] Cf. Buchan, *Domestic Medicine*, 15, 6, 424.

[51] Porter, ' "I Think Ye Both Quacks" '; Brian, *Piss Prophet*.

[52] John Aubrey, quoted in Hunter, *John Aubrey and the Realm of Learning*, 128.

53 Freudians have their own theories as to why Georgian culture was fascinated by excrement: Brown, *Life against Death*; 126f.

54 Buchan, *Domestic Medicine*, 406ff., 612f.

55 Jones, *Mysteries of Opium Reveal'd*.

56 Shorter, *Bedside Manners*, 62.

57 Cheyne, *Essay on Health and Long Life*; Buchan, *Domestic Medicine*, 441, 754.

58 Astruc, *Treatise on all the Diseases Incident to Women*; Loudon, 'Chlorosis'; Figlio, 'Chlorosis'; Crawford, 'Attitudes to Menstruation'.

59 Quoted in Schwarz, *Life in Johnson's London*, 100; Robinson, *Theory of Physic*, 78, recommended frequent sex, on the grounds that retention of semen was harmful. Cf. Porter, '"Secrets of Generation Display'd"'.

60 Stengers and Van Neck, *Histoire d'une Grande Peur*.

61 Fildes, *Breasts, Bottles and Babies*, 98f.; Mauriceau, *Diseases of Women with Child*, viii; Astruc, *Treatise on all the Diseases Incident to Women*.

62 Bonnard (ed.), *Edward Gibbon: Memoirs*, 186.

63 Coleridge (ed.), *Memoir and Letters of Sara Coleridge*, I, 164.

64 Temkin, *Galenism*; Beier, *Sufferers and Healers*, 63-4.

65 Rosenberg, 'Therapeutic Revolution'; *idem*, 'Text and Medical Context'. Ellis (ed.), *Works of Anne Bradstreet*.

66 Latham and Matthews (eds), *Diary of Samuel Pepys*, VIII, 422.

67 Fremantle (ed.), *Wynne Diaries*, I, 212.

68 Swift, *Journal to Stella*, 254; for discussion of Swift's prudery and excremental vision, see Brown, *Life Against Death*; Nokes, *Jonathan Swift*; Siebert, 'Swift's Fiat Odor'. Cf. Kassler, 'Breaking Wind'.

69 Home (ed.), *Letters and Journals of Lady Mary Coke*, II, 393.

70 Fremantle (ed.), *Wynne Diaries*, I, 131, 143, 223.

71 King and Ryskamp (eds), *Letters and Prose Writings of William Cowper*, IV, 64.

Compare Gibbon's awkwardness in discussing with his friend, his hydrocele: I must at length withdraw the veil before my state of health though the naked truth may alarm you more than a fit of the gout. Have you never observed through my *inexpressibles* a large prominency which, as it was not at all painful and very little troublesome I had strangely neglected for many years? (Norton (ed.), *Letters of Edward Gibbon*, III, 359.)

72 Fitzgerald (ed.), *Correspondence of Emily, Duchess of Leinster*, III, 255.

73 Wagner, *Eros Revived*.

74 Rolleston, *A Philosophical Dialogue Concerning Decency*, 9.

75 Ibid.

76 Mandeville, *Virgin Unmask'd*. Betsey Wynne noted in 1798, 'the fashion now is to be almost naked'. Fremantle (ed.), *Wynne Diaries*, II, 205. Cf. 'Introduction' to Rousseau and Porter (eds), *Sexual Underworlds of the Enlightenment*.

77 Porter, 'Libertinism'.

78 Perrin, *Dr Bowdler*, 3f.; Jaeger, *Before Victoria*, 139f.

79 Bonnard (ed.), *Edward Gibbon, Memoirs*, 89, 29.

80 Christie (ed.), *Diary of the Rev'd William Jones*, 241. To overcome such squeamishness, Lady Harriet Spencer's father insisted that she touch remains in charnel houses. See Bessborough and Aspinall (eds), *Lady Bessborough and Her Family Circle*, 23-4.

81 Home (ed.), *Letters and Journal of Lady Mary Coke*, III, 385. The autopsy revealed cancer, as had been expected.

82 Climenson (ed.), *Elizabeth Montagu*, II, 204.

[83] Porter, 'Rise of Physical Examination'; *idem*, 'A Touch of Danger'; Donnison, *Midwives and Medical Men*; Schnorrenberg, 'Is Childbirth any Place for a Woman?'; Lewis, *In the Family Way*.

[84] Wagner, *Eros Revived*; *Onania*, ch. 1, opening: 'Self pollution is that unnatural Practice, by which Persons of either Sex, may defile their own Bodies'.

[85] Camporesi, *Incorruptible Flesh*, 3; Sterne, *Life and Opinions of Tristram Shandy*, 557:

It was not only a laconic way of expressing – but of libelling, at the same time, the desires and appetites of the lower part of us.

[86] Brockbank and Kenworthy (eds), *Diary of Richard Kay*, 20.

[87] Ewing, *Dress and Undress*, 41f.

[88] Calder-Marshall, *Grand Age of the Lady*, 36f.

[89] Duffy, *Englishman and the Foreigner*.

[90] Marchand (ed.), *Byron's Letters and Journals*.

[91] As criticized by Beddoes, *Hygeia*. Cf. Williams, *Powder and Paint*.

[92] Brockbank and Kenworthy (eds), *Diary of Richard Kay*, 20, 46, 56, 93.

[93] Home (ed.), *Letters and Journal of Lady Mary Coke*, IV, 93.

[94] Hillam, 'Development of Dental Practice'.

[95] Home (ed.), *Letters and Journal of Lady Mary Coke*, III, 105.

[96] Collier (ed.), *Scandal and Credulities of John Aubrey*, 132.

[97] Rogers, *Eighteenth Century Encounters*, 1.

[98] Marquess of Anglesey (ed.), *Capel Letters*, 139. 'Georgy' was a daughter of Caroline Capel.

[99] Williams, *Powder and Paint*; Gunn, *Artificial Face*; Kanner, *Folklore of the Teeth*, 90; Woodforde, *False Teeth*, who discusses (p. 98f), George Washington's struggles with false teeth, which he wore from his early forties. Pelling, 'Appearance and Reality'.

[100] Ariès, *Hour of Our Death*; Gittings, *Death, Burial and the Individual*, 151f. Richardson, *Death, Dissection and the Destitute*, 3f.

[101] Polhemus (ed.), *Body as a Means of Expression*, 13f.; Miller, *Body in Question*.

[102] Norton (ed.), *Letters of Edward Gibbon*, III, 317.

[103] Burton (ed.), *Autobiography of Alexander Carlyle*, 319; Bonnard (ed.), *Edward Gibbon: Memoirs*, 37.

[104] Hankin (ed.), *Life of Mary Anne Schimmelpenninck*, II, 127.

[105] Bond (ed.), *The Spectator*, II, 531.

[106] Quennell (ed.) *Private Letters of Princess Lieven*, 29: 'In England the worst of misfortunes is to have a vulgar nose.' The sexual connotations of noses were exploited, of course, by Sterne.

[107] Sterne, *Life and Opinions of Tristram Shandy*, 232.

Chapter 4:
Embodiment and Self

The body thus remained the mystery of mysteries, provoking contradictory feelings. 'A poor thing but mine own', it excited mingled pride and shame. But even more intractable, perhaps, was the problem of how precisely this animated carcass related to the knowing, willing, thinking, feeling, and suffering self. Were there indeed two separate entities, mind and body, the soul merely serving time trapped in the terrestrial cage of flesh?[1] Or were they just different modalities of a unity, head and tails of the self-same coin? Sometimes it seemed one, and sometimes the other.

In certain circumstances individuals would own their bodies and call them 'myself'; in other, they would just as readily point to a leg or a tooth – especially when it was damaged – and address 'it' in the third person.[2] Certain parts of the body were more 'disownable' than others: traditional opinion regarded the womb as alien, an 'animal within an animal'; the penis was likewise unbiddable, possessing a life of its own, or not. Moreover, the mind, in turn, was no less many-headed than the body. Age-old familiarity with such phenomena as dreaming, trance, sleepwalking, and possession, and not least the late-Enlightenment fad of mesmerism, offered convincing proof that the mind was no simple unity, but rather multiple strata of consciousness, each possessing a 'mind of its own'. Conventional metaphysics itself spoke of many faculties – the will, judgement, and the various 'souls' (rational, animal, vegetable) – with distinct offices in directing life. Perhaps the problem was, thus, less how the body related to the mind, than how the various properties of the body related to the different chambers of the conscious self.[3] To those practised in a certain mental detachment, this very disconnection could itself provide wry amusement. Racked with gout, Gibbon commented: 'I hope with Philosophy. My legs *depend* on a single cushion.'[4]

Such questions of how far one controlled – indeed, how far one *was* – one's own body, were, of course, extremely pertinent to sufferers trying to order their lives, and cope with pain in bodies which all too often seemed possessed less by their own selves than by alien diseases or even spirits. But they also raised profound general philosophical and religious dilemmas. If they were to uphold the Christian creed, and indeed, the common conviction of man's unique dignity, then consciousness – whether defined as mind, spirit, understanding, soul, or *cogito* – had to be seen as ontologically independent of, prior and superior to, mere 'blood and gut'. It had to be shown to survive the shuffling off of this mortal coil, proving that flesh and bones were, after all, no other than a transit van. Mary Anne Schimmelpenninck explained why it was of such paramount importance – both dogmatically and personally – to sustain the autonomy of the soul:[5]

> The connexion between the visible and invisible world is one of the greatest of all questions, and it must ever remain a subject of deepest concern, especially to *regenerate* man, – that creature distinguished not only from the brutes by his intellect, but from the fallen human race by the renovation of his spirit, and who, thus connected with the animals by his body of dust, with man by his intellect, and with the Church above by his renovated spirit, stands on the verge of two worlds.

Only if man possessed a self-moving spirit did Christianity's hopes of life eternal, or *homo sapiens*'s sense of his unique dignity, make sense. Similar notions of the integrity of mind form the reference frame – one, of course, far more ironical – against which David Hume, hardly a man of piety, when dying of cancer, could write to William Strahan, 'My body sets out tomorrow by Post for London; but whether it will arrive there is somewhat uncertain'.[6]

This Christian humanist dualistic vision of mind over matter entailed certain basic tenets for man considered as a whole. It was the job of reason to rule the body as a rider would bridle his horse, or a king command his subjects. The flesh was bound to prove a snakepit of agony, embarrassment, and anguish, but the mind should soar above such tribulation and bear it with fortitude. John Locke's friend, Damaris Cudworth, thus recognized her duty to stand aloof from bodily woes. She suffered, she told Locke, many painful trials:[7]

> It is not long you Know since I Bury'd my Brother, Since that I have also lost my Sister, My child has beene in the Greatest Danger Possible of the same Fate, and I am not yet freed from the Feares of it Besides this I have Freqent Assaults of the most Painefull of Distempers, of which I had no Apprehension till very latly.

Nevertheless, she claimed, 'I would not have you suppose me when you have read This, Under any Violent Griefe, I am grown such a Stoick'. It was especially important to certain Christians, to show the superiority of the pious soul to physical temptation or mere somatic pain.

From all quarters, the counter-view – the prospect that there was nothing to man but matter,[8] and that consciousness itself might be only a function of organization – was execrated. Inherently degrading, it was seen as flinging open the door to immorality, anarchy, and atheism.[9]

So the mind's duty was to master what Walter Shandy libelled as his 'ass'. Thus, Parson Malthus reflected that, despite the searing pain of toothache, he could transcend the agony when engrossed in writing his *Essay on Population*.[10] By contrast, the urgent appetites of the body ought not reciprocally to unsettle the mind. Or, put another way, those physical fits which, overwhelmingly and unavoidably, overturned the mind's customary sway were to be defined as abnormal, pathological exceptions: they were *sickness* itself.[11] Man was sick when his body was out of control. Such bouts of sickness could be physical – fever, for example – so devastating as to render the mind unable to command the body, upsetting the mental equilibrium itself; or worse, they could actually be diseases of the mind, thereby suspending or terminating the empire of reason. The Georgians championed the rule of the mind; but they acknowledged that there must be exceptional circumstances – which needed to be strictly defined – in which it was waived.[12]

Such a philosophy – established in Platonism, Christian theology,[13] and, subsequently, Cartesianism – in which the mind's separation from, and dominion over, the body were axiomatic, entailed a programme of health responsibilities. For one thing, it meant duties of self-government and regimen, to discipline and civilize the body.[14] Threats to such superiority needed to be overcome. Over-indulgence in carnal appetites – in fornication, lying abed, tippling, or whatever – would erode the controlling will. Vices readily became habit-forming; especially when reinforced by alcohol and narcotics, addiction would be the consequence, and the cravings of the body, for stimulus, pain relief, or mere oblivion, would, if not resisted, ultimately enslave the will. As we shall explore below, the perils of addiction and obsession dominated the Georgian pathological imagination. Occasional abuses would turn into physical necessities; at first, these would merely elude mind control; eventually, the mind itself would collude in self-subjugation; thus, vice begat physical malady, which then begat mental illness over three degenerations.[15]

Mind-body dualism thus obliged the healthy mind to control the healthy body. In recompense, it also allowed exculpations. Precisely because it was seen as relatively distinct from the self, the body could in the same manner ultimately be disowned.[16] Damaris Cudworth could excuse to Locke the disability of sickness along these lines, 'it being onely in my Power to Governe my Mind, and not my Body'.[17] Thus no blame was *necessarily* attached to becoming ill (unless, of course, it was self-inflicted, the product of recklessness or excess); and the state of being sick could thus legitimately be regarded as deserving compassion, not condemnation.[18] Feeling bad did not make you bad; being innocently unwell did not make you a worse person. (In his utopian or distopian fantasy, *Erewhon*, the Victorian, Samuel Butler, later explored, by contrast, a social code in which it was a crime to be sick.)[19]

In other words, under special circumstances – legitimate sickness – people were permitted to dissociate themselves from, to disown, bodies that were temporarily disobedient and disgusting. This offered scope for a certain strategic somatization – in other words, for attributing disorders and disturbances to the flesh as a way of distancing oneself from them, ensuring that the nobler faculties were not implicated.[20]

A person was subject to disturbing feelings, pains, lowness of spirits. How was that to be evaluated? The Georgian sufferer would repudiate the possibility that his mind was truly disordered, for in the scale of disease, mental affliction always had a grave, and, indeed, stigmatizing, ring. Neither did he wish to believe that his pains were moonshine, mere imagination or malingering; for the *malade imaginaire* drew suspicion and satire. Nor would he gladly lie in limbo, uncertain of what was the matter. Far better to pin down the pains to some named organ as part of a physical diagnosis. Thereby the sickness was authenticated, no blame was (most probably) attached, and the definite somatic diagnosis removed the anxiety of uncertainty. Pre-modern patients and doctors alike, coping with those complaints liable to be called hypochondria, hysteria, the vapours, the spleen, and so forth – we might say 'neurotic' symptoms – commonly pinned them on some physical defect.

The autobiography of the post-Restoration Nonconformist, Richard Baxter, affords an instance. When he fell sick with mysterious pains, his physicians initially sought a somatic aetiology (kidney stones were suspected), found they could not agree, and began to suspect that all the trouble lay in Baxter's imagination. For his part, the patient resented the implication that he was merely suffering from – or indeed basking in – 'the hypochondriac melancholy'. Hence, he had to formulate his own rival diagnosis of his complex symptoms: 'I thought myself, that my disease was almost all from debility of the stomach, and extream acrimony of blood by some fault of the liver'. Far better that the liver be to blame, than that Baxter himself – or worse still, the Devil – be the guilty party.[21]

Doubts about Dualism

This vision of mind and body as constituting a dualistic hierarchy had dazzling attractions. It gave plenty of explanatory leeway and flexibility. By privileging the mind and permitting holding the body at arm's length, it emphasized a general duty of the self to safeguard well-being, while sufficiently exonerating itself from blame in most cases of sickness.

Dualism's difficulty was that it could not be consistently sustained. For one thing, it lost its coherence when faced with all those intractable anatomical and philosophical dilemmas thrown up in the wake of Descartes. If psyche and soma were separate, but mind could act on the lower faculties, through which physical channels did it operate? Descartes's proposal that the pineal gland formed this magic motorway had become an object of merriment in the satires of Swift and others. Yet what other putative pathway seemed more plausible? Few Georgians wished to conflate mind and brain; but they clearly needed some axis of interchange. All thus seemed obscure: as the Scottish doctor, William Buchan, put it: 'How mind acts upon matter will, in all probability, ever remain a secret'.[22]

More seriously, the basic proposition of strict mind-body independence simply flew in the face of the facts of life. For daily experience was enough to convince everyone of the absolute inseparability – identity even – of mental disposition, feelings, and bodily states – a point Laurence Sterne merely confirmed when stating in *Tristram Shandy*,[23] 'A man's body and his mind, with the utmost reverence to both I speak it, are exactly like a jerkin, and a jerkin's lining; rumple one – you rumple the other.' – in short, what a 'junketting piece of work [there is] betwixt [our bodies] and our seven senses'. Obviously, the passions of the soul were inflected in the body. In anger, the blood boiled, and one went crimson; when terrified, one trembled, one's hair stood on end, one developed goose-flesh; one shook with excitement; one's heart pounded with grief or stood still with shock, and so forth. Social life, in fact, *relied* upon those systematic correspondences between mental feeling and physical manifestation – were things otherwise, would not all gesture and expression be a mockery? And would not the acme of mind-body dualism be the sly hypocrite, whose actions would never betray his intentions?[24]

Inner states did not merely express themselves through the body; it was universally accepted that mental turbulence could actually reduce the body to sickness.[25] As one Oxford undergraduate explained in 1781, there are[26]

> Cases where actual diseases of the body were evidently occasioned by perturbations of the mind. Instances of the force of imagination in pregnant women are notorious. Convulsions and fainting are common effects of fear, an extreme degree of which has been said to turn the hair white. And I have heard an odd story of a man at Edinburgh that was persuaded, by the stratagem of some physician, into a fever.

Psychosomatic views of this kind were not the daring speculations of the intellectual *avant garde*; they were utterly commonplace. As George Cheyne emphasized, 'The *Passions* have a greater Influence on *Health*, than most people are aware of'. He detailed their great range:[27]

> 2. All *violent* and *sudden* Passions, dispose to, or actually throw People into *acute* Diseases; and sometimes the *most violent* of them bring on *sudden* Death.
> 3. The *slow* and *lasting* Passions, bring on *chronical* Diseases; as we see in Grief, and languishing hopeless Love . . . .
> 5. Men of lively Imaginations and great *Vivacity*, are more liable to the *sudden* and *violent* Passions, and their Effects.
> 6. Thoughtful People, and those of good Understanding, suffer most by the *slow* and *secretly consuming* Passions.
> 7. The *Indolent* and the Thoughtless suffer *least* from the Passions: The *Stupid* and Ideots *not at all*.
> 8. The *Diseases* brought on by the Passions, may be cured by *Medicine*, as well as those proceeding from other Causes, when once the Passions

themselves cease, or are quieted. But the *preventing* or *calming* the Passions themselves, is the Business, not of Physick, but *Virtue* and *Religion*.

Cheyne's final point was crucial. The solution for mentally-induced disorders of the body did not lie in medicine: only spiritual means would avail, to produce the requisite calm.[28]

The symptoms of Mary Clarke were communicated to John Locke through her husband. She copied down her complaint thus:[29]

I find when any thinge doss afectt and disturbe my mind, it doss thuss refenge it selfe upon my body, beyond the common rate that it dose att other times, and by thiss meanes keeps me very leane and low sperrited, and hindred me as I beleve from Gathering that stranth by the bath waters as mr lock expectted.

Her first-person account perfectly illustrates Cheyne's point. Parson Jones recorded the sad death of a parishioner, Mrs Webb, in her twenties, whose maladies appeared similarly psychological:[30]

She languished for many months. I saw her frequently during her illness. She never appeared to have any bodily complaint which medicine could relieve. She certainly died of a broken heart arising from the unhappy state in which she & her husband lived together.

There is, of course, no suspicion of 'witchcraft' or 'maleficium'. Nor does the vicar find the happening surprising. It is plain as a pikestaff to him that consciousness can oppress the body. Contemporaries were well aware of the power of the emotions to induce physical disease symptoms. John Taylor recorded a case, treated by Dr Brooke, of a woman who had first suffered from sexual fears, and had then actually been sexually assaulted:[31]

Brooke said he had attended a lady who suffered under a contracted throat, which occasioned her great difficulty in swallowing. She said that she traced the cause to the following circumstance. When she was a young woman, and in bed with her mother, she dreamed that she was on the roof of a church, struggling with a man who attempted to throw her over. He appeared in a carman's frock and had red hair. Her mother ridiculed her terrors, and bade her compose herself to sleep again, but the impression of her dream was so strong, that she could not comply. In the evening of the following day, she had appointed to meet her lover at a bowling-green . . . She had passed over one field in hopes of meeting the gentleman, and sung as she tripped along, when she entered the second field, and accidentally turning her head, she beheld, in the corner of the field, just such a man as her represented, dressed in a carman's frock, with red hair, and apparently approaching towards her.

She tried to escape, but he caught her and assaulted her. The man was caught, and was brought to trial for rape.[32]

> The lady, however, was too ill to come into court, but appearances were so strong against him that he was kept in close custody, and when she was able to give evidence . . . she was struck with terror at the sight of him, and fainted, but gave evidence; the culprit was convicted and executed. The medical gentleman added, that when she had finished her narrative, she declared that she felt the pressure of the man's hand on her neck while she related it, and that her throat had gradually contracted from the time when the melancholy event occurred. At length her throat became so contracted, that she was hardly able to receive the least sustenance.

Note that it is the woman herself who makes the association between the rape and the constriction of the throat. Neither Brooke nor Taylor, it seems, stooped to Freudian speculations as to whether the woman in question was merely hysterical, having fantasized it all; nor did they hypothesize about anatomical analogues for the throat; nor did Taylor state whether recounting the story served as a talking auto-cure and relieved the constriction. The point, however, is that all parties clearly perceived and accepted the psychosomatic origins of the malady.

Indeed, the faculty of imagination was accepted as exercising enormous sway over bodily states. Congreve, complained Swift, 'gave me a pain in the great toe, by mentioning the gout'.[33] Not least, it was still widely believed that whatever 'conception' possessed a woman's imagination when she 'conceived' would be imprinted on her foetus.[34] Indeed, the even more impressive phenomenon of the *couvade*, phantom male pregnancy and labour, was well known, though ponderers such as John Ward might ask 'what may bee the reason why husbands sympathize with their wives in their breeding and bringing forth'.[35] Above all, in the hypochondriac, imagination could suggest itself into all manner of physical diseases. As a correspondent informed Mr Spectator:[36]

> I am one of that sickly Tribe who are commonly known by the name of Valetudinarians; and do confess to you that I first contracted this ill Habit of Body, or rather of Mind, by the study of Physick. I no sooner began to peruse Books of this Nature, but I found my Pulse was irregular, and scarce ever read the Account of any Disease that I did not fancy my self afflicted with. Doctor *Sydenham's* learned Treatise of Fevers threw me into a lingring Hectick, which hung upon me all the while I was reading that excellent Piece. I then applied my self to the Study of several Authors, who have written upon Phthisical Distempers,

and by that means fell into a Consumption; till at length, growing very fat, I was in a manner shamed out of that Imagination. Not long after this I found in my self all the Symptoms of the Gout, except Pain; but was cured of it by a Treatise upon the Gravel, written by a very Ingenious Author, who (as it is usual for Physicians to convert one Distemper into another) eased me of the Gout by giving me the Stone. I at length studied my self into a Complication of Distempers; . . . .

Mental agitation caused physical distress, provoking the young David Hume to write that 'to keep my Mind at rest & my Body in motion seems to be the best Recipe'.

Thus, the mind and the passions produced physical responses unwittingly, 'insensibly' (the Georgians' near-equivalent of 'unconsciously'), and agonizingly. But the pathways were clearly two-way. For everyone knew that physical malaise would also inevitably disturb the mind and the spirits. It was the experience of the toughest person and the most resolute Christian; as even Elizabeth Fry put it:[37]

My spirit is so much broken within me, and bowed down, that I cannot write much. As the body so much affects the mind, I feel the more sunk under our trials from my state of illness, still the Lord sustains me in mercy and in love.

Satirists mocked the magnificent *homo sapiens* whose mind was so prey to aberrations of the gut and the bowels. In Swift's phrase, 'the corruption of the senses is the generation of the spirit'. Ever irreverent, Byron made capital of the notion that the most idealistic sentiments and spiritual torment were in reality thrown up by lower causes. What of his own troubles? pish! –[38]

a *broken heart* means nothing but *bad digestion*. I am one day in high health – and the next on fire or ice – in short I shall turn hypochondriacal – or dropsical – whimsical I am already – but don't let me get tragical.

Overall, the Georgians could not reject the duet of self and soma; theirs was a vision holistic through and through – equally psychosomatic and somato-psychic. The mysteries of the organism had their wretched side. Voyaging to the West Indies, the Rev. William Jones fell sick of body and spirits: 'My poor Tabernacle is racked with pain. My flesh and bones are entirely a prey to Disorder . . . Bodily Pains and Lowness of Spirits have filled up most of this day.'[39] Such misery could equally be represented in the grotesque mode. Smollett has one of his characters in *Humprhy Clinker* sardonically gloss this holism,[40]

I find my spirits and my health affect each other reciprocally – that is to say, every thing that discomposes my mind, produces a correspondent

disorder in my body; and my bodily complaints are remarkably miti-
gated by those considerations that dissipate the clouds of mental
chagrin.

There was no single, all-explanatory *theory* of operations of the intricate
symbiosis of mind and body. But everybody acknowledged this interplay in
healthy subjects, and recognized that sickness entailed a further labyrinthine
complexity, something else out of control. Take epilepsy. The peasant poet,
John Clare – who, of course, spent the last thirty years of his life in an asylum –
attempted to get to the root of his own epileptic seizures:[41]

> my indisposition, (for I cannot call it illness) originated in fainting fits,
> the cause of which I always imagined came from seeing when I was
> younger a man name Thomas Drake after he had fell off a load of hay and
> broke his neck the gastly palness of death struck such terror on me that I
> coud not forget it for yers and my dreams was constantly wanderings in
> church yards, digging graves, seeing spirits in charnel houses etc in my
> fits I swooned away without a struggle and felt nothing more then if I'd
> been in a dreamless sleep after I came to my self but I was always warnd
> of their coming by a chillness and dithering that seemd to creep from
> ones toe ends till it got up to ones head, when I turnd sensless and fell;
> sparks as if fire often flashd from my eyes or seemd to do so when I
> dropt, which I layd to the fall.

Clare thus seemingly believed suggestion and imagination were the origin of
his condition, which returned 'every spring and autumn since the accident
happend when my fears are agitated to an extreem degree and the dread of
death involves me in a stupor of chilling indisposition'. Medical means,
however, were of avail:[42]

> – these fits was stopt by a Mr Arnold M.D. of Stamford, of some
> notoriety [*sic*] as a medical gentleman and one whom I respect with
> gratful remembrances for he certainly did me great benefit as usual.

Nerves

Traditional medicine, of course, possessed a familiar idiom for explaining the
complete permeability of mind, body, and behaviour – consciousness and
physical behaviour: humoral theory. For humours were organic (body fluids),
yet they also paralleled the temperament (temper), and the complexion
(appearance).[43] In other words, one single, self-contained system governed
disposition, mien, and constitution.

Over time, humoral physiology lost its purchase, although the idiom itself
enjoyed life after death. The new terminology, increasingly in vogue during
the eighteenth century, for depicting the intricate interlinkage between
consciousness and embodiment, was that of 'nerves'. In the educated mind,

the notion of 'nerves' perfectly captured the intuition that some internal physical medium must be responsible for the inscrutable interaction of psyche and soma in cases of agitation, feverishness, or depression. 'Nerves' (as Thomas Trotter put it), perfectly explained this secret 'sympathy':[44]

> There is a species of sympathy among certain organs of our body, that points out a more intimate connection with the mind; than what is possessed by others. The lungs and heart, in the thorax: the stomach, intestines, liver, and all the viscera subservient to digestion, have an innate sympathy with our emotions. During strong impressions on the mind, the heart beats quick and tremulous, and is said to palpitate; the motion of the ribs and diaphragm grows irregular and involuntary; and the action of the lungs so unequal as to make respiration hurried and convulsed; hence sobbing, sighing, and panting take place.

The nervous system had, of course, been familiar ever since Antiquity.[45] But during the eighteenth century, it acquired a dominant role in medical theorizing through the new fascination with the reflexes, sensation, and irritability. Did individual organs possess intrinsic powers of sensation and motion, independently of central brain activity and conscious volition? (Reflex action could provide a model for this.) Or was the only ultimate site of activity the mind or brain itself, in which case all sensation needed to be channelled through the nerves into the cortex, registered as pleasure or pain, and transformed into the motor response through this central nervous centre? In Britain, Robert Whytt's emphasis upon unconscious yet purposive mental activity offered a popular reading of the subterraneous interconnectedness of brain, body, and behaviour.[46]

Meanwhile, in the same intellectual milieu, the enormously influential Edinburgh medical professor, William Cullen, argued in a complementary way that all disease was strictly speaking 'nervous', i.e., typified by pain mediated through nervous stimuli. Through the central nervous system the body responded to dysfunction or infection, wiring up sensitive tissues with the higher structures of brain and mind.[47]

Georgian doctors embraced the language of the nerves. Patients were bombarded with this talk. They read about it in popular health manuals, in magazines, and in novels. Despite a satirical tinge, the fashionable Bath doctor, James McKittrick Adair, claimed they embraced it with open arms, as the latest fashionable medical explanation:[48]

> Upwards of thirty years ago [Adair noted] a treatise on nervous diseases was published by my quondam learned and ingenious preceptor Dr. Whytt, professor of physic, at Edinburgh. Before the publication of this book, people of fashion had not the least idea that they had nerves; but a fashionable apothecary of my acquaintance, having cast his eye over the book, and having been often puzzled by the enquiries of his patients

concerning the nature and causes of their complaints, derived from thence a hint, by which he readily cut the gordian knot – 'Madam, you are nervous!' The solution was quite satisfactory, the term became fashionable, and spleen, vapours, and hyp were forgotten.

Patients may have been rather more sceptical over what occasionally seemed a new-fangled nonsense. David Garrick reported a 'terrible malignant Fever':[49]

> my health has been very delicate, & capricious – I have had no less than Eight Physicians, yet I am alive & in Spirits, tho somewhat ye Worse for Wear and tear – Dr Gem, Physician to ye Embassy, has exerted all his Skill & Knowledge . . . . – I have no Fever at present, I have head-Aches, & Indigestions, & I have lately been convinc'd that I have Nerves.

Nevertheless, presumably through medical proselytization, the idiom of the nerves became the élite way of representing the subtle sympathies of consciousness and physical state. If the nerves were 'high', or 'highly strung', the mind was bright, and the body felt sensations acutely; were the nerves 'low', the mind was dull and the body sluggish. Or one could simply be 'nervous' as a blanket term, suggesting a diffused heightened sensibility, febrile delicacy, vulnerability to excessive feeling, and a brittleness of temper.

Nervousness was not automatically identified as sickness *per se* – a point rather bunglingly made by George III in the first of his bouts of insanity, when he insisted, 'I am nervous, I am not ill, but I am nervous; if you would know what is the matter with me, I am nervous'.[50] Yet nervousness dipped into illness along a sliding scale. 'I'm sorry to find how very nervous (or what's called so) I am when the least thing ails me, or hurries or fatigues me', apologized Caroline Fox to her sister Emily.[51]

Talk of nerves triggered assumptions with profound ambiguity. It could be a way of establishing an entitlement to sickness status, without encumbering oneself with a stigmatizing disease (one was ill in the nerves, not *mad*). It could, on the other hand, be a way of enlisting sympathy, while denying illness, as with George III. And it had the advantage of being sufficiently somatic (nerves after all were anatomically tangible, unlike the elusive black bile) to head off hints of malingering. As George Cheyne put it:[52]

> Often when I have been consulted in a Case, before I was acquainted with the Character and Temper of the Patient, and found it to be what is commonly call'd Nervous, I have been in the utmost Difficulty, when desir'd to define or name the Distemper, for fear of affronting them or fixing a Reproach on a Family or person. . . . Notwithstanding all this, the Disease is as much a bodily Distemper (as I have demonstrated) as the Smallpox or a Fever.

The attractions for the sick of 'nervousness' as an expression for generalized malaise, physical and mental, were undoubtedly great. In the long run, the risks, perhaps, were even greater. For as the medical profession steadily enlarged the bounds of 'nervous disorders', they wove a web wherein lay people entangled themselves at their peril. The Victorian John Addington Symonds thus felt he had to cut himself free from the labelling of those psychiatric doctors who 'would claim me as neurotic'. He was, he admitted, delicate:[53]

> I shunned the society of masculine boys, disliked physical exercises of a violent kind, preferred solitude and study to games, because subject at the age of puberty to excessive involuntary losses of semen, stammered for a period in my speech; in short I exhibited many of the symptoms which Krafft-Ebing and his school recognize as hereditary neuroticism predisposing its subject to sexual inversion. . . . compared with the average of men, I may be pronounced to have exhibited an abnormal strain of nervous energy.

Yet he resented the attempts of doctors to appropriate his condition.[54]

> But is it either logical or prudent to diagnose so marked a specimen of the artistic temperament as morbid? . . . Here we approach too near to the paradox that genius is a species of madness.

In the eighteenth century, the laity retained some say in nervous diagnoses, establishing them, rather like Renaissance 'melancholy', as marks of distinction. It was mainly in the Victorian era that medical power turned nervousness into a stigma.[55]

Obviously, this new language of nervousness was class-biased through and through. Only high society could be highly strung. Cheyne and many others insisted that the lower orders lacked the tingling feelings which alone would experience refined pain.[56] Paradoxically, therefore, the implication was that the upper classes, thanks to their own more refined nervous constitution, would inevitably 'tune in' more to malaise than the masses. Certain illnesses were exclusive to top people. Yet fashionable diseases, like all other fashions, descended the social scale, and talk about nerves became vulgar. At the beginning of the nineteenth century, Thomas Trotter identified the predominant malaise of the society at large – of the petty bourgeoisie no less than fine gentlemen and ladies – as being 'the nervous temperament':[57]

> a sensible, irritable, and mobile condition of nerves; by which different organs of the body, from slight causes, are urged into violent and involuntary action; and their motions and sympathy often reversed; giving birth to false perceptions and erroneous judgment; and sometimes accompanied with pain of the acutest kind.

Was all this just fashionable baloney? Such was the claim of critics such as James McKittrick Adair.[58] But talk of nerves also met very real needs. It verbalized what would otherwise have been a silent series of sensations, generally painful, whose precise origin, nature, and location were unclear. It expressed that heightened sensitivity appropriate to the introspective bent of a high-pressure, fashionable, polite society, where public visibility was so important.[59] Or, to put it another way, with secularization those existential anxieties traditionally expressed in the idiom of religion – the dark night of the soul – were now translated into the language of bodily pain and mental anxiety – real or imaginary. For, as we will show below, these were believed to be times of rampant hypochondria.[60]

Sickness and Shame

Precisely because the body was unthinkable except when coupled with mind, all prescriptions about health and illness necessarily involved a moral dimension. Sickness was interleaved with vice and virtue; disease presupposed notions of personal responsibility and exoneration, which, socially contextualized, we may call the 'sick role'.[61] It was a lay medical culture in which mind, mentality, morals, and medicine were mutually defining. Every disease, every pain, had its meaning, and meanings typically had their moral. Generally implicitly, sometimes explicitly, most stories of sickness were exemplary of correct and incorrect attitudes and actions. On the grand scale, the idle, the feckless, and the debauched were those who were expected to succumb to disease – perhaps including the idle rich no less than the improvident poor. Many diseases seemed like self-inflicted punishments, above all, of course, venereal infections and mental maladies – often the one was seen to lead to the other. It seemed fitting that the treatments for vice diseases should themselves be painful.

The Therapeutic Psyche

But if states of mind *produced* sickness, such a penalizing, even victim-blaming, view had its positive side: mental power could equally sustain good health or speed recovery. 'My bile is quite gone', proclaimed Sir Walter Scott, 'I really believe it arose from mere anxiety. What a wonderful connexion between the mind and body.'[62] So good spirits were essential for good health, as Locke explained to Philip Van Limborch:[63]

> Since nothing so promotes and restores the health of the body as does tranquillity of the mind, you cannot doubt that your most enjoyable letters, evidence of your affection and good will, have been the greatest comfort to me in my protracted condition of poor and variable health. Often when utterly weary of other people's remedies I was refreshed by those ever delightful specifics of yours.

Sick people attempted to put preaching into practice. When Lady Louisa

Conolly had a nervous complaint ('my nerves are miserably affected by
obstructions'), she battled against it in her mind:[64]

> I *fight* against it, which I believe is the only way, though I can't always do
> so as much as I wish. I have been in the warm bath, which I hope will do
> me good. If not, I'll try something else, for I would do anything to get rid
> of miserable feels. Pray don't mention it, for I cannot bear to speak of it.

In short, the sick person's duty lay in mustering good spirits to drive away the
disease.

Overall, such a theory of recuperation – congruent with the positive
regimens for health discussed above in chapter 2 – involved self-help and self-
management; not all could be left to doctors or medicine. Indeed, it pointed to
a *duty* of the patient to help himself. When Dr Denton reported Mary Verney
low-spirited and 'much worse' in 1663, Sir Ralph Verney, her father-in-law,
responded that 'all the Phisick in the World will not cure her, unless she
strive against her Malancholly, & in a good measure proove her owne
Doctor'.[65] The truth of this lay in the placebo effect – so galling to regular
doctors since it mocked their powers, reducing them to a par with charlatans,
and implying that medicine was hardly better than magic. Still, who could
deny that if patients had faith in doctors or drugs, these trebled in effective-
ness? The bedside manner was extremely powerful. Dr Peter Shaw offered an
instance:[66]

> The great Bartholine declares, he once, by Mistake, gave to a Patient a
> Bottle of fair Water, instead of another Bottle of Liquor designed for an
> Emetic; and that the Patient's Imagination was so affected by the
> Expectation, that the Water operated as a Vomit.

From such cases, Shaw drew the obvious conclusion:[67]

> if People may be sick by Imagination, Physicians should endeavour to
> cure by Imagination . . . . I would not be suspected of endeavouring to
> degrade the Art of Physic; or of looking upon Physicians as useless. I
> acknowledge the Effects of Medicine, and am satisfied that Cures have
> been wrought by the Rules of Art: but I say, at the same time, that many
> Cures are performed by Nature, Accident, and Imagination.

In particular, there was no hope for hypochondria – increasingly seen as a
mind-forged malady – unless the sufferer showed a capacity for self-healing.
For the doctors' attempts would, by their very assiduity, paradoxically
increase dependence, producing a descending spiral. Doctor-dependence was
one of the most frightening of the addictive malaises.[68]

Notes

1. O'Neill, *Five Bodies*, 2; Broadbent, 'Image of God'; Leder, 'Medicine and Paradigms of Embodiment'.
2. Bakan, *Disease, Pain and Sacrifice*.
3. Whyte, *Unconscious Before Freud*; Ellenberger, *Discovery of the Unconscious*; Porter, ' "Under the Influence" '; Weidhorn, *Dreams in Seventeenth Century Literature*.
4. Norton (ed.), *Letters of Edward Gibbon*, III, 164. See also Lain Entralgo, *Doctor and Patient*.
5. Hankin (ed.), *Life of Mary Anne Schimmelpenninck*, I, 225.
6. Greig (ed.), *Letters of David Hume*, II, 315.
7. De Beer (ed.), *Correspondence of John Locke*, III, 218. Yet she also added that she was afraid melancholy 'should Grow a Disease upon me'.
8. Cf. Cherno, 'Feuerbach's "Man is What he Eats" '.
9. Yolton, *Thinking Matter*.
10. See Gallagher, 'The Body', 83. Malthus admitted that the effect could not be sustained.
11. Sontag, *Illness as Metaphor*, 3-4.
12. [Martineau], *Life in the Sick-Room*, spells out many of the above assumptions.
13. Bottomley, *Attitudes to the Body*, 31f.
14. Vigarello, *Le Corps Redressé*.
15. Trotter, *View of the Nervous Temperament*; Porter, 'Drinking Man's Disease'; *idem*, 'Love, Sex and Madness'; *idem* (ed.), 'Introduction' to Trotter, *Essay on Drunkenness*.
16. Penal theory and practice exemplifies this: Georgian punishments remained largely corporeal, from whippings to executions. See Ignatieff, *Just Measure of Pain*; Foucault, *Discipline and Punish*.
17. De Beer (ed.), *Correspondence of John Locke*, II, 550. She added 'which I beleeve you know is of a very Unphilosophical Constitution'.
18. Mechanic, 'Concept of Illness Behaviour'.
19. Cf. Porter, 'Body Politics'.
20. For somatization see Kleinman, *Patients and Healers*; *idem*, *Social Origins of Distress*; *idem* and Good (eds), *Culture and Depression*.
21. Excellently discussed in Wear, 'Puritan Perceptions of Illness'.
22. Buchan, *Domestic Medicine*, 139.
23. Sterne, *Life and Opinions of Tristram Shandy*, 174. Sterne specifically presents this view in the context of the impossiblity of Stoicism.
24. Porter, 'Making Faces'; Shortland, 'Skin Deep'.
25. For that strand of modern dynamic psychiatry that sees all physical disease as mental in origin, see Groddeck, *Meaning of Illness*.
26. Evans (ed.), *Letters of Richard Radcliffe and John James*, 155.
27. Cheyne, *Essay on Health and Long Life*, 169.
28. Ibid., 171.
29. De Beer (ed.), *Correspondence of John Locke*, V, 342.
30. Christie (ed.), *Diary of the Revd William Jones*, 101.
31. Taylor, *Records of My Life*, 48. Along the same lines, the *Spectator* also noted that 'The Fear of Death often proves Mortal'; Bond (ed.), *Spectator*, I, 107.
32. Taylor, *Records of My Life*, 48.
33. Williams (ed.), *Swift, Journal to Stella*, 38.
34. Boucé, 'Imagination, Pregnant Women, and Monsters'; *idem*, 'Les Jeux Interdits'. The 'imagination' theory was contested by some doctors, such as James Blondel, as an old superstition with no scientific basis. Imagination also, of course, was held to account for false pregnancy. More generally, see Rather, 'Old and New Views of the Emotions'.

35 Plot, *Natural History of Oxfordshire*, 193. Severn (ed.), *Diary of the Rev'd John Ward*, 278.
36 Bond (ed.), *Spectator*, I, 105-6.
37 Fry and Cresswell (eds), *Memoir of the Life of Elizabeth Fry*, II, 493.
38 Marchand (ed.), *Byron's Letters and Journals*, IV, 26.
39 Christie (ed.), *Diary of Revd William Jones*, 10.
40 Smollett, *Humphry Clinker*, 187. There is an excellent discussion of the general point in Haley, *Healthy Body and Victorian Culture*. One strand of historiography asserts that in the post-Cartesian world, mind and body became totally separated: see Berman, *Re-enchantment of the World*; Capra, *The Turning Point*. But this philosophical analysis was clearly foreign to the actual experiences of real people. See Porter, 'Barely Touching'; Tomaselli, 'The First Person'.
41 Robinson (ed.), *Autobiography of John Clare*, 16.
42 Ibid.
43 Barkan, *Nature's Work of Art*, 13.
44 Trotter, *View of the Nervous Temperament*, 82.
45 Spillane, *Doctrine of the Nerves*, 111f.
46 Porter, *Mind Forg'd Manacles*, ch. 4; C. Lawrence, 'Nervous System and Society in the Scottish Enlightenment'.
47 Cheyne, *English Malady*, 260.
48 Adair, *Essays on Fashionable Diseases*, 6.
49 Little and Kahrl (eds), *Letters of David Garrick*, II, 451. See also Rousseau, 'Nerves, Spirits and Fibres'; *idem*, 'Psychology'.
50 Barrett (ed.), *Diary and Letters of Madame D'Arblay*, IV, 289. Compare Maria Edgeworth's remark about the Princess Sophia in 1818: she 'is not insane – only nervous and weak – this is the truth, and *nervous* is not here used as a soft equivocal word'. Colvin (ed.), *Correspondence of Maria Edgeworth*, 127.
51 Fitzgerald (ed.), *Correspondence of Emily, Duchess of Leinster*, I, 270; Todd, *Sensibility*, 88f.
52 Cheyne, *English Malady*, 260-2.
53 Grosskurth (ed.), *Memoirs of John Addington Symonds*, 64.
54 Ibid.
55 Drinka, *Birth of Neurosis*.
56 Porter, 'Rage of Party'.
57 Trotter, *View of the Nervous Temperament*, 197.
58 Adair, *Essays on Fashionable Diseases*, 5f.
59 Turner, *Body and Society*.
60 Fischer-Homberger, 'Hypochondriasis'; Baur, *Hypochondria*, 13.
61 Parsons, *Social System*.
62 Quoted in Brett (ed.), *Faber Book of Diaries*, 456.
63 De Beer (ed.), *Correspondence of John Locke*, III, 300.
64 Fitzgerald (ed.), *Correspondence of Emily, Duchess of Leinster*, III, 315.
65 Verney (ed.), *Memoirs*, IV, 42.
66 Shaw, quoted in Hunter and Macalpine, *Three Hundred Years of Psychiatry*, 314.
67 Ibid.
68 Porter, 'The Patient in the Eighteenth Century'.

Chapter 5:
The Ages and Stages of Life

Peering back, the Rev. William Jones recorded that the instant of his entry into this world had so nearly been the moment of his departure from it:[1]

> I was *still-born*. The officious care of an old . . . mid-wife blew up the dormant spark of life . . . she stimulated or excited 'my excitability', – by burning feathers under my nostrils, and with other sage expedients.

This perception of life in death and death in life haunted him all his days; in his mature years, he kept a coffin in his study as a *memento mori*; unfortunately, he grew too fat to be borne off in it when the time came.[2]

'The world's a bubble', Francis Bacon had elegized, 'And the life of man/ Less than a span'.[3] The notion of a finite, almost predestined, allotment of days from womb to tomb was pregnant with meaning to the pre-moderns. Each chapter carried its hints of life to come, each was also scarred by its own characteristic diseases and dangers. The idea of the ages of man – four, or perhaps seven, scenes played on life's stage – was, of course, one with roots deep in literature and divinity and medical theory. From first through to second childhood (*sans* everything), every picture told its story.[4] We should not suppose, of course, that real people routed their journeys down life's highway according to pre-planned itineraries. Nevertheless, individual expectations and broader social pressures ensured that age, stage of life, and rites of passage all mattered. Every succeeding year was never just another twelve-month, but one step nearer the grave. Moreover, as Gideon Mantell insisted at the very opening of his journal, with thirty years already expired of his own portion, each remaining year took on a lachrymose meaning all of its own.[5]

Infancy and Childhood
Unlike their Victorian and present-century successors, Georgian autobiographers recorded little about their earliest times. Romanticism and Freudianism have since endowed infancy with a portentousness that would have astonished eighteenth-century minds. When the fictional hero of Thomas

Amory's *Life and Adventures of John Buncle Esq* says 'The things of my childhood are not worth setting down', he is being very Georgian.[6] Edward Gibbon, not a little proud of his memory, confesses that he relied on outside information for the first four years of his life.[7] Many eighteenth-century autobiographers were looked after – or sometimes neglected! – in their early life by a temporary nurse who subsequently disappeared off the scene; this may further explain why in later life the recollection of their time as toddlers was so hazy.

Getting a good start was hazardous in the extreme. Contemporaries were acutely aware of all the mishaps incident upon a foetus in the womb (a mother's 'imagination' or vices could, it was assumed, inflict permanent damage on the embryo). Birth was itself extremely dangerous for both mother and child, as were the succeeding weeks with their risks of post-natal infections (septicaemia, etc.). Small wonder that popular tradition hardly considered the neonate a fully-fledged and established human until it had survived the initial nightmares of the world and thereby established its own title to life.[8] It is perhaps, however, a sign of growing fascination with the newly-born, that the eighteenth century provides some accounts of being born – albeit, of course, fictional. Richard Steele imaginatively recreated the trauma of being expelled from the mother's womb into a persecuting world.[9]

I lay very quiet, but the Witch [i.e., midwife], for no manner of reason, or provocation in the world, takes me and binds my head as hard as possibly she could, then ties up both my legs, and makes me swallow down a horrid mixture. I thought it an harsh entrance into life to begin with taking physic, but I was forced to it or else must have taken down a great instrument in which she gave it me . . . I was bred by hand and anyone that stood next me gave me pap if I did but open my lips, so much that I was grown so cunning as to pretend myself asleep when I was not, to prevent my being crammed.

Things went from bad to worse. His nurse, the baby tells us:[10]

downright starved me, insomuch that I daily pined away, and should never have been relieved had it not been that on the thirtieth day of my life a fellow of the Royal Society who had written on cold baths came to visit me and solemnly protested I was utterly lost for want of this method, upon which he soused me head and ears in a pail of water where I had the good fortune to be drowned.

Laurence Sterne, of course, treated the birth and early moments of his hero, Tristram Shandy, as totally disastrous. Thanks to his calamitous conception, he was deprived from the start of his animal spirits. A forceps birth, he lost his nose in the process; he then suffered a fit, and was assumed to be at death's door, thus accounting for the botched christening which gave him the sad

name, Tristram, instead of the potent, Trismegistus,[11] precursor of many
future sad losses, including his foreskin and apparently his virility too.

Sterne's fiction depicted a baby who at least survived. Millions didn't.
Historians have recently underlined the devastating infant and maternal
mortality rates throughout the pre-modern period. Lawrence Stone has
argued that so many infants died, that parents had to keep a psychological
distance from their babies. There may be truth in this view. Many eighteenth-
century parents clearly could not, or would not, even remember precisely how
many offspring they had produced or when they had been born (many had
died along the way). Gibbon availed himself of just that distancing effect,
when writing about his siblings, who, without exception, died in their early
years, leaving him as sole survivor: 'my five brothers, whose names may be
found in the Parish register of Putney, I shall not pretend to lament'.[12]

Yet, as Linda Pollock has emphasized, the fact that life was so precarious for
babies did not preclude the most intense affections being lavished upon them:
maybe the reverse. Bitter experience proved that babies had no life tenure:
'The painful task has devolved upon me', wrote Muzzy Capel to her grandmother, the Dowager Countess of Uxbridge:[13]

> to acquaint you with the death of our dear little Baby . . . Sunday
> Morning at about 6 she was taken suddenly worse – Mamma was
> immediately alarmed by the fixed & glassy look of her beautiful eyes – &
> Mr. Doratt, who was sent for, said she could not outlive the day – Mama
> insisted upon holding her in her arms – everything which could be
> thought of was tried – but without effect, & the little angel expired with
> her face on Mama's breast, at a little past eleven, but so peaceably that
> we did not perceive it till several minutes had passed.

There followed scenes of aching grief and beatification:[14]

> – Dearest Mama gave her Baby one kiss – & Papa supported her, while
> we removed the child, & laid it out, washed & Dressed it ourselves –
> Since that, Mama has never left its side – And behaves like a perfect
> Angel – I sat up with it last night for I loved it so much, and held its little
> cold hand all the time – Oh! My dearest Grand Mama, you can have no
> idea of any thing so lovely as she looks. – Mama's resignation is
> admirable, I never can forget it – But she was *such* a treasure, *So* angelic
> *so* beautiful she was the admiration of the town – & we were so proud of
> her.

Survivors looked back upon their own earliest years with jagged pain.
Samuel Johnson recalled being born 'almost dead'. He became scrofulous,
thanks to the infected milk of his wet-nurse, awkward in his gait, and sickly,
and had dim recollections of being hauled up to London by his mother at the
age of three to be touched by Queen Anne for the King's Evil. These

'memories' were incorporated into his enduring sense of self, explaining, excusing and justifying his poor eyesight and hearing, his ungainliness, his sense of being alien, almost a monster, whose badge or burden he bore all his life.[15]

Edward Gibbon's recollections of his early physical trials are comparable. He suffered early mistreatment:[16]

> I was a puny child, neglected by my Mother, starved by my nurse, and of whose being very little care or expectation was entertained . . . [without the care of my aunt] I should either have been in my grave, or imperfectly lived a crooked ricketty monster, a burthen to myself and others.

His mother was too engrossed in his father to have any time for him. In any case, she herself died in childbed when he was just nine.[17] There followed a childhood of constant sickness:[18]

> I was successively afflicted by lethargies and fevers; by opposite tendencies to a consumptive and a dropsical habit; by a contraction of my nerves, a fistula in my eye, and the bite of a dog most vehemently suspected of madness: and in the list of my sufferings from my birth to the age of puberty few physical ills would be omitted.

His sufferings, however, made him special. In particular, he was surrounded by all the great doctors of the day, rather like Christ receiving homage from the Elders:[19]

> From Sir Hans Sloane and Dr Mead, to Ward and the Chevalier Taylor every practitioner was called to my aid: the fees of Doctors were swelled by the bills of Apothecaries and Surgeons: there was a time when I swallowed more Physic than food; and my body is still marked with the indelible scars of lancets, issues and caustics.

Like Johnson, Gibbon used childhood illness to explain later physical gaucheness and deformity (the historian of the Roman Empire was under five feet tall, and quickly ran to fat, being dubbed 'Mr Chubby Chub'). Yet early sickness served different mythologizing functions for Gibbon. For he turned into a healthy adult, eager to project himself as debonair and detached – not least from his body. Thus, sickness defined infancy as a stage of life thankfully consigned to the past. The child had been the slave of sickness; the adult, loftily amused by his gout, was its master. Gibbon pointedly discredited Thomas Gray's sentimental longings for childhood innocence ('Where ignorance is bliss, 'Tis folly to be wise'). Manhood stood for Roman strength and maturity.[20]

Letters and journals tell us about infant and childhood years principally at

second hand, via adults' observations upon their own children and those
around them. They flesh out historical demographers' findings that the early
years were ones of frequent, dangerous, and often fatal sickness.[21]

Bells toll endlessly for the death of children: sons and daughters, brothers
and sisters. Parson Holland recorded that four of his own children died in a
scarlet fever outbreak 'within a fortnight'.[22] The Quaker, Hannah Allen,
depicted the shocking story of a neighbour's child, the nine-years-old Richard
Corder:[23]

> Brother George saw him in the street, and five minutes after the dear
> child had replied in answer to his greeting, 'Quite well', he suddenly fell
> . . . and died immediately.

Childhood death was particularly chilling. It had to do, Elizabeth Holland
perceived, with 'a sensation in a mother's breast at the loss of an infant that
partakes of the feeling of instinct. It is a species of savage despair'.[24]
Registering the death of her own son, Henry, from water on the brain, Lady
Bessborough evoked just that kind of despair:[25]

> Of all disorders, this most horrible one is the worst to see. For the last
> twelve days of poor little Henry's life, he has lain in his bed & one
> constant round of changes from fever to deathlike paleness & feebleness,
> then convulsions & sometimes quite reviving, every trace of illness gone
> for a short time, & just as one began to hope, dreadful stupor again, & all
> the same sad round till Sunday when at about eleven at night after three
> deep sighs, he expir'd. William, Barbara, Sally & I scarcely ever left
> him, & to see them hanging over him & trying to warm his little cold
> hands in theirs made my heart ache almost to breaking.

So how did Georgian parents feel about, and cope with, their children's
sicknesses? The testimony of letters and diaries requires caution. Such
documents abound with touches of adult concern, as when Lady Jerningham
inquires after her new grand-daughter (an 'Elegant Extract'), or Lord
Pembroke depicts the decline of his tubercular daughter, Charlotte.[26] But how
are we to interpret their silence? – are they marks of indifference? In any case,
letters are hardly the places we would expect to find callous indifference
positively expressed.

Whatever the quality of parent-child affections, there can be no doubt that
the Georgians took – and prided themselves upon taking – an energetic
interest in child-rearing methods, in both theory and practice. Scores of books
were published on childbirth, post-natal care, infant feeding, children's
sickness, education, manners, and the like.[27] Such manuals were clearly much
read, and advice-conscious parents (the 'Locke-generations') argued the
superiority of modern over traditional modes of child management, and used
their infants as guinea-pigs in testing the new.

Progressive parents broke with the old ways of childbirth, infant feeding, and baby rearing. They used male accoucheurs in place of the old granny-midwife. These new obstetricians seemed better trained, more skilful as anatomists, more attentive, less aggressive; and in the last resort, they also had access to instruments, forceps above all. Progressive parents replaced wet-nurses or dry-feeding with the mother's own breast. They abandoned the age-old dosing of the newly-born with spicy alcoholic cordials; they rejected overheated, stuffy nurseries; they denounced swaddling, and clad their babies in loose clothes instead; and so forth. Following Locke, such parents denounced 'coddling' as weakening, and expressed faith in a cool regime, simple food, maternal suckling, and free movement as nature's way. All these developments have been amply documented in recent scholarship by Stone, Shorter, Pollock, Wilson, Fildes, Lewis, and others, and there is no need to pile on further illustrations here.[28] The philosophy underpinning the new is expressed in Thomas Bewick's repudiation early in the nineteenth century of the bad old habits:[29]

> With respect to the health of children, I fear the present management is not right. The mistaken indulgence of parents, in pampering and spoiling the appetites of children lays the foundation of a permanent train of diseases, which an endless supply of medicines and nostrums will never restore to its pristine vigour. Skilful medical aid may, indeed, be of use, but nothing is so sure as recurrence to a plain diet, temperance, and exercise.

But there lay the rub. For, as Bewick hints, the Georgian age was one of affluence and leisure, a time when the polite, relishing domesticity, actually lavished greater attention upon their homes, households, children – even their pets – than formerly.[30] The result was paradoxical. On the one hand, a commitment to bringing up children in the ways of sturdiness; on the other, a regime which in practice fussed, spoilt and cosseted. John Baker's diary shows him fretting over his daughter, Pattie's, minor ailments.[31] Likewise Caroline Fox's letters gush endlessly over the ailments of poor 'poor dear Ste', her son Stephen, from infancy to adolescence.[32] Weak and sickly, the boy suffered occasional mild fits, and (it seems) what we might generally call 'backwardness'. His mother thought he had St. Vitus' Dance, though she was anxious about his failure to develop the settled sickness profile necessary for definitive diagnosis: 'his illness changes from day to day without our being able to find out what make him better or worse with any certainty'.[33] Like Gibbon, he was fed a whole menu of medicines for a while, then Dr Duncan ordered an end to medication, confused by then as to which aspects of his symptoms were *bona fide* illness and which mere by-products of medication. Letters such as the following suggest that all that was wrong with him was having a nervy mother and a bevy of doctors to boot:[34]

I am obliged to you [his mother writes to her sister] for your receipts. Ste
is not worse but not at all better than he was that day I wrote you word he
was so vastly mended, which was last Thursday; I rather fear he is not
quite so well, he got a little cold in his feet. Poor dear boy, he is mighty
untractable about his health, the distemper itself makes him so. When I
consider tho', how much better he is than he was three weeks ago I can't
help flattering myself he will get over it this summer; he continues the
powder.

Lady Caroline's correspondents clearly thought her attentions smothering,
and that illness was a device whereby the child – whom they thought a brat –
manipulated his mother and gained attention. The common view was that the
cosseted child was father to the hypochondriac.[35]

Lady Caroline engulfed her son with physicians.[36] Bringing in doctors for
children's complaints was becoming a more common practice. The evidence
of seventeenth-century diaries, such as Ralph Josselin's and John Evelyn's,
suggests that doctors were not traditionally summoned to see children even
when they were perilously sick.[37] Physicians themselves had been loth to
meddle with infant diseases; unable to 'take a history' from a child, they
lacked the means of arriving at a confident diagnosis.[38] Attendance upon sick
children became more common, however, in the eighteenth century.[39] This
was probably a side-effect of the greater deployment of male obstetricians.
Once a practitioner had brought a baby into the world, he was likely to be kept
on to supervise the child's growth.[40]

Nevertheless, summoning practitioners for children's illnesses, and indeed
physicking them in general, were bones of contention. Parents and commentators alike were dubious, arguing that the young simply had to go through the
illnesses of childhood, which they would just grow out of naturally. John
Byrom instructed his wife not to physick their children, but to regulate their
well-being by diet alone.[41] Excessive doctoring, many feared, was bound to
make a child delicate, indeed to create a patient for life. To admit the doctor
into the nursery was to grant him a life income.[42] People remained undecided.
In 1786, Lady Duncannon was debating whether her son John, aged five, was
'too young' to see a dentist, though 'his back teeth are gone'.[43]

Youth

The child who survived became a youth, a stage Lord Chesterfield judged
began at nine, though others saw as commencing with puberty. Since the
Victorians, adolescence has become deeply problematic, both physically and,
above all, psychologically. By contrast, as Patricia Spacks has contended,
there was a strong perception in Georgian England that it was the prime of life:
'Youth's the season made for joys', rang the refrain.[44]

Youth enjoyed some independence. Teenagers typically got out from under
the shadow of their parents by being apprenticed or sent into service. Such
young labour was often harsh and cruel, but it precluded that protracted
period of tutelage in the parental home responsible for such deep psychosom-

atic problems – withdrawal, depression, rebellion – in the modern family. Yet if the young had 'escaped', they had not yet contracted too many responsibilities. Marriage and parenthood were typically ties of one's twenties, not teens. People could go on being regarded as 'youths' till some rite of passage, such as matrimony, supervened.

Yet things were perhaps changing. Anxieties over youth were emerging, at least in the pages of medical manuals and advice books (those one might call professional 'anxiety makers').[45] Authors made much of the so-called diseases of youth, typically regarded as the side-effects of the onset of sexuality, premature or delayed, frustrated or misdirected. Unmarried pubescent girls were, it was said, particularly at risk, especially of succumbing to the 'green sickness' or chlorosis. [46] Known by its physical symptoms (pallid skin, loss of appetite, amenorrhoea), and accompanied by behavioural disturbance (lethargy, solitariness), this condition was associated with widespread fears of 'wasting'.

Home medicine manuals and expert tracts such as Jean Astruc's *Treatise on all the Diseases Incident to Women* describe such conditions in profuse detail:[47] almost any oddity of behaviour seems to be included. Bernard Mandeville's *Treatise of the Hypochondriack and Hysterick Diseases* investigates the case of a sickly teenage daughter who has become vapourish; the doctor blames the dull, constricted life she has to lead, warns her parents against medicines, advises air, exercise, and distraction, and if all else fails, marriage, to cure her condition.[48]

First-hand evidence confirms that many teenage girls were indeed wasting – wasting their time, and wasting away physically. James Watt poured out his fears to Erasmus Darwin about the deteriorating condition of his teenage daughter, Jessie; and the correspondence between the two Lunar scientists shows that they conceptualized her condition very much as a teenage disorder, somewhat psychological in character, which could be overcome by stimulating the stomach and the mind.[49] It may be significant that we know nothing of her own perception of her condition.

Professional medicine and medical folklore alike saw the onset of menstruation as problematic. Yet it remains debatable whether diagnoses such as 'green sickness' were primarily labels pinned upon awkward and wayward adolescents by others (parents, doctors, patent medicine advertisers, scaremongers);[50] were they 'owned' – or indeed, contested – by the girls themselves? The writings of mothers do not in the event seem to display great anxieties about the psycho-physical development of their pubescent daughters. One surmises that they expected the girls to grow out of these 'difficult stages', thereby reflecting the commonplace that marriage and childbearing would resolve the problems of the teenage girl.

Teenage masturbation is likewise hard to interpret. The Georgian age was snowed under with *exposés* of self-abuse, most famously *Onania* (1710), which went through multiple editions. This and other works, such as Tissot's popular *Onanism*, denounced self-pollution as physically, morally, and mentally harmful, though, by contrast to the nineteenth century, progressive organic deterioration, not insanity, was seen as its likely outcome.[51]

But how should we interpret this new *grande peur*? Other sexual manuals did not denounce masturbation in the same way; and erotica such as Cleland's *Fanny Hill* accept it as a natural pleasure. In any case, the probability is that prurient works such as *Onania* were actually read as aids to indulgence in the very sins they purported to denounce. Conspicuously absent from the diaries and correspondence of Georgian parents are terrors about auto-erotic activities of their teenagers – indeed, parents seem remarkably unconcerned with teenage sexuality at all.

Did the masturbation scare worry the young themselves? Works such as *Onania* teem with letters supposedly penned by anxious youngsters confessing their vile habits, seeking advice, lamenting how self-pollution has ruined their health, morals, prospects, indeed lives. Were all or any of such letters authentic? We do not know. Even if they were, we could not know how representative they were. Yet patent medicines dealing with what was often known euphemistically as 'debility' were certainly popular, suggesting that there was, indeed, a worried clientèle, possibly created by 'anxiety makers'.[52]

Overall, the first-hand evidence of attitudes to masturbation is slight and confusing. Boswell, predictably, was anxious about his own auto-erotic habits. While still a teenager, he asked his friend Temple to get him a copy of *Onania*.[53] He indulged much in the vice when young: 'that madness passed'.[54] Another account of teenage masturbation – from the diary of the Taunton apprentice, John Cannon – is self-censorious about the practice, the diarist playing super-ego to his living self; but does not show deep guilt:[55]

> Amongst the many books I delighted in I got Aristotles Masterpiece wch cost two shillings wch I gott to the Secrets of Nature Especialy of the female sex wch book I confess was very pernicious to youth for it was not only the reading part but gave me occasions of many temptations to watch the Servant Maid when especially at the Necessary house wch further curiosity I had made holes thro' the boards near the seat, & so planting my self at a small distance in an adjoining [illegible] house I could plainly see that parts my Lustfull thought provoked a stirr'd me up unto And then to remedy it the aforementioned practice of my fellow school fellows was sometimes put in practice [i.e. masturbation], wch was not without a remorse of serious reflexion on the vanity of such folly So that it might be said, twas . . . [illegible]. Sin upon sin we heap. Yet for all those temptations I as yet never attempted to any Carnal familiarity with any female whatsoever for wch I am bound to praise God forever for his enabling me with grace to resist.

It is thus not easy to sift reality from myth regarding the sexual malaises of the young or how to evaluate the incipient moral panic. It would be silly, however, to minimize the real health dangers the young faced. In particular, consumptive disorders became more prevalent, amongst men and women, in town and country, leading to the romanticization of the beautiful death.[56] Moreover, adolescents remained ultra-susceptible to infections. Because they were recruited to institutions such as schools and the armed services, and because the labour market required them to be mobile, in particular moving to service in towns, youths were constantly exposed to communicable diseases, which cut off many in their prime.

Manhood and Womanhood
The health histories of male and female children and youths seem comparable. Girls were cosseted more than boys, who were allowed greater freedom; but the differential may not have been great: Locke and others advocated the same treatment for both sexes.[57] But all changed as people outgrew their youth, when the health histories of adult men and women diverged markedly. From perhaps the early twenties onwards, those successfully reaching manhood might expect that the next twenty or thirty years would form the healthiest of their lives. After all, by then, most men would already have been exposed to infections and so would have built up some immunity. Not least, folk wisdom had it that marriage was good for men's health. It was precisely the opposite for women. As the Duchess of Newcastle put it, 'all the time of their lives is ensnared with troubles, what in breeding and bearing children'.[58]

Some women, of course, married and bore plenty of children with no difficulty whatsoever. The Duchess of Leinster was always breeding – her sisters scolded her for it: she had twelve surviving children by her first husband and another two by her second (who, mildly scandalously, had been her children's tutor).[59] 'Mrs Wedgwood yesterday morning presented me with another fine girl', Josiah Wedgwood informed his partner, Bentley, as though he were invoicing a shipment of clay, '& with as little trouble to herself & family as could be expected':[60]

> She sent for the midwife whilst we were bowling (after making tea for us as usual in the afternoon) without so much as acquainting me with the matter, slipt upstairs just before supper & we had not risen from table before the joyfull tiding of a *safe delivery & all well* was brought to us.

Indeed, progressive medical opinion abandoned the traditional elaborate ritual of childbirth, with its special darkened and heated lying-in room, crowd of 'gossips', and so forth; for, as Erasmus Darwin argued, 'parturition is a natural, not a morbid process'. As such, the more 'natural' the birth, the better.[61] Once it had been *de rigueur* for women to lie-in for a month. 'It is becoming fashionable here', Josiah Wedgwood commented on changing practices, 'for the Ladies in the Straw to become well and leave it as soon as they are able.'[62]

But if some women had it easy and doctors played it cool, in reality common experience was different. Pregnancy itself was frequently painful, exhausting, and fearful. 'My deare wife under great feares she shall not doe well of this child', confessed Ralph Josselin in 1647, 'one night ill as if she should have dyed.'[63] There had frequently been far too short an interval between pregnancies, with no time for recuperation (in those pre-contraceptive times, husbands were to blame). Women themselves often wanted large families, but they knew the advisability of spacing births sensibly.[64] A doctor was surprised to find a pregnant woman who actually looked well.[65]

Not least, giving birth could be a nightmare, both painful and protracted. Hester Thrale called it the sentence of a convict: 'confinement with hard labour'.[66] Historians of childbirth have detailed all the appalling risks of giving birth. The mother's weakness often meant that her contractions did not spontaneously expel the baby.[67] Sometimes pelvic deformities – the result of rickets – trapped the foetus. Babies were often already dead in the womb or died during prolonged labour. Occasionally, recourse had to be made to surgical instruments, which lacerated, and which we know were supremely efficient carriers of infection. Not uncommonly, the mother herself died in childbed, either while giving birth, or shortly afterwards, of haemorrhage or sepsis, as happened to such notables as the Princess Charlotte and Mary Wollstonecraft.[68] Thus, Elizabeth Iremonger retailed, to her friend Mary Heber, the tragic story of her niece:[69]

> Eleanor's hour came on! and, after a long & tedious time, she was safely and very well delivered of a fine Boy . . . On the second evening, when least expected, a Shivering & Sickness seized her, followed by fainting fits, obstruction & fever that baffled all art and, on the ninth morning, she sunk finally to this World!

Even where the birth was successful, women would often remain weak for months afterwards, especially if they chose to breast-feed,[70] which brought further sicknesses. Not least, there were commonly long-term complications; such as tears, fistulas, and prolapsed uteruses. Above all, women commonly simply exhausted themselves from breeding too much. Lady Stanley remarked of Maude Scott in 1841: 'I wonder if a different husband would have made her a different woman, perhaps not if she had had as many children for she seems almost worn out, poor thing.'[71]

Other gynaecological disorders were the curse of Eve. Elizabeth Pepys had a long-standing malady of her genitals, quite possibly the product of some venereal infection her philandering husband had given her. This may explain their childlessness.[72] Thomas Turner's wife had a diseased womb, probably cancerous. She suffered immensely before it killed her.[73]

What is noteworthy is the hardihood with which so many women habitually faced the perils of childbearing. Were they fatalistic? Did wives simply accept that their husbands could not be thwarted? Perhaps. But their readiness to embark upon marriage and its inevitable childbearing may have been coloured by the myth of the old maid's malady, the idea that barrenness gave birth to malaises of its own. Popular sexual advice manuals such as *Aristotle's Master-*

piece argued that it was healthier to be married, a mother, than a spinster (and, of course, marriage was preferable in terms of social status).[74]

Equally worrying was infertility, which was usually blamed on the woman. It was obviously a social stigma; it was also believed symptomatic of some underlying malady. Health advice books for women were preoccupied with recipes for fertility. Taking the waters was one of the main cures.[75]

Old Age

Middle age turned to old age; the moment of transition was elastic. Some, like James Yonge, the Plymouth surgeon, thought the crucial divide was sixty-three, the so-called climacteric year of the Bible and Eastern culture.[76] All agreed with Edward Young that 'there is a great difference between *middle* and *old age*. Hope is quartered on the middle of life, and fear on the latter half of it.'[77] As historians have recently emphasized, age did not automatically confer authority, far from it: 'In my esteem age is not estimable', thought Byron.[78]

Old age was a worry, indeed 'a disease of itself', judged Burton early in the seventeenth century, long before modern medicine could be accused of 'medicalizing' it.[79] 'I see you are weary of taking any more physicall things', writes Sir Ralph Verney to a friend, 'but those that are either old or infirm must be content to do it some Times.'[80] Women began to perceive themselves ageing earlier than men. This was partly a product of repeated pregnancies, partly also because beauty and bloom counted so much more in a woman. We have already noted that Lady Mary Coke was astonished how the Duchess of Portland looked after the loss of her teeth.[81] But the perception of fading beauty was largely in the mind, reflecting the social convention that the married woman was past her prime once she had passed her mid-twenties. At twenty-seven Elizabeth Inchbald noted, 'extremely happy but for the still nearer approach of age'; a year later: 'still happy, but for my increased appearance of declining years'.[82]

The flight of the years terrified the Wynne sisters even in their teens. Elizabeth Wynne thought herself at seventeen 'prodigiously old . . . not far from twenty':[83]

> Sunday, April 19th. . . . a very dull birthday as at the bottom of my heart I was very sad to think I was beginning the eighteenth year of my life and that till now I had wasted my time in a very foolish way but I took resolutions to begin to be more applied to things that will be of more use to me in future and to enjoy life as it is very short. I was quite Philosophical.

Things got worse. A year later, she was forced to reflect, 'This is my birthday. I am eighteen years old. It does not please me much I shall soon be an *old lady*.' A generation later, Queen Victoria almost echoes her: 24 May 1837, 'Today is my 18th birthday! How old!'[84] As Patricia Spacks has noted, Georgian adolescents felt no special urgency to grow up.[85]

The late twenties were a crucial time. 'On Monday I was 28 years old!!!
Alas! Alas!', lamented Lady Elizabeth Holland in 1799. [86] Her view echoed a
remark made by her grandmother, Caroline Fox, in a letter to her sister Emily,
the Countess of Kildare, some forty years earlier:[87]

> October the 18th [1759]. Yesterday was your birthday dearest siss,
> twenty-eight I think; don't the near approach to thirty make you
> feel old? I think that's the age it strikes one most, all pretensions to
> youth are then over. God send you health and spirits to enjoy many
> many more; 'tis astonishing when one reflects how the time slips away;
> il s'en va, as Madame Sévigné says, et nous emporte avec lui very fast
> indeed.

Emily took the advance of years so much to heart she eventually provoked a
rebuke from her elder sister:[88]

> What do you mean, dear siss, by lamenting growing old, as you call it?
> So much I think, indeed, that turning thirty is the first step one feels to
> take towards old age, and consequently one minds it most; but why is it
> so dreadful I can't find out, tho' I'm near forty. I had no pleasure at
> twenty I don't enjoy to the full as much now. I'm told you look as
> handsome as ever you did, therefore you need not yet regret the loss of
> beauty.

Life was a pleasure, thought Lady Mary Wortley Montagu, but for the 'd-d,
d-d quality of growing older and older every day'. [89]

The Biblical three score years and ten notwithstanding, some men also
clearly felt themselves old at a very early age. 'I am old and the times sickly',
wrote Sir Ralph Verney in 1643: he was forty.[90] John Stuart Mill thought
likewise: 'hardly anybody continues after my age to have the same vigorous
health they had in early youth'.[91]

But social pressures did not weigh so heavily upon men. Of course, many
occupations prematurely wore men out. Southey remarked that the lead
miners on Alston Moor were old at thirty and seldom reached fifty. Yet it was
assumed that men remained eligible sexual and marriage partners for far
longer, although, of course, ancient male lechers, such as Dr Richard Mead in
his dotage, were targets of satire.[92] Men could still feel in their prime until well
into their fifties or sixties. Both William Cobbett and Francis Place boasted in
their sixties that none of their faculties had decayed. In his late seventies, John
Wesley, still riding thousands of miles a year and preaching more than once a
day, remarked on his state of preservation:[93]

> I have now completed my seventy-fourth year; and by the peculiar
> favour of God, I find my health and strength, and all my faculties of body
> and mind just the same as they were at four-and-twenty.

Particularly for men, the recipe for continuing fighting fit was activity. Thus, William Hutton recalled at 'the age of eighty-two I considered myself a young man. I could, without much fatigue, walk forty miles a day.' Things had changed however:[94]

> But, during the last six years, I have felt a sensible decay; and, like a stone rolling down the hill, its velocity increases with the progress. The strings of the instrument are, one after another, giving way, never to be brought into tune.

The advisability of retirement was often discussed. Erasmus Darwin, like Wesley, deprecated the idea: it could lead only to idleness; that would reduce the body tone, that, in turn, producing melancholy, depression, and even suicide:[95]

> It is a dangerous experiment, and generally ends either in drunkenness or hypochondriacism. Thus I reason one must do something (so country squires fox-hunt), otherwise one grows weary of life, and becomes a prey to ennui.

Vigorous activity was the secret of health. Darwin recommended to the hypochondriacal Watt that he should[96]

> Remember the philosophical experiment Monsr Rabelais determined to try upon himself for the good of the Public – which was 'to try how long an ingenious and agreable man might last, if taken good care of'.

Yet ageing was a worry. 'The worst thing I find now,' Erasmus Darwin confided to his friend, Richard Dixon, in his sixties, 'is this d–n'd old age, which creeps slily upon one, like moss upon a tree, and wrinkles one all over like a baked pear'. It moved him to eloquence:[97]

> Ye days, which are past! – when I could have pursued the rolling Taw with spirits light as air; and limbs supple as the bending grass blade; when I could have crept through an Alderman's thumb-ring! – where are ye – Corpulency of body, hebetude of mind, or in one word old age I feel your irresistible approach.

Darwin was one of those, like Godwin, to entertain hopes of prolonged life through medical improvements.[98] Obviously, age brought with it its pains, or as the proverb put it, 'age breeds aches'. It also meant social penalization. In England, old age was accorded no special status. For the poor, it increasingly meant the workhouse.[99]

People tried to fight age, some with nostrums and cordials, charms, potions, and spells.[100] Quacks such as Samuel Solomon made fortunes out of restoratives

guaranteed to bring back potency and vigour. Cheyne advised the aged to keep
well out of the cold.[101] John Ward was gloomier: 'there is no physick against
old age'.[102]

Some followed the light regimes, advocated by Cornaro, and popularized by
the vegetarian, James Graham, aimed to slow down the wearing-out of the
parts.[103] (Graham claimed one could live to 150; he himself expired at forty-
nine.) Others thought the ageing body, above all, needed increased stimulus.
Thomas Trotter, normally a critic of stimulants, recommended that at forty
the body needed two glasses of wine a day, at fifty, four, and at sixty, six. A
variation on this was the old advice, revived with success by Philip Thicknesse, to inhale the breath of young virgins:[104]

> The brisk and lively motion in the blood of young people is the cause of
> their health, vigour and growth; and I see no reason to doubt but that the
> re-respiring their breath may rouse the sluggish circulation of men
> advanced in years.

Some, however, became resigned, following the Christian and Stoical
advice of such books as John Smith's *The Pourtraict of Old Age* (1676). For
despite attempts to preserve the body, old age would encroach, and later,
senility. These were fearsome prospects. 'I have for some years', Thomas
Jefferson pondered, 'dreaded nothing so much as the living too long.'[105] It was
a grim prospect. 'In old age' concluded Gibbon,[106]

> the consolation of hope is reserved for the tenderness of parents who
> commence as new life in their children; the faith of enthusiasts who sing
> Hallelujahs above the clouds; and the vanity of authors who presume the
> immortality of their name and writings.

NOTES

1   Christie (ed.), *Diary of the Revd William Jones*, 265. His aunt, who was present, said
    '*Never mind the brat*', rather 'attend to the Mother'.
2   Ibid., 262.
3   Quoted in Dick (ed.), *Aubrey's Brief Lives*, 10.
4   Sampson and Sampson, *Oxford Book of Ages*; Sears, *Ages of Man*. In the Middle
    Ages, the seven ages were thought to correspond with the seven planets. Anne
    Bradstreet, in the seventeenth century, wrote of the 'Four Ages of Man'. Here the
    analogy was often to the four seasons. Ellis (ed.), *Works*; cf. Lynch, *Guide to Health
    though the Stages of Life*.
5   Curwen (ed.), *Journal of Gideon Mantell*.
6   Amory, *Life of John Buncle*, 2.
7   Bonnard (ed.), *Edward Gibbon. Memoirs*, 27.
8   Pollock, *Forgotten Children*, 97f. Crawford, ' "The Sucking Child" '.
9   *The Tatler*, no. 15, 14 May 1709. Swift's *Gulliver's Travels* equally evokes the sensation
    of being tiny and powerless.

10 *The Tatler*, no. 15, 14 May 1709.
11 See Cash, 'Birth of Tristram Shandy'. George Crabbe's poem 'Infancy – A Fragment' waxes lyrical on the miseries of infancy and childhood, and suggests this is emblematic of miseries to come.
12 Bonnard (ed.), *Edward Gibbon. Memoirs*, 24.
13 Anglesey (ed.), *Capel Letters*, 140. Muzzy Capel was Maria, the daughter of Lady Caroline Capel.
14 Ibid.
15 Porter, 'The Hunger of Imagination'. Wain, *Samuel Johnson*, 17f.
16 Norton (ed.), *Letters of Edward Gibbon*, III, 45. Bonnard (ed.), *Edward Gibbon. Memoirs*, 28.
17 Ibid.
18 Ibid., 29.
19 Ibid.
20 Ibid., 44. Spacks, *Imagining a Self*. Cf. the valuable discussion in Geyer-Kordesch, 'Cultural Habits of Illness'.
21 Wrigley and Schofield, *Population History of England*.
22 Ayres (ed.), *Paupers and Pig Killers*, 25.
23 Allen (ed.), *Life of Hannah S. Allen*, 35.
24 Ilchester (ed.), *Lady Holland's Journal*, 135.
25 Bessborough and Aspinall (eds), *Lady Bessborough*, 265. Crawford, ' "The Sucking Child" '; Bayne-Powell, *English Child*, 157ff. Some of the most heart-rending accounts of grief over a dying child are to be found in Toynbee (ed.), *Diaries of William Charles Macready*, 97ff.
26 Castle (ed.), *Jerningham Letters*, I, 259; Herbert (ed.), *Pembroke Papers*, 220f. The chief physician, Sir Lucas Pepys, told Pembroke that he could at best palliate the disease.
27 Hardyment, *Dream Babies*.
28 Lewis, *In the Family Way*, 85f; Pollock, *Forgotten Children*; idem, *Lasting Relationship*; Stone, *Family Sex and Marriage*; Shorter, *History of Women's Bodies*; Wilson, 'William Hunter and the Varieties of Man-Midwifery'; idem, 'Participant or Patient?'; Fildes, *Breasts, Bottles and Babies*.
29 Weekley (ed.), *Memoir of Thomas Bewick*, 161.
30 Trumbach, *Rise of the Egalitarian family*, 119f.; Davidoff and Hall, *Family Fortunes*, 149f.; Waterson, *Servants' Hall*.
31 Yorke (ed.), *Diary of John Baker*.
32 Fitzgerald, *Correspondence of Emily, Duchess of Leinster*, I, 195.
33 Ibid., I, 210.
34 Ibid., I, 219. Many were worried about overmedicating children. 'Let me beseech you not to destroy the powers of her [a child's] stomach with medicine. Nature alone can re-establish infant organs', wrote Thomas Jefferson to his daughter: Randolph, *Domestic Life of Jefferson*, 216.
35 Mandeville, *Treatise of the Hypochondriack and Hysterick Diseases*, 306f.
36 Fitzgerald (ed.), *Correspondence of Emily, Duchess of Leinster*.
37 Macfarlane (ed.), *Diary of Ralph Josselin*; idem, *Family Life of Ralph Josselin*; De Beer (ed.), *Diary of John Evelyn*.
38 Harris, *Treatise on the Acute Diseases of Infants*, 3.
39 Stott, 'Medical Practice of George Chalmers'.
40 Wilson, 'Participant or Patient?'; idem, 'William Hunter and the Varieties of Man-Midwifery'; Loudon, *Medical Care and the General Practitioner*; Lane, 'Provincial Surgeon and his Obstetric Practice'.
41 Talon (ed.), *Selections from the Journals and Papers of John Byrom*, 111.

42 Quoted from Nelson, *Essay on the Government of Children*.
43 Bessborough and Aspinall (eds), *Lady Bessborough and Her Family Circle*, 38.
44 Spacks, *Adolescent Idea*, 89f.
45 And perhaps with some teenagers themselves. Thus James Boswell:

The Truth is, with regard to me, about the age of seventeen I had a very severe illness.
I became very melancholy. I imagined that I was never to get rid of it. I gave myself
up as devoted to misery. I entertained a most gloomy and odd way of thinking. I was
much hurt at being good for nothing in life.(Pottle, *James Boswell: The Earlier Years,
1740-1769*, 43.)

46 Loudon, 'Chlorosis': Figlio, 'Chlorosis and Chronic Disease in Nineteenth-Century
Britain'.
47 Astruc, *Treatise on All the Diseases Incident to Women*, 94.
48 Mandeville, *Treatise on the Hypochondriack and Hysterick Diseases*.
49 King-Hele (ed.), *Letters of Erasmus Darwin*, 245ff. Jessie died shortly afterwards.
50 MacGregor, 'Eighteenth Century V.D. Publicity'; Solomon, *Guide to Health*; Senate,
Medical Monitor; Brodum, *Guide to Old Age*.
51 Hare, 'Masturbatory Insanity'; R.H.MacDonald, 'The Frightful Consequences of
Onanism'; Stengers and Van Neck, *Histoire d'une Grande Peur*.
52 Comfort, *Anxiety Makers*.
53 Pottle, *James Boswell: The Earlier Years*, 30.
54 Ibid.
55 Diary of John Cannon (Taunton Record Office). We owe this quotation to the
kindness of John Brewer. *Onania*; Wagner, 'Veil of Science and Morality'; Boucé,
'Les Jeux Interdits de L'Imaginaire'.
56 See ch.14.
57 Locke set out good reason why girls should be cared for identically to boys:

And since I should rather desire in my wife a healthy constitution, a stomach able to
digest ordinary food, and a body that could endure upon occasion both wind and sun,
than a puling, weak, sickly wretch, that every breath of wind or least hardship puts in
danger, I think the meat drink and lodging and clothing should be ordered after the
same manner for the girls as for the boys. (De Beer (ed.), *Correspondence of John
Locke*, II, 686.)

58 See classically Charles Darwin's discussion, itself sensitively discussed in Macfarlane, *Marriage and Love in England*, 4ff.; Prior, *Women in English Society*, 195.
59 Fitzgerald (ed.), *The Correspondence of Emily, Duchess of Leinster*.
60 Quoted in Wedgwood and Wedgwood, *Wedgwood Circle*, 71-72.
61 Quoted in King-Hele, *Doctor of Revolution*, 255. William Hunter was of the same
view.
62 Wedgwood and Wedgwood, *Wedgwood Circle*, 61.
63 Macfarlane (ed.) *Diary of Ralph Josselin*, 108. On the weaknesses of women see
Withers, *Observations on Chronic Weakness*.
64 Fitzgerald (ed.), *Correspondence of Emily, Duchess of Leinster*, I, 69.
65 Poynter (ed.), *Journal of James Yonge*, 156.
66 Hayward (ed.), *Life and Writings of Mrs Piozzi*, 69.
67 Shorter, *History of Women's Bodies*, 71f.
68 Tomalin, *Mary Wollstonecraft*, 216f.
69 Bamford (ed.), *Dear Miss Heber*, 221.
70 Fildes, *Breasts, Bottles and Babies*, 188.
71 Mitford (ed.), *Ladies of Alderley*, 7.
72 Latham and Matthews (eds), *Diary of Samuel Pepys*, II, 24; III, 3, 44, 82, 111, 112, etc.

73 Vaisey (ed.), *Diary of Thomas Turner*, 212ff.
74 Porter, ' "Secrets of Generation Display'd" '; Blackman, 'Popular Theories of Generation'; Beall, 'Aristotle's Masterpiece in America'.
75 Quinton, *Treatise of Warm Bath Water*, I, 95.
76 Poynter (ed.), *Journal of James Yonge*, 228.
77 Pettit (ed.), *Correspondence of Edward Young*, 237.
78 Marchand (ed.), *Byron's Letters and Journals*, IX, 37.
79 Burton, *Anatomy of Melancholy*, 829.
80 Verney (ed.), *Memoirs*, IV, 421.
81 Home (ed.), *Letters and Journal of Lady Mary Coke*, 93.
82 Littlewood (ed.), *Elizabeth Inchbald*, 129.
83 Fremantle (ed.), *Wynne Diaries*, II, 24.
84 Esher (ed.), *The Girlhood of Queen Victoria*, I, 190.
85 Fremantle (ed.), *Wynne Diaries*, II. 84. Spacks, *Adolescent Idea*.
86 Ilchester (ed.). *Lady Holland's Journal*, I, 232.
87 Fitzgerald (ed.), *Correspondence of Emily, Duchess of Leinster*, I,261.
88 Ibid., I, 265.
89 Johnson (ed.), *Letters from Lady Mary Wortley Montagu*, 224. Quoted in Gibbs, *Admirable Lady Mary*, 149.
90 Verney (ed.), *Memoirs*, III, 50.
91 Quoted in Mazlish, *James and John Stuart Mill*, 112.
92 *Old Cornutor of Seventy-Five.*
93 See Wesley, *Journal*, IV, 105. Three years later he was still just as energetic.

I can hardly think I am entered this day into the seventy- eighth year of my age. By the blessing of God, I am just the same as when I entered the twenty-eighth. This hath God wrought, chiefly by my constant exercise, my rising early, and preaching morning and evening. (Ibid., IV, 190.)

What was the explanation?

Fri. 28. I entered into my eightieth year; but, blessed be God, my time is not labour and sorrow: I find no more pain or bodily infirmities than at five and twenty. This I still impute, 1. To the power of God, fitting me for what he calls me to; 2. To my still travelling four or five thousand miles a year; 3. To my sleeping, night or day, whenever I want it; 4. To my rising, at a set hour; and, 5. To my constant preaching, particularly in the morning. (Ibid., IV, 236.)

By the time he was eighty-six things had changed:

I now find I grow old. My sight is decayed, so that I cannot read a small print, unless in a strong light. My strength is decayed, so that I walk much slower than I did some years since. My memory of names, whether of persons or places, is decayed, till I stop a little to recollect them. What I should be afraid of is, if I took thought for the morrow, that my body should weigh down my mind, and create either stubbornness, by the decrease of my understanding, or peevishness, by the increase of bodily infirmities. (Ibid., IV, 478)

94 Jewitt (ed.), *Life of William Hutton*, 308. Hutton commented:

Suppose a man endeavours after health, and his endeavours are blessed with such success that, by a proper use of his animal powers, he can, at fourscore, walk thirty miles a day. Suppose him, by assiduity and temperance, to have obtained a complete independency, can reside in a house to his wish, with a garden for use and amusement, is blessed with a son and a daughter of the most affectionate kind, who attentively watch his little wants with a view to supply them: add as an appendage to this little family a pair of old and faithful horses, who are strangers to the lash, and whose value increases with their years. Still add to a taste for reading the benefits arising from a library of choice authors, which cost £1500. Would you pronounce this a *happy man*? That man is myself. Though my morning was lowering, my evening is sunshine.

[95] King-Hele, *Doctor of Revolution*, 231.

[96] King-Hele (ed.), *Letters of Erasmus Darwin*,181.

[97] Ibid., 238.

[98] King-Hele, *Doctor of Revolution*, 229. Darwin offered a full and instructive account of the medical dimensions of old age in Additional Note VII to *The Temple of Nature*, p. 23f. He argued that old age could be retarded by due attention to quantity of stimulus to the body. See Trimmer, *Rejuvenation*, 58ff.

[99] R.M. Smith, 'Structured Dependency of the Elderly'; Pelling, 'Old People and Poverty in Early Modern Towns'; Richardson, 'Old People's Attitudes to Death'; Thane, 'Perception and Experience of Old Age'; Bosanquet, 'Old Age – Present and Future', all in *Bulletin of the Society for the Social History of Medicine*, no. 34 (1984), 35-55.

[100] Brodum, *Guide to Old Age*; Solomon, *Guide to Health*; Collins, 'Two Jewish Quacks in Eighteenth-Century Glasgow'; J. Hill, *Old Man's Guide*; Hufeland, *Art of Prolonging Life*.

[101] Cheyne, *Essay on Health and Long Life*, 205.

[102] Severn (ed.), *Diary of the Revd John Ward*, 249.

[103] Porter, 'Sex and the Singular Man'.

[104] Gosse, *Dr Viper*, 290, quoted from the *Valetudinarian's Bath Guide*. Thicknesse said he had done this 'whenever they lay in my way', as a result of which he felt none of the usual 'infirmities' of men in their sixties. The subject had, of course, interested Francis Bacon. See Rees, *Francis Bacon's Natural Philosophy*.

[105] Randolph, *Domestic Life of Thomas Jefferson*, 287. Jefferson was only sixty. In 1803, Benjamin Rush advised Jefferson on how to take care of himself in the decline of life. Butterfield (ed.), *Letters of Benjamin Rush*, II, 856. Compare Rush's advice to Horatio Gates: II, 870.

[106] Bonnard (ed.), *Edward Gibbon. Memoirs*, 189.

Sickness

Chapter 6:
The Phenomenology of Pain

'And how does every body get on?', inquired Byron of Augusta Leigh in 1820, 'How is your rabbit-warren of a family? I gave you an account of mine by last letter. The child Allegra is well – but the Monkey has a cough – and the tame Crow has lately suffered from the headache. – Fletcher has been bled for a stitch – & looks flourishing again'.[1]

We have argued so far that pre-modern culture waxed warm about health. This was, of course, because, as Byron's facetiousness indicates, pain and illness were ubiquitous. 'Sick – Sick – Sick . . . O Sick – Sick – Spew ', complained Garrick to his brother George in 1767; 'Sick! Sick! Sick! Sick!', echoed Laurence Sterne. Little wonder, in Sterne's case in particular.[2] Like his fictional *alter ego*, Parson Yorick, Sterne himself, or rather the 'leaky bellows' of his lungs, succumbed to tuberculosis while he was still middle-aged. He had had his first 'bed full' of blood when a Cambridge undergraduate in the 1730s.[3] By the late 1750s, the condition was worsening, and he was eventually to suffer 'the most violent spitting of blood mortal man experienced'.[4] Tortured by 'long and obstinate coughs and unaccountable hemorrhages',[5] he fled to France in the quest of health, hoping the air, mildness, and asses' milk would preserve 'this weak taper of life'.[6] This unavailing,[7] he returned 'like a bale of cadaverous goods consigned to Pluto',[8] finally dying of pleurisy and consumption in 1768.

Sterne's own wasting constitution served him as a *memento mori*. But reminders were hardly needed, for affliction and death already enshrouded him. All but one of his children were stillborn or died shortly after birth,[9] and his sole surviving daughter, Lydia, languished with asthma and probably epilepsy.[10] Moreover, his wife, Elizabeth, grew disordered in her wits, probably spending some time in a private lunatic asylum, where she ruled as Queen of Bohemia.[11]

The fictional world of *Tristram Shandy* thus in many ways mirrors the author's life itself. For it is a chronicle of disasters and diseases from cradle to grave ('Alas, poor Yorick') – and (we might say, *therefore*) full of characters extolling the inestimable value of health, because they cannot escape pain's omnipresence. When Dr Slop, the bungling man-midwife, wants to punish the servant, Obadiah, for being responsible for slicing his thumb, he can think of nothing better than to hurl down execrations against all the members and functions of his body.[12]

> May he [Obadiah] be cursed in eating and drinking, in being hungry, in being thirsty, in fasting, in sleeping, in slumbering, in walking, in standing, in sitting, in lying, in working, in resting, in pissing, in shitting, and in blood- letting! May he be cursed in all the faculties of his body! May he be damned in his mouth, in his breast, in his heart and purtenance, down to the very stomach. May he be cursed in his reins, and in his groin, (God in heaven forbid, quoth my uncle Toby) – and in his thighs, in his genitals, (my father shook his head) and in his hips, and in his knees, his legs, and feet, and toe-nails.

In short, for Sterne, this is 'a dirty planet' whose 'strange fatalities' rain down blows against 'the delicate and fine spun web of life'.[13]

In 1805, the less literary, but utterly gouty Parson Holland visited a 'young girl dying of consumption, of the name David. She seemed wasted to the bone'. A couple of months later, he went back and found the house a veritable hospital:[14]

> She is greatly emaciated and in a lamentable state yet very sensible, very grateful for anything done and attentive to what is said and also resigned. In short, she is the most interesting girl I ever attended. Her mother who takes care of her is a miserable object too. She has got a cancer come on in her breast so that she will soon be in sad state. The husband has most shocking health and they are all poor to the greatest degree.

What did all such suffering mean? 'Alas the misery there is in this world, the ways of Providence are very mysterious.'[15]

Thus pain's curse was hard to escape, and most of all for the poor. Yet wealth did not provide immunity. 'I am all over bug bites', grumbled the Marchioness of Kildare in 1761, 'tormented all night with these bugs; could not sleep.'[16]

The imperial sway of suffering seemed self-evident to thinkers as diverse as the optimistic Deist doctor, Erasmus Darwin, and the sombre Christian, Samuel Johnson. Both as a working physician and in philosophical poems such as the *Temple of Nature,* Darwin personified disease as a foul fiend, a Devil visiting evil and destruction upon innocents:[17]

> Behind in twilight gloom with scowling mien
> The demon Pain, convokes his court unseen;
> Whips, fetters, flames, pourtray'd on sculptur'd stone,
> In dread festoons, adorn his ebon throne;

Each side a cohort of diseases stands,
And shudd'ring fever leads the ghastly bands;
O'ver all Despair expands his raven wings,
And guilt-stain'd Conscience darts a thousand stings.

Darwin's dramatization has a Manichean flavour: disease is a real evil, an alien, destructive superpower.[18]

Johnson, by contrast, tended to view physical pain as built into man's bones, integral to his existence as embodied reason and feeling, inescapably part of 'the pain of being a man'. Johnson, of course, had multiple disorders, and his last decade was almost permanently discomforted by bronchitis, asthma, and dropsy; not least, he suffered a stroke a year before his death. Yet for him, physical tribulation was primarily exemplary and thus ultimately trivial in the sublime scales of vice, sin, and mental anguish. Sickness of the mind, however, was altogether more terrible, because it might jeopardize the salvation of the soul. Having, as he saw it, inherited a 'vile melancholy' from his father, Johnson suffered fits of depression all his life, feared he would go mad, and vouched he would gladly have a limb amputated if it would heal his stricken understanding.[19]

'The world is full of Misery and Heartbreak, Pain, Sickness and Oppression', sighed Keats.[20] Disease did not merely mean of temporary pain and the prospect of death; it frequently carried with it permanent disablement. Take smallpox. Many died of that dread disease, especially of the 'malignant' or 'confluent' sort; up to one sufferer in seven during some epidemics.[21] But survivors would commonly carry with them some permanent scar: the pock-marks disfiguring the skin and destroying beauty (as with Lady Mary Wortley Montagu, such blemishes could scar the mind as well),[22] or worse still, impotence and blindness. Nicholas Saunderson, the prodigious blind professor of natural philosophy at Cambridge, had lost his sight through childhood smallpox.

Christian theodicy made sense of the lottery of life by treating pain and suffering as probationary in a cosmic epic started by Original Sin.[23] Pain was due punishment for the Fall, and its constant reminder. The Dissenting doctor, Richard Kay, besought the God of Justice but also of Mercy:[24]

Have Mercy upon us, O Lord . . . . We know we must die: there is no Discharge in that War. Man that is born of a Woman is of few days and full of Trouble; yea, Man at his best State is altogether Vanity. This World is a State of Probation and Exercise: our Way lies thro' a Vale of Tears: This is the unalterable Appointment of thee who art the great God of Nature.

Yet orthodox Christians had to make sense of suffering. One resource was to see illness as a reprieve.[25] The Christian struggle to understand why a God of love should send sickness is well conveyed in Anne Bradstreet's seventeenth-century verses, 'Before the Birth of One of Her Children'. The poet commended the pious acceptance of adversity:[26]

> All things within this fading world hath end,
> Adversity doth still our joyes attend;
> No tyes so strong, no friends so dear and sweet,
> But with death's parting blow is sure to meet.
> The Sentence past is most irrevocable,
> A Common thing, yet oh inevitable,
> How soon, my Dear, death may my steps attend,
> How soon't may be thy Lot to lose thy friend.

She was concerned for the welfare of her children in case she should die:[27]

> And when thy loss shall be repaid with gains
> Look to my little babes my dear remains.
> And if thou love thy self, or loved'st me
> These O protect from step Dame's injury.
> And if chance to thine eyes shall bring this verse,
> With some sad sighs honour my absent Herse;
> And kiss this paper for thy loves dear sake,
> Who with salt tears this last Farewel did take.

Thus even a natural event such as childbirth, which, as the epitome of Creation itself, should have been a cause for joy, terrorized a mother's heart. Such fears were allayed by a faith that took suffering as man's just deserts and treated all things earthly as fleeting and as naught, *sub specie aeternitatis*.[28]

Yet in so rationalizing pain, Christians certainly did not explain it away or make light of it. In a magnificent sermon, evoking the Old Testament plagues, John Donne portrayed sickness as the most fearsome evil under God: 'Put all the miseries that man is subject to together, *sicknesse* is more than all . . . *Phalaris* could invent a bull; and others have invented Wheels and Racks; but no persecutor could ever invent a *sicknesse* or a way to inflict a *sicknesse* upon a condemned man.'[29] When writers such as Soame Jenyns, under the spell of Enlightenment philosophical optimism, attempted to prove that sickness was a boon in a world-order in which all was for the best – the blind often had their other senses sharpened, disability drew forth pity – such casuistry was dismissed by Samuel Johnson with the contempt it deserved.[30]

Christian culture strove to tread a middle path. Fortitude was required. Mary Anne Schimmelpenninck recalled of her childhood, 'my father and mother constantly desired me to bear pain like a Philosopher or a Stoic'. She remembered her own exceptional bravery in the teeth of the dentist:[31]

> I well remember one day when George Bolt, the Friends' Dentist, came
> to examine my teeth. I agreed to have my front teeth drawn before my

mother came in from her walk, that I might puzzle her as to my classification, as I should want the four teeth in the upper jaw, the distinctive mark of the Primates. I sat still and had them all out, that it might be over when she arrived. George Bolt said I was 'the best little girl he had ever seen;' and took from his pocket a paper of comfits as my reward. But I drew up, and said, 'Do you think Regulus, and Epictetus, and Seneca, would take a reward for bearing pain; or the little Spartan boys?' He laughed heartily; and my mother just then coming in, he said, 'Thy little girl is too much of philosopher to be rewarded for bearing pain, but still I hope she is enough of child to like these comfits, as a mark of love and kindness;' to which I acceded with great delight.

Yet Christianity did not demand Oriental indifference to suffering (that smacked too much of Manicheism), or the heroic asceticism of martyrs. Robust Protestants and sceptics such as Gibbon even distrusted the praeternatural endurance of medieval saints – might it be fraudulent, or, indeed, masochistic perversion? In any case, even Stoicism was suspect in an age of feeling. The gout, mused Edward Young, was 'one of the best Antidotes against Stoical Opinions'. As with Johnson kicking the anti-Berkeleyan stone, Stoicism was instantly refuted by the unanswerable prick of pain.[32] 'Mortifications never come single', commented Horace Walpole:[33]

> Pain not only makes its *prerogative* felt, but deprives one of collateral satisfactions that might compensate. It annuls promises, and like other imperial tyrants, roots out both wishes and virtues.

Being in Pain
The medical *ancien régime* had scant resources against illness and accident. The absence of effective ('antibiotic') drugs meant diseases generally took their full course. There were many pains medicine could not help or heal. Defective understanding of diet and deficiency diseases meant that conditions potentially easily prevented or rectified, in reality caused enduring suffering. Scurvy, for instance, remained widespread – extremely painful and sometimes fatal – beyond the eighteenth century, because the countervailing power of fresh fruit and vegetables was not widely understood.[34]

Sydney Smith wrily viewed hay fever as medicine's Waterloo; Henry Matthews thought worst of all was sea sickness ('mind can not conceive, nor imagination paint, the afflicting agonies of this state of suffering'); and David Garrick expostulated against 'ye damn'dest Cold that Ever made a poor Mortal Snuffle'.[35] It was, however, the mortification of toothache that stirred Burns's muse:[36]

> My curse upon thy venomed stang
> That shoots my tortured gums alang;
> And through my lugs gaes many a twang

Wi gawing vengeance;
Tearing my nerves wi bitter pang
Like wracking engines.

When fevers burn or ague freezes,
Rheumatics gnaw or cholic squeezes;
Our neighbour's sympathy may ease us
Wi' pitying moan;
But thee, thou hell of all diseases
Aye mocks our groan.

The last years of the poet's life were, of course, a dire tale of inner, 'nervous' complaints, exacerbated by alcoholism. 'I have been ill the whole winter', he writes early in 1790, 'incessant headache, depression of spirits and deranged nervous system.'[37]

If little in the mocking profusion of the pharmacopoeia effectively abbreviated or overcame disease, so likewise there were few reliable painkillers. Alcohol was, of course, the favourite analgesic. The eighteenth century became the golden age of medically-prescribed opiates, and in the nineteenth century, chloroform made anaesthetized surgical operations possible.[38] Yet all these pain-killers produced pains of their own, being habit-forming and destructive of the gut.[39]

Many recorded their pains. Anne Bradstreet versified a fever in 'Upon Some Distemper of the Body'. There was, as she saw it, no human help: it was a storm in which one must wait upon nature and call upon God:[40]

In anguish of my heart repleat with woes,
And wasting pains, which best my body knows,
In tossing slumbers on my wakeful bed,
Bedrencht with tears that flow'd from mournful head.
Till nature had exhausted all her store,
Then eyes lay dry, disabled to weep more;
And looking up unto his Throne on high,
Who sendeth help to those in misery;
He chac'd away those clouds, and let me see
My Anchor cast i'th'vale with safety.
He eas'd my Soul of woe, my flesh of pain
And brought me to the shore from troubled Main.

But if some recorded their ailments copiously, the annals of pain remain selective and, read at face value, rather misleading. Almost inevitably, the deadliest strokes, the most acute fevers, have left the fewest records. *De profundis*, people had neither strength, time, nor wish to pen their pains; as they lapsed into coma or delirium, reflections became otiose or impossible. Millions died of raging fevers, but none (so far as we know) chose to lash themselves to the mast, as it were, and talk to their diaries till the pen literally dropped from their hands. It is a rare diary that breaks off in mid-flight, showing that the sufferer was writing almost up to death itself.

Likewise, those most susceptible to life-endangering diseases, the very young, left no eyewitness records.[41] The same goes for the mentally ill. Most surviving records of being mad were written after recovery or during 'lucid intervals'.[42] Innumerable mothers died in childbed: all had better things to do than document their own demise; even Mary Wollstonecraft was too poorly to leave any record of her last days.[43] We seem to have no first-hand accounts of actually *experiencing* a stroke: we are lucky to possess Samuel Johnson's moving account of awakening to find he had suffered such a blow, systematically testing his own faculties, and then, though partly paralysed and unable to speak, methodically organizing his own welfare through a chain of written messages.[44]

First-hand accounts of sickness are thus much more forthcoming with some disease types than others. Chronic complaints leave more record than acute, those attacking visible parts are described in greater detail than those of the internal organs. Thus gout is richly recorded.[45] It was, for one thing, widespread amongst the articulate; but gout produced precisely the kind of pain sufferers could readily write about: tedious enough to be capable of description (what can be said about instantaneous spasms?), severe enough to command attention, yet not so deranging as to preclude writing; not least, because of its recurrent nature, close observation of gout might lead to prophylaxis. And it was intriguing. As Charles Greville put it,[46]

> Very strange disorder, affecting different people so differently; with me very little pain, much swelling, heat, and inconvenience, more like bruised muscles and tendons and inflamed joints; it disables me, but never prevents my sleeping at night.

Stomach disorders had similar properties, permitting them to be written about *ad nauseam*;[47] the old also wrote extensively about their own pains, perhaps because they were often solitary, and time hung heavily on their hands.[48] Consumption, too, was much portrayed, because it killed gradually.[49]

Experiencing pain was one thing; finding expression for it another.[50] Not infrequently sufferers did not get beyond words such as 'unspeakable'. Indescribability, of course, conveys sublimity. But putting pain into words was always difficult. Particularly, perhaps, in the seventeenth century, diary reports were laconic: sufferers commonly penned the naked monosyllable 'pain', unqualified even by a single adjective. Such telegraphic reporting continued. The Duchess of Northumberland recorded for 6 May 1760: 'went home; voided a large stone. Tired to death. Went to ball; tired to death. A bad supper. Miss Townshend drunk.' How painful was voiding a stone, or indeed the rotten supper or Miss Townshend's company? She doesn't say.[51] The late seventeenth-century diary of William Tyldesley is one long record of pain, particularly arthritic, but it defies qualitative evaluation:[52]

> June 15. – In great payne [through gout] . . .
> June 16. – In paines alover . . .
> June 17. – In great payne; seized in my joynts with ye gout.

– and so it drones on, day after wretched day. Of course, we must never assume that silent sufferers suffered least. And what do we make of this kind of understatement? – 'I was very indifferent all day', wrote Elizabeth Wynne, 'and safe deliver'd of a little girl soon after five o'clock': is 'very indifferent' a little poorly or nigh unto death?[53]

Swift's health deteriorated: he had a whole mass of complaints including deafness, vertigo, and rheumatic problems. He confides his pains to Stella, without ever expatiating on them. Yet his sufferings were severe and vexed his peace of mind. 'I am plagued with these Pains in my Shouldr', he complained to her, rubbing it with Hungary water. 'Tis plaguy hard . . . you must know I hate pain'. [54]

Later in the eighteenth century, and presumably symptomatic of refined introspection of the age of sensibility,[55] accounts of sickness seem to become more expansive and intimate, especially, of course, in the valetudinarian sub-culture. One penalty of progress, it was argued, was increased sensitivity to pain; thus the civilized found that sickness hurt them worse than savages. In the West Indies, the Rev. William Jones decided that blacks bore sickness better than the whites because they felt it less; just as well, since they had more of it.[56]

Reports tell of people suffering unbearable pain, and longing for release. After weeks of excruciating suffering with ruptured intestines, Queen Caroline at last began to slip away; Horace Walpole reports her relief: 'I feared I should not have died of this.'[57] The last months of Elizabeth Wynne's mother make terrible reading. 'Poor mamma was in shocking pain again today', the daughter wrote in July 1798; she worsened. Next spring Elizabeth is writing, 'Mamma was so much worse today and towards night in such excessive pain and agony that we thought she was going to expire'. Yet she was still suffering in autumn, when Elizabeth comments, 'Mama is almost quite out of her mind. She is obliged to take 120 drops of Laudanum a day, and this convulses her in a shocking manner and at times deprives her of her senses'. It was another month before she was released from her agonies.[58]

Where we lack autobiographical accounts of pain, we often possess abundant eye-witness reports from their nearest and dearest. These documents create a circle of suffering, the pains of the sick chiming with the torments of spouses, friends, and children who watch and are often about to become bereaved. Such secondary suffering is especially acute where children are involved.[59] Very occasionally in childhood sickbed scenes, the voices of the infant are heard: frightened or brave, begging their parents' grace, as John

Evelyn's diary or Arthur Young's letters reveal;[60] but often they are mute, and we have to imagine their condition mirrored through their parents, or at best through accounts written long after the event, as when forty years on, Gibbon remembered the 'excruciating pain' of the 'nervous' complaints he bore as a child and for which he was ineffectually treated at Bath.[61]

Painful Medicine

There were thus the pains of being sick and of watching the sick. But there were also the pains of treatment: 'The disease torments us on one side', Montaigne lamented, 'and the remedy on the other'.[62] Medication sometimes seemed like leaping out of the frying-pan into the fire. 'I took physic today', moaned Elizabeth Wynne, 'it gave me the Belly ake all day and made hardly no effect.'[63] Byron, as ever, ridiculed the whole business:[64]

> I have been most painfully ill [he told Hobhouse in 1812], cupped on the loins, glystered, purged & vomited, *secundum artem*, & am condemned to the strictest regimen & the most durable of disorders for the residue of my life.

It sounds as though being physicked was his illness.

Pre-modern medicine tasted foul (we owe the sugar-coated pill to the enterprise of quacks).[65] This fact was given its moral by Johnson: 'life is a pill which none of us can bear without gilding'.[66] Moreover, medicines were meant to produce unpleasant effects, so many being laxatives or emetics, designed to evacuate, fast and furiously, the 'peccant humours' or poisons that were causing sickness. Diarists often report purges yielding up to twenty motions – whereat they were delighted, for it meant that the physick 'worked' – that is, produced the desired physical response.[67] Without such shaking, could medicine be efficacious? Others, however, retorted that such drastic medicines made bad worse. Thus, Thomas Gray, ever suspicious of doctors, worried about 'forcing medicines':[68]

> Poor Mr. Chute has now had the Gout for these five days with such a degree of pain & uneasiness, as he never felt before. Whether to attribute it to Dr. La Cour's forcing medicines, or to a little cold he got as soon as he came hither, I know not, but for above forty hours it seem'd past all human suffering, & he lay screaming like a man on the rack. The torture was so great, that (against my judgement & even his own) he was forced to have recourse to infusion of Poppy-heads.

Were these 'iatrogenic' pains – those inflicted by doctors – worth it? People wondered. Recalling her childhood, Mary Anne Schimmelpenninck confirmed that she had 'suffered many things of many physicians, and became more and more shattered in nerve'.[69] What had caused this?

The source of the evil was believed to be in the spine, and my parents at this time heard of a machine invented by a certain Mr. Jones, which was esteemed an infallible means of supporting the spine, and this instrument it was determined I should wear: which I accordingly did, from the time I was eleven till I was eighteen years old. My parents, full of kindness to me and hope for my benefit, little realised the continued and often severe pain occasioned by the application of this machine. It was taken off only at night, and during the hour and a half when I was allowed to lie down in the day; nor did they perceive the deleterious effect of a plan which for so many years, from childhood to womanhood, absolutely precluded the use of any vigorous bodily exercise.

Such episodes confirmed the widespread fear that medicine created more pains than it cured.

For some conditions, the approved treatments were recognized to be excruciating. The radical cure of syphilis was salivation with mercury. The metal – a poison in its own right – induced an artificial fever, whose effects, heightened by sweating, were meant to expel the infection.[70] Fetid breath, noisome smell, loosened teeth, endless spitting, aching joints, and fever were amongst the side-effects. One of the boasts of patent and quack medicines for venereal and other ailments was that here at last were medicines less troublesome – less harmful, even – than the disease.[71] Regulars countered that desperate afflictions required desperate remedies. Common wisdom, however, was willing to accept – in the abstract at least! – that the only cure that was tangibly working was one that hurt. 'Gentle purges and slight phlebotomies are not my favourites, they are Popgun batteries, which lose time and effect nothing', was Samuel Johnson's verdict.[72]

Surgery could, obviously, be even more painful. Recent scholarship has challenged the old myth of the swashbuckling 'sawbones', drawing the knife at every possible opportunity.[73] The education, training, and skills of surgeons were improving, and amputation was probably only the very last resort.[74] Nevertheless, surgical procedures remained characteristically painful, distasteful and messy – even routine treatments such as bloodletting, the making of 'issues' (deliberately inflicted minor wounds, artificially kept open, to encourage pus to suppurate), seatons (the insertion of threads under the skin, for the same purpose), and blisters, produced by hot irons or caustics.[75]

The pain sustained by those undergoing radical surgery is almost unthinkable. Farington thus quoted surgery performed upon his friend, West, whose ankle-bone had mortified: [76]

West said 'He could bear pain' – The wound was again laid open & a *caustic* applied to the *Bone* for 48 hours during which time the pain was excessive. The caustic was then removed & with it came the *exfoliated bone*, on seeing which the surgeon told Him all wd. now be well which proved to be the case after a little time. – West said that He was confined 6 months to His bed, & 2 months more to his chamber.

Amputating limbs, removing bladder stones, excising tumours – all were excruciatingly painful in the pre-anaesthetic era (the only palliatives were alcohol, and heavy pressure applied by attendants, creating diversionary pain). Fanny Burney, then living in Paris, has left us an extraordinarily detailed account, worth quoting in full, of her own breast cancer and the radical mastectomy she underwent at the surgeon's knife:[77]

About August, in the year 1810, I began to be annoyed by a small pain in my breast, which went on augmenting from week to week, yet being rather heavy than acute, without causing me any uneasiness with respect to consequences: Alas, 'what was the ignorance?' The most sympathising of Partners, however, was more disturbed: not a start, not a wry face, not a movement that indicated pain was unobserved, & he early conceived apprehensions to which I was a stranger. He pressed me to see some Surgeon; I revolted from the idea, & hoped, by care & warmth, to make all succour unnecessary. Thus passed some months, during which Madame de Maisonneuve, my particularly intimate friend, joined M.d'Arblay to press me to consent to an examination. I thought their fears groundless, and could not make so great a conquest over my repugnance.

Eventually, as the tumor worsened, she recognized she must face reality: 'All hope of escaping this evil being now at end, I could only console or employ my Mind in considering how to render it less dreadful.'[78] She consulted with surgeons, who pronounced her trouble cancer, and deemed surgery necessary:[79]

M. Dubois had pronouced 'il faut s'attendre à souffrir, Je ne veux pas vous tromper – Vous Souffrirez – vous souffrirez *beaucoup*!' – M.Ribe had *charged* me to cry! to withhold or restrain myself might have seriously bad consequences, he said. M. Moreau, in echoing this injunction, enquired whether I had cried or screamed at birth of Alexander [her son] – Alas, I told him, it had not been possible to do otherwise; Oh then, he answered, there is no fear! – What terrible inferences were here to be drawn! I desired, therefore, that M. d'A. [her husband] might be kept in ignorance of the day till the operation should be over. To this they agreed, except M. Larrey, with high approbation: . . . I obtained with difficulty a promise of 4 hours warning, which were essential to me for sundry regulations. From this time, I assumed the best spirits in my power *to meet the coming blow*; – & support my too sympathising Partner. They would let me make no preparations, refusing to inform me what would be necessary; . . . Dr. Moreau instantly entered my room, to see if I were alive. He gave me wine cordial & went to the salon. I rang for my Maid & Nurses, – but before I could speak to them, my room, without previous message, was entered by seven men in black, Dr. Larry, M. Dubois, Dr. Moreau, Dr. Aumont, Dr. Ribe, & a pupil of Dr. Larry & another of M. Dubois. I was now awakened from my stupor – & by sort of indignation – why so many? & without leave? – But I could not utter a syllable. M. Dubois acted as Commander in Chief. Dr. Larry kept out of sight; M. Dubois ordered a Bed stead into middle of the room. Astonished, I turned to Dr. Larry, who had promised that an Arm chair would suffice; but he hung his head, & would not look at me. Two *old mattresses* M. Dubois then demanded, & an old sheet. I now began to tremble violently, more with distaste & horrour of preparations even than of the pain. These arranged to his liking, he desired me to mount the Bed stead. I stood suspended, for a moment, whether I should not abruptly escape – I looked at the door, the windows – I felt desperate – but it was only for a moment, my reason then took command, & my fears & feeling struggled vainly against it. I called to my maid – she was crying, & the two nurses stood transfixed at the door. Let those women all go! cried M. Dubois. This order recovered me my voice – No, I cried, let them stay! *qu'elles restent!* This occasioned a little dispute, that re-animated me – The Maid, however, & one of the nurses ran off – I charged the other to approach, & she obeyed. M. Dubois now tried to issue his commands *en militaire*, but I resisted all that were resistable – I was compelled, however, to submit to taking off my long robe de Chambre , which I had meant to retain – Ah, then, how did I think of my Sisters! – not one, at so dreadful an instant, at hand to protect – adjust – guard me – I regretted that I had refused Me de Maisonneuve – Me Chastel – no one upon whom I could rely my departed Angel ! – how did I think of her ! – . . . I mounted, therefore, unbidden, the Bed stead – & M. Dubois placed me upon the Mattress, & spread a cambric handkerchief upon my face. It was transparent, however, & I saw, through it that the Bed stead was instantly surrounded by the 7 men & my nurse, I refused to be held; but when, bright through the cambric, I saw the glitter of polished Steel – I closed my Eyes. I would not trust to convulsive fear the sight of the terrible incision. A silence the most profound ensued, which lasted for some minutes, during which, I imagine, they took their orders by signs, & made their examination – Oh what horrible suspension! – I did not breathe – & M. Dubois tried vainly to find any pulse. This pause, at length was broken by Dr. Larry, who, in a voice solemn melancholy, said 'qui me tiendra ce sein?'– No one answered; at least not verbally; but this aroused me from my passively submissive state, for I feared they imagined the whole breast infected – feared it too justly, – for, again through the Cambric, I saw the hand of M. Dubois held up, while his forefinger first described a straight line from top to bottom of the breast, secondly a Cross, & thirdly a circle; intimating that the whole was to be taken off. Excited by this idea, I started up, threw off my veil, &, in answer to the demand 'Qui me tiendra ce sein?' cried 'C'est moi, Monsieur!' & I held my hand under it, & explained the nature of my sufferings, which all sprang from one point, though they darted into every part. I was heard attentively, but in utter silence, & M. Dubois then replaced me as before, &, as before spread my veil over my face. How vain, alas, my representation! immediately again I saw the fatal finger describe the Cross – & the circle – Hopeless, then, desperate, & self-given up, I closed once more my Eyes, relinquishing all watching, all resistance, all interference, & sadly resolute to be wholly resigned.

My dearest Esther, – & all my dears to whom she communicates this doleful ditty, will rejoice to hear that this resolution once taken, was firmly adhered to, in defiance of a terror that surpasses all description, & the most torturing pain. Yet – when the dreadful steel was plunged into the breast – cutting through veins – arteries – flesh – nerves – I needed no injunctions not to restrain my cries. I began a scream that lasted unintermittingly during the whole time of the incision – & I almost marvel that it rings not in my Ears still! so excruciating was the agony. When the wound was made , & the instrument was withdrawn, the pain seemed undiminished, for the air that suddenly rushed into those delicate parts felt like a mass of minute but sharp & forked poniards, that were tearing the edges of the wound, – but when again I felt the instrument – describing a curve – cutting against the grain, if I may so say, while the flesh resisted in a manner so forcible as to oppose & tire the hand of the operator, who was forced to change from the right to the left – then, indeed, I thought I must have expired, I attempted no more to open my Eyes, – they felt as if hermettically shut, & so firmly closed, that the Eyelids seemed indented into the Cheeks, The instrument this second time withdrawn, I concluded the operation over – Oh no! presently the terrible cutting was renewed – & worse than ever, to separate the bottom, the foundation of this dreadful gland from the parts to which it adhered – Again all description would be baffled – yet again all was not over, Dr. Larry rested but his own hand, & oh Heaven! – I then felt the Knife [rack]ling against the breast bone – scraping it! – This performed, while I yet remained in utterly speechless torture, I heard the Voice of Mr Larry, – (all others guarded a dead silence) in a tone nearly tragic, desire every one present to pronounce if any thing more remained to be done; The general voice was Yes – but the finger of Mr. Dubois – which I literally *felt* elevated over the wound, though I saw nothing, & though he touched nothing, so indescribably sensitive was the spot – pointed to some further requisition – & again began the scraping! – and, after this, Dr. Moreau thought he discerned a peccant attom – and still, & still, M. Dubois demanded attom after attom – My dearest Esther, not for days, not for Weeks, but for Months I could not speak of this terrible business without nearly again going through it! . . .

To conclude, the evil was so profound, the case so delicate, & the precautions necessary for preventing a return so numerous, that the operation, including the treatment & the dressing, lasted 20 minutes! . . . When all was done, & they lifted me up that I might be put to bed, my strength was so totally annihilated, that I was obliged to be carried, & could not even sustain my hands & arms; which hung as if I had been lifeless; while my face, as the Nurse has told me, was utterly colourless. This removal made me open my Eyes – & I then saw my good Dr. Larry, pale nearly as myself, his face streaked with blood, & its expression depicting grief, apprehension, & almost horrour.

Burney was, of course, a novelist, and perhaps no one but a novelist could have left such a graphic account of the psycho-physical trauma of an operation. Did its rather macabre ritual, did the pious deceptions that had been played upon her, lessen or worsen the pangs?

In other accounts, we experience the pain mainly at second-hand, often through the surgeon's own account of the patient's incredible sufferings and resolve. Heroic bravery is apparent in an operation for cancer recorded by John Ward in the seventeenth century:[80]

A cancer in Mrs Townsend's Breast of Alverton taken off by 2 surgeons the one's name was Clark of Bridgnorth, another's was Leach of Sturbridg. First they cutt ye skinne cross and laid itt back; yn they workt their hands in ytt one above and the other below and so till their hands mett and so brought it out. They had their needles and waxt threads ready but never used them, and also their cauterising irons, but they used them not. Shee lost not above 6 ounces of blood in all . . . . Every time they dressed itt they cutt of something of ye cancer yt was left behind. Ye chirurgions were for applying caustick, but Dr. Needham said 'No, not till ye last, since [she] could endure ye knife'. They prepared her body somewhat, yn let her blood ye day before.

Ward notes of the woman, 'she endured it with infinite patience all along, not offering to lay her hand uppon it to ease it, but a warme cloth to ye other breast all the time'. 'One of the surgeons told her afterwards', he concludes, 'that shee had indured soe much yt he would have lost his life ere he would have suffered ye like'.[81]

Without anaesthetics, even the best surgery was torture. Nevertheless, patients dutifully submitted. A Mrs Driver was operated on by Richard Kay for cancer. He removed a breast; the wound healed, and she was well for some months. A new schirrous knot appeared beneath the old wound. The woman returned, 'she being determined to undergo a second amputation '. It proved ghastly, for examination showed growths around 'six or seven inches square':[82]

I took off the Skin . . . so that from below where her Breast formerly was

down her Ribs to her Belly I dissected from her at a moderate Compu-
tation five hundred different distinct Schirrous Knots or young Cancers;
she was sick and very poorly after the Operation.

Nevertheless, Kay reported on the next day, 'I left Mrs Driver pretty easy'.
   Patients were not ignorant of the pains of surgery, or automatically docile to
doctors' orders. Rather, they submitted out of a rational calculus of pain.[83]
When Samuel Johnson's dropsy worsened, his surgeon tapped off the fluid.
Johnson begged him to make deeper incisions, rebuking him for fearing to
give him pain, when what he craved was the prolongation of life.[84] Similar
priorities were at work when Josiah Wedgwood's tubercular leg became a
useless encumbrance in the 1760s. The master-potter was eager to submit to
amputation. It is some mark of his business-like fortitude when faced with a
possibly life-threatening procedure that he left no record at all of his
operation.[85] When Pepys developed a bladder stone in the 1650s (alas, before
he started his diary), he was confronted with a choice of enduring pain; hoping
to dissolve it by medicines; or of surgery. He opted for the knife – a brave
decision, since the operation commonly led to fatal sepsis.[86] It proved a
success, though the diarist continued to experience pain in his bowels, belly,
and 'cods', as he reported in 1663:[87]

> Up full of pain, I believe by cold got yesterday. To the office, where we
> sat; and after office, home to dinner, being in extraordinary pain. After
> dinner, my pain increasing, I was forced to go to bed; and by and by my
> pain is to be as great for an hour or two as ever I remember it was in any
> fit of the stone, both in the lower part of my belly and in my back also.
> No wind could I break. I took a glister, but it brought away but a little
> and my height of pain followed it.

Pepys was always quite business-like when faced with pain. He would act at
once to remedy it:[88]

> 15. *Lords day*. Rose, and as I had intended without reference to this pain,
> took physic and it wrought well with me. My wife lying from me
> tonight, the first time she did in the same house ever since we were
> married I think (unless while my father was in town that he lay with me);
> she took physic also today, and both of our physics wrought well; so we
> passed our time today, our physic having done working, with some
> pleasure talking; but I was not well, for I could make no water yet but a
> drop or two with great pain, nor break any wind.

Though Pepys submitted himself to surgery, he was loth for his wife to
undergo the same fate. She suffered frequent trouble in her genitals. A
surgeon was called in, and a possible operation discussed. When he
pronounced it unnecessary, Pepys was greatly relieved. Did he fear that the

excisions would spoil his/their sex life? Did he hate the idea of a surgeon tampering with Elizabeth's *'chose'*? Whichever, his wife's condition hurt him as much as it pained her: 'My wife so ill of late of her old pain', he wrote on 31 October 1660, 'that I have not known her this fortnight almost, which is a pain to me.'[89]

In the late Enlightenment, Jeremy Bentham enunciated his Utilitarian philosophy based upon the felicific calculus. Mankind so acted as to maximize pleasure and minimize pains. We largely remember the 'pursuit of happiness'. To pre-moderns, pain was of far greater moment.[90]

NOTES

1   Marchand (ed.), *Byron's Letters and Journals*, VII, 227. Barclay Fox, in 1832, had numerous diary entries about his sick monkey. Brett (ed.), *Barclay Fox's Journal*, 40.
2   Little and Kahrl (eds), *Letters of David Garrick*, II, 557; Sterne, *Tristram Shandy*, 461.
3   For Sterne's life see Cross, *Life and Times of Laurence Sterne*; Cash, *Laurence Sterne*.
4   Curtis (ed.), *Letters of Laurence Sterne*, 367; Cross, *Life and Times of Laurence Sterne*, 329, 330, 367.
5   Curtis (ed.), *Letters of Laurence Sterne*, 229.
6   Sterne, *Journal to Eliza*, 152.
7   Curtis (ed.), *Letters of Laurence Sterne*, 318.

About a week or ten days before my wife arrived at Paris I had the same accident I had at Cambridge, of breaking a vessel in my lungs. It happened in the night, and I bled the bed full, and finding in the morning I was likely to bleed to death I sent immediately for a surgeon.

8   Ibid., 346.
9   Ibid., 43-5; Cash, *Laurence Sterne*, 134.
10 Cross, *Life and Times of Laurence Sterne*, 195.
11 Curtis (ed.), *Letters of Laurence Sterne*, 85; for Sterne's wife and daughter see Cash, *Laurence Sterne*, 285; Curtis (ed.), *Letters of Laurence Sterne*, 85.
12 Sterne, *Tristram Shandy*, 189; Porter, 'Against the Spleen'; Porter, 'Barely Touching'.
13 Sterne, *Tristram Shandy*, 164.
14 Ayres (ed.), *Paupers and Pig Killers*, 112, 114.
15 Ibid.
16 Fitzgerald (ed.), *Correspondence of Emily, Duchess of Leinster*, I, 100.
17 Darwin, *Temple of Nature*, 10-11; Cf. Thompson, *Sickness*.
18 For analysis see McNeil, *Under the Banner of Science*, 148f.
19 Porter, 'Hunger of Imagination', 68f.
20 Gittings (ed.), *Letters of Keats*, 95.
21 See Razzell, *Conquest of Smallpox*; Miller, *Adoption of Inoculation for Smallpox*; J.R. Smith, *Speckled Monster*, 17f.
22 Halsband, *Lady Mary Wortley Montagu*.
23 Bottomley, *Attitudes to the Body in Western Christendom*.
24 Brockbank and Kenworthy (eds), *Diary of Richard Kay*, 160.
25 Turner (ed.), *Oliver Heywood*, I, 203.
26 Ellis (ed.), *Works of Anne Bradstreet*, 'Before the Birth', 393.
27 Ibid.

28 For the culture of suffering associated with pregnancy see Shorter, *History of Women's Bodies*.

29 Donne, 'Sermon 20', quoted in Coope (ed.), *Quiet Art*, 159.

30 Wain, *Johnson*, 195-200.

31 Hankin (ed.), *Life of Mary Anne Schimmelpenninck*, I, 6-7.

32 Pettit (ed.), *Correspondence of Edward Young*, 189.

33 Toynbee (ed.), *Letters of Horace Walpole*, XI, 29.

34 Carpenter, *History of Scurvy and Vitamin C*, 233-38, 249-51.

35 Matthews, *Diary of an Invalid*, 4; Little and Kahrl (ed.), *Letters of David Garrick*, I, 181.

36 Quoted by Anderson, 'Robert Burns, His Medical Friends', 55.

37 Ibid.

38 Porter, 'The Drinking Man's Disease'.

39 Berridge and Edwards, *Opium and the People*, 11f.

40 Ellis (ed.), *Works of Anne Bradstreet*, 392-3.

41 See Chapter 8 below.

42 Porter, *Mind Forg'd Manacles*, ch. 5.

43 Tomalin, *Mary Wollstonecraft*, 222.

44 Chapman (ed.), *Letters of Samuel Johnson*, III, 32f. Mulhallan and Wright, 'Samuel Johnson: Amateur Physician'.

45 Rogers, 'Rise and Fall of Gout'.

46 Reeve (ed.), *Greville Memoirs*, II, 187.

47 Woodforde's diaries offer a good instance.

48 The writings of George Crabbe, when in old age, are an instance.

49 Sontag, *Illness as Metaphor*; F.B. Smith, *Retreat of Tuberculosis*.

50 Keele, *Anatomies of Pain*; Scarry, *Body in Pain*, 161f.; Wear, 'Historical Aspects of Pain'.

51 Greig (ed.), *Diaries of a Duchess*, 15.

52 Gillow and Hewitson (eds), *Tyldesley Diaries*, 136-7. Compare the following entries:

February 26. – Alday in paine . . .
February 27. – In paine of grips . . .
February 28. – Alday in paine, and sometimes sicke.
March 2. – Bad in paine.
March 25. – Very bad with payne of ye gra-ll.
March 26. – In very great payne all day off ye gravell.
March 27. – My payne of gra-ll continewd.
March 28. – My payne increased. Not able to move without helpe.

53 Fremantle (ed.), *Wynne Diaries*, III, 76. It evidently became a habit with her: cf. 30 August 1807, 'I felt extremely uncomfortable all day but walked out and dined at table. Mr. Tookey was sent for in the evening and towards twelve o'clock I was happily delivered of another boy.'

54 Williams (ed.), *Swift: Journal to Stella*, 527.

55 Todd, *Sensibility*, 10f.

56 On the hypochondriac see Fischer-Homberger, 'Hypochondriasis'; Baur, *Hypochondria*, 11f.; Porter, 'The Patient in the Eighteenth Century'; and below, Chapter 12. For an eighteenth-century view of Negroes and pain see Christie (ed.), *Diary of William Jones*, 32f.

57 Walpole, *Memoirs of George II*, 295. On the excruciating deaths of royalty, see Ray, *Deaths of the Kings of England*; Crawford, *Last Days of Charles II*; Yearsley, *Le Roy Est Mort!*

58 Fremantle (ed.), *Wynne Diaries*, III, 1, 9, 11.

59 For contrasting views on attitudes to children see Stone, *Family, Sex and Marriage*, 105f.; see also Pollock, *Forgotten Children*, chs 1 & 2; *idem, Lasting Relationship*; Crawford,' "The Sucking Child" '.

60 See, for example, Evelyn's grief-stricken accounts of the deaths of his children: De Beer (ed.), *Diary of John Evelyn*,III, 206-211, IV, 418-432, 461-465; Gazley, *Life of Young*, 545f.

61 Bonnard (ed.), *Edward Gibbon. Memoirs*, 39.

62 Taylor, *Montaigne*, 109.

63 Fremantle (ed.), *Wynne Diaries*, I, 143.

64 Marchand (ed.), *Byron's Letters and Journals*, II, 161.

65 Porter, 'Language of Quackery'.

66 Wain, *Samuel Johnson*, 266.

67 Robinson and Adams (eds), *Diary of Robert Hooke*, 18.

68 Toynbee and Whibley (eds), *Correspondence of Thomas Gray*, III, 479.

69 Hankin (ed.), *Life of Mary Anne Schimmelpenninck*, I, 259. On 'iatrogenesis', see Illich, *Limits to Medicine*, 39f.

70 Buchan, *Observations Concerning the Prevention and Cure of Venereal Diseases*.

71 Bynum, 'Treating the Wages of Sin', 15.

72 Chapman (ed.), *Letters of Samuel Johnson*, II, 394.

73 Loudon, *Medical Care and the General Practitioner*, 24f.; Beier, *Sufferers and Healers*, 51f.

74 Holmes, *Augustan England*, 166f.

75 Woodall, *Surgion's Mate*, 23f.

76 Cave (ed.), *Diaries of Joseph Farington*, IX, 3250. One recalls that Sterne's Uncle Toby spent several years in bed recovering from the wound he received at the siege of Namur.

77 Hemlow (ed.), *Journals and Letters of Fanny Burney*, VI, 598f. Burney is writing in 1811.

78 Ibid.

79 Ibid.

80 Severn (ed.), *Diary of John Ward*, 244-6.

81 Ibid., 246.

82 Brockbank and Kenworthy (eds), *Diary of Richard Kay*, 142-3.

83 For the obedience of patients see Porter and Porter, *Patient's Progress*, ch. 6; Lane, ' "The Doctor Scolds Me" '.

84 Chapman (ed.), *Letters of Samuel Johnson*, III, 84.

85 Wedgwood does, however, provide some interesting details of the care he took about obtaining a comfortable artificial leg:

Dear Sir.
    My first wooden leg was made by Mr. Addison, lay figure maker in Hanover Street, Long Acre; this was about 18 years ago, and I have heard nothing of him since. I do not know whether he is now alive or dead. An ingenious joiner in his neighbourhood is making me a new one, which I believe is nearly finished. He has made me one or two before and had the care of the old for many years and it has received so many repairs from him that it is now become almost like the sailor's knife, which has so many blades and so many hafts. (Finer and Savage (eds), *Letters of Josiah Wedgwood*, 314.)

86 Beier, *Sufferers and Healers*, 174.

87 Latham and Matthews (eds), *Diary of Samuel Pepys*, IV, 150. Pepys suffered

persistent though not life-threatening pain. In October 1663, he underwent 'one of the best-documented attacks of flatulence in history': ibid., IV, 324ff.
88   Ibid., 150.
89   Ibid., I., 279.
90   Halévy, *Growth of Philosophical Radicalism*.

Chapter 7:
Pain Experienced

Pre-modern times were thus watermarked by a plenitude of pain. The culture permitted the expression of suffering, though within an idiom circumscribed by moral dictates setting a premium upon individual responsibility and the maintenance of self-control.[1] It was admirable to bear pain with fortitude.

In this chapter we shall explore the capacity of certain individuals for coping with sickness. We shall begin with episodes thought not life-threatening – ones likely to have finite courses of development, containment, and recovery. We shall then proceed to look at chronic unwellness, in a case in which life itself did not seem seriously threatened. We shall also examine a case of acute, disorienting pain, and – far worse – profound anxiety, where the pain could not easily be assimilated within familiar diagnostic patterns, the prognosis was uncertain, and life itself lay possibly at risk. We shall review the defences available for handling agonies that made life itself a mockery. And, finally, we shall examine an instance of one whose sickness brought him to death itself. Did narrating the descent into dying enable those in such a plight to transform pain and terror into stories they felt better able to handle?

Certain threads, discussed earlier, run through all these cases. There is the envisaging of an interplay between mind and body, the experience of pain in limbs and organs simultaneously regarded as integral to self yet also, because diseased, as somehow alien.[2] There is the attempt to 'incorporate' the unfamiliar, to mount a look-out for patterns, causes, pointers. We see people alert to the requirements of realism, torn between hope and despair; and, as disorders develop, there are signs of roles changing, particularly the dawning recognition that life itself is endangered.

Not least, being ill had consequences. Sickness maketh man. Mary Anne Schimmelpenninck, born into a middle-class West Midlands Quaker family in the late eighteenth century, was a delicate child. She was seized with 'violent spasmodic asthma':[3]

> How long it lasted, I cannot now say, but the time then appeared interminable and my sufferings were very great. I especially remember,

once, when I was very ill, that a lady, out of kindness, to amuse me, read to me the story of Apollyon and Giant Despair in 'The Pilgrim's Progress': the fearful visions and terror it occasioned nearly cost me my life. It was many days before I recovered from its effects.

Thus physical sickness could be worsened by the pains of being treated as a sick person. 'Nothing could exceed the vigilant kindness of my dear mother in this heavy visitation', continued Mary Anne, perhaps confiding more than she meant. Her mother told her the edifying story, out of Aesop, of the courtier, who, to prove his utter obedience, agreed to eat a bitter fruit, at his King's behest, 'without complaint, or asking the reason why':[4]

'My dear child', my mother continued, 'God is our kind King, who surrounds us with every sort of benefit, and has done so ever since we were born. Hast thou, like Aesop, thanked Him every day for His goodness? And art thou not willing to submit patiently to the first thing He has given thee which is really bitter?'

Schimmelpenninck's reaction is interesting. The moral ploy did not work as planned. She notes how, instead of (as intended) enabling her to surmount the sickness, it left a psychosomatic scar:[5]

I never forgot the story. I will only add that the distress of this asthma and the weakness it left upon my organs of respiration laid, I think, at this time the foundation of that timidity and nervous apprehension which has tried me so much through life, and which my mother in vain attempted to counteract.

Once more, her mother attempted to conquer her fear of pain, but in a way that merely confirmed her physical debility:[6]

To prove my fears were groundless, she would often send me in the dark to find something she might want, and I remember rushing along the passages and lobbies of Barr, almost expecting to see some ghastly face peep out from behind one of the many doors.

There was, however, a happy ending. Her mother could not comfort, but God could:[7]

Yet even this trouble wrought for my good, since I found my only comfort and support under it was to look to God, and to realise the sense of being under His care; so that my very fears seemed, by His blessing, to lay a foundation for that confidence in His mercy, and turning to Him as my refuge, which I have found at times an unspeakable benefit in the real calamities of life.

Through examples such as this, we shall explore how sickness shaped the self, making people, but marring them too. And sickness *is* social relations as well: though focusing upon the socialized self that diaries typically evoke, we shall also glimpse how incapacity required renegotiation of relations with others – family, friends, and finally doctors.[8]

James Woodforde and Trivial Complaints

The journal is the man. Parson Woodforde's diaries were as copious as he was himself; they project the image of a happy broad-bottomed Georgian, following what, generously interpreted, may be called a moderate regime of life. He ate with relish, never drank himself under the table, and had no other vices that endangered his health. Indeed, he enjoyed a good measure of wellness, which perfectly complemented his generally optimistic, easy-going Anglicanism and his unruffled sense of the churchman's place as a man of the world, quiet hero of a bucolic idyll.[9]

More days than not, from 1758 to 1802 in Woodforde's diary, someone in his circle was unwell. Yet Woodforde expected ailments would find treatments, alleviations if not cures. There was always something or other to be done. Very frequently, he had recourse to minor home self-medication, which he practised upon himself, his niece, Nancy, who for many years kept house, his servants, and other villagers (it is Woodforde himself, and not Nancy, who appears to manage household medicine).[10] He relied on standard home-medicine texts such as Buchan's *Domestic Medicine*, which first appeared in 1769.[11] He had no particular faith in the healing power of nature, but displayed an implicit confidence in the powers of the hearty body, blessed with a good constitution, to combat malaise. For Woodforde, the mark of health was a healthy appetite.

But as well as auto-diagnostic home care, he also drew gratefully upon the services of local doctors. He trusted these men, cultivating connections both sociable and professional; he sought their advice and even abided by it. Woodforde did not share the common scepticism towards the medical profession.[12] He did not search out quacks, nor was his temper disposed towards spiritual remedies. For Woodforde, sickness was one of life's bothers, more a nuisance than a revelation, to be managed rather as pregnant maids, leaky roofs, or wet summers that ruined the harvest. A pinch of forbearance and charity would provide some balm. 'Very bad all day in the toothache', Woodforde wrote on 3 June 1776: the next day he took action:[13]

> My tooth pained me all night, got up a little after 5 this morning, & sent for one Reeves a man who draws teeth in this parish and about 7 he came and drew my tooth, but shockingly bad indeed, he broke away a great piece of my gum and broke one of the fangs of the tooth, it gave me exquisite pain all the day after, and my Face was swelled prodigiously in the evening and much pain. Very bad and in much pain the whole day

long. Gave the old man that drew it however 0.2.6. He is too old, I think, to draw teeth, can't see very well.

Woodforde's diary records scores of minor conditions like this, which he took in his stride. On 8 February 1793, his face came up. Next day, he reported, 'My face swelled rather more this Morning', but, as usual, piety enabled him to look on the bright side: 'not very painful, thank God for it'.[14] Indeed, he still managed a 'neck of mutton, boiled', for dinner. By the tenth, things were worse: 'my face much swelled this morning'; now 'painful' really was the word and it began to affect his spirits: 'it made me rather low, having duty to do at Church'. All the same, 'I walked to Church in the Afternoon with my face quite exposed', reading prayers and preaching. 'Pray God my face might not suffer.' His prayers were, it seems, answered. On his return 'I thank God! that I did not find myself worse in my face . . . Dinner today Loin of Veal rosted &c.'[15]

Fortunately, recovery came with care and time. 'Feb 12, Tuesday . . . My face near the same as Yesterday, tho' I used Hartshorn last night and kept part of my face very warm with flannell all Night.' He had been unable to sleep, 'but thank God not in much pain'. During the day, gout flared in his toe, which Woodforde clearly linked with the improvement in his face. 'The pain in my face and swelling much abated this Evening, but my great Toe more and more painful. Nancy complained of the Wind Cholic this Evening.' The day ended companionably: 'We both took some Rhubarb going to bed'.[16]

Thus ended a typical Woodforde week. He and his niece had been sick enough for the episode to be worth recording (partly because he recorded everything, and partly specifically to log a condition that might have turned more serious, thus requiring full diagnostic information). The facial swelling educed no complex medical theorizing; he advanced no hypotheses about the cause, nature, or identity of the complaint – beyond worrying that the cold would make it worse. He felt no need to summon professional aid, expecting home remedies would work (the hartshorn, the flannel, keeping warm, and the final touch of rhubarb for luck). Nor did he attempt to plumb Providential meanings in the manner of those Nonconformists who spied Divine warnings in every wen. In this, Woodforde was quite typical of Georgian parsons.

A further illustration will clarify Woodforde's pragmatism with minor sickness interludes. In September 1794, his ankle started giving him trouble. He felt he knew why. Having had a sore on it, he had applied a plaster made up to a family recipe. Believing it would quickly heal, he had not changed the bandage regularly. He blamed himself for this negligence, for the sore had 'corroded'.[17] On the twenty-fifth of the month, he reported, 'My ankle very painful in the night at times . . . dismal dreams'. Next morning things were no better, so he sought help:[18]

My ankle having given so much Pain last Night & having applied nothing at all to it but our Family Plaster, soon after breakfast I sent to John Reeves at the Heart [Inn] who practises something in the doctoring

way, for some Yellow Basilicum Ointment, which I immediately applied
to my ankle, & wch. Dr Buchan recommends, pray God! it may do
good.

Despite this recourse to local, amateur aid, he was quite apprehensive: 'I have
my doubts [i.e., fears] of its turning out a very serious matter – I mean my
ankle which I am afraid is much worse than it appears to be – very dangerous.
It makes me I confess very low.' Why? Eighteenth-century pathological
notions believed that distempers readily migrated round the body. The ankle
disorder might settle upon some more dangerous part; hence Woodforde's
fear. Things, however, improved. Next morning, it hurt less ('better I believe
from my applying the Basilicum Ointment Yesterday'). His anxiety dispelled:
'my Spirits (thank God) much better today . . . I relished my Dinner very well
to day & eat heartily.'[19]

Though things were better still the next day, Woodforde sent his servant,
Ben, to the local doctor, Mr Thorne, who advised a poultice. On Tuesday 30,
Thorne called, removed the poultice, assured Woodforde that there was no
inflammation (evidently his worry); Thorne dressed it with 'some dry Lint,
and on that something like Turner's Cerat [i.e., a waxy ointment with which
Woodforde would have been familiar, for it was mentioned in Buchan] on
Linen, and then bound it on quite tight with a Bandage'. The doctor delivered
a sermon on regimen:[20]

Mr Thorne would not have me eat any salt Meat nor drink any Wine &
but little Malt Liquor. I might eat Mutton, Veal or Chicken & Puddings.
He recommended me to lay my Leg upon a Stool as much as I could in
the day time. He says, that there is a kind of Stuff in the part which must
be eat down with some red precipitate before it can possibly heal, wch. I
am to have from him this Evening with some Turners Cerate, which I am
to send after.

Nancy had dressed mutton and goose for supper; showing noble asceticism,
Woodforde abstained from the goose. 'Pray God! The Medicines made use of,
may do good.' The doctor also sent with them 'some Calomel Pills' – i.e., a
strong purge – 'to take 4. every Night and to begin to night'. At this, the
parson baulked: 'I would not take them to Night nor indeed any of them at any
time': Woodforde liked laxatives, but violent purges were another matter.[21]

Woodforde had a bad night, but he naturally did not attribute this to his
refusal to take the doctor's purgative: 'if I had taken the four mercurial Pills,
they would have half if not quite killed me'.[22] Rather, his restlessness was due
to 'living Yesterday much below par' – that is, not stimulating his stomach
with sufficiently appetizing food and drink (the goose was on his mind).
Hence, after breakfast, once his maid Betty had dressed the ankle with the
doctor's ointment, he knocked back a 'Good Glass of Rum & Water, as I felt so
queerly in my Stomach . . . seemed to do me much good. Living to[o] low

wont at all agree with my gouty Constitution and past fifty four Years of Age.'[23] (Like most Englishmen, Woodforde believed that ageing had to be compensated by stiff external stimulus.)

The next night was bad; the part treated with the red precipitate was agonizing ('like a Dog almost gnawing it'). 'I am afraid', he recorded, 'it will turn out bad in the End, if it does not soon mend.'[24] Thorne, however, visited and reassured him that all was well.

Little changed over the next couple of weeks, when he remained 'uneasy about my Ankle'.[25] Then on 21 October a fit of gout broke out, shedding welcome light on the whole episode: 'glad rather than sorry in having the Gout'. Like many others, Woodforde knew he was on familiar ground once strange disorders transformed themselves into gout. Thus reassured, he felt able to disobey the doctor with impunity on the matter of diet, eating beef, etc. The ankle then seemed to mend. On 25 October, and every couple of days thereafter, Thorne came to dress it. Then Woodforde took a turn for the worse, just at the moment that he became anxious that his maid, Molly, was pregnant.[26] By early November, however, all seemed almost well, and he started dressing the wound himself, rather than relying on the doctor. By mid-November, he was leaving off the bandage, and could triumph in his diary, 'No Doctor this day',[27] though, not to tempt fate, he grudgingly kept to doctor's orders: 'Dinner to day, a Bullock's Heart boiled (according to Dr Thorne's recommendation) and a pheasant rosted. N.B. a Bullock's Heart boiled is a Bullock's H. spoiled. We think a rost one far preferable.'[28]

And so, despite one further alarm in November, when he feared that 'there is some kind of humour arising from it', Woodforde recovered, convalescing over the course of two months.[29] The episode was lengthy – in those days, minor infections, abrasions, and ulcers seem to have been slow to heal. The diary presents Woodforde as a sick person anxious until he had put himself under the control of the doctor, who was able to afford him full reassurance about the prognosis – the most valuable service any doctor in these circumstances could perform. Woodforde was obviously happy enough to follow Thorne's general recommendations, while feeling entitled to disobey on details. He formulated his own views about a healthy regime, based upon the need to 'live high', and drawing upon common folklore about gout (if you were disposed to gout, it was best to have a fit of it, for it would absorb and drive away other ailments).

Pain Persistent: Robert Hooke

Woodforde's sickness experiences punctuated a generally healthy, active, and serene existence. Many seventeenth- and eighteenth-century diaries show a very different pattern, that of a life fretted by more or less daily symptoms – not necessarily severe enough to be life-threatening, but requiring vigilance, and casting a cloud on life. Samuel Pepys was like that. Not surprisingly, perhaps, for someone who had survived serious surgery and who lived in plague-ridden London, Pepys rarely went more than a few days without becoming apprehensive of threats to his own health, or that of his wife and household. He was no hypochondriac, but, as befitted a scientific bureaucrat, was always on the alert for the multitude of health risks afforded by the weather, environment, and infected people.[30]

A member of Pepys' wider circle who, *prima facie*, merits the label 'hypochondriac' is Robert Hooke, possibly the greatest polymath of the Restoration. Hooke's childhood probably triggered his health worries, for his contemporary biographer tells us that he was weak from birth, 'all which time his chief Food was Milk, or things made thereof, and Fruits, no Flesh in the least agreeing with his weak Constitution'. From his mid-teens, he developed a crooked back, and he remained 'pale and lean, and latterly nothing but Skin and Bone, with a meagre Aspect'.[31] His 'restless, indefatigable Genius' was accompanied, as so often in those anxious, competitive times, by a temper 'Melancholy, Mistrustful and Jealous'.[32]

Many of Hooke's contemporaries kept journals for religious purposes, to confess their inmost thoughts to God. Hooke's, by contrast, is quite secular, recording in matter-of-fact prose his day-to-day dealings, business, and meetings – it seems more like the experimental notebook of a methodical, meticulous mind for whom scientific observation was a way of life, possibly a man obsessionally needing to keep tabs on existence, or to account for himself. Hooke was hooked on minutiae, listing every visit to the coffee-house, every last halfpenny jar of ale. Not least, he recorded his health.

Hooke's health was probably neither better nor worse than most people's; he gives the impression, however, of having been extremely delicate, precisely because he registered his complaints so particularly, in context of all relevant factors, including his eating and drinking habits, changes in the weather, his orgasms, his state of mind, and the maladies of his friends and household (he was, of course, writing just after the plague of 1665). He evidently paid great attention to regulating his routines with a view to protecting his health, and we may surmise that he experimented on his body, testing out foods, drugs, and regimens for their effects. He was ever watchful and self-absorbed. 'Much disturbed with a guiddiness in my eyes and head after drinking new ale and eating mutton pottage, slept a little after it', he writes on 1 January 1673:[33]

> better after eating pullet and drinking ale . . . was somewhat better after drinking tea and cleering right nostill after Beet Juice . . . I took a clove of garlick in drink: at night I slept pretty well but had a strange noyse in right ear upon waking like a horne or bell. Towards bed I spitt very much and my right nostill was cleerd which I ascribe in part to juice of beet and part to garlik swallowd and to tea drunk.

A frequent companion of London physicians, Hooke often consulted with them on an equal footing, and tried out their suggestions: thus his personal viligance over health was no expression of hostility to the profession. But he also resorted to unorthodox medicines, often taking 'mountebank's drink', or

'Andrew's drink' and suchlike; a confirmed empiricist, he would try anything. Often, a spell of self-observation would indeed culminate in consulting with physicians. Thus he fell sick on Christmas Eve, 1672. 'I took a clyster after which working but once I was very ill and giddy'. He then slept badly: 'Worst night I ever yet had, melancholly and giddy, shooting in left side of my head above ear.' On Christmas Day, he rose, but 'on eating broth, very giddy'. The successive entries show him trying self-dosing, and when this failed, he summoned the physician, yet apparently carried on self-medicating too:[34]

> Mr Godfrey here but made noe effect. Eat plumb broth, went pretty well to bed but slept but little and mightily refresht upon cutting off my hair close to my head and supposed I had been perfectly cured but I was somewhat guiddy; (26) next day and tooke Dr. Godderds 3 pills which wrought 14 times towards latter end. I was again very giddy and more after eating, which continued till I had taken a nap for 1/2 howr about 5 when I was very melancholly but upon drinking ale strangly inlivend and refresht after which I slept pretty well and pleasantly. Dreamt of riding and eating cream. (27) After I was up I was again guiddy and was soe for most part of the day . . . Borrowed Mr. Colwalls ale, agreed not, guiddy head, benummed and guiddy. Made oyle of bitter almonds, put some in right ear . . . Slept ill. (28) With Lamot at Lord Brounkers. Mr. Haux at home. At Guidlys I made an issue in my Pole. Dr. Chamberlaine was here and directed. He made it with caustick, I gave him 5sh. slept ill.

Hooke thus constantly treated and monitored himself: 'Slept ill after cheese. Dremt of viragoes and other strange phenomena.'[35] Yet he rarely overtly commented on, or analysed, what he recorded. He never presents a formal diagnosis of his health; he explores no theories; neither does he deploy an elaborate vocabulary of pain or disease. Even the connections he presumably drew between cause and effect in his illnesses must be inferred from the sequence of events recorded and the implied force of forms of expression ('better after eating pullet').

Convinced of the necessity of moderation, he clearly believed rich viands and strong liquor made him ill. 'Drunk claret which made me sick', he records once, [36] and, later, 'at home and to bedd. I had drunk canary 3 glasses. Slept ill but purgd much yellow snot next morn which releivd me.'[37] Likewise having sex with his serving maids (which he marked with an 'X' sign) often upset him ('Nell X sweat and was ill').[38]

But, then, so many things made him feel bad, including the medicines he constantly swallowed. So routinely did he drug himself that he actually found it worth recording on Sunday 3 August 1673, 'took noe physick'.[39] Yet Hooke lived to a ripe old age, with little impairment of his faculties: quite possibly his medications – the steel, diet drinks, etc. – were the prime source of his troubles.

Above all, Hooke tried to inch his way, much like Pepys, through a hazardous environment. All eventualities had to be kept in mind, to understand what precisely put one's health at risk, and how to react. 'Yesternight I woke with an intolerable pain in head.' So whatever was wrong? This, he said,[40]

> I found to be from cold having cut my hair a week before and not putt on
> a thicker cap, but upon keeping my head warmer my head recovered.
> my losse of smell was rather worse and my ill tast continued.

Duty-bound to look after his own health, Hooke sought advice and collected recipes. 'Mr Axe told me that my Lady Portman receivd the greatest ease of collick paines by a clyster of Venice treacle' – eloquent testimony to the lay medical-grapevine.[41] He also garnered information about other people's health, recording on 4 July 1673, the death of Sir Robert Moray, 'choked with flegme in indeavouring to vomit. He had dind at Lord Chancellers and about an howr before his death drank 2 glasses of cold water.'[42] Hooke presumably made a mental note to beware rash indulgence in cold water.

Hooke never thought of himself as a valetudinarian (when he noted he had 'hypochondriack wind', he simply meant cholic).[43] We might so call him, on the grounds that he was morbidly preoccupied with trivial complaints to a counter-productive degree, becoming touchy and suspicious as a result. Yet in one important sense, Hooke was no true hypochondriac: he never gave rein to his imagination, nor convinced himself he was suffering from ever more desperate diseases. Perhaps he was simply too literal-minded, too stalwart an empiricist, for that. Nor – so far as his written remains allow us to judge – did he ever develop some larger 'mythology', 'biography', or 'psychopathology' of being ill. Sickness was merely a presence that had to be controlled, checked, and recorded.

Pain Insupportable

James Woodforde's life shows occasional bouts of sickness, managed through hand-me-down knowledge and nursing that dispelled anxiety and facilitated coping. Robert Hooke's diary displays ill health as more vexatious, but seemingly successfully patrolled by permanent vigilance. Not all were so fortunate. Many suffered severe afflictions that remained mysterious, defying attempts to define or limit them, or even to frame prognoses. In such cases, the very lack of specificity produced a numbing helplessness. The tormented life of Anne Conway offers an instructive instance.

Born in 1631 into an illustrious family, Anne Finch suffered fever when she was twelve. She recovered, but the bout seems to have left a legacy of appalling headaches, both frequent and persistent, which plagued her without remission for the next forty years up to her death in 1679. In 1651, she married Edward Conway, who became a career diplomat; contrary to optimistic forecasts, however, neither matrimony nor motherhood alleviated her headaches. Her only child, Heneage, was born in 1658, succumbing a couple of years later to smallpox.

Anne Conway passed most of her married life as chatelaine of Ragley Hall in Herefordshire, where she kept in close touch with her beloved brother, the amiable John Finch. On going to Christ's College, Cambridge, Finch developed a great admiration for his tutor, Henry More, the Cambridge Platonist; and through his good offices, Anne and More established a lifelong correspondence and informal 'tutorial' relationship. From her sickbed – and she seems increasingly to have been confined to her chamber – she dedicated herself, under More's guidance (he called her 'my heroine Pupil'), to religion and philosophy.

The correspondence stretching over some thirty years between Lady Conway and her husband, John Finch, Henry More, and a few others, is a testament to continuous suffering. She herself records it. 'Sir, I have been extremely troubled with a violent fitt of the headache these 3 or 4 dayes', she tells More in 1653, in a message endlessly repeated over the years.[44] But things grew even worse,[45] in particular in 1658, when she suffered an unparalleled 'fit' (it turned out she was pregnant), and then in 1666-7, when her husband thought she was 'near her last'.[46] During 1664 she recorded the worsening of the condition:[47]

> I received yours both of the 26 of March and the 26 Aprill, though my sickness hath rendered me from giving you an account of them. I have formerly given you some intimation of the great increase of my distemper and other indispositions since this last winter, which doeth not yet abate upon me but contrarily I have been so much worse then I was when I writt last that since good fryday I have not been able to goe abroad, and am very little off of my bed. I find myself very faint and weak, but yet as little strength as I seeme to have, I still indure those violent paines (which I always thought would be accounted intollerable by a stronger body then I ever had), and that more frequently then ever. I cannot dissemble so much as not to professe myself very weary of this condition.

The ebb and flow of her correspondence reflects her trials. In later life, her pains speak through silences: she felt too ill to respond to the stream of well-wishing letters.

At all times, her friends urged her to pious and philosophical resignation, or in More's phrase, to add 'Stoicisme to Christianity'.[48] 'Resigne yourself wholy to the will of God', he advised, casting himself in the role of 'both Physician and Patient', for God was 'the great Physician of soul and body'.[49] Warning against 'melancholy' – a self-destructive indulgence, and possibly the Devil's work – More's nostrums were 'Reason, Philosophy and Relligion'.[50] Indeed, she seems to have accepted his advice.

Early on, hopes for a cure ran high. Her friends showered her with physical advice. Thus, her brother wrote to her in good Polonian vein in April 1652 with maxims for her regimen:[51]

> I am exceeding sorry to heare that your Rheume is not quite vanquish'd yet. I am very fearfull you take cold and if my conjecture be true assuredly the warmth of the summer will cure you: and I am apt to thinke you drinke too much small beere the summer will also manifest unless you either increase your quantitiy of drink or cool your stomach by fruits. Take heed of overcooling your selfe for your temper being naturally hott to take perpetuall cool thinges is to cure not your disease but to disturb your temper which to preserve in its first constitution is to restore you to your health but in regard you have been accustomed to an ill diet and custome is a second nature doe not alter your old course on a suddain but gently by degrees wean your selfe from too many cool things, for if you make a violent change I am afraid of some Feavour or disease. Let the meat you eat be little and of easy digestion and rather of good nourishment then quelque chose, such as Mutton, in the first place, Veal, Lamb, and all sorts of White Fowl. Other things I shall leave to your discretion, for I would not tye you to live by a Rule, but if you eat of any thing lesse convenient eat the lesse of it. Pray keep good houres of going to bed; in truth to make it twelve of the clock before you are in bed is such a thing that you will never be well whilst you breath and doe so.

Her friends also suggested no end of medicines. Her brother at one point thought the answer lay in Tachenius's medicine made up of 'volatile salt of vipers';[52] and though he once told her, 'my Dear I shall never advise you whilst I breath to a Mountebank', he later sent a quack cure, about which she was highly sceptical (she exercised her own judgement when swallowing medicines).[53] When regular boluses and electuaries failed, More himself came up with a special red powder made by a Welshman,[54] 'an admirable sovereign virtue for curing, as it is told me, all diseases'.[55]

She tried regular physicians, including the nonpareil William Harvey (the Finches feared that as a clinician he showed more 'imagination' than 'judgment'; in any case, he was aged). She experimented with the nostrums of the famous, including Robert Boyle's 'Ens Veneris'.[56] She showed interest in such faith healers as Matthew Coker; when Valentine Greatrakes (the 'Stroker') came to England, he was summoned to Ragley, and his services tried, though to no avail.

During the first decade of her headaches, Anne was active in searching for therapies, reading medical works such as Nicholas Culpeper's *Practice of Physick*. She tried a great variety of preparations, including a 'red powder', a 'blue powder', assorted plasters, a water douche, an opium-based medicine of Dr Ridsley,[57] Van Helmont's 'universal medicine', coffee, and tobacco. She underwent nauseating salivation with mercury on two occasions.[58] She gave a try to quackish remedies such as an 'Elixir' her husband sent her.[59] And, presumably in desperation, she went, on her own initiative – indeed, it seems, on her own – to France to get herself trepanned, though it appears that the operation was not, in fact, performed.[60] More was sympathetic, but rather disapproving: 'I am sorry you are forced to try so desperate a remedie as the Trepan'.[61]

As she aged, the migraines worsened and she underwent 'extremities of paine'.[62] Anne herself came to the conclusion – in which she was apparently seconded by her circle – that no cure was likely. She abandoned her therapeutic experiments – something she had apparently been threatening for some while, since her brother had written to her as early as 1653, 'I like your resolution not to try many experiments on your own body in Physick, considering the small encouragement you have had by the [rest]'.[63] More (himself absorbed with his own health) agreed, talking disarmingly of his 'sullen conceit' that medicines would not avail where Nature would not repair itself through exercise and diet:[64]

> I do not at all mislike your resolution in giving over Physick if there be not better effect of it. Ease of minde, fresh ayr and diet, may leasurely do that, which Physick could not effect so suddenly. And you must absteine not onely from reading but from thinking too intensely.

The later correspondence falls silent on these issues. She was, in short, 'discouraged by the paine and feaverishnesse' accompanying her medication.[65] Thus, Anne Conway underwent a transition, from being sick to becoming an invalid. She abandoned physic and took to religion. In mid-life, she devoted herself to an uplifting Christian Platonism; at a later stage – and much to her husband's distress – she leant towards the Quaker persuasion, finding solace in its peace.

What are we to make of Anne Conway's headaches and her enactment of the sick role? It is fruitless to speculate whether her headaches were 'real' (organically caused) or 'psychosomatic'. Her friends sometimes suspected an element of the latter, as when More warned her not to let 'phansy' make things worse.[66] Sickness certainly had compensations; it enabled her – unlike most married women – to lead a congenial life of retirement with her books and writing in 'the privacy of her closett'. It also bound her brother and his onetime tutor to her in ties of intimate friendship; their enduring support possibly meant more than her husband's. Both Finch and More (himself perennially on a 'course of Physick')[67] loved sharing confidences of their own illnesses with her in their medical *ménage à trois*. Of course, the fact that she had a child shows that Anne did not straightforwardly use the sick role to escape conjugal duties; in later life, however, when her husband came down to Ragley she was, she said, sometimes too sick to see him.

Overall, the precise impact of sickness upon Lady Conway's life remains debatable. It probably confirmed an early disposition to retirement and intellectual pursuits; it certainly gave her exemption from the glittery ambassadorial life she might have been obliged to follow in tow to her husband. It fostered her Platonism and her Quaker-leanings (decidedly aberrant in a woman of her rank). What we are left with is the evidence of an adult life dominated by torturing pain.[68]

Pain Unto Death: Gideon Mantell

In this chapter, we have surveyed how pain intruded into three lives, in cases of increasing severity. Woodforde's pains were a pinprick; Hooke's formed a grumbling ground-bass; Anne Conway's agonies proved progressively disabling. Finally, we examine a case in which a crippling disease reduced a successful person to a wreck, before finally killing him.

Born in 1790, Gideon Mantell appeared to have an enviable existence: a successful medical practitioner in rural Sussex, and one of the nation's leading palaeontologists, remarkable for his discoveries of dinosaur remains and for his éclat as a scientific popularizer.[69] The reality was more complicated. Leading a double career taxed his energies to breaking-point, firing envy against the metropolitan gentlemen geologists with their command of means and leisure. His private life proved painful. A brother, Joshua, became insane and ended up confined in Ticehurst House asylum. Several of his children died young, including a beloved teenage daughter, Hannah; and in 1840, his wife left him (an intense man, he was probably difficult to live with).

From 1841, Mantell's journal begins to record appalling pain in his lower back - he attributed it to the constant stooping required in nursing his daughter, an explanation that smacks of the 'martyr'.[70] Over the next few years, his wail of pain rose to a crescendo. 'Almost dead from pain and fatigue', 'I am half dead', 'sorrow and sickness' – these are typical of 1841 and the succeeding year.[71] 'Suffering very much all the year' was his summary of 1842 as a whole. Individual entries testify to acute pain: 'every night I have suffered intensely from Neuralgia', 'still suffering severely', 'suffering martyrdom from Neuralgia', 'I end this year in a state of great suffering from neuralgia'; and so forth.[72]

1843 proved no better. 'All night and day almost frantic with pain', 'suffering dreadfully', 'almost worn out with suffering' – similar expressions echo down through the year.[73] He never got better, and in the remaining decade of his life, before his death in 1852, kept up the shriek of pain: 'Alas! suffering as usual both in mind and body – no remission of bodily pain or mental affliction'.[74] His thoughts turned ever more to death. 'Another night of intense suffering: how I live on is a mystery to me: so little sleep – so seldom free from pain'; 'another night of suffering and distress. Went yesterday to my poor child's grave: Oh! that I were lying in peace beside her!!!'[75]

Mantell's troubles were not eased by the fact that, though a doctor, he could not frame a satisfactory diagnosis. Having in vain tried such treatments as hot baths and self-dosing with laudanum, aconitina ('cost 7/6, but of no use whatever'), and prussic acid, he consulted numerous top London physicians and surgeons, including Dr William Fitton ('were this man not an Irishman, I should think him demented')[76] but the experts only contradicted each other and compounded his troubles:[77]

[28 September 1842] Went to London and consulted Sir Benjamin Brodie. Well may the unmedical sufferer exclaim, 'Who shall decide when doctors disagree?' – when I am at a loss to decide upon the conflicting opinions upon my case! Sir Benjamin Brodie and Mr Lawrence believe there has been periostitis and that there is diseased bone, but not of the bodies of the vertebrae; and that an abscess has formed and will probably require to be opened, but perhaps some exfoliation will take place. But the one recommends entire rest in a horizontal position, and blisters, moxa or some other external stimulant; while the latter advises no external application, gentle carriage exercise, and sarsaparilla.

He also visited the surgeons Liston and Coulson, who believed there was no bone disease at all, but merely an abscess. Mantell himself, by contrast, was inclined to believe he had cancer. He viewed the metropolitan doctors with contempt, but one suspects he felt similar contempt at his own ineptitude, as a doctor, to heal himself.

If diagnosis failed, so did therapy and even pain control. He tried external applications of iodine, prussic acid liniments, and caustics. In the end, he took to inhaling vast quantities of ether and chloroform, but these achieved little more than secondary nausea; their relief was only temporary. Chloroform, he wrote, 'threw me into a deep but wretched state of stupor for a short time; the neuralgia returned as severe as ever':[78]

28 Friday. – Passed a night of intense suffering; at four could bear it no longer, and therefore inhaled Chloroform which made me insensible for half an hour, when the spasms in the nerves of the thighs came on as bad as ever.

In the end, it is hard to tell whether pain killers were more agonizing than his disease: 'terribly ill from the chloroform still', or, a little later, 'at home sick and ill all day, from the opiate'.[79] In his last years, his opium consumption increased dramatically: on 19 May 1852, he wrote that he 'took 1 oz of liq[uor] opii sedati[vu]s in the night' – about thirty-two times the usual recommended dose; and his death eventually came, deliberately or not, from an opium overdose.[80]

Mantell offers a poignant instance of a life overwhelmed by pain – all the more so because here the patient was a doctor. What is fascinating is that – so far as the records permit one to judge – the affliction remained totally external to the victim. As we shall explore in chapter 12 below, some sufferers digest disease, internalizing it as an extension or expression of their selves. It becomes integral to their being, changing their personality. Mantell, however, experienced pain simply as a negative, meaningless, arbitrary alien force, a cruel 'torture'.[81] Whatever one might surmise about his 'unconscious', for Mantell the diarist, disease had no redeeming features, led to no maturation in his consciousness, produced no catharsis, no epiphanies. It did not even generate an elaborate self-explanatory, self-vindicatory mythology.[82] Perhaps Mantell offers an instance of the mind of the doctor divorced from the body of the patient.

'Wee all look like People risen from the dead', wrote Dorothy Osborne to her fiancé, William Temple, in 1653. She was referring to herself, her father, and her eldest brother, all of whom were recovering from ague (malaria).[83] And for her, the tyranny of sickness had been compounded by the medical regime she had endured. Her medical attendants, she wrote, so 'governe mee that I am neither to eate drink nor sleep without their leave, and sure my Obedience derserv's they should cure mee or else they are great Tyrants to very little purpose. You cannot imagine how cruel they are to mee and yet will persuade mee tis for my good.'[84] Thus disease was a tyrant; but so could medical regimes be as well – in this case, not of professional doctors but rather of her own family (had they enforced the same tyranny on themselves?). The empire of pain had many minions.

NOTES

[1]   Macfarlane, *Origins of English Individualism*.
[2]   That sense of alien parts is strongly emphasized throughout Bakan, *Disease, Pain and Sacrifice*; and also Sacks, *A Leg to Stand on*, 83f.
[3]   Hankin (ed.), *Life of Mary Anne Schimmelpenninck*, I, 56-7.
[4]   Ibid., I, 58.
[5]   Ibid. For asthma and the psyche see Gabbay, 'Asthma Attacked?'.
[6]   Hankin (ed.), *Life of Mary Anne Schimmelpenninck*, I, 58.
[7]   Ibid.
[8]   See Wear, 'Puritan Perceptions of Illness'; Locker, *Symptoms and Illness*.
[9]   Beresford (ed.), *Diary of a Country Parson, passim*.
[10] Hultin, 'Medicine and Magic in the Eighteenth Century'. For Woodforde's role as family healer see, e.g., Beresford (ed.), *Diary of a Country Parson*, III, 90.
[11] Ibid., III, 11.
[12] See, Porter and Porter, *Patient's Progress*, ch.2.
[13] Beresford (ed.), *Diary of a Country Parson*, I, 183.
[14] Ibid., IV, 6.
[15] Ibid., IV, 7.
[16] Ibid.
[17] Ibid., IV, 136.
[18] Ibid.
[19] Ibid., IV, 137.
[20] Ibid., IV, 144.
[21] Ibid., IV, 145.
[22] Ibid.
[23] Ibid.

24   Ibid.
25   Ibid., IV, 147.
26   Ibid., IV, 148.
27   Ibid., IV, 154.
28   Ibid.
29   Ibid., IV, 155. The ankle worsened again the following April.
30   Porter, 'Patient's View'; Beier, *Sufferers and Healers*, 154f.
31   Robinson and Adams (eds), *Diary of Robert Hooke*, xvi. The quotation is from Robert
      Waller. There is a good discussion in Beier, *Sufferers and Healers*, 139f.
32   Robinson and Adams (eds), *Diary of Robert Hooke*, xvi.
33   Ibid., 19.
34   Ibid., 18. Hooke also occasionally used his dreams to direct his medication: '(31)
      Rose about 10, but guiddy. Eye much distorted (Dremt of a medicine of garlick and
      the night before I drempt of riding and of eating cream with Capt. Grant) . . . . Mr.
      Haux bough garlick and beet', ibid., 18
35   Ibid., 92.
36   Ibid., 39.
37   Ibid., 74.
38   Ibid., 38. Sometimes sex seemed therapeutic: 5 July 1674, 'Slept after in Gowne. X.
      somewhat better'; ibid., 111.
39   Ibid., 54.
40   Ibid., 36.
41   Ibid., 21.
42   Ibid., 49.
43   Ibid., 25.
44   Nicolson (ed.), *Conway Letters*, 71; cf. Fraser, *Weaker Vessel*, 345-52.
45   Ibid., 259.
46   Ibid., 224.
47   Ibid., 100.
48   Ibid., 100, 107.
49   Ibid., 126.
50   Ibid., 63.
51   Ibid., 89.
52   Ibid., 88, 226. Finch stresses that 'common country people' believe in mountebanks
      because they are 'the most ignorant people under heaven': 87.
53   Ibid., 105.
54   Ibid.
55   Ibid., 225.
56   Ibid., 76.
57   Ibid., 91. Reviewing her case and the use of salivation, Thomas Willis reported 'I
      found not the harvest worth the paines'; ibid., 91.
58   Ibid., 226.
59   Ibid., 106.
60   Ibid.
61   Ibid., 245.
62   Ibid., 77-8.
63   Ibid., 92.
64   Ibid., 396.
65   Ibid., 100.
66   Ibid., 74.
67   Obviously, mental illnesses would fall into this category. We have decided not to
      handle these in detail in this book as they have already been discussed in Porter, *Mind*

Forg'd Manacles; idem, *Social History of Madness*.

[68] Curwen (ed.), *Journal of Gideon Mantell*.

[69] Post mortem showed lateral curvature of the lumbar spine. It might have arisen as a result of a carriage injury he recorded in October 1841.

[70] Curwen (ed.), *Journal of Gideon Mantell*, 151, 148.

[71] Ibid., 161, 161-5 *passim*.

[72] Ibid., especially 165-70, but see *passim*.

[73] Ibid., 213.

[74] Ibid., 221, 217.

[75] Ibid., 211.

[76] Ibid., 163-4.

[77] Ibid., 220, 241.

[78] Ibid., 265, 289.

[79] Ibid., 289.

[80] Ibid., 264.

[81] Ibid., 164.

[82] G.C.M. Smith (ed.), *Letters of Dorothy Osborne*, 40.

[83] Ibid.

Chapter 8:
Conceptualizing Illness

Charles II's Archbishop of Canterbury, Gilbert Sheldon, is reported as having offered[1]

> £1000 to any person who would 'help him to the gout', looking upon it as the only remedy for the distemper in his head, which he feared might in time prove an apoplexy; as in time it did and killed him.

It is a revealing anecdote. It shows, of course, that even archbishops did not entirely entrust their health to the Lord. It confirms that people beyond the holy circle of the medical profession held strong views of their own about maladies and their management. And it also, obviously, proves that a lay folklore of sickness was alive and well, not least at the apex of society. Gout, a bothersome but not fatal complaint, was seen as a rather distinguished disease – one whose presence had the almost talismanic power of protecting its victims against the onslaughts of other ailments. It was abnormal (people thought) to suffer from two major distempers at the same time – for, as the phrase went, one disease drove out another. Hence, the archbishop's £1000, if lavished on someone successful at giving him the gout, would have been an insurance premium against some more fatal disease taking root.

In this chapter, we shall explore lay ideas of the nature of sickness and disease. We do not intend to imply that these differed greatly from those of the faculty itself. The assumptions underlying Sheldon's story were not some antediluvian lay superstition but would broadly have been endorsed by his physicians (though things did change: a century later, the eminent clinician, William Heberden, dismissed this piece of lore, complaining of the proliferation of so-called lay expertise [2]). But we do wish to stress how popular strategies with sickness hinged upon forming an understanding of illness itself, and upon recognizing the various particular maladies.

What had happened when you fell sick? It might be said, you had caught a disease to make you ill; but maybe such talk was just a form of words and begged all the questions. So was a distemper something you 'got' or 'had'? Or was it a 'humour', an internal upset? Or was it simply the way you felt? Was 'disease' then a real thing, or merely a name, perhaps no more authentic than all those so-called occult forces and scholastic virtues that had been the scandal of natural philosophy before the Scientific Revolution exploded such verbal hocus-pocus. Molière ridiculed the nonsense of saying that opium made you sleep because of its 'dormitive faculty': if you said you were diseased because you had bad humours – was not that no less circular?

Yet words could not be brushed aside that easily. For illness had to be explained somehow. So fearful were its terrors, it was vital for sufferers to define and describe it, thereby confronting the unknown and assimilating it within the familiar. Ignorance is unbearable; naming leads to knowing and knowing to controlling. Labelling a clutch of symptoms, hazarding a diagnosis, was no less crucial to the sick person than to his physician.[3]

In some cases, of course, arriving at an identifying word was easy enough, for visible symptoms presented themselves, prompting a reassuring disease name. It was easy to say someone had a 'stroke', a 'fit', a 'seizure', for the word matched the disorder, even if the disorder itself remained fearsome. Oliver Goldsmith died, people said, of 'purple fever'. Parson Woodforde reported Mrs Custance's son being dangerously ill of the 'whitethroat' – a graphic term, not to be found in medical dictionaries, but one that comfortingly identified the condition (perhaps what we would call 'tonsilitis') and at least ruled out something worse.[4] When someone's skin and eyes turned yellow, it reduced anxieties to call it 'jaundice' – or if darkish-yellow, the word was 'black jaundice'.[5] Vaginal discharges were called the 'whites': the word implicitly ruled out a venereal infection; 'scarlet fever' specified that type of fever when the tongue went bright red; 'speckled fever' described a particular sort of spots; 'whooping' cough named a particular cough by its sound.

Such terms, graphically descriptive and even onomatopoeic, were ingrained in the common culture; others were invented ad hoc when new clusters of symptoms cropped up and required a new word. Thus, it was fashionable for a while to speak of the 'Pelham sore throat', so named when prime minister Henry Pelham's two sons died of what was presumably some virulent form of diphtheria.[6] In 1781, Thomas Marshall was reporting 'Chinese cough' in the East Midlands: the term must have conveyed some special exotic menace.[7]

All such names were maps to render the unfamiliar familiar. Yet it still remained difficult to fix *le mot juste* for baffling symptoms. In 1778, Lady Louisa Conolly wrote to her sister, the Duchess of Leinster, about the condition of Charlotte, Emily's daughter. Assuredly, she was unwell, but what did she have? 'She certainly coughs a great deal, and complains of the pain in her side and breast'. Lady Louisa hoped against hope it was not serious, and to translate hope into words, ventured that it 'may be nervous'. 'Nervous cough' – by which she certainly did not mean a purely psychosomatic tic – is a phrase that is probably best left vague. But its tacit message was evidently that the condition was relatively superficial and remediable, the nervous system being *so* delicate as always to be in danger of disorder. Yet she had to admit that she feared something worse ('it keeps one in a fidget'), doubtless 'consumption' – the graphic term for what medicine subsequently relabelled tuberculosis.

Other opinions are offered: 'Mr Power [the physician] thinks she has an intermitting complaint' – seemingly implying a fever such as malaria. Lady Conolly herself was prepared to endorse that: 'I should not be surprised at her having an ague after being so lowered as she was' (note the assumption that weakened constitutions laid people low and exposed them to external infections). At least malaria, unlike consumption, would probably not prove fatal. She concludes, ominously, that a whole tribe of doctors is about to descend.[8]

What precisely was wrong with Charlotte is now beside the point. It is important, however, to gauge the resonances of the diagnoses bandied around by those groping for a label realistic yet reassuring; just as it is to tease out the distinct nuances about the nature of sickness that they implied. Above all, we must see the urgency of framing a diagnosis.

In 1712, Jonathan Swift developed 'a small pain on the tip of my left Shoulder'. What was up? He was unsure. 'It grew worse & spread for 6 days', finally becoming truly troublesome:[9]

> then broke out by my collar, & left side of my neck in monstrous red Spotts, inflamed, & these grew to small Pimples. for 4 days I had no rest nor nights for a Pain in my neck; then I grew a little better; afterwards where my Pains were a cruell Itching seised me beyond what ever I could imagine, & kept me awake severall Nights; I rubbd it vehemently but did not scratch it. Then it grew into three or four great Sores like Blisters.

As this fiendish monster materialized, Swift formed, and reformed, his ideas of his complaint. At one point, he tells his physician to regard the disorder as the body's attempt to expel bad humours; thus the spots must be used 'like a Blister'. For this, he applies flannel and astringents to bring out the sores. As a result, he could write on 24 April that though he had 'never suffered so much in my life', 'I am daily mending'.[10]

He spoke too soon. Over a fortnight later he admits to Stella, 'My Pain continues still in my Shouldr and Collar. I keep Flannel on it, and rub it with Brandy, and take a nasty Dyet Drink I still itch terribly, & have some few Pimples.' Still, it seems, thinking his complaint rheumatic, Swift continues: 'I am weak & sweat, & then the Flannell makes me mad with Itching; but I think my Pain lessens'.[11] By now, however, the Dean was having to modify his conception of what was wrong. The doctors were insisting upon their own diagnosis: 'In answer to your good opinion of my Disease [he tells Stella], the Drs sd they never saw any thing so odd of the Kind; they were not properly Shingles, but Herpes miliaris, and 20 other hard names.'[12] Swift was both fazed and flattered by the oddity of his condition: 'I can never be sick like other People, but always something out of the common'.[13]

Yet once the doctors had reached their diagnosis, and Swift accepted it, he felt some reassurance, that it was, at least, nothing worse: 'The Doctors say it would have ended in some violent Disease if it has not come out thus'. Certain at last what was wrong, he could confidently predict, 'I shall now recover fast'. At least he no longer had to fear he had 'miliary fever'; hence he was 'in no danger of Life'. As the old proverb had it, 'a disease known is a disease half cured'.[14]

The sick person and his doctor were thus engaged on a disease hunt. Internal pains – severe but often diffuse – and external symptoms had to be interrogated for clues about the disorder at large. Some pain or abnormality is felt. Will it worsen, presaging something graver? It needs to be pinned down. Semiotic skills are required for decoding the sign. An aetiology must explain what produced it in the first place, and thereby provide a basis for prognosis. Yet piecing clues together into the complete illness profile was often perplexing for physician and lay person alike. 'He suffers from his complaints (what ever they are) being grown so much worse', wrote Lady Louisa Conolly about her brother, Charles. He looked poorly in so many ways that it was confusing, exhibiting 'symptoms of several' different diseases, which 'altogether make a very bad jumble'. All that could be said for sure was that 'there is some humour about him, that sometimes wastes itself in pain, or else falls upon his nerves'.[15] But this vagueness created anxiety.

Or take Thomas Turner, the Sussex grocer, going down with a mysterious complaint. He begins to feel a 'stitch-like pain' in his side, breast, and back (trade was very slack: did he have business worries? Was time simply hanging heavy on his hands behind the counter?). He called in the surgeon to bleed him, yet felt no better. He gave his trouble no name: was this because he was baffled, or was he terrified of something unmentionable, such as cancer? Certainly, he suspected the worst: 'I am fearful whether I shall ever get the better of it'. In the succeeding days, he gropes for an acceptable diagnosis. 'I am very doubtful that my disorder in my side etc is of a strumous [i.e., scrofulous] kind, and what gives me the greater room to think so is that the left parotid is very much swelled.' Rumination only deepens his suspicions. He begins to fantasize about his inner organs, possibly after poring over medical books. 'Very ill all day, and I am very fearful my liver is cirrhous . . . Oh how uncertain is the health of poor mortal man!' (He soon forgot about it, however.)[16]

In short, no sooner was something wrong than sufferers needed to know *what* was wrong.[17] The writings of the sick bulge with attempts to develop such knowledge, tracking the pathways to sickness, both with an eye to present relief (not least, of uncertainty) and as prophylactics against future difficulties. In 1718, William Abel made an approach to Ralph, Lord Fermanagh, about selling his town property. He needed to give over business (he explained) because of the decrepit state of his health; and he regaled the nobleman with a hard-luck story of how this had come about. He had been commendably health-conscious. To cleanse his blood and forestall a gout bout, he had drunk freely of diluent fluids (presumably barley water, etc.). By doing so, he had, alas, brought on a 'diabetes' (in those days this primarily meant excessive urine discharge). This was distressing, for diabetes was 'much the more dangerous distemper of the two'. The upshot was that he had been forced to go down to Bristol Hot Wells spa 'for a cure'.[18] In this tale we see exemplified once again the common view that a latent disposition to sickness could materialize in diverse forms. Thus disease was protean, capable of many disguises, yet, by being thus malleable, in principle manageable.

Of course, lay attempts to theorize their ills might often be seen as so much pseudo-learned stuff and nonsense; Sterne mocked Walter Shandy's obsession with 'consubstantials, impriments and occludents' – discussing all of which instead of curing, merely heightened his apoplexy.[19] Notwithstanding these difficulties, to safeguard one's health it was vital to be on the *qui vive*, plotting the chains of cause and effect, of illness in general and understanding what made oneself sick in particular. Dorothea Lieven told her lover about the sad fate of a certain Hardenbrot:[20]

> It is less than three weeks since he came to call on me. I was alone with him. He told me that he was sometimes seized by fits of madness, during which he was not responsible for his actions. At this alarming information, I went up to the bell-cord and stood sentinel until the Duke of York came in and rescued me from our tete-à-tete. Afterward, I told my husband that I thought Hardenbrot was talking very incoherently. He made enquiries and was told that he was in excellent health and had never shown any sign of madness. Two days later, he went off his head. He was put in charge of two doctors from Bedlam and died yesterday in a violent fit of madness.

The sage Princess had no doubt about the medical moral: 'Don't ever think of eating lobster after dinner; that is what the poor lunatic used to do'.

The Language of Illness
In their terminology, these lay self-diagnoses were largely congruent with those advanced by regular practitioners. This is hardly surprising. After all, sick people often picked up medical talk through consultations with their physicians and by reading medical books. And conversely, doctors striving to form a diagnosis remained, through the eighteenth century, utterly dependent upon scrupulous attention to the 'histories' recounted by patients themselves. Pre-modern medicine could function only as a dialogue. Without some common language, the enterprise would have juddered to a halt.[21]

Yet there was no single, fixed medical vocabulary. Alongside common lay parlance there were what Swift banteringly called the 'hard names' of the faculty. All conditions went under a multiplicity of aliases: various labels were applied by doctors (technical Latin terms, standard English, colloquial), others were used solely by the laity, including vulgarisms, dialect words, and so forth. The choice of one term in preference to another often involved fraught issues of fashion, power, and moral connotations. Not least, the medical profession itself did not possess an unequivocal, rigid, scientific lexicon. 'I was told some time ago Ld Grantham was dying of a leprosy', wrote Mary Coke, ''tis a distemper one so seldom hears of, that it surprised me.'[22] The good lady had 'Biblical' leprosy in mind; but she was probably victim of ambiguity produced by the semantic versatility of 'leprosy', whose connotations ranged from the classic Biblical disease through to almost any severe skin disorder, as well as serving as a euphemism for syphilis.[23]

In time, of course, the profession came to pride itself upon being able to detect diseases through diagnostic techniques independent of patients' presentations of their pains. One step in this direction lay in the emergence, during the eighteenth century, of a more specialized, systematized disease language amongst certain cadres of the medical profession. Scientific medicine as taught in the Enlightenment university encouraged progressive doctors to rely more heavily upon technical disease names within the framework of systematic taxonomies and nosologies. William Cullen's highly popular noso-logical scheme, expounded at Edinburgh, classified diseases on the basis of common pathological features (fever, inflammation, wasting, etc.). That developed by Erasmus Darwin – never popular, but symptomatic of the quest for a scientific terminology – depended upon attributing disease aetiology to basic physiological processes such as sensation, perception, volition, etc. Medical institutions such as hospitals leant increasingly heavily upon a disease vocabulary derived from professional training rather than from the complaints presented by the sick themselves. There always had been some give-and-take between lay and professional medical terms; possibly the balance was tipping in favour of professional language.[24]

However that may be, the pretensions of doctors in inventing their own fancy words were always a target of fun. The idea of the complete itemization of disease was, for instance, turned into carnival in the *Chelmsford Chronicle* in 1765, when it published a spoof 'Exact List of Maladies Suffered by the Townsfolk of Chelmsford'. The roster included 100 youths of both sexes suffering from 'vertigo', twenty husbands with 'blindness on one side', forty wives stricken with 'deafness in one ear', two 'pretenders to wit' suffering from 'false conceptions', and one parson with 'unnatural delivery'.[25]

What Was Disease?

Ever since the Greeks, the medical profession had disputed the precise nature of disease. This involved a multiplicity of issues. There was the question of causation: was disease an outside, invasive being, or was it generated within the body itself? There was the question of nature: was disease a thing, a separate entity (seeds, a micro-organism, a poison, etc.), or simply a dysfunction indexed by pain? Thus, were such features as feverishness and diarrhoea disease proper, or merely its symptoms? And there was the question of significance and interpretation: was sickness to be regarded as an evil, an enemy to be countered? Or was it the body's own attempt to cope? – in which

Conceptualizing Illness 139

case, sickness should be appropriately encouraged, as part of the healthy reactive, adaptive life-process.

Lay writers occasionally engaged explicitly in these rather abstract issues. Coleridge, for example, mused about why certain epidemic diseases conferred immunity whereas others didn't:[26]

> There are two grand divisions under which all contagious diseases may be classed: – 1. Those which spring from organized living beings, and from the life in them, and which enter, as it were into the life of those in whom they reproduce themselves – such as small-pox and measles. These become so domesticated with the habit and system, that they are rarely received twice. 2. Those which spring from dead organized, or unorganized matter, and which may be comprehended under the wide term malaria.

All the same, it would be misleading to suggest that lay people often plunged into theorizing about sickness and disease. When smallpox strikes, no academic debates fill the Verney family correspondence as to whether it is, or is not, 'contagious' – or, indeed, about what precisely 'contagiousness' might mean. The Verneys simply take time-honoured practical action, like staying away from infected people and places. People did not need to figure out a subtle theory of the nature of 'miasmas' to be convinced that low-lying marshlands gave you 'marsh-fever' or ague.[27]

Colds and Fevers

Perhaps the most pervasive disorders of all hardly required any speculations about the essence of disease, because they were so immediately felt. Colds and fevers made up, between them, a high percentage of actual disorders and played a significant part in defining conceptions of sickness. Having a cold or fever was a direct experience of discomfort and malfunction. Explanations drew upon time-honoured humoral assumptions about imbalances in the body fluids, which directly reflected the symptoms themselves. The shivering and runny nose of a cold were immediate proof of the excess of cold and wet humours, i.e., phlegm. The hot flushes, prickly skin, and dry mouth of fever were, by contrast, marks of a superfluity of choler.[28] Chills and fevers were thus reassuringly tangible: they were overt distempers, not subtle, silent, invisible enemies. Moreover, and equally reassuring – except when fatal! – they also ran pretty predictable courses.

This applied also to the question of aetiology. Experience taught that cold and damp surroundings led to colds. They were particularly common in winter. But other forms of chilling could produce the same effect – sudden cooling, e.g., through drinking cold refreshments, after hot summer's exertion, or the draught produced by an open window on a warm but breezy day. Sudden temperature changes were perilous. Fanny Burney thus complained of her 'imprudent' builder who 'made himself very ill t'other day, by going

from the violent heat of extreme hard work in his garden to drink out of a
fresh-drawn pail of well-water . . . a dreadful headache ensued.' Luckily, she
was a resourceful home-medicator: 'two days' confinement, with James's
powders, have but just reinstated him'.[29]

Thus the well-being of the body depended upon maintaining a proper
equilibrium with the environment. Prudence required precautions, such as
wrapping oneself up properly. Samuel Pepys, for instance, was constantly
rebuking himself for catching colds and chills, through forgetting to wear his
cloak when rowing down the damp and misty Thames.[30]

As for colds, so for fevers. Everyone knew that fevers – those presenting in
rashes and spots, such as measles, smallpox, and typhus; those mainly
affecting the bowels, such as gastro-enteritis; and those chiefly causing
prostration, such as ague or malaria – were more common in the warmer
seasons. The tropics were notorious for their fevers, and the English were no
strangers to the deadly effects of the summer sun on exhausted or drunken
harvesters. Fever often followed strenuous exercise or the overheating effects
of feasting and carousing.

Nobody made light of fevers. But – although the Princess Lieven gaily
declared that colds were 'nothing'[31]– the pre-moderns also saw colds as
potentially serious. Pepys was perhaps more worried about colds than any
other sickness except the legacy of his bladder stone and his deteriorating
eyesight.[32] This was, doubtless, because pre-modern domestic and travelling
arrangements made keeping warm and dry difficult. But it was also because
colds were villains in complex stories about how the body worked.

Cold, it was believed, produced dangerous physiological changes. It caused
the pores to close (heat, sweating, and open pores obviously went together).
Closed pores prevented perspiration. Perspiration was a crucial means
whereby the body rid itself of wastes. Without adequate perspiration, the
system would suffer a form of auto-poisoning. Thus, on catching cold, it was
imperative to induce sweats. Warm clothes, hot drinks, special 'diaphoretic'
or 'sudorific' (sweat-inducing) medicines, were all recommended. Yet, as
always, the pendulum could swing too far: excessive perspiration could also be
a bad sign. It worried William Holland when he found his head sweating too
much: excessive blood must be flowing there, 'which is the cause of the pains
in my face'.[33]

If colds had their dangers, fevers formed the direst disease family. Fevers at
least made themselves highly conspicuous, with their eruption of blotches,
pimples, and rashes, their parched throat, headache, nausea; their sweating
brow or palms; the accompanying faintness, exhaustion, vomiting, and/or
diarrhoea, and, in extreme cases, a wandering mind, convulsions, coma and
finally death itself. Fevers developed fast, and ran a predictable course.
Though dangerous, they were at least familiar, following patterns of onset and
symptom-development that left them readily identified, particularly when
epidemic. Sufferers and their attendants would thus seek to identify as early as
possible the variety of fever in question. Knowing your enemy might not make
much therapeutic difference (most eruptive fevers were treated rather simi-

larly),[34] but it would affect the prognosis. It would be a great relief, for example, to know that one had chickenpox or measles, not smallpox.[35]

Thus, lay as well as medical opinion energetically differentiated infections. Was optimism or pessimism in order? Was it safe to visit? It was known that smallpox conferred a certain immunity to itself but not, say, to other infections such as erysipelas. Hence, it was worth developing expertise at distinguishing the bright red tongue of scarlet fever; the petechiae of typhus (commonly known as jail fever, hospital fever or ship fever, from the environments in which it prevailed);[36] the red rash of measles; the pustles and crusts of smallpox, and so forth. Sometimes, the fever was identified by the specific organ it affected most, as with 'brain fever' (probably today's meningitis, though occasionally a euphemism for insanity).[37]

Fevers were further differentiated by their severity and their rhythm. Certain seasons brought outbreaks which contemporaries ominously labelled 'malignant'. Terms such as 'intermittent', 'recurrent', and 'relapsing' were used to distinguish those remaining in the system – above all, ague – from once-and-for-all afflictions such as smallpox. Amongst the agues, such terms as 'quotidian', 'tertian', or 'quartan' identified how frequently the fit returned (in a tertian ague, on the third day, in a quartan, on the fourth).[38] Amongst the fevers, there were special advantages in identifying ague, because it was one of the few severe afflictions for which a specific existed: Peruvian bark (Jesuit's bark, or simply 'bark'; today's quinine). 'I am sorry Jack ague hathe catched you by the heels', wrote William Vickers to Lord Fermanagh in 1717, 'you must Bark at him Lustily, and then he will leave you.'[39]

As with colds, fevers were regarded as marks of a debilitated body, often precipitated by fluctuating or adverse environmental conditions. Reporting on the death of his clerical acquaintance, Dean Clerke, Edmund Pyle explained how it had come about:[40]

He died of an ague; caught by living in that vile damp close of Salisbury, which is a mere sink; and going to a church, daily, that is as wet as any vault; and which has destroyed more, perhaps, than it has saved.

Abnormal weather conditions – mild winters, chilly summers, autumn drought, and so forth – were all regarded as ominous. This helped explain why fevers came in waves, striking down not just individuals with vitiated constitutions or unwholesome habits, but droves of people indiscriminately. Fevers thus had an 'epidemic' quality. 'In the last moneth', commented the Glaswegian, Robert Wodrow, 'and the beginning of this, ther was the most generall cold and cough, with a feaver, seized almost everybody that I ever kneu. Not one of fifty escaped . . . It proved deadly to severalls.'[41] 'In the beginning of this year', reported William Stout in 1737, 'there was a general distemper of violant coughs and coulds all over the nation, of which many died. I was sorely afflicted with it nigh two months.' Typically, the Quaker Stout sat it out: 'it went in time without using any means but patience'.[42]

Calling fevers 'epidemic' signalled their prevalence. Epidemic fevers threatened the social fabric. Their effect ('crisis mortality') could be quite devastating in the micro-social environment: many members of one household
might be stricken and even die of 'spotted fever', 'malignant fever', or 'putrid
sore throat' (diphtheria) – children were particularly vulnerable. Not least,
such epidemics changed from year to year. Seventeenth-century eye-witnesses
were especially perturbed by the succession of 'new diseases' – though aid
could be forthcoming: 'If you have a new dises in your toun, pray have a car of
yourself . . . drinck good ale for tis the gretest cordall that is: I live by the
strength of your malt', advised Lady Fanshawe in mid-century.[43]

To call fevers epidemic did not prejudge the question of their cause, or
endorse any particular theory of their nature: it merely described their
prevalence. Experience taught that smallpox was highly contagious – a fact
underlined when the introduction of inoculation showed the disease could be
artificially passed from arm to arm. But in other cases, epidemicity did not
seem conclusive proof of contagiousness. Why otherwise did some people in
one family succumb to miliary fever or the bloody flux, whereas others did
not? Fevers continued to be viewed as products of a concatenation of
circumstances, in which atmosphere, environment (both natural and man-
made), and the quality of the individual constitution ('crasis') all played a part.

Disease and the Constitution

To succumb to sickness was widely seen as the mark of a vitiated constitution
(often called 'cachexia'). For within the contemporary understanding of
physical health and disease, disorders did not typically afflict just one specific
organ, or produce an invariable battery of symptoms. Disease was a barometer
of the body as a whole.

Of course, some were localized; for example, a stone concreting in the
bladder. Ear and eye complaints might likewise be seen as local, susceptible to
specific treatments. Parson Woodforde had great faith in a 'rosted onion'
wedged in the ear for earache,[44] and Nicholas Blundell copied into his recipe
book twenty-nine separate recipes for sore eyes.[45] Commonly, as with
Gibbon's hydrocele, surgery was required.[46]

But most complaints were believed to be iceberg-like in nature. Only the tip
showed; but in reality, they ran far deeper. Skin complaints such as boils,
ulcers, and abrasions, for example, were not just skin-deep but were regarded
as the surfacing of some subcutaneous peccant humour. If, as often, they
healed but slowly, that was itself a token of the underlying constitutional
disorder. Take, for instance, scurvy.[47] Various individual symptoms
appeared: purple blotches on the skin, a fetid odour, the swelling of the gums
and loosening of the teeth which made eating almost impossible; lassitude and
fainting fits. These were surface manifestations, visible and unmistakable.
The ensemble was typically called 'scurvy', because all were seen to be
interlinked. The ultimate cause was much disputed, but many assumed that
the root lay in a 'scorbutic constitution', vitiated through poor life-style, bad

air, bad morals, diet, or whatever. Thus, when a leg sore refused to heal, Elizabeth Purefoy believed she had a 'scorbutic humour' – 'I cannot learn when it is to be well', she groaned.[48] With hindsight, we might say that this conviction that complaints were typically constitutional possibly delayed the conquest of diseases such as scurvy. For it aroused suspicions against specifics, against the very possibility that there might be a 'pill for every ill'. Such a notion seemed too 'superficial', smacking of quackery. Hence, in the case of scurvy, although fresh vegetables and citrus fruits were empirically seen to be effective, medical scientists continued to search for its real nature, cause, and cure, often with disastrous results.

Pains and feverishness were thus commonly seen as indices of deep-seated malaises; minor disorders might be symptomatic of serious, local, or systemic complaints. Alternatively, a topical trouble (maybe an infected sore, or perhaps gonorrhoea) would, if not speedily rectified, descend into the constitution itself, perhaps through the blood.[49]

For the body was regarded as a single integrated system, in which pain and dysfunction in one area or organ had ramifications for the entire organism. Hence, sufferers often interpreted quite localized manifestations in terms of general 'constitutional' health. Thus, piles would be seen not just as swollen veins, but as a warning sign of plethora, a superabundance of blood;[50] various treatments might be required to reduce or dilute the blood. Headaches likewise signalled problems extending well beyond the head, as the discussion of Anne Conway in Chapter 4 has suggested. Hence, it often seemed best to treat symptoms indirectly, e.g., by bleeding and purging, to expel toxins and clear the system, or by the application of 'topical' blisters to other regions of the body, to serve as counter-irritants, decoying the disorder to a safer place.

Distempers were 'mobile'. Like an invading army, a malaise could surface in one location or organ and spread or retreat to another. In so moving, it would thereby become more or less serious – typically *more* serious if it migrated from a relatively external and peripheral member to one more internal and pivotal. Thus, a cough might begin in the throat. If it descended on to the lungs, that was a danger sign. A gout, safe if confined in a toe, could become a real health peril if it moved 'metastasized' into the heart or brain.[51] A key strategy of pre-modern therapies was thus to conduct disorders from vital to less important regions of the body. In 1794, William Hutton had trouble with his foot. 'The continuance of the wound in my leg brought a humour', which 'seemed to baffle the skill of the surgeon'. He was recommended 'a course of physic' to cure it, but declined, 'lest it should injure the constitution, therefore tried Lady-Well Bath, which in two months effects a cure'.[52]

Parallel to this was belief in the importance of forcing a disease 'out'. Trapped within the body, poisons would damage it. Rather than allow disorders to remain latent, it was better to expel them. This could obviously be done through purges, phlebotomy, and sweats; but also by encouraging fevers, rashes, and boils to erupt, thus carrying 'humours' to the surface, where they would break and disperse.

Thus, diseases were not seen as distinct, generic fixed entities but rather as

temporary concentrations of humours, fluids, or spirits, like clouds gathering
and then melting in the sky. One 'disease' might mutate into another,
according to precipitating circumstances. Whether a distemper erupted as
measles or smallpox might depend primarily upon the individual constitution.
Thus Pope was not being wholly facetious when he informed Lord Orrery,
soon after making Thomas Thompson his doctor, 'I have indeed a new
Physician; who . . . has chang'd the nature of my disease, from an Asthma
into a Dropsy'.[53] Above all, the disposition of one's humours would be crucial
in how precisely a disorder would settle. Local complaints might always be put
down to internal toxins and processes, requiring general treatments. When
Caroline, Lady Holland, advocated sea-water bathing for her son, Stephen's,
deafness, she had 'great hopes' for the treatment, believing 'his deafness
proceeds from humours in his glands'.[54]

Other internal entities were also thought to possess fluid physiological
properties and flexible explanatory powers. Common talk of 'spirits', 'nerves',
and 'vapours' thus further sustained the idea of the organism as an active,
dynamic entity, liable to localized dysfunctions indicative of some more
general failure.

This taken-for-granted 'holism' was obviously of great significance for
therapeutics. For it created a disposition towards general – 'whole person' –
cures rather than specifics. An aching tooth might be more than just that,
indeed symptomatic of a nervous disorder, which, in turn, might be due to
viscid blood or a corrupted gut. Thus, the antidote might well involve
bleeding and a tonic. In particular, scores of disorders were laid at the door of
the stomach, regarded as the crucible of the metabolism. For, as discussed
above, the body was typically viewed as a through-put machine, requiring
efficient digestion and speedy waste disposal.[55]

Much thus hinged, many thought, on the stomach, 'an organ' according to
the late eighteenth-century practitioner, Thomas Trotter, 'endued by nature,
with the most complex properties of any in the body, and forming a centre of
sympathy between our corporal and mental parts, of more exquisite qualifica-
tions than even the brain itself.'[56] Gastro-intestinal disorders – commonly
known as colic, hysteric colic biliousness, or colloquially as the 'blue devils' –
were the daily plague of Georgian society, accustomed to rich food and drink.
'The Bile', wrote David Garrick, 'which is my chief complaint . . . comes
upon me like a Thief in ye Night.' He had just had 'such an overcoming
Sickness that I was half dead for near 3 hours.'[57] Over-indulgence in hard
liquor was commonly blamed. Vine Hall, whose bane was biliousness, was
frequently intoxicated: 'drunkenness, horrible depravity', he records in his
diary on one occasion, and, some time later, 'drunkenness, six days drunk'. To
save himself, he became a Methodist, apostasized into drink, and was
suddenly brought to his senses when his minister asked him point-blank, 'Do
you love porter better than Christ?'[58]

The point is that what Byron termed 'the horrors of digestion' were viewed
not merely as a local disease, but rather as intrinsic to the whole constitution.
When Parson Woodforde had indigestion – as he did, frequently, presumably

from simple over-eating – he typically saw it as symptomatic of a graver condition, such as 'gouty Wind'.[59] Charles Darwin's meticulous sick notes show him as not simply crucified by his stomach, but a man convinced that a disordered stomach was a dire omen. Ironically, his trouble was compounded if not created by self-dosing and by health anxiety.[60]

Woodforde responded, like many others, by fortifying the stomach. Thus when his niece, Nancy, fell ill with pains and vomiting, he attributed it to 'what she eat at Dinner and after . . . some boiled Beef rather fat and salt, a good deal of a nice rost duck, and a plenty of boiled damson pudding. After dinner, by way of desert, she eat some green-gage Plumbs, some Figgs, and Raspberries and Cream.' But after all that, by way of cure, Woodforde got her to drink half a pint of rum and water; more rum, rhubarb, and ginger followed. She got well. Next day she was guzzling again on 'rost Neck of Mutton'.[61] William Cowper, whose stomach was 'the plague of [his] life', preferred the evacuant method, dosing himself with tartar emetic ('one abomination in order to get rid of half a dozen').[62]

Seen as closely allied to stomach complaints were such disorders as dropsy and jaundice, the latter typically regarded as a drinker's disease.[63] These demonstrated failure to dispose of wastes, and were classically identified as marks of systematic decay. Thus, Alexander Carlyle recorded his father's death in 1765: 'He had been for some years declining, and of late had strong symptoms of dropsy, a disease of worn-out constitutions.'[64] Therapeutic interventions were attempted – diuretics to pass the waste, and stimulants to reactivate the kidneys or bowels. But dropsy was unmistakably symptomatic of a constitution in its last throes, and medication might actually speed the process. Edmund Pyle recorded the demise of the Archbishop of Canterbury, Thomas Herring:[65]

> He was filling again in the dropsical way. And one day, in the beginning of the last week, was prevailed upon to take a dose of the medicine, which he has used since the regular physicans could do no more for him. It wrought as it used to do, that is pretty strongly, in the diuretic way (I take it); but he was then so unequal to the operation that it hastened his end, perhaps, a few days.

In many cases, as with Samuel Johnson, dropsy was accompanied by respiratory difficulties. He was bled for the asthma and tapped for dropsy. Interestingly, his physicians explained to him that the asthma was due to 'cold', encouraging hopes that he might survive in a warmer climate.[66]

Another grave disorder equally indicative of a failing constitution was consumption, seen as a wasting disease: as Samuel Garth described it in the *Dispensary*,[67]

> Whilst meager Phthisis gives a silent Blow;
> Her Stroaks are sure; but her Advances slow.

As with other such constitutional malaises, the signs were obvious enough –
coughing up blood, the red spot on the cheek, the hectic flush, pallor, general
wasting – and the prognosis dire:[68]

> That is blood from my mouth [exclaimed Keats] . . . I know the colour
> of that blood; – it is arterial blood; – I cannot be deceived in that colour;
> that drop of blood is my death warrant. I must die.

When Parson Woodforde's best servant, Molly Dade, grew emaciated and
weak, he realized she was consumptive and turned her off – not, it seems,
because he thought consumption infectious, but because she could no longer
do her work, and was sure to get worse. A good constitution could overcome
specific ailments, but illness springing from broken constitutions boded ill
indeed.[69]

Conformably with broader disease lore, it was typically believed that
consumption might result from some other distemper 'falling' on the lungs, or
even from weakening physicking. Worried about the health of Henriette,
Charles Lennox's illegitimate daughter, Lady Sarah Lennox, her aunt,
demanded that the doctors make up their minds whether or not she was
suffering from worms. For if she were, she would fall into fever unless they
were smartly treated; whereas if she were worm-free but were treated for them
unnecessarily, the depletive effects would cause her to fall into a consumption.[70]

As before, however, we must beware of automatically assuming that one
single, fixed 'ontological' disease was meant by the word 'consumption', its
synonym, 'phthisick' – or indeed by most other diagnostic labels. Diseases
were rather *sui generis*, marking states not things. Tobias Smollett spent his
last years in a decline, suffering with his lungs. But, though a professional
physician as well as a writer, it is far from clear that he thought of himself as
being the victim of one particular disease, 'consumption'. He rather used a
variety of 'symptomatic' terms, such as 'asthma' and 'catarrh'. Above all, he
acknowledged that his 'constitution' was broken, partly because so many
other complaints kept breaking out, such as skin rashes, which he suspected
were 'scurvy', i.e., further marks of constitutional decay.[71]

Cancers, too, were seen as constitutional distempers. Tumours were merely
visible manifestations of disorder within – as was proved by the tendency of
new swellings to metastasize. As with consumption, it was the wasting that
was the critical symptom; in his last letters, David Hume saw rapid weight loss
as proof of its lethal nature.[72] Falling flesh presaged constitutional collapse. 'I
am most truly ye Knight of ye Woefull Countenance', complained Garrick,
after a 'bilious fever' had struck, '& have lost legs arms belly cheeks &c & have
scarce any thing left but bones & a pair of dark lack-lustre Eyes that are retir'd
an inch of two more in their sockets.'[73] – 'invalids will prate of their ailments',
he shrugged, self-deprecatingly.

Relating to Disease

People monitored their disorders with care, like sailors scanning the skies to tell the weather. The most terrifying disorders were the least predictable, such as strokes, epilepsy, or the convulsions that carried off so many infants like a thief in the night. Good and bad signs were well known. Fortunately, many diseases, such as fevers, took predictable courses, while others, like gout, were amenable to management, through sensible diet, living habits etc. Once disease signs appeared, received wisdom was that it was best that they should develop quickly, regularly, and without hindrance. Fever, diarrhoea, pustules, etc., were seen as hopeful signs: by collecting poisons, they helped expel them from the body. By contrast, it was desperate when in smallpox the rash did not 'come out' but remained 'blind' ('struck in'). Stimulants might be tried to bring them out – mirroring the view behind the philosophy of the classic hot regime with smallpox, with its faith in heated rooms, hot drinks, and heavy bedclothes to sweat the disease out.

When any disease came out, it was thought a favourable sign. Caroline Fox's son, Stephen, languished with what she called St Vitus' Dance; she was perturbed because no positive manifestations appeared, for 'suppressed fits' were worse than manifest ones. 'Mr Compton's disorder used to come by fits', she wrote . . . 'I know some of our physical people told us the having fits made it easier to be cured.'[74] It would be going too far to say that the Georgians regarded having an illness as healthy; they did believe, however, that it was advisable that disease should take its course.

Coda

This chapter has not attempted to map the major diseases from which the Georgians suffered, but rather to pinpoint those that preoccupied them, and to explain the ideas underlying them. Some of the worst afflictions were little discussed. There seemed little to say about the fits that killed off so many infants: the blow was too sudden and apparently random. By contrast, the nature of other distempers encouraged luxurient ruminations – gout, for instance, a disorder of the leisured that provided further enforced leisure for reflection.

Gout is one of those rich disease labels – familiar to eighteenth-century minds and mystifying to ours – used to denominate a great diversity of pains striking different regions of the body – not just the joints, but also the inward parts, the stomach, and the head.[75] Like hysteria, its local manifestations knew no bounds, even if all were assumed to be localizations of some root condition. 'Gout flying about me today I think', recorded Woodforde.[76]

Gout was widely seen as the rich person's status symbol, the product of intemperance, especially hard drinking. William Cadogan, the society doctor, attributed it to 'indolence, intemperance and vexation'. One reason, then, why sufferers might take gout in their stride was because it was a proof of affluence, a sort of success tax. Edmund Pyle called it 'fit for a man of quality'.[77]

But people also came to terms with gout by regarding it as a preservative. 'I have a touch of Gout Spring and Fall which I look upon as highly salutary', the Rev. John Forster informed Jeremy Bentham.[78] If diseases rarely coexisted in one body, gout would surely drive others away; hence the 'immunity' theory with which this chapter opened. 'Perhaps it is a prerequisite of my time of life, to have the gout or some formidable illness', wrote Sydney Smith, in his sixties.[79]

Gout could thus be almost a bodyguard, or at least the foe you knew (Gibbon called it 'a fair and honourable Enemy').[80] Edmund Pyle imagined it as almost medicinal, praising it for having 'made an effort to relieve me' of a slow fever.[81] In a more extravagant conceit, David Hume declared, 'All the World allows that Privilege to the Gout, that it is not to be cur'd. It is itself a Physician',[82] adding with a deadly Parthian shot, 'and, of course, sometimes cures and sometimes kills.' What made gout a safe disorder was that it was self-limiting and seemed to be capable of management, through sensible regimen. Gibbon confidently emigrated to Lausanne, believing that the clean, high, dry air would do his gout the world of good.[83] So much for lay wisdom, retorted Dr Thomas Beddoes some twenty years later: the historian should have laid off the madeira.[84]

Susan Sontag has deplored the spawning of metaphorical accretions around disease:[85] such mythologies can prove more dangerous than the diseases themselves. That was a view commonly expressed at the time, by doctors and laity alike. With haughty disdain, Charles Greville surveyed the cholera panic sweeping Europe from 1831. He deplored the spread of the rumour that cholera was in reality mass-poisoning by governments:[86]

> It is remarkable that the common people at Berlin are impressed with the same strange belief that possessed those of St. Petersburg that they have been poisoned, . . . they believe there is no such disease, and that the deaths ascribed to that malady are produced by poisons administered by the doctors, who are bribed for that purpose; that the rich finding the poor becoming too numerous to be conveniently governed, have adopted this mode of thinning the population, which was employed with success by the English in India; that the foreign doctors are the delegates of a central committee, which is formed in London and directs the proceedings, and similar nonsense.

Things were no better in Britain itself, where talk of the new disease speedily fanned equally wild and far-fetched stories.[87]

> In the first place, what has happened here proves that 'the people' of this enlightened, reading, thinking, reforming nation are not a whit less barbarous than the serfs in Russia, for precisely the same prejudices have been shown here that were found at St. Petersburg and at Berlin.

Greville was appalled at the proliferation of rumour, fear and panic at all levels of society:[88]

> Fresh claims have been raised about cholera morbus. A man at Port Glasgow insists upon it, without much apparent reason, that it prevails there; so we have sent a medical man down, in order to quiet people's minds and to set the question at rest. Lord Grey, who is credulous, believes the Glasgow man's story, and spread the news in his own family, who immediately dispersed it over the rest of the town, and yesterday nobody could talk of anything else; not believing it very much, and not understanding it at all, for if they did they would not be so flippant. Lady Holland wrote to Lord Lansdowne to desire he would recommend her the best Cholera doctor that he had heard of.

Greville enjoyed his own aloof pose, but was it not inevitable that sickness led to elaborate stories about the inner transformation of the body, about cause and cure, about susceptibility? For sickness was traumatic, terrifying, and unpredictable. Verbalizing it at least familiarized it. And the stories integral to Georgian disease lore were appropriate to the times and their needs. They tended to see disease as a condition, rather than ontologically as a thing, an invasive agent. Such ideas of disease thus related symptoms to the inner constitution, and saw its manifestations as mobile. All these features reinforced the perception that disease was an individual matter – for which the individual might, of course, be blamed, but over which he himself had some control. A disease that is an expression of one's own constitution is something which one can, perhaps, manage.

Notes

[1] Quoted in Warter (ed.), *Southey's Common-Place Book*, 551.
[2] Heberden, *Commentaries*, 32f.
[3] Helman, *Culture, Health and Illness*. Cf. Dirckx, *Language of Medicine*.
[4] Beresford (ed.), *Diary of a Country Parson*, II, 16.
[5] Bourne (ed.), *Letters of the Third Viscount Palmerston*, 35.
[6] Gosse, *Dr Viper*, 88. Thicknesse's wife and two of his children died of it.
[7] Hardstaff and Lyth, *Georgian Southwell*, 82.
[8] Fitzgerald (ed.), *Correspondence of Emily, Duchess of Leinster*, III, 341.
[9] Williams (ed.), *Swift: Journal to Stella*, 530.
[10] Ibid.
[11] Ibid., 531.
[12] Ibid.
[13] Ibid., 532.
[14] Ibid.
[15] Fitzgerald (ed.), *Correspondence of Emily, Duchess of Leinster*, III, 59-60. For ideas about 'nerves' see Walker, *Nervous Diseases*; Drinka (ed.), *Birth of Neurosis*.
[16] Vaisey (ed.), *Diary of Thomas Turner*, 204-5.
[17] Reiser, *Medicine and the Reign of Technology*, 1f.; Bynum and Porter (eds), *Medicine and the Five Senses*.

18   Verney (ed.), *Verney Letters*, II, 56.
19   Sterne, *Tristram Shandy*, 393.
20   Quennell (ed.), *Private Letters of Princess Lieven*, 86.
21   Slack, 'Mirrors of Health'; G. Smith, 'Prescribing the Rules of Health'; Porter, 'Lay Medical Knowledge in the Eighteenth Century'; Reiser, *Medicine and the Reign of Technology*; Brody, *Stories of Sickness*, 41f.
22   Home (ed.), *Letters and Journals of Lady Mary Coke*, II, 363.
23   Crook and Guiton, *Shelley's Venomed Melody*, 91f. for a discussion of 'leprosy'; Quincy, *Lexicon Physico-Medicum*, 233.
24   Lawrence, 'Medicine as Culture'; Risse, *Hospital Life in Enlightenment Scotland*; and see in particular Fissell, 'Physic of Charity'. We deal with this issue in Porter and Porter, *Patient's Progress*, ch. 6.
25   Dobson, 'Population, Disease and Mortality in Southeast England', 398.
26   Coleridge, *Table Talk*, 157. Cf. Brett (ed.), *Barclay Fox's Journal*, 222:

     Dr Calvert called. We talked of the malaria, which is now supposed to be caused by sulphuretted hydrogen generated by the decomposition of vegetable matter (especially the cruciform plants, which contain much sulphur) in salt water.

27   Temkin, 'Historical Analysis of the Concept of Infection'; Engelhardt, 'Concepts of Health and Disease'; Risse, 'Health and Disease'; *idem*, ' "Typhus" Fever in Eighteenth-century Hospitals'.
28   Helman, 'Feed a Cold, Starve a Fever'; *idem*, *Culture, Health and Illness*, 95f.
29   Hemlow (ed.), *Journals and Letters of Fanny Burney*, III, 332.
30   See Latham and Matthews (eds), *Diary of Samuel Pepys*, IV, 318; V, 277; VI, 1; IX, 224, etc; and discussion in Porter, 'Patient's View'.
31   Quennell (ed.), *Private Letters of Princess Lieven*.
32   Porter, 'Patient's View'.
33   Ayres (ed.), *Paupers and Pig Killers*, 214. Cf. Buchan, *Domestic Medicine*, 156ff., 312f.
34   Though there were two ways with fevers. The much-revered Thomas Sydenham had introduced and popularized the 'cooling method', emphasizing plentiful cool drinks, light bed clothes, and cool rooms to counter the excessive heat of the fever. Often, this was supplemented by 'lowering' forms of therapy, including very light diet, purges, and the like. But many lay people believed that strengthening and fortification were required to help the body resist such powerful enemies. Thus, for example, wine was frequently used as an antidote to malaria.
35   Miller, *Adoption of Inoculation*; J.R. Smith, *Speckled Monster*, 15f.
36   D. C. Smith, 'Medical Science, Medical Practice, and the Emerging Concept of Typhus'; Risse, ' "Typhus" Fever in Eighteenth-century Hospitals'; Bynum and Nutton (eds), *Theories of Fever*.
37   Hartshorne (ed.), *Memoirs of a Royal Chaplain*, 285. Cf. Buchan, *Domestic Medicine*, 322f.
38   Dobson, *Chronology of Epidemic Disease and Mortality in Southeast England*; *idem*, *From Old England*. For the 'double tertian' see De Beer (ed.), *Diary of John Evelyn*, III, 243.
39   Verney (ed.), *Verney Letters*, I, 397.
40   Hartshorne (ed.), *Memoirs of a Royal Chaplain*, 285.
41   Fyfe (ed.), *Scottish Diaries*, 387.
42   Marshall (ed.), *Autobiography of William Stout*, 22.
43   Verney (ed.), *Memoirs*, III, 390. Stevenson, ' "New Diseases" '.
44   Beresford (ed.), *Diary of a Country Parson*, I, 307.
45   Bovill, *Country Life in England*, 222.

[46] Norton (ed.), *Letters of Edward Gibbon*, III, 364. Gibbon's hydrocele became a matter for conversation. Mr Pollen, friend to Lord Holland, recommended radical surgery. Ilchester (ed.), *Lady Holland's Journal*, 223.

[47] Carpenter, *History of Scurvy and Vitamin C*; Loudon, 'Leg Ulcers'.

[48] Mitchell (ed.), *Purefoy Letters*, 100.

[49] Bynum, 'Treating the Wages of Sin'; Ober, *Boswell's Clap*.

[50] Buchan, *Domestic Medicine*, 425f.

[51] Nicolson, 'Metastatic Theory'.

[52] Jewitt (ed.), *Life of William Hutton*, 258.

[53] Spence, *Anecdotes*, I, 261.

[54] Fitzgerald (ed.), *Correspondence of Emily, Duchess of Leinster*, I, 443.

[55] Buchan, *Domestic Medicine*, 368.

[56] Trotter, *View of the Nervous Temperament*, 203.

[57] Little and Kahrl (eds), *Letters of David Garrick*, II, 507. Shortly earlier, he had written that he had headaches and indigestions and feared he had 'nerves': II, 451.

[58] Ponsonby (ed.), *More English Diaries*, 180-1.

[59] Beresford (ed.), *Diary of a Country Parson*, II, 179.

[60] Colp, *To Be an Invalid*.

[61] Beresford (ed.), *Diary of a Country Parson*, II, 217.

[62] King and Ryskamp (eds), *Letters and Prose Writings of William Cowper*, III, 188. Cf. the advice of Squirrell, *Maxims of Health*.

[63] Bliss (ed.), *Reliquiae Hearnianae*, III, 33.

[64] Burton (ed.), *Autobiography of Alexander Carlyle*, 463.

[65] Hartshorne (ed.), *Memoirs of a Royal Chaplain*, 296. Very similar was the deterioration of Gibbon's father: Norton (ed.), *Letters of Samuel Johnson*, III, 133.

[66] Chapman (ed.), *Letters of Samuel Johnson*, III, 133.

[67] Garth, *Dispensary*, 106. Cf. F.B. Smith, *Retreat of Tuberculosis*; Bryder, *Below the Magic Mountain*.

[68] Hale-White, *Keats as Doctor and Patient*, 52. Keats almost certainly caught tuberculosis from his brother, Tom. At the time, it was not commonly believed that consumption was infectious.

[69] Toynbee (ed.), *Letters of Horace Walpole*, XI, 337.

[70] Fitzgerald (ed.), *Correspondence of Emily, Duchess of Leinster*, II, 301.

[71] Knapp, *Tobias Smollett*, 245 ff. Asthma is a medical term whose meaning has undergone profound changes: see Gabbay, 'Asthma Attacked'.

[72] Mossner, *Life of David Hume*, 590f.

[73] Little and Kahrl (eds), *Letters of David Garrick*, II, 425.

[74] Fitzgerald (ed.), *Correspondence of Emily, Duchess of Leinster*, I, 245.

[75] Rogers, 'Rise and Fall of Gout'; Cadogan, *Dissertation on the Gout*; For a cough as a 'preservative' in old age, see Bamford (ed.), *Dear Miss Heber*, 205.

[76] Beresford (ed.), *Diary of a Country Parson*, II, 179.

[77] Hartshorne (ed.), *Memoirs of a Royal Chaplain*, 103; Cadogan, *Dissertation of the Gout*. 3.

[78] Sprigge (ed.), *Correspondence of Jeremy Bentham*, II, 207.

[79] N.C. Smith (ed.), *Selected Letters of Sydney Smith*, 148.

[80] Norton (ed.), *Correspondence of Edward Gibbon*, II, 239. Gibbon later refered to the 'decline and fall' of his gout: ibid., II, 375.

[81] Hartshorne (ed.), *Memoirs of a Royal Chaplain*, 103.

[82] Greig (ed.), *Letters of David Hume*.

[83] Norton (ed.), *Correspondence of Edward Gibbon*, III, 28.

[84] Beddoes, *Hygeia*.

[85] Sontag, *Illness as Metaphor*.

86   Reeve (ed.), *Greville Memoirs*, II, 197. For cholera see Pelling, *Cholera, Fever and English Medicine*; Durey, *Return of the Plague*; Morris, *Cholera 1832*; *idem*, 'Religion and Medicine'.
87   Reeve (ed.), *Greville Memoirs*, II, 284.
88   Ibid., II, 172.

Chapter 9:
Understanding Causes

In the previous chapter, we examined the general disease lore of the Georgians: what people thought happened to the body when it sickened; the relations between symptoms and underlying physiological processes, between local manifestations and constitutional stamina itself; and the names and classes of maladies. We emphasized the plurality of ideas in circulation – sufferers never left theorizing about sickness to the medicos, and, of course, lay ideas commonly dovetailed with the profession's.

The present chapter shows this body of disease lore in action by examining the explanations individuals advanced when faced with a world full of sickness, or as to why they fell sick. These were, of course, life-and-death concerns that people pondered meticulously. Elizabeth Iremonger thus gave a detailed 'history' of her sickness to her friend, Miss Heber:[1]

> I came up to Mrs Shipley's towards the end of October . . . to put myself under the direction of Dr. Fraser for a continuance of alarming, periodic head-achs, which did not yield to the treatment of the Country practitioners, who evidently appeared at a loss both as to cause & effect.
>
> Doct. Fraser soon discovered the Complaint to be inflammatory Spasm, & in such a state of fullness were all my vessels that, for the first 6 weeks, he put me into an uninterrupted course of Epsom salts & nitric; nor would this suffice. Bleedings were frequently necessary & indisposable. None of this plan has weakened me, as you would naturally suppose it might; a plain proof that it was requisite. At length, however, I am become sufficiently reduced, and Dr. Fraser is enabled now to apply himself chiefly to the attendant irritability by giving me warmer, soothing medicines, such as Hemlock & assafetida, from which I at present receive the greatest benefit & am quite another creature. From living with a hard, wiry pulse of 96, I am now restored to a soft pulse of 74.

Poring over one's maladies in this way may sometimes have been morbid.

Typically, however, people had practical and constructive reasons for such minute self-examination, with regard to the future. Close scrutiny would afford prognostic clues. Would one recover? By divining the cause of an ailment, could one gauge how to relieve or cure it? Or, perhaps still more important, could one take a check on one's constitution as a whole, to activate wider schemes for body maintenance and repair? Not least, could one prevent future bouts?

Prognostic concerns were paramount. Herein lay one of the attractions of the astrological medicine widely practised throughout the Stuart Age. From Simon Forman and Richard Napier at the beginning to Samuel Jeake at its close, doctors and laymen alike cast horoscopes both to determine a general humoral profile, and to gain advance warning of heavenly conjunctions that would endanger health. The papers of Elias Ashmole show a busy astrologer using his skills – for himself, his friends, and clients – to preview the medical future: would X recover? was Y pregnant? would Z prove fertile? and so forth.[2]

In the Georgian age, astrological techniques lost credit as the basis of medical prognoses amongst the educated classes, as did other 'occult' forms of futurology such as fortune-telling or palm-reading.[3] The late seventeenth-century antiquarian, John Aubrey, collected stacks of omens and portents about health; he recorded numerous instances in which people had seen corpses in their bed, or shadows in a mirror, only to die shortly afterwards. It is unlikely that Aubrey was merely *preserving* such lore, without according it any credence. Later folklorists, by contrast, typically distanced themselves from the omens and divinations that they collected.[4]

Such beliefs and skills, drawing upon the esoteric sciences, nevertheless remained lastingly important in popular circles. Best-selling almanacs continued to purvey medical advice, derived from planetary positions. Readers of popular manuals such as *Aristotle's Works* found plenty of information about health and sexuality based upon astrology, palmistry, metaposcopy (reading of the forehead for life-signs), etc.[5]

Did other prognostic devices arguably smacking of occultism or superstition similarly lose élite credence in the cool light of Enlightenment reason? Ever since Antiquity, people had examined their dreams to gain forewarnings of sickness and confront their own deaths. Simple techniques of dream interpretation (substitution, reversal, etc.) would yield predictions about crucial life events such as marriage, childbirth, and accidents. Georgian diarists commonly recorded their dreams, anxious about omens. Most were unsure what 'truth' to attribute to them. Few seemed to believe that God was literally speaking to them in dreams, or that they were authentically providential. Many, however, took dreams of disaster and death very seriously, possibly not primarily as prophetic but often as symptoms of emotional and even physical turmoil. A powerful current deriving from Hobbes and Locke, portrayed dreaming as in itself pathological, the mark of a sick, over-active imagination (not to say a stomach that had supped too well).[6]

People scrutinized their attitudes and acts of commission and omission – to judge what made illness supervene. Often, as Pepys' diary shows, there was real doubt as to which of several factors was the most important:[7]

> This is the day, seven years, which, by the blessing of God, I have survived of my being cut of the stone. And am now very perfect good health and have long been. . . . Now I am at a loss to know whether it be my Hares-foot which is my preservative against wind, for I never had a fit of the Collique since I wore it – and nothing but wind pain – or keeping my back cool; for when I do lie longer then ordinary upon my back in bed, my water the next morning is very hot – or whether it be my taking of a pill of Turpentine every morning which keeps me always loose – or all together.

On another occasion Pepys experienced a multitude of complaints:[8]

> Having lain there a while, I then to the Abbey and there called Mitchell; and so walked in great pain, having new shoos on, as far as Fleet-street; and there got a coach, and so in some little ease home – and there drank a great deal of small beer. And so took up my wife and Betty Michell and her husband, and away into the fields to take the ayre – as far as beyond Hackny, and so back again. In our way drinking a great deale of Milke, which I drank to take away my Heartburne, wherewith I have been of late mightily troubled. But all the way home I did break abundance of wind behind – which did presage no good, but a great deal of cold gotten. So home and supped; and away went Michell and his wife – of whome I stole two or three salutes. And so to bed, in some pain and fear of more – which accordingly met with, for I was mightily in pain all night long, of the Winde griping of my belly and making of me shit often, and vomit too – which is a thing not usual with me.

So what had made him sick, with both cold and cholic? 'But this I impute to the milk that I drank, after so much beer. But the cold, to my washing my feet the night before.'[9]

As can be seen from this example, when people contemplated their life patterns to discover what made them sick, they highlighted particular events. Guilt might lead them to blame some personal misdeed; anger might provoke them to condemn the malign role of others (as, of course, crucially in witchcraft accusations, which, however, do not surface in Georgian diaries). Often, as Mary Fissell has argued, people attributed their maladies to events dating back many years, spotlighting seminal happenings in their own lives.[10] It was rare, however, for people to express total bafflement about what caused them to fall sick. The explanations offered fall into patterns, for they conform to prior programmes of expectations.

The Invasive Environment

Prominent amongst the factors to which sickness was ascribed was the total milieu within which the sick person lived. Geographical and meteorological conditions combined to precipitate ill health.[11]

Altitude, the lie of the land, exposure to winds, the composition and porosity of the soil, landscape features such as rivers, forests, lakes, and mountains, proximity to the sea – all these were believed to impinge on health, and thus critical when choosing a residence or travelling.[12] Tracts of marshy ground were particularly to be avoided: Romney Marsh, the Thames flats, and the Fens were notorious for ague or marsh fever.[13] Elevated land, by contrast, was seen as relatively healthy, away from the miasmas exuded by standing waters, and fanned by refreshing summer breezes. In Peacock's *Crotchet Castle*, Mr Firedamp is adamant on this issue: 'Wherever there is water, there is *malaria*'. He has the answer: 'The great object of a wise man should be to live on a gravelly hill'.[14]

In choosing somewhere to live, climate was no less important. Excessive moisture was bad for the lungs and the joints. People were advised against areas of high rainfall; but they were also worried about the damps, mists, and fogs of river estuaries and coastal flatlands. Thus, commiserating with Anne Conway for her continuing wretched health, Henry More told her, 'I was in good hope that your returne into English Ayre would contribute something towards a better enjoyment of your health than in Ireland'.[15] There was little fear that any region of England was too hot for health, but with the growth of empire overseas, discussion raged whether Britons could acclimatize success-fully to the tropics.[16]

Weather was important not only in respect of the prevailing climate. Health-conscious people spied danger in all sorts of meteorological conditions. Atmospheric extremes were often associated with disease. Certain sorts of winds supposedly brought particular ailments. Thus James Watt – ever the hypochondriac – wrote to Joseph Black in 1796:[17]

> My health for some time after my Bath jaunt was better than its usual Standard, to which it seems now relapsing, the late east winds brought back my Rheumatic affections in the arms sides breasts and shoulders and by the same time I had got them a little subdued, the West Winds have brought on an attack of my dyspnea, so troublesome that yesterday I begun to try the effects of the Hydrocarbonate air upon it, seemingly with some success but I cannot be sure yet, as I have kept out of the wind all this day. It however has done no harm as I take it in doses which cause the least possible vertigo, having experienced upon others that in general it is not necessary to produce that effect to any troublesome degree. It rather encreases the dyspnea immediately after taking it, which may be owing to the unnatural method of inhaling it, after an hour or two its sedative powers take effect, what the ultimate success is I shall inform you.

Weather abnormally hot or cold for the time of year, sudden changes of wind direction, freak squalls, and thunderbolts, were all judged potentially pestilential. For the astrologically-primed John Manningham in the early seventeenth century, eclipses were perilous, for 'dangerous diseases breed in bodyes naturall by putrefaction springing out of the sunnes eclipse'.[18] Likewise, dramatic changes in the weather presaged ill. Writing to his son in 1825, George Crabbe expressed his delight at his family's good health, 'because I had fears that your Caroline might have felt these Changes of Weather which we & I suppose you have'.[19] Of course, this was simply a variant upon the standard notion that sudden extremes of temperature were intrinsically dangerous. Miss Weeton explained catching cold:[20]

> Went to Miss Dannett's to tea: the heat of the room was such, that on coming away and plunging into the cold night air, I received a violent cold, and was for several days in a burning fever; and at the same time an inflammation in my mouth, and gathered gums. By Saturday following, I was recovered.

In a whole host of ways, the atmosphere posed a major health hazard. Indoors or even outdoors, the air all too easily became close, fetid, rank, dank, stale. Open windows, fresh breezes, air currents, and through draughts were amongst the great desiderata. Damp was also hazardous. The Georgians endlessly complained how all manner of rheumatisms, shooting pains, colds, catarrhs, and sciaticas, were due to damp rooms, unaired clothes, musty bed-linen, etc. Parson Woodforde thus recorded the demise of a relation, 'owing to laying in a Pair of damp sheets on his return from my house'.[21]

One major problem facing the Georgians was to decide whether town or country was better for health. The urbane Georgians loved city life, at least for the winter and the 'season'. Yet they were all too aware of the mass of maladies associated with sardine living in insalubrious towns, where poor water supply, sanitary arrangements, and the sheer press of people precipitated epidemic disorders. Plagues had always triggered an exodus from town.

Certain diseases were especially associated with the city; thus when Samuel Johnson had bronchitis and asthma, he was advised to flee London's smoke and rusticate himself (he was somewhat sceptical). Consumption and rickets were both notoriously urban distempers.[22] The received wisdom was expressed in Thomas Holcroft's novel, *Hugh Trevor*:[23]

> Mr Evelyn not only read all the best authors, but went to London, every winter, and assiduously maintained an intercourse with the most able men, attended their lectures, was present at their operations, and fully informed himself of their differences both in opinion and practice.
>
> But his frame was delicate, a too long abode in London always occasioned pulmonary symptoms, and experience taught him that his native air was more healthful and animating than any other.

Thus, the generally superior quality of country air was much touted. It was
certainly believed to be the best place to recruit one's health. As the Marchioness of Kildare wrote from the depths of Kildare to her husband, *à propos* of a
confirmed town mouse:[24]

> Lady Barrymore talks of coming there to me by way of recovery, which
> she thinks the country air will contribute to. Only think of her allowing
> that any good can come of the country! What a change! Indeed, it's true
> the town is very sickly. Seven people died in High Street one day of
> spotted fevers; Mr Sharman, my shoe-maker, was one of them. Mrs
> Cutts Harman is dead of that disorder.

Overall, we must never underestimate the sensitivity of the Georgians to
environmental factors, when attempting to explain ill health and safeguard
their constitutions. Such attentiveness shines through in the following epistle
sent to Miss Heber, with its celebration of 'getting away':[25]

> My friend Louisa Shipley has had a bad relapse again of her Cold &
> Cough soon after she left the balsamic air & charming Scenery of Bristol-
> Wells. She has since been to the Sea-Side with her Mother, where she
> entirely recovered again by constantly Riding & Sailing, & gained such a
> look of Health as She never had before. She is returned home scarcely
> above a Week & this surprising Cold is beginning to come again.

Comments like these explain the vast attractions of travelling in search of
health. The asthmatic Tobias Smollett – no less than his sworn enemy, the
consumptive Laurence Sterne – went to France in hopes of benefiting from the
milder, drier climate. Henry Fielding, dying of dropsy, sailed to Lisbon on
medical advice. The gouty Edward Gibbon was glad of a medical excuse for
emigrating to Switzerland, for 'the Gout is much less frequent on the
Continent than in our Island'.[26]

Epidemics

The physical environment was thus a Pandora's box of maladies for the
individual residing in the wrong locale for his constitution, following the
wrong occupation, wearing the wrong clothes, and failing to acclimatize
properly. But contemporaries also believed the environment posed a much
more terrible health threat, endangering not just isolated individuals but
populations at large. For out of such surroundings sprang epidemics.

Since Pasteur, we have grown accustomed to view epidemic disease as
caused by invasive micro-organisms. Bacteriology and virology have established the importance of contagion, of person-to-person, or person-vector-
person transmission chains, and of specificity (constant agents, constant
symptoms). In this modern view, the physical environment is relatively
secondary, indeed at most a 'seedbed'. The Georgians, however, conceptualized epidemics in a fundamentally different way. Far from regarding

epidemic diseases as distinct in origin from environmental maladies, they commonly viewed them as a special case – by far the most serious – of disease induced by the environment.

When dysentery, enteric fever, spotted fever, putrid sore throat, or most of the other terrible Georgian epidemics spread – usually worsening through the summer into the autumn – the data observers garnered to grasp what was happening were primarily to do with environmental variables. What had been the weather pattern? In which locations was it spreading? Were some places apparently exempt? Were towns stricken worse than the countryside? Were certain trades particularly affected? – for example, were farm livestock or particular industrial premises implicated? Implicit or explicit was the conviction that the total interaction of all physical conditions must be generating lethal effluvia or miasmas. Minor local variations of milieu explained why certain people succumbed and others did not.

Interpreting epidemics in this way meant that overall little could be done to eradicate them (short of becoming the mad astronomer in Samuel Johnson's *Rasselas*, who claimed to command the weather). On the small scale, however, prophylactic action was indicated. Individuals could insulate themselves with some success (it was claimed) against such miasmas. Health-care books, above all, insisted on the paramount importance of currents of fresh air, flowing freely. Close atmospheres always bred pestilence. Health lay in open windows, abundant ventilation, the cool and fresh condition.

Such works also insisted upon cleanliness. Readers of manuals such as Buchan's *Domestic Medicine* were constantly exhorted to keep their own bodies spruce, scrub their clothes, change bedclothes in the sick-room, mop, swab and scour the floor, sprinkle lemon juice or vinegar, use fumigation, and so forth. Surrounded by a dangerous macro-environment, the vigilant could stockade themselves within a safer micro-environment, and then attend religiously to the non-naturals.[27]

Thus environmentalism and epidemics did not leave people helpless and fatalistic. True, the environment seemed laden with poisons. But these threats were invitations to action. In some ways, collectively: to drain marshes, remove feculent refuse heaps, widen streets, and so forth (Georgian public health initiatives still await study);[28] in other ways, individually: by taking domestic and personal action to armour-plate oneself against an infectious environment, or indeed by moving to a healthy one.

Thus, environmentalism as a disease explanation spelt out messages of personal responsibility. This is, of course, confirmed by the one major epidemic condition for which a remedy was developed during the Georgian era: smallpox. Once inoculation had been tested and become widely available, its implementation came to be viewed as a duty. Parish authorities arranged for inoculation of the poor; individuals such as Parson Woodforde paid out of their own pockets for their households. And, conversely, those neglecting the act were blamed if they then fell victim. Thus Woodforde, as a ratepayer, condemned one of his parishioners:[29]

Poor Js. Pratt died this afternoon in the Small Pox in the natural way. He never could be prevailed on to be inoculated. He has left a wife just ready to be brought to bed, with 6 more small children.

Enemies Within

So one of the main reasons why people fell sick, according to the Georgians, was that they lived in a dangerous environment: everyone ought to guard his health. But internal causes generated sickness no less than external. How much the more responsible were people for ailments tangibly within their own control!

As argued in the previous chapter, the Georgians regarded many sorts of disease as manifestations of vitiated constitutions. Clearly, in this mutable world, nobody's system would last for ever, and, as we have seen, the culture allowed for the frailties of gender, infancy, and age: a constitution might be corrupt from birth, inherited perhaps from diseased parents, just as it would become superannuated. Some even held the view – a sort of medical Calvinism – that the length of a man's days was determined from the beginning: the eccentric physician, James Barry, taught that each embryo had its allotment of heartbeats, believing, as Johnson put it, that 'a Man's pulse wore [him] out'.[30]

All the same, the diseases of a vitiated constitution were chiefly blamed on the vices of its owner. 'I verily beleeve [Dr Baines] will kill himself ere long by his intemperance', lamented Lady Conway.[31] Much wretched health was thus self-generated by destructive living. Its paradigm was gluttony ('the present luxurious and fantastical manner of Eating'), or, at least, the pernicious diet indulged in by a nation of 'gullet-fanciers'.[32] Notorious for heavy eating, the English were, as the proverb ran, digging their graves with their teeth. 'The stomach of the Irish went & came', so ran the popular saying, 'but that of the English came & stayed'.[33] Philip Thicknesse believed wine did no harm:[34]

But where is the turtle-eater, the venison glutton, or a devourer of high dishes, to be found, who has filled himself . . . without being over-whelmed with bodily misery? After 40 years experience I know 20 intemperate eaters die early in life to one intemperate drinker – provided they were boon companions and wine and not dram drinkers.

'Purging and vomiting almost the whole day', lamented Parson Woodforde on 18 July 1786, 'I believe I made too free Yesterday with Currant Tarts and Cream &'.[35] It is a common tale. John Carrington, likewise, discovered the hard way that gourmandizing destroyed first his stomach and then his health. Though a lover, above all, of 'Butock of beef', he noted how, at one dinner, he dined on 'Roasted heart & a hasht heart & boyled Sholdr of Motton & onions, puding etc . . . Plenty of punch & good company', and the next day duly paid the price: 'Theese fine made dishes did not agree with me, purged me very much all next day, I am for plane food.'[36] But too late! The next few months see entry after entry reading 'canot eate nor drink', 'no stomake to eat', and so forth. His belly had rebelled; he declined and died.[37] 'Papa mismanages himself terribly', wrote Lady Palmerston in 1822:[38]

> Ate pickled Salmon for Supper the other night. There is nothing really wrong about him, but these continual attacks of Stomach and then dosing must in the end be very bad for him, and certainly weakens him very much – It is very vexatious that he will not think a little of his health.

So many Englishmen abused their stomachs. Social habit and the temptations of self-indulgence gratified their consuming passions; yet a ruined digestion brought nemesis. 'Last night I suffered horribly', wrote Byron in 1821:[39]

> from an indigestion, I believe. I *never* sup – that is never at home. But, last night, I was prevailed upon by the Countess Gamba's persuasion, and the strenuous example of her brother, to swallow, at supper, a quantity of boiled cockles, and to dilute them, not reluctantly, with some Imola wine. When I came home, apprehensive of the consequences, I swallowed three of four glasses of spirits . . . All was pretty well till I got to bed, when I became somewhat swollen, and considerably vertiginous. I got out, and mixing some soda powders, drank them off. This brought on temporary relief. I returned to bed; but grew sick and sorry once and again. Took more soda-water. At last I fell into a dreary sleep. Woke, and was ill all day, till I had galloped a few miles. Query – was it the cockles, or what I took to correct them that caused the commotion? I think both. I remarked in my illness the complete inertion, inaction, and destruction of my chief mental faculties. I tried to rouse them and yet could not – and this is the *Soul*!!!

If heavy eating was bad, heavy drinking was thought still more constitutionally destructive. Erasmus Darwin, who gave up hard liquor in his twenties and left off beer and wine in the 1780s, saw alcohol as 'the greatest curse of the christian world'.[40] No wonder. Gargantuan quantities were consumed. Sylas Neville records halcyon days as a medical student in Edinburgh:[41]

> Sun. Sep 17. Dined at the Fox & Goose, Musselburgh with Gerald & Shiel, who have lodgings in that town. Lucky I did not go yesterday, as a company of only 8 or 10, chiefly Shiel's friends, drank 27 bottles of claret & 12 of port besides Punch & were all beastly drunk.

As Steele put it in *The Tatler*, drunkards 'died by their own hands' – a view endorsed by Samuel Richardson in his *Familiar Letters*. For the benefit of the barely literate, he composed what he saw as the standard warning from father to son against liquor:[42]

In the first place, with respect to *health*, the greatest jewel of this life, it is
the most destructive of all vices: *asthma's, vertigoes, palsies, apoplexies,
gouts, colics, fevers, dropsies, consumptions, stone,* and *hypochondriac
diseases,* are naturally introduced.

'Oh! that baneful liquor; that mankind should be so infatuated as to give way
to anything for an opportunity to drench themselves with such a slow and
lingering poison', lamented the grocer, Thomas Turner, resolving yet again to
abandon the village carousing that routinely left him utterly incapable.[43]
   'I buried poor Thos Barnes this afternoon', reported Parson Woodforde in
1770. This sad fellow had been 'a long time killing himself by Liquor' – 'he
was, I believe', concluded the irenic parson, 'no man's enemy, but to himself a
great one.'[44] Woodforde himself was no mean toper, yet he heeded the health
hazards, and succeeded in keeping his habits in check (coping with a drunkard
brother was a sobering experience). 'I drank but very little Wine Yesterday',
he wrote in August 1790, 'only 2 or 3 Glasses. I used myself before and all last
Winter to near a Pint of Port Wine every Day and now I believe did me much
harm.' As with many, Woodforde's attitudes towards alcohol were complicated not just by social duty – drinking 'healths' – but by the fact that he
swigged port medicinally, as 'a strengthening Cordial twice a day', while also
drinking rum for 'wind cholic'.[45]
   Many Georgians ruined their health with drink, indeed drank themselves to
death, not least James Boswell, who declined into an old soak. Shortly after his
death – largely due to kidney failure – Malone explained his demise thus: 'He
seemed to think himself entitled to more than usual indulgence, in which he
went on so rapidly that I had no longer, as formerly, any kind of influence over
him.'[46] Contemporaries were convinced habitual toping was a major cause of
disease and death; or, as the old proverb put it, 'to drink health is to drink
sickness'. Princess Charlotte explained to Miss Elphinstone in February 1814
the deteriorating health of the Prince Regent. Dr Henry Halford had been
called in, and (she reported) 'he attributes this violent attack to *drinking* wh. he
had been doing a vast deal lately. *Laudanum,* his old enemy, was administered
first, but at first did not remain in his stomach; however he is *dosed* with it *now*
to assuage the pain.'[47] Similar fates befell ordinary people too. While a student
at Oxford, John James wrote to his father about a doorkeeper who made the
mistake of going drinking with students:[48]

[He] was invited to drink, which he did, first rum and then shrub, in
such quantities that he presently fell to the ground sensless. In this
condition he was removed by some of the college servants to an adjoining
public-house, but as nobody would take him in, was left for three hours
during a very cold night in the street. He was next day carried home in a
high fever and delirium, accompanied with a violent strangury, and died
the day following.

Doctors warned of its dangers. That great missionary of moderation, George Cheyne, denounced it as a giant evil: 'The running into *Drams*' is giving up one's health; 'for neither *Laudanum* nor *Arsenick* will kill more certainly, although more quickly.'[49] Or, as Thomas Trotter commented in the same vein, 'May men never forget that the vine sometimes produces very bitter fruit, – disease, pain, repentance, and DEATH!'[50] It is significant, in the light of the earlier discussion of epidemics, that when cholera reached England, outbreaks were commonly laid at the door of its 'victims', characterized chiefly as drunkards. Lady Stanley noted in 1849: 'The cholera is creeping on here, 8 cases since Sunday; most of them may be accounted for as predisposed from drunkenness, unhealthy dwellings or previous weakness.'[51]

Of course, alcohol was not the only drink accused of polluting the springs of health. Tea was widely condemned as deleterious. Like coffee and soda water, tea (argued critics both lay, like Jonas Hanway, and medical, such as Thomas Beddoes) habituated the stomach to artifical stimulus, leaving it incapable of absorbing plain and simple fare, and thus debilitated and unfit for action.[52]

Tea-drinking was seen largely as a female vice; other habits of the sex were thought no less destructive of health, not least fashions in clothes (as the adage went, 'the chief disease that reigns this year is folly'). For decades, strait-lacing and corseting were condemned for constricting the intestines and distorting the rib-cage.[53] Yet when whalebone stays went out of fashion things did not improve. For the gauzy, stayless garments of the 1790s had their own dangers. 'The doctors tell me', wrote Lady Sarah Napier in 1794, 'that the new fashion of being so thinly clothed in our damp climates checks nature by degrees . . . they perceive a great increase of complaints on the breast amongst young women.'[54] 'Formerly youth was seldom ill', Lybbe Powys remarked in 1805, 'now, from thin clothing and late hours, you hardly see a young lady in good health, or not complaining of rheumatism, as much as us old ones!'[55] Cosmetics were similarly condemned. The corrosive lead base of the white face make-ups did not merely ruin the skin, but descended upon the nervous system, contributing to general poisoning.[56]

Overall, women were widely criticized (by men, women, and doctors alike) for pursuing beauty and a fashionable delicacy at the expense of health. They grew physically weak, unable to cope with routine biological functions such as childbirth. Erasmus Darwin thus complained that 'parturition' had become more dangerous to the ladies of high life because of their:[57]

> greater general debility from neglect of energetic exercise, their inexperience of the variations of cold and heat, and their seclusion from fresh air. To which must be added, that great source of the destruction of the female grace and beauty, as well of female health, the tight stays, and other bandages, with which they are generally tortured in their early years by the active folly of their friends, which by displacing many of the viscera impedes the relation of one part to another, and affects even the

form and aperture of the bones of the pelvis, through which the nascent child must be protruded.

This chapter has not sought to itemize Georgian opinion about the causes of disorders, disease by disease. Nor has it pursued a discussion of aetiology as understood by medical texts. Instead, it has aimed to lay bare the main causes of illness as seen by the Georgians. The health-conscious person had to negotiate the physical environment with great judgement. Only a fool ignored the hazards of living in a dangerous milieu. For all that, theories of disease causation gave great prominence to the individual's initiative. With know-how, Providence, or luck, he could negotiate environmental hazards. With self-discipline, he could preserve himself from the diseases of excess bedevilling polite society. Danger, blame, responsibility, and mastery thus formed a continuum in the pre-modern medical mind.

NOTES

[1] Bamford (ed.), *Dear Miss Heber*, 204-5.
[2] Josten (ed.), *Elias Ashmole, passim*; see also Lilly, *Christian Astrology*; Hunter and Gregory (eds), *An Astrological Diary*; Capp, *Astrology and the Popular Press*.
[3] Leventhal, *In the Shadow of the Enlightenment*. In gauging how far Georgian polite society continued to subscribe to popular folk omens, superstitions, etc., with regard to health, a problem obviously arises: we possess only their written remains – highly considered reflections; we have no access to fears that flitted across their minds or beliefs never committed to paper.
[4] Hunter, *John Aubrey and the World of Learning*.
[5] Porter, 'Secrets of Generation Display'd'; Blackman, 'Popular Theories of Generation'; Beall, 'Aristotle's Masterpiece in America'.
[6] Weidhorn, *Dreams in Seventeenth Century Literature*; Price, 'Future of Dreams'; Bond, *Essay on the Incubus*.
[7] Latham and Matthews (eds.), *Diary of Samuel Pepys*, VI, 67.
[8] Ibid., VII, 207.
[9] Ibid.
[10] Fissell, 'Physic of Charity'.
[11] Riley, *Eighteenth Century Campaign to Avoid Disease*, 3f.
[12] Corbin, *Foul and the Fragrant*, 11f; Wear, 'Perceptions of Health and the Environment'.
[13] Dobson, 'Population, Disease and Mortality'.
[14] Garnett (ed.), *Novels of Thomas Love Peacock*, 661.
[15] Nicolson (ed.), *Conway Letters*, 231.
[16] Livingstone, 'Human Acclimatization'.
[17] Robinson and McKie (eds.), *Partners in Science*, 227.
[18] Sorlien (ed.), *Diary of John Manningham*, 80. Manningham added, 'the world is governed by planets'.
[19] Faulkner (ed.), *Letters and Journals of George Crabbe*, 319.
[20] Hall (ed.), *Miss Weeton*, II, 253; cf. Helman, 'Feed a Cold'.
[21] Beresford (ed.), *Diary of a Country Parson*, I, 297.
[22] F.B.Smith, *Retreat of Tuberculosis*.

23 Holcroft, *Adventures of Hugh Trevor*, 309.

24 Fitzgerald (ed.), *Correspondence of Emily, Duchess of Leinster*, I, 141.

25 Bamford (ed.), *Dear Miss Heber*, 46-7.

26 Norton (ed.), *Letters of Edward Gibbon*, II, 352.

27 Buchan, *Domestic Medicine*.

28 Porter, 'Cleaning up the Great Wen'.

29 Beresford (ed.), *Diary of a Country Parson*, I, 244.

30 Chapman (ed.), *Letters of Samuel Johnson*, III, 119.

31 Nicolson (ed.) *Conway Letters*, 266.

32 Marrs (ed.), *Letters of Charles and Mary Lamb*, II, 155; the quotation is from *Hell Upon Earth*, 28. Cf. Drummond and Wilbraham, *Englishman's Food;* Oddy, *Making of the Modern British Diet; idem, Diet and Health in Modern Britain;* Mennell, *All Manner of Foods*.

33 Clifford (ed.) *Dr Campbell's Diary*, 43.

34 Gosse, *Dr Viper*, 285.

35 Beresford (ed.), *Diary of a Country Parson*, II, 258.

36 *Carrington Diary*, 171.

37 *Carrington Diary*, 174-6.

38 Lever (ed.), *Letters of Lady Palmerston*, 102. William Withering's cases involving the use of foxglove wonderfully demonstrate just how frequently hard drinking led to diseases such as asthma and dropsy. Withering, *Account of the Foxglove*.

39 Marchand (ed.), *Byron's Journals and Letters*, VIII, 51.

40 Porter, 'Drinking Man's Disease'.

41 Cozens-Hardy (ed.), *Diary of Sylas Neville*, 226.

42 Steele, *The Tatler*, 24 October 1710; Richardson, *Familiar Letters*, 41; Beresford (ed.) *Diary of a Country Parson*, I, 99. A few years earlier, Woodforde had recorded the death of Milly Chiche: 'she was good to everyone, but herself, and I am afraid that drinking was her death': ibid., I, 40. Oliver Heywood took much the same view in recording how all the drunkards he knew fell sick and died. Turner (ed.), *Oliver Heywood*, II, 281, etc.

43 Vaisey (ed.), *Diary of Thomas Turner*, 34. Gin, he thought, was 'surer to kill than even a cannon bal': p. 49. Cf. Porter, 'Drinking Man's Disease'.

44 Beresford (ed.) *Diary of a Country Parson*, III, 205.

45 Ibid., III, 174, 274.

46 Pottle and Brady, *Boswell: The Later Years*, 490.

47 Aspinall (ed.), *Letters of Princess Charlotte*, 112.

48 Evans (ed.), *Letters of Richard Radcliffe and John James*, 201.

49 Cheyne, *Essay on Health and Long Life*, 54.

50 Trotter, *View of the Nervous Temperament*, 93.

51 Mitford (ed.), *Ladies of Alderley*, 261. Her friend, Lady Eddisbury, wrote, 'None of the people here are the least contagionists, so we have not that folly to contend with': p.251. For the wider dimensions of victim-blaming see Gilman, *Disease and Representation*; Sontag, *Illness as Metaphor*; Groddeck, *Meaning of Illness*; Pelling, *Cholera and English Medicine*; Morris, *Cholera, 1832*; Durey, *Return of the Plague*. For contagionism see Cooter, 'Anticontagionism'; Ackerknecht, 'Anticontagionism'.

52 Trotter, *View of the Nervous Temperament*.

53 Ewing, *Dress and Undress*.

54 Fitzgerald (ed.) *Correspondence of Emily, Duchess of Leinster*, II, 350-1.

55 Climenson (ed.), *Diary of Mrs Philip Lybbe Powys*, 357.

56 Williams, *Powder and Paint*.

57 See the anecdote about Erasmus Darwin and the 'Duchess of D——' in Hankin (ed.), *Life of Mary Anne Schimmelpenninck*, I, 153.

Chapter 10:
Interpreting Meanings

We have been examining lay views of the laws of cause and effect governing health and sickness. Maladies originated from physical causes. Many of these stemmed from outside the individual, and were thus to some degree beyond his control. Other complaints arose from malfunctionings of the sick person's internal system, for which he was held more responsible.

But falling sick – and in particular, falling *seriously* sick – could not be wrapped up like that, all neat and tidy, in a parcel of medico-scientific laws. Affliction cried out for profound answers – explanations of why this was a world of sickness at all, why innocent babes died, why pain proliferated so agonizingly, why upright, blameless individuals were seemingly victimized by disease, no less than the feckless and the reckless. People needed grander explanations – stories, mythologies, cosmologies, theodicies, call them what you will – to make sense of pain and pathos. How were they to interpret the empire of illness as a whole? Or come to terms with their own personal sicknesses, fitting suffering into their sense of life's meaning, the private epic of the self?

These were sharp questions, causing much distress. Boswell was always desperately seeking solutions from Johnson as to why Providence permitted such apparent evils as smallpox epidemics. Could one rationalize such outbreaks, as one could executions, as being compatible with God's moral government of the world?[1] Even parsons did not have all the solutions, or had answers that sound more like puzzles. 'Heard of Mrs Morris's death', wrote William Holland, 'a young woman and left six children – sad news indeed – mysterious are the dispensations of Providence.'[2]

Clearly everybody was not agonizing over these fundamentals all the time. Diarists took life as it came: typical entries about health are quite laconic, balancing 'felt sick' against 'took physick'. And some were more pragmatic (should one say, 'phlegmatic'?) than others. Samuel Pepys and the Rev. Ralph Josselin were contemporaries, one a London bureaucrat, the other an Essex vicar. Pepys responded to sickness in a down-to-earth manner, concentrating on physical causes and remedies. Even so terrible a blow as what he feared was encroaching blindness wrung from him none of that pride of martydrom voiced by his near-neighbour John Milton. Pepys did not think of himself as Samson, eyeless at Gaza by the mill, or as blessed with spiritual insight to compensate for the loss of his outward eyes.[3]

The vicar of Earl's Colne, by contrast, is often straining to descry the hidden meanings of sickness within Providence's continual revelation to man. On one occasion he writes:[4]

Sept 5. 1644: Stung I was with a bee on my nose, I presently pluckt out the sting and layd on honey, so that my face swelled not, thus divine providence reaches to the lowest things, lett not sin, oh Lord that dreadful sting bee able to poyson me.

Josselin saw illness as a divine rap over the knuckles to the pious, a foretaste of torments in store for the ungodly.[5]

Aren't we here simply seeing the predictable difference of world-view between a layman and a man of God? Yet this is too simple. For one thing, Pepys himself was far from deaf to suggestions that sickness played its part in the grand divine drama; even he trembled before the plague, fearful of God's wrath.[6] For another, it is easy to identify clergy through the Georgian era – Prebendary Pyle for instance – whose response to sickness was even more mundane than Pepys's, and laymen – not least, doctors, such as Richard Kay – no less absorbed than Josselin with penetrating Providence.

Of course, falling sick required wider rationales. It was painful, and apparently arbitrary (why did epidemics lay some people low and not others?). Designating physical causes normalized it and so went some way towards resolving the mystery; accepting blame for self-negligence could, at least, be a step towards a better future. Yet more was needed. For affliction challenged expectations about a loving God. It could also create the social stigma of uncleanliness.

A deformed child is born. The mother is distressed, the community aghast at such a monstrosity, possibly demonic in origin. It is too scary to ignore. Explanations proliferate. Eighteenth-century physicians, for their part, were increasingly likely to put it all down to mere physical causes, bad blood, poor nourishment; but this did not satisfy people at large. Pre-moderns sometimes saw such an event as a Divine portent. Or was it due punishment for the (perhaps secret) life of vice the mother was evidently leading? – folklore ascribed monstrous births to bestial intercourse. She might exonerate herself from such an accusation by claiming her 'misconception' was due to some accident – seeing a monkey, or whatever – which had impressed itself upon her imagination while pregnant. Thus, threatening medical occurrences were defused by providing stories to explain them. Each account staked out a position, explaining why the anomalous event had happened to the particular party, thus rendering it innocuous to people at large (so long as they avoided vice).[7] Disease meant stigma. Thus in a letter home, the medical student,

Hampton Weekes, records a critical incident at St Thomas's Hospital. A man had applied for treatment; he had been pronounced venereal. He fiercely denied the implication of immorality, saying he had been married twenty years. When he died, his widow struggled to get the hospital to clear his name.[8]

For obvious reasons it was sudden, bizarre and scandalous afflictions (death especially) that generated the most elaborate stories. (The gradual onset of a chronic disorder such as rheumatism seemed, by contrast, 'natural'.) Someone is suddenly struck down by an apoplectic fit. Why? Moral explanations provide reassurance. He was surely a notorious drunkard (or maybe a secret tippler). Let the stroke be a warning to others – yet also a comfort to them: such a fate will not befall the sober.[9] One's neighbour's affliction was always one's own deliverance. Sufferers exonerate themselves from sickness, but the tribulations of others are their just deserts, the wages of sin, or the visitations of God. The Nonconformist, Oliver Heywood, recorded the grisly fates of ill-livers and backsliders with grim pleasure.[10]

The philosopher-anthropologists of the Enlightenment speculated that primitive man's vulnerability when faced with the mysterious and threatening state of nature, and, in particular, the incomprehensibility of death, gave birth to religion.[11] Coping with affliction – above all annihilation – nevertheless remained the great terror even *within* religion for so many Georgians – Boswell and Johnson, in their different ways, both knew fear and faith were of a piece.[12] Christianity thus mythologized the visitations of illness. But explaining sickness was also central to the 'anthropologies' of social progress emanating from the Enlightenment. Drawing upon such epics, individuals could piece together their own distinctive alibis. Perhaps, in Catholic nations, the orthodox rituals of the Church standardized attitudes towards illness; individualist, Protestant Britain, by contrast, had a priesthood of all the sick. Many people made sense of their afflictions through religion; but religion afforded many different parables.

Religious Meanings

To provide an *entrée* into early Stuart opinion we might take the patients of Richard Napier, the Buckinghamshire parson-physician, and Robert Burton's scholarly *Anatomy of Melancholy* (1621). Napier's patients, Napier himself, and Burton all believed that visitations of sickness, both physical and mental, were frequently manifestations of cosmic struggle between Higher and Nether powers.[13] Burton was sure Satan could inflict sickness and take it away: 'the Devil is an expert Physician'. He also saw disease as a demonic Trojan horse; he who fell sick was more likely to despair and curse God, thus providing a fertile seedbed for Satan.[14]

Such ideas had a long life ahead of them. Later folklorists were still encountering countless items of medical wisdom ascribing sickness to Satan, or more generally to evil forces.[15] Blaming witchcraft for malaise (seen as *maleficium*) persisted in pockets of popular culture even into the nineteenth century.[16]

Nevertheless, from the Restoration onwards, polite society ceased to interpret illness in general, or particular bouts of it, as diabolical in origin. Belief in the Satanic armies of the night was undermined in the general assault on 'enthusiasm', and, in particular, scepticism grew about the capacity of Evil to intervene in the mundane world.[17] If someone ailed of a sudden with 'praeternatural' symptoms such as convulsions, fainting, delirium, dislocated speech, etc., the temptation was, of course, to blame the Devil. But that was terrifying, implying that Satan possessed the soul, and hence the prospect of eternal damnation. There was thus every incentive to seek alternative explanations, characteristically a natural cause, organically located.[18] During the eighteenth century, divines such as the Dissenter, Hugh Farmer, and doctors such as Richard Mead alike, began to interpret even the evil spirits of the Bible in terms of physical sickness.[19]

Towards the end of the eighteenth century, Erasmus Darwin sometimes bantered of diseases as the doings of the Prince of Darkness: 'You know there is a perpetual war carried on between the devil and all holy men', he assured James Watt, by 'holy men' alluding to Lunar Society members like himself:[20]

Sometimes one prevails in an odd skirmish or so, and sometimes the other. Now, you must know this said devil has played me a slippery trick, and, I fear, prevented me from coming to join the holy men at your house, by sending the measles with peripneumony amongst nine beautiful children of Lord Paget's. For I suppose it is a work of the devil! Surely the Lord could never think of amusing himself by setting nine innocent little animals to cough their hearts up. Pray ask your learned society if this partial evil contributes to universal good?

For Darwin, the Devil had been reduced to *un façon de parler* – compare the 'blue devils' as a term for dyspepsia. No Christian, his irony questioned how epidemics, decimating innocent children, could be compatible with a loving Father's pastorship. The dethroning of the Devil from his role in wreaking medical havoc was not universal, however; indeed, it was powerfully countered by Methodism. John Wesley's journals show how frequently he ascribed sickness – both physical and spiritual – directly to Satan.[21]

But if progressive culture deleted the Devil from the drama of disease, religion continued to provide the common framework for making sense of sickness. During the seventeenth century above all, but also still widely in the eighteenth, meaning was given to falling sick by reference to Providence and Design. This was not, of course, unproblematic: why should a loving, benevolent, and omnipotent God permit sickness? Various theodicies were proposed.

As we have hinted in Chapter 6, one scenario vindicating God's ways to the sick regarded disease as endemic to the human condition since the Fall and expulsion from Eden. Lapsarian man had been justly sentenced to the curses of Labour, disease, and death itself, due penalties of Original Sin, voluntarily committed. Subsequent generations had inherited Adam's sin; thanks to Eve, all women would hereafter bring forth in pain. Illness registered man's radical unworthiness, his self-inflicted woes. If man was sometimes crucified with disease, what better reminder that God's only Son had Himself been crucified? Early Christians had suffered martyrdom for the faith: latter-day believers must bear their own cross.[22]

Scripture thus explained affliction. Natural theology, so popular amongst Anglican divines, offered further support, derived from reason and nature. 'Population' Malthus, for instance, at the close of the eighteenth century, suggested that, working through the laws of nature, God deployed disease on a global scale for more sublime purposes. Alongside war and famine, epidemics completed a triple alliance of checks wisely preventing disastrous over-population blighting the earth.[23] (In his more secular formulation, Erasmus Darwin hinted that because disease decimated the feeble, the strong would thereby thrive, contributing to evolutionary progress – perhaps thereby answering his own question about 'partial evil' and 'universal good'.)[24]

These arguments from evidential and natural theology gave some explanation why disease necessarily, indeed beneficially, existed as a general phenomenon. But how could it account for the individual case: *why me*? Here what counted was the direct will of God, or Providence. 'It pleased God to visit me with a rhumatisme', mused Sir John Reresby in the late seventeenth century; 'Though I paid dear for the experience, I must own a great deal to Providence for the discovery of this medicin milke.'[25] 'Deare Ned', Lady Brilliana Harley addressed her son, explaining good and bad health all at once, 'It hath pleased God that I haue beene ill euer since you went; but yet I reioyce in Gods mercy to me, that you enjoy your health.'[26] When she miscarried, Lady Brilliana attributed it to 'the will of god'.

Thanking God for afflictions evidently made such disasters bearable, by removing their sinister, unknown aura. God had His reasons, which man might, or might not, divine. Ascribing sickness to Providence familiarized it, even if, as was frequently emphasized, the ways of Providence remained unfathomable. Defoe puzzled how one could be sure, in cases of sickness, of the Divine will and its consequent human duties (did God want one to fly the plague?).[27] Tracing the dictates of Providence was never easy, and to our eyes, sometimes involved casuistry, an easy conscience, or inordinate confidence. James Clegg, the Derbyshire Dissenting minister-cum-medical practitioner, was worried about failing health and the disastrous effects his passing would have upon godliness in the locality:[28]

> But God can provide, and on him I rely. With a view to this I have a Ticket purchased for me in the Irish Lottery. If Providence shall favour me with a prize, I have determined that one halfe of it shall be applied to that use or to some other that shall appear more pious and charitable.

Some zeal-of-the-land-busies found gaming and Providence hard to square. It is reassuring, however, that Clegg believed the Irish Lottery would receive Divine benediction, and that God would be pleased if he went fifty-fifty with his Providential winnings.

Clearly, Providence plied the rod of sickness. But why should God smite particular people? One reason, it was widely said, was to draw attention to their dependence under the Divine Governor. As Harriet Martineau put it,[29]

> Happy they, who have been brought up in allegiance to Duty, more or less strict; and happiest they whose loyalty has been the strictest! In the hour of nature's feebleness, and apparent decay, they find themselves under the eye and hand of the Physician of souls, who has for them a cordial of heavenly virtue, but of no virtue to such as have let their moral nature take its chance, and who, in their hour of extreme need, are no more capable of spiritual enterprise than a bodily flight beyond the precincts of their pain.

Another explanation was that God meant some to bear special crosses, as tests of their faith, or because broadest backs should bear most. The Rev. Henry Newcome saw his own tribulations in this light: 'My crosses have beene, 1, poverty. 2, Pride. 3, Crosseness. 4, Sickness.'[30] Or they might primarily be punishments, perhaps for general iniquity, or as direct Divine retribution for specific offences. On Sunday 27 September 1663, Pepys was crippled with pain in his breast, head, and ear. Why? He knew only too well. 'It is a cold' – the old trouble again – 'which God Almighty in justice did give me while I sat lewdly sporting with Mrs Lane the other day with the broken window in my neck.'[31] John Wesley, for his part, had no doubt pain was a scourge:[32]

> This evening, I believe before I had done preaching, a remarkable instance of divine justice appeared. A man in the street was grievously cursing another, and praying God, 'to blast his eyes'. At that instant he was struck blind. So I suppose, he continues ever since.

The perception of sickness as a sentence was widespread amongst all social and religious groups, more especially in the seventeenth century. When the Dissenting practitioner, Richard Kay, fell ill, he spoke of it sometimes as a 'Thorn in the Flesh, a Messenger of Satan to Buffet me', and sometimes as a 'rod of correction', which he vowed would prove the 'school of instruction', beseeching God, 'Lord, May every Affliction be a proper warning to me to get ready for my last Affliction'.[33]

The Nonconformist minister, Oliver Heywood, saw the Divine scourge in scores of cases of sickness and mortality. Practically all those whose grim and gruesome deaths he listed were adulterers, whoremongers, gamblers, or Anglicans. One notorious curser exemplarily got it in the mouth.[34] Divine anger or favour were thus manifest in the bestowal of Providential sickness. As

late as 1857, an Anglican preacher, the Rev. R. S. Hawker, was still tracing
these patterns with zestful *Schadenfreude*:[35]

> For twenty years Typhus has never raged in this, my Parish, and I have
> been accustomed to link its absence with the sound of the daily bell for
> daily prayer. And now, strange to say, it has not smitten down the
> Church People – but its ravages have been among the Wesleyans.

Yet sickness did not have to be a punishment from above. It could be a
blessing, or at least a divine mark. The convalescent Maria Edgeworth could
write in 1843:[36]

> I thank God not only for my recovery but for my illness . . . my illness
> was a source of more pleasure than pain to me, and that I would willingly
> go through all the fever and weakness to have the delight of the feelings
> of warm affection and the consequent unspeakable sensations of grati-
> tude. When I felt that it was more than probable that I should not
> recover . . . I felt ready to rise tranquil from the banquet of life; where I
> had been a happy guest; I confidently relied on the goodness of my
> Creator.

Oliver Heywood regarded it as a favour when his family was ill or suffered
accidents. But for God's goodness such incidents might have been *fatal*; they
were, indeed, 'rescues'.[37] This truly pious sense of Divine deliverance was
experienced by a traveller John Wesley met:[38]

> I preached at four to a large congregation, and rode to Sandhutton that
> night. Two or three miles short of it we overtook a man . . . On my
> saying, 'We ought to thank God it is a fair night', 'Oh Sir, (said the man,)
> so we ought; and I thank Him for everything. I thank Him that I am
> alive; and that the bull which tossed me to-day only broke two or three of
> my ribs, for he might have broken my neck.'

William Ewart Gladstone's father, a staunch Evangelical, also knew how to
count his Blessings. Late in life, he suffered a spectacular fall downstairs. 'As
good sometimes comes out of evil, whilst I bless God for my providential
escape, I think the consequences have been decidedly beneficial to my general
health'.[39] George Williamson similarly appreciated the at first sight devious
ways of the Lord when he fell parlously sick in 1809:[40]

> It has pleased the Almighty to throw this in my way, for the purpose of
> chastening my aberrations from my duty, or to prove my resignation and
> patience. We are told, and I sincerely believe it, that *all things* work
> together for the good of those who serve Him. My sickness, though
> happening at a time when to human prudence and foresight it must seem

highly disastrous to me, may be followed with beneficial and happy consequences.

In short, being so obviously Heaven-sent, argued Charles Wesley, sickness must be a blessing: the nearer the grave, the closer to Heaven:[41]

> While sickness shakes the house of clay,
> And, sapp'd by pain's continued course,
> My nature hastens to decay,
> And waits the fever's friendly force.

There were other positive reasons why Providence smote people with disease. It could be a warning to deviants from the Divine ways. One Sunday, Parson Woodforde cut his face shaving. What was this but an admonition not to profane the sabbath? He vowed to mend his ways.[42]

Above all, it could be a divine forewarning of death. Pious folk believed that Providence sent disease specifically to work humility, penitence, and reconciliation. George Whitefield told a parable of the 'most remarkable swearer' aboard his ship *en route* to Georgia. Normally, he scoffed at Whitefield's religious warnings:[43]

> But tonight he sent for me trembling and burning with fever; he told me what grievous sins he had been guilty of, and prayed most fervently for repentance. Two or three of the same stamp have been taken in the same manner . . . Sinners must bend or break.

Sickness could, of course, induce such confessions in more secular frameworks. In the nineteenth century, a whole volume of medical stories was published – purportedly from life – centred on melodramatic deathbed repentances.[44]

As well as a warning, disease was God's medium of instruction. 'Sickness', wrote Burton,[45]

> may be for the good of their souls; 'tis parcel of their destiny; the flesh rebels against the spirit; that which hurts the one must help the other. Sickness is the mother of modesty, putteth us in mind of our mortality.

Disease might, for instance, awaken people to the canker of their soul, suggested Charles Wesley, who had, of course, been sorely sick himself. His 'Physician's Hymn' used medical analogues to urge higher, spiritual healing. 'Physician, heal thyself' proves futile for those whose maladies are spiritual:[46]

> Myself, alas! I cannot heal,
> But thou shalt every seed expel
> Of sin out of my heart;

Thine utmost saving health display,
And purge my inbred sin away,
And make me as thou art.

Through mention of the earthly doctor, Providence called to mind the fact
that Christ was the only true physician.

God also used disease for probationary purposes, as a Job-like test of faith.
It was thus said of Charles Kingsley that sickness 'in his eyes, seemed always
to sanctify and purify'. Sweet were the uses of other people's adversity.
Kingsley 'would say, with the utmost modesty, that the patient endurance of
the poor taught him day by day lessons which he took back as God's message
to the bed-side from which he had learnt them.'[47] The memorials of the Harris
family, good Quakers, record sickness almost as a resident guest. Regarded as
the somatization of sinfulness, an organic hairshirt,[48] for them it was not
primarily to be fought or cured (such would be vanity itself). Rather, it was an
aid to reflection, a pang calling people to focus their thoughts upon God.

Indeed, many saw sickness as a summons. Riven with toothache in 1739,
Richard Kay prayed, 'O my Tooth, my Tooth, no Remedy takes Effect, I've
had continual Pain of it all Day. Lord, look upon mine Affliction, and my
Pain, and forgive all my Sins.' It could concentrate the mind on the hereafter.
'Tis better for me to endure the Pains of a gripping Stomach', confided Kay,
'than that of a gripping Conscience.'[49]

The complement to all such views was that relief and cure were God's alone.
Charles Wesley, as usual, provided the hymn:[50]

> AFTER A RECOVERY FROM SICKNESS
> And live I yet by power divine?
>   And have I still my course to run?
> Again brought back, in its decline,
>   The Shadow of my setting sun?
>
> Jesus to my deliv'rance flew,
>   Where sunk in mortal pangs I lay:
> Pale Death his ancient conquerer knew,
>   And trembled, and ungrasp'd his prey!
>
> The fever turn'd its backward course,
>   Arrested by almighty Power;
> Sudden expired its fiery force,
>   And Anguish gnaw'd my side no more.

After all, 'Is not Jesus himself the great Physician?' mused Hannah Allen's
daughter.[51] Isabella Harris, for her part, called the Lord 'the Physician of
value'.[52]

Thus sickness demanded prayer. Such calling upon the Lord, Samuel
Johnson emphasized, was not crudely 'magical': one was not to expect prayers

to be answered; what counted was obeisance.[53] Prayer in time of sickness continued a major Christian office; as late as 1832, public fasts were still being called to beg for divine help against the cholera.[54] When Charles Wesley fell mortally ill of a fever, prayer was followed by recovery: 'Jesus touched my hand, and rebuked the fever, and it left me.'[55] The Wesleys eagerly promoted healing by faith. John recounted the story of one Mary Special:[56]

> She said,'Four years since, I found much pain ago my left breast broke, and kept running continually. Growing worse and worse, after some time, I was recommended to St. George's Hospital. I was let blood many times, and took hemlock thrice a day, but I was no better . . . When, yesterday se'nnight, I went to Mr. Owen's, where there was a meeting for prayer, Mr. Bell saw me, and asked, 'Have you faith to be healed?' I said, 'Yes'. He prayed for me; and, in a moment, all my pain was gone; but the next day, I felt a little pain again. I clapped my hands on my breasts and cried out, 'Lord, if thou wilt, thou canst make me whole.' It was gone; and from that hour I have had no pain, no soreness, no lumps, or swelling, but both breasts were perfectly well, and have been so ever since'.
>
> Now here are plain facts. 1.She was ill. 2.She is well. 3.She became so in a moment. Which of these can with modesty be denied?

Yet such faith did not, of course, clash with trust in medical means (or, in Ben Franklin's cynical formula, 'God heals, and the Doctor takes the fee').[57] After all, John Wesley himself believed in herbal remedies and medical electricity.[58] In England's self-help Protestant climate, God helped those who helped themselves. Hence, the pious prayed to God to bless the means (i.e., medications) they employed. As Elizabeth Iremonger explained to Mary Heber, Providence was not an alternative to human healing, but rather its sanctification:[59]

> Bad Health, like every other allotment of Providence, I have always considered as given us for the exercise of certain peculiar Duties, & those not merely of the patient, resigned, quiescent kind, though I allow them their due merit, but to call our attention to the wonderful Structure of the Human Frame, to it's delicacy & liability to be disordered, & to the kindness of Providence in placing it within our own powers often to relieve these inconveniences while it pleases him that our Lives should be continued.

No sect excluded the use of medical means on religious grounds, as Christian Scientists were soon to do.[60] Far more typical was the sentiment of Lady Brilliana Harley, when her son, Tom, took a purge: 'I hope the Lord will bles it to him: his noose bleeds every fit'.[61]

Belief that Providence worked through medicine is apparent with smallpox inoculation. *Prima facie*, inoculation could present special doctrinal problems. It might be seen as meddling with Providence, forestalling God's epidemic thunderbolts against wicked mankind. Moreover, in so far as inoculation entailed deliberately injecting disease (to prevent a more serious one), and some inoculees died, the practice might thereby be held to contravene the sixth Commandment. Objections along these lines were, indeed, occasionally raised in England. The Quaker, John Woolman, for instance, protested that inoculation tampered with the unknown ways of Providence; anyway, smallpox was a good thing, the 'messenger from the Almighty . . . an assistant in the cause of virtue'.[62]

Woolman's view chimed with widespread Christian sentiments, perhaps rather similar to those expressed by John Evelyn in accepting his daughter, Elizabeth's, death from smallpox as a 'chastisement' for her parents' 'unworthiness'.[63] Nevertheless, the Anglican clergy strongly backed inoculation, arguing that God had revealed the practice to fortify man against sickness for fulfilling his regular duties. The chief entrepreneurial inoculator, Daniel Sutton, employed a clergyman to publicize his operation from the pulpit.[64] Of predestinarian leanings, Scottish Presbyterianism, by contrast, entertained greater suspicion towards inoculation, which spread more slowly North of the Tweed. As one Scottish minister noted in 1795:[65]

the people are in general averse to inoculation from the general gloominess of their faith, which teaches them, that all diseases which afflict the human frame are instances of the Divine interposition, for the punishment of sin; any interference, therefore, on their part, they deem an usurpation of the prerogative of the Almighty.

Taken as a whole, this religious culture of sickness prompts numerous questions. Can its professions simply be taken at face value? Are we encountering the heartfelt attempts of mortal man, brought to his knees by sickness, to relate to his God; or superstitious pledges and pious platitudes, empty verbal formulae, equivalent to today's 'bless you' at a sneeze? Surely, everything points to the former. The complex syntax and tangled thoughts of such expressions suggests that believers were commonly agonized, wrestling with problems of fate and faith. It would be insensitive to slight such personal expressions, communicated in the privacy of the sickbed or study, in a Protestant country with few collective ecclesiastical rituals for the sick and dying.

Richard Kay's diary, for example, bears witness to a living faith in the Christian theodicy. 'We live here in a very uncertain World, in a World full of Changes; yet one Event happeneth to all', muses the young doctor, uttering a pious commonplace which he proceeds to develop in his own personal way:[66]

I am yet alive, Blessed by God, but have been often sensibly touched with the Death of a Friend; a fresh Instance I now have of the Death of a near Relation . . . Cousin Richard Kay is dead, he has left this World and gone into an invisible State; O, the Account is heavy and shocking, it toucheth me in a tender Part, it grieves me sore. I believe in the Immortality of the soul.

Faith that affliction had ultimate religious rationales afforded comfort. Moreover, it was a rehearsal for the finality of death and so reinforced expections for spiritual life after bodily dissolution. Pious management of disease was vital in a society that practised Christian death.

Christian ways with sickness did not, however, lack critics. Dwelling on disease, they claimed, encouraged morbidity, glamorizing suffering and hindering recovery. Erasmus Darwin, amongst others, argued that Methodist emotionalism actually made converts ill – indeed, was itself disease. He recalled a specially gruesome case of a Wesleyan neophyte convinced that God required of him extreme mortification, to cleanse the soul. Hardened against persuasion, the patient wasted away and died.[67] As a teenager, George Whitefield himself experienced a great loathing of the flesh and fasted avidly.[68] Such exercises became associated in the 1830s with Tractarianism and the Oxford Movement. Criticism of Christianity for encouraging sickly attitudes was reiterated by Harriet Martineau, on the basis of first-hand experience. Her views will be explored in chapter 12.[69]

Darwin was a Deist, Martineau a lapsed Unitarian *en route* for Positivism. Do we, however, find ardent believers in doubts as to the transcendental meanings of sickness? Difficulties arose chiefly with respect to the particular case, as to precisely how to pinpoint the Providential footsteps. Take Boswell, whose faith was a volatile cocktail of childhood Calvinism, laced with more liberal outlooks, and spiced with superstition. He records on 10 April 1784:[70]

Saturday 10 April. Riding to Glasgow this morning from Kingswell, I attempted to pass a cart quickly upon a causeway near the Gorbals. My Horse fell and threw me off before him, close by the track of the cart. *Providentially* (I *will* say) the horse which drew the cart, heavy-laden with sacks of meal, started a little to one side, so that while I lay on the ground the wheel next me missed my head by about an inch. It went over my hat, which had come off my head . . . It left a fright upon my imagination. I most sincerely returned thanks to Almighty God for my preservation.

Boswell's italicization of '*will*' hints that he suspects others will think his certainty superstitious.

Whether God used dreams for communicating medical messages posed severe problems. Parson Woodforde was unsure whether his own dreams contained authentic religious messages:[71]

May 28 Thursday. I breakfasted, dined, etc. again at home. Nancy

breakfasted, dined, etc. again home. I had a very odd Dream last Night,
I dreamt that I should die the Friday before the fifth of Nov[br] next; not
my Will O Lord but thine be done, if it be thy good pleasure thus to fulfil
the same. And may thou O Good God forgive me all my Sins.

Woodforde was not quite sure what to make of dreams but treated them with a
sense of foreboding:[72]

Feb. 26 . . . I dreamt a good deal about Jenny Woodforde Frank
Woodforde's Wife, of her being dressed all in white, looked exceeding
pale but very handsome. I hope my Dream portends no ill to her.

But dreams could equally appear to be revelations of cures. Aubrey recorded
of Wren:[73]

When Sir Christopher Wren was at Paris, about 1671, he was ill and
feverish, made but little water, and had a pain in his reins [kidneys]. He
sent for a physician, who advised him to be let blood, thinking he had
plurisy: but bleeding much disagreeing with his constitution, he would
defer it a day longer: that night he dreamt, that he was in a place where
palm-trees grew, (suppose Egypt) and that a woman in a romantic habit,
reached him dates. The next day he sent for dates, which cured him of
the pain of his reins.

Writing at the turn of the nineteenth century, the Rev. William Jones wrestled
with the tremendous problem of the divine uses of disease. Disease at large
was Providential, no doubt. But did God smite individuals with particular
diseases for His own special purposes? Jones had no pat answer, but he
doubted whether mere mortal men could confidently trace Providence's
finger: that smacked of presumption (and, presumably, of Methodism and
enthusiasm). He instanced the case of a much-hated parishioner, Rogers:[74]

My old friend, Cheney, who has quitted this life but a few weeks,
persisted to the last in declaring his firm persuasion that this wretched
man's case, (which is truly a most uncommon complaint), is a plague, a
stroke, or judgement of Heaven inflicted on him for his excessive,
unbounded villainy.

Rogers had machinated against Jones's appointment as vicar: did God punish
him for that?:[75]

It is very remarkable that, just at this time, he was seized with his
complaint . . . & Mr. James, the surgeon, assured me that it exhibited
fatal symptoms the Michaelmas following. Ever since that time he has
been literally 'dying by inches'. The agony & tortures which he has

endured, have been represented to me as extreme, & his cries & groans have been heard throughout the neighbourhood.

So was Rogers being Divinely punished for his anti-social, anti-Jonesian behaviour? A Heywood or a Josselin, a century or so earlier, would have been in a little doubt. Jones, however, characteristically ducks the issue:[76]

Such sufferings, one would think, would be enough to subdue the hardiest, proudest spirit; but they have not hitherto had that effect on him. Instead of humbling himself under the mighty hand of God & supplicating his mercy for the pardon of his past offences, & the renewal of a right spirit within him, his heart is & still hardened, like Pharaoh's, & every interval of respite & comparative ease is employed in pouring out the most shocking oaths & curses, to which his mouth had been so long accustomed! Shocking abuse of God's goodness!

In Jones's time, the old certainties were dissolving. Disease, however, still made many look on high. 'Who can tell', thumped John Wesley, 'how many of those diseases which we impute altogether to natural causes may really be preternatural? What disorder is there in the human frame which an evil angel may not inflict?'[77]

Secular Myths

As a historical religion, Christianity was able to spin stories of sickness resolving the problem of pain through temporalizing man's condition, suspended in a continuum between Fall and Resurrection, and emblematic of both. These religious scenarios of sickness had their secular analogues. The age of Enlightenment was especially prolific in attempts to explain the essence, potential, and destiny of man in naturalistic terms. Imaginative history provided crucial intellectual elbow-room. Speculative surveys of human development, starting from some putative initial condition – a state of nature, primitive savagery, or (for a minority at least) a pristine civilization – explained the paradoxes of the human predicament in the present and pointed pathways to the future.

Above all, Enlightenment political economy and socio-political analysis argued that the notion of man as a progressive being offered the key to social change, past, present and future. Man had developed via a series of economic stages from a hunter-and-gatherer existence, through a slave society, to feudalism, and finally to agrarian, mercantile, and industrial capitalism.[78] Thanks to the increasing division of labour, production had become more efficient. Thanks to the growth of political liberty, free markets had liberated human energies. Thanks to discoveries in knowledge and science, technology had advanced (as Francis Bacon put it) for the 'relief of man's estate'. Overall, as frequently-drawn contrasts between the West and tribal societies in Africa or Polynesia claimed, the march of mind was enabling man to dominate his environment. Man was more powerful, more secure, more prosperous, more free. Progress, apologists proclaimed, was producing human happiness. Must it not also be making men healthier as well? After all, environmental hazards were being mastered, famine had been conquered, medicine itself was sharing in the benefits of the Scientific Revolution. Had not inoculation been implemented? Had not the discovery of the Orient and the New World brought back to Europe potent new items of *materia medica* such as opium and the Peruvian bark? Many voices sang the song of medical progress. And yet things were obviously not so simple.[79]

Anybody could see that disease had neither been conquered nor had simply withered away. Many analysts, indeed, believed that the aggregate population of Britain was decreasing; a population failing to reproduce itself was a sure sign of biomedical crisis.[80] Above all, it was argued that far from ending health problems, 'progress' might actually exacerbate them. Hence, people were faced with the dilemma of aligning sickness to social development. What were the relations between disease and civilization?

The answer, as articulated by lay people and doctors alike, was that civilization actually seemed to breed sickness. On the basis of empirical knowledge of – or fantasizings about – present-day primitives, it was widely contended that Britons of bygone times had been hardy, sturdy peoples (Tacitus provided many hints). Life had been simple and healthy. Needs were few, exercise plentiful, food plain and wholesome. Necessity made men hardy, and hardiness inured them to pain. Such had been pristine health. Thomas Trotter claimed that 'true health and vigour of body' did not come from civilization but were 'the inheritance of the untutored savage'. Diseases were the brood of 'excess' or 'debauch'. They were unknown in the age of the patriarchs. Things had changed:[81]

> In the present day, this class of diseases, forms by far the largest proportion of the whole, which come under the treatment of the physician. Sydenham at the conclusion of the seventeenth century, computed fevers to constitute two thirds of the diseases of mankind. But at the beginning of the nineteenth century, we do not hesitate to affirm that *nervous disorders* have now taken the place of fevers, and may be justly reckoned two thirds of the whole, with which civilized society is afflicted . . . nervous ailments are no longer confined to the better ranks in life, but rapidly extending to the poorer classes.

The communities of primitive peoples were small and isolated, thus minimizing epidemics. For all these reasons, they were less afflicted by disease. As Pacific explorers such as Captain Cook were well aware, Polynesian islanders had few diseases. Generous as ever with gifts, Europeans gave the natives smallpox, influenza, and, not least, syphilis. The spread of trade, Gibbon insisted, was the spread of disease.[82]

However people evaluated progress – and there were few outright Rousseauvians who thought that the transition from savagery to civilization, from rudeness to refinement, was wholly bad – many feared that economic advance bred disease. As Mr. Escott put it, over dinner, in Peacock's *Headlong Hall*:[83]

> The first inhabitants of the world knew not the use either of wine or animal food; it is, therefore, by no means incredible that they lived to the age of several centuries, free from war, and commerce, and arbitrary government, and every other species of desolating wickedness. But man was then a very different animal to what he now is: he had not the faculty of speech; he was not encumbered with clothes; he lived in the open air; his first step out of which, as Hamlet truly observes, is *into his grave*. His first dwellings, of course, were the hollows of trees and rocks. In process of time he began to build: thence grew villages; thence grew cities. Luxury, oppression, poverty, misery, and disease kept pace with the progress of his pretended improvements, till, from a free, strong, healthy, peaceful animal, he has become a weak, distempered, cruel, carnivorous slave.

The wealth of nations thus jeopardized the health of nations. Progress had involved a vast extension of dangerous occupations, with their hazardous fumes, heat, steam, and dust, their grossly excessive physical demands upon men's strength, or their sedentary nature. Progress meant the proliferation of towns, cramped, poorly ventilated and drained, their inhabitants huddled on top of each other, producing pestilence. Progress had brought about a proletarianization in which the pauperized classes grew ever larger, more indigent and more demoralized, severed from the access to land which had traditionally safeguarded their livelihoods and health. Not that the élite necessarily benefited from their own affluence. The industrious rich worked their health away; the idle rich squandered it in ways directly ruinous to health: rich food, floods of alcohol, harmful fashions, irregular hours, excess.[84] Overall, civilization spelt a deleterious life-style. All this luxury, chorused the critics, was bad for morals, bad for political liberty, and, not least, bad for health.

John Wesley added a further twist to the evils of civilization. If they happened to fall sick, our ancestors found relief through self-help. This sensible recourse was being undermined by medical imperialism, a professional ramp with a vested interest in illness.[85] Dryden put it in a nutshell:

> The first physicians by debauch were made:
> Excess began, and sloth sustains the trade.

Many – sufferers, doctors, and moralists alike – thus blamed vitiated manners for the descent into degeneracy. Certain maladies were specially marked out as the diseases of civilization: gout, stomach disorders, nervous conditions, and, not least, insanity itself, as people grew deranged under the strains of *la dolce vita*.[86]

Responses, of course, differed. Many doctors and *laudatores temporis acti* lamented the demise of old frugality, and told luxury-lubbers to imitate the hardy lives of the virtuous poor – yeoman smallholders tilling family acres. The simple life was the healthy life. William Cadogan, physician to the fashionable, thus emphasized how 'the Poor, I mean the laborious', had as their reward 'Health and Posterity.'[87]

Yet this image of civilization begetting its own monstrous brood of disease could be given a different twist. For it could be used to *abrogate* responsibility for health. The élite could imply that the price to be paid for promoting this sophisticated, progressive, polite society was social strains and personal pressures that could not but tax the system. Hence, health was bound to be jeopardized. Indeed, delicate health could even be prized as a mark of distinction (echoing all those smart playhouse jibes about how boorish it would be to possess rough, rude health). Above all, amongst certain ranks at least, sickness would require to be excused. For being sick was not, in this view, a dereliction of social obligation; it was the cost of playing one's part in the social round. Hence, the invalid could rightly demand attention and sympathy. The result was a certain glamorization of sickness itself, through its identification with the social cream. Doctors such as James McKittrick Adair complained that in a fashionable society, the thing most in fashion was sickness.[89]

These last two chapters have shown how people come to terms with sickness by normalizing it in context of a natural order of cause and effect, and by endowing it with heightened, personal meaning, in the contexts of sacred and profane history. By revealing its place and purposes, disease was thereby robbed of its terrors. Precisely how individual sufferers additionally made sense of sickness in respect of the unfolding of their own personal lives, will be examined in the final section of this book.

NOTES

[1]   Lustig and Pottle (eds), *Boswell: Applause of the Jury*, 249.
[2]   Ayres (ed.), *Paupers and Pig Killers*, 25.
[3]   See the discussion in Porter, 'The Patient's View'; *idem*, 'Medicine and Religion in Eighteenth Century England'.
[4]   Macfarlane (ed.), *Diary of Ralph Josselin*, 19; Wear, 'Puritan Perceptions of Illness'; Beier, 'In Sickness and in Health'; *idem*, *Sufferers and Healers*, 182f.
[5]   See discussion in Beier, 'In Sickness and in Health'.
[6]   Latham and Matthews (eds), *Diary of Samuel Pepys*, VII, *passim*.
[7]   Porter, 'Monsters and Madmen'; Rousseau, *Tobias Smollett*; Morley, *Memoirs of Bartholomew Fair*, 316.
[8]   Ford (ed.), *Medical Student at St. Thomas's Hospital*, 203.
[9]   For an instance see Marshall (ed.), *Autobiography of William Stout*, 140.
[10] Turner (ed.), *Diary of Oliver Heywood*.
[11] Manuel, *Eighteenth Century Confronts the Gods*; Porter, *Edward Gibbon*, ch.5.
[12] Porter, 'Hunger of Imagination'; Hagstrum, 'Dr Johnson's Fear of Death'.

13 MacDonald, *Mystical Bedlam*; Sawyer, 'Health, Disease and Healing'; Porter, *Mind Forg'd Manacles*, ch. 2.

14 Burton, *Anatomy of Melancholy*, 114.

15 Hand, 'Folk-Healer'; Porter, 'Medicine and the Decline of Magic'.

16 Thomas, *Religion and the Decline of Magic*, 794f.; Trimmer, 'Medical Folklore and Quackery'.

17 Walker, *Decline of Hell*; Thomas, *Religion and the Decline of Magic*, 681f.; Stock, *Holy and the Daemonic*; Knox, *Enthusiasm*.

18 Porter, *Mind-Forg'd Manacles*, ch. 2.

19 Ibid., 73; compare Mead, *Medica Sacra*; Zuckerman, 'Dr Richard Mead', 173.

20 King-Hele (ed.), *Letters of Erasmus Darwin*, 104. Elsewhere, Darwin wrote of the 'infernal Divinities, who visit mankind with diseases': ibid., 84.

21 Porter, *Mind-Forg'd Manacles*, ch. 2; Hill, *Wesley Among the Physicians*.

22 Bottomley, *Attitudes to the Body in Western Christendom*, 93f.

23 Malthus, *Essay on Population*.

24 MacNeil, *Under the Banner of Science*.

25 Browning (ed.) *Memoirs of Sir John Reresby*, 226.

26 Lewis (ed.), *Letters of the Lady Brilliana Harley*, 78.

27 Defoe, *Journal of the Plague Year*, 32.

28 Doe (ed.), *Diary of James Clegg*, III, 844. See, more generally, Sheils (ed.), *Church and Healing*; Barry, 'Piety and the Patient'.

29 [Martineau], *Life in the Sick-Room*, 170-1.

30 Heywood (ed.), *Diary of Henry Newcome*, 6.

31 Latham and Matthews (eds), *Diary of Samuel Pepys*, III, 318.

32 John Wesley, *Journal*, IV, 349-50.

33 Brockbank and Kenworthy (eds), *Diary of Richard Kay*, 24, 37, 55.

34 Turner (ed.), *Oliver Heywood*.

35 Byles (ed.), *Reminiscences of Hawker*, 296.

36 Colvin (ed.), *Correspondence of Maria Edgeworth*, 297.

37 Turner (ed.), *Diary of Oliver Heywood*, 196-7.

38 John Wesley, *Journal*, II, 127.

39 Checkland, *Gladstones*, 285.

40 Williamson, *Autobigraphy*, 33.

41 Jackson (ed.), *Journal of Charles Wesley*, 232.

42 Beresford (ed.), *Diary of a Country Parson*, I, 85.

43 Whitefield, *Journal*.

44 L. F. C. (ed.), *Extracts from the Diary of a Living Physician*.

45 Burton, *Anatomy of Melancholy*, 499.

46 Jackson (ed.), *Journal of Charles Wesley*.

47 Kingsley (ed.), *Charles Kingsley*, I, 186.

48 Harris (ed.), *Family Memorials*.

49 Brockbank and Kenworthy (eds), *Diary of Richard Kay*, 26, 23.

50 Jackson (ed.), *Journal of Charles Wesley*.

51 Allen, *Life of Hannah S. Allen*, 44.

52 Harris (ed.), *Family Memorials*, 16.

53 Boswell, *Life of Johnson*, I, 302.

54 Morris, *Cholera 1832*. Elizabeth Fry feared it would not be taken very seriously. Fry and Cresswell (eds), *Memoir of the Life of Elizabeth Fry*, II, 101.

55 Jackson (ed.), *Journal of Charles Wesley*, 232.

56 John Wesley, *Journal*, III, 77.

57 Franklin, *Poor Richard's Almanack*, year 1744.

58 Hill, *John Wesley Among the Physicians*; Rousseau, 'John Wesley's *Primitive Physick*'.

[59] Bamford (ed.), *Dear Miss Heber*, 177-8; Wear, 'Puritan Perceptions of Illness'.

[60] Inglis, *Natural Medicine*, 58.

[61] Lewis (ed.), *Letters of the Lady Brilliana Harley*, 120.

[62] Whittier (ed.), *Diary of John Woolman*, 153.

[63] De Beer (ed.), *Diary of John Evelyn*, IV, 465-6, (27 August 1685).

[64] Farr, 'Medical Developments and Religious Belief'; Miller, *Adoption of Inoculation for Smallpox*; Porter, 'Religion and Medicine in Eighteenth Century England'; J.R. Smith, *Speckled Monster*, 74.

[65] Quoted in Farr, 'Medical Developments and Religious Belief'.

[66] Brockbank and Kenworthy (eds), *Diary of Richard Kay*, 145.

[67] King-Hele (ed.), *Essential Writings of Erasmus Darwin*, 74.

[68] Whitefield, *Journal*, 20.

[69] Martineau, *Autobiography*.

[70] Lustig and Pottle (eds), *Boswell: Applause of the Jury*, 202.

[71] Beresford (ed.), *Diary of a Country Parson*, II, 108. Compare II, 193, 8 June 1785.

[72] Ibid., II, 177. Others were, of course, more cavalier: 'Let us make the most of life, and leave dreams to Emanuel Swedenborg'. Marchand (ed.), *Byron's Letters and Journals*, II, 97-8.

[73] Aubrey, *Miscellanies*, 39. There are scores of similar tales in Aubrey. Of course, folklore through the nineteenth century attributed superstitious powers to dreams. See Collison, *Story of Street Literature*, 138ff.; Carlton, 'The Dream Life of Archbishop Laud'. Traditionally, dreaming of suffering pain was a portent of gladness. If a sick man dreamt he had no nose, it spelt death.

[74] Christie (ed.), *Diary of the Revd William Jones*, 152-3.

[75] Ibid.

[76] Ibid.

[77] Wesley, *Works*, 1842, VI, 358.

[78] Bryson, *Man and Society*.

[79] See discussion in Porter, 'Was There a Medical Enlightenment in Eighteenth Century England?'

[80] The view of James Graham. See Porter, 'Sex and the Singular Man'; MacKenzie, *History of Health*; Buchan, *Domestic Medicine*, 3f.; cf. Inglis, *Diseases of Civilization*.

[81] Trotter, *View of the Nervous Temperament*, xvi- xvii.

[82] Porter, *Edward Gibbon*, ch. 6.

[83] Garnett (ed.), *Novels of Thomas Love Peacock*, 27; Trotter, *View of the Nervous Temperament*. See also Sekora, *Luxury*.

[84] Cheyne, *English Malady, passim*.

[85] Wesley, *Primitive Physick*; Rousseau, 'John Wesley's *Primitive Physick*'.

[86] Porter, 'Rage of Party'; Sekora, *Luxury*.

[87] Cadogan, *Gout*, 17. Rogers, 'Rise and Fall of the Gout'; Rousseau, 'Nerves, Spirits and Fibres'; *idem*, 'Psychology'.

[88] Adair, *Essays on Fashionable Diseases*.

Suffering & the Self

Chapter 11:
The Sick Role

The Rev. William Jones tells the story of one Mr C——, a healthy, debonair Irish adventurer, chasing promotion in the Anglican Church. He knew that the appointment of the Bishop of Man was vested in the Athol family. When the see became vacant near the close of the eighteenth century, the Duchess-dowager, who hoped her second son would accede to the mitre in a few years, looked out, as a stop-gap, for some broken-down old clergyman 'whose candle of life would be likely to be extinguished in about 12 years'. Mr C—— boxed clever. He secured an introduction:[1]

> previous to which he had his face painted in such a manner as to give him the appearance of age; & counterfeiting an asthmatic cough, he was admitted into the presence of the Duchess . . . she soon determined to appoint him to the Bishopric.

He was consecrated, and naturally presented himself at Court, where he met the Duchess once more:[2]

> But how shall I attempt to describe the Duchess's surprise & indignation, when, instead of a *poor, sickly, asthmatic being*, she surveyed a *fine, upright,* man who had scarce attained the middle age, in all the vigour of health, and set off with a very handsome *cauliflower-wig*!! The Dowager was known to be very violent & impetuous; &, I am told, she occasionally, in spite of her high rank, condescended to vent her passion in the same vulgar language as the dames of Billingsgate are wont to do. I cannot take upon me to write that she wholly abstained from this, when she discovered the imposition that had been practised upon her. She went up to him in the Drawing-room, &, in the most menacing tone, exclaimed, – 'You are not the *ill-looking, old rascal* to whom I gave the Bishopric!' – 'Ah!', said he, very coolly, 'Your Grace can hardly imagine what a good thing a bishopric is to cure an asthma'.

We have so far been examining the attitudes and experiences of the sick person. In the final part of this book, we now turn to investigate the broader cultural implications of suffering. Obviously, analysis of the integration of the sick within, or their dis-integration from, the wider circles of their fellows is crucial if we are to gauge the stigma or support the sick attracted. Illness is disruptive. Normal social intercourse is suspended, because sickness puts the suffering beyond the reciprocities of social exchange, or one might say – and herein lay the great ambiguity – because the sufferer, by *choosing* to 'go down sick', has elected, temporarily at least, to opt out of society and into the 'sick role'.

As Talcott Parsons emphasized, he who adopts the sick role makes special demands on his fellows. They will probably be prepared for him to assume that role – indeed, will be accused of unneighbourly and unChristian behaviour unless they do so. Sickness exerts a power of its own, the power of helplessness. He who resents and rejects the claims of the sick exposes himself to disapproval and guilt.[3]

Because illness affords scope for exploitation, the sick person generates ambivalence. Hence the emotional force of William Jones's anecdote. Jones evidently has very mixed feelings towards Mr C————: envy at his audacity (Jones was no toady and must have been pleased to see the Duchess outwitted); and grievance at the success of his roguery – after all, Jones had himself long suffered from real ill health, but had never received the slightest promotion.

Sickness thus perplexes, but it also disarms. Precisely because its legitimate claims upon others are so great, it arouses suspicions of malingering, apprehensions that its moral leverage is all too readily exploited, annoyance that it commands power without responsibility. Take this report about the dying days of a *grande dame*:[4]

[it was reported in London] that the poor Duchess of Devonshire had applied to the Duke [of Devonshire] for Succour in her Pecuniary State of Affairs, and that the Duke told her in so positive a manner that He had engaged himself never to do more in the Business, having paid enormous sums, that the Duchess in despair of ever prevailing in this her last and only Ressource, fell ill.

The illness, if wretched, was also highly convenient, and hence put the Duke on his guard:[5]

the first days the Duke supposed the illness a little put on, but when He understood that She was so bad and in danger of her life, he entreated the Doctor who sat up with her, if She had a lucid interval to assure Her that every wish she had should be complied with, and that He would purchase her Health with any thing she could command. But, poor thing, I suppose it was then too late. I pity the Duke who, they say, is very much affected. And well He may!

No one wants to be duped by sickness 'put on'. But once its genuineness established itself, it wielded more power than the Duchess could have commanded when well. And when death then flexed its muscles and claimed his victim, the guilt – and the social disapproval – were overpowering.

The sick person thus sends out contradictory signals. On the one hand, he stirs sympathy. In the sixteenth century, Montaigne had emphasized the mutual feeling linking the invalid with the bystander:[6]

> The very sight of another's pain does materially work upon me, and I naturally usurp the sense of a third person to share with him in his torment. A perpetual cough in another tickles my lungs and throat. I more unwillingly visit the sick I love, and am by duty interested to look after, than those I care not for, and from whom I have no expectation. I take possession of the disease I am concerned at and lay it too much to heart, and do not at all wonder that fancy should distribute fevers, and sometimes kill such as allow too much scope, and are too willing to entertain it.

That kind of sympathy for sickness drips from Sterne's *Tristram Shandy*, as in the Le Fever interlude. But Sterne's contemporary, Adam Smith, displayed greater scepticism. It was his belief that the sick in reality commanded remarkably little intuitive sympathy from others.[7] This resulted from the ways sickness presented itself. There were, of course, all the familiar symptoms of pain: grimaces, writhings, wincings, tears, howls. Yet these were double-edged, for they also created a distance, exciting disgust. They could also be 'put on', an act. Moreover, the roots of pain probably remained hidden, in the internal organs. It was a case of 'out of sight, out of mind'. What could not be seen could not excite great pity.

Smith may also have suspected that such hidden springs of sickness provoked doubts: were they real? Illness was worrisome because it was so deceptive. This was obviously true with mental illness, where mad-doctors were arguing that one of insanity's most frightening features was its bizarre capacity to mimic normalcy. A man might be utterly crazed within, while presenting a rational face to the world.[8] Could not physical 'illness' be similarly deceptive, only inside-out, as it were? Might not a devious person convincingly feign sickness, while being perfectly healthy? Indeed – worse still – might not his *imagination* convince him that he was sick, despite A-1 health? The Georgians were haunted by the hypocrite who masked his true self. The malingerer and the hypochondriac both seemed varieties of that diabolical species. A man could, indeed, smile and smile and be a villain; might he not wince, moan, and groan and be a villain too?[9]

That pain had its pleasures was no secret. James Boswell, celebrating the bittersweet delights of 'hypochondria', explicitly acknowledged the appositeness of Smith's discussion, and especially his remark that 'a time of indisposition is not altogether a time of misery'.[10] Gibbon, too, recalled how he had found it a positive relief to be ill while a child:[11]

> Instead of repining at my long and frequent confinement to the chamber or the couch, I secretly rejoiced in those infirmities which delivered me from the exercises of school and the society of my equals.

Not surprisingly, then, those basking in what Harriet Martineau called the 'gains and sweets of invalidism' were disturbing.[12] Would-be bishops were not the only beneficiaries. With the development of the Poor Law, ever more paupers were in receipt of poor relief for sickness, lameness, and general disability.[13] Moreover, charity hospitals also mushroomed. Would not the poor take to shamming sickness to exploit charity and gain a hospital bed, shelter, and food?[14]

The up-market version of the pauper shammer was, of course, the hypochondriac or valetudinarian. The art of invalidism evolved through the Georgian era, and delicacy came into vogue, claiming attention, exemption, sympathy, and excuse.[15] It might even just be an agreeable way of filling the time. In this vein, Ralph Varney's doctor, Dr Denton, once informed him that he, unlike others, did not have the 'leasure to be sick'.[16]

Society distrusted those suspected of simulating sickness. Dorothea Lieven wrote cattily about Madame de Princetau, for whom 'it is very becoming . . . to be taken ill'.[17] Garrick assured Peter Fountain that he 'never had a political illness in my life' – in other words, had not invented sickness to wriggle out of an engagement; behind Garrick's defence is the implication that it was a common ploy.[18] Indeed, explaining to Benjamin Bailey why he had been so remiss a correspondent, Keats jokingly ran through all the sickness excuses in the book:[19]

> . . . I have sunk twice in our Correspondence, have risen twice and been too idle, or something worse, to extricate myself – I have sunk the third time and just now risen again at this two of the Clock P. M. and saved myself from utter perdition . . . [he goes on to explain why he has not written] . . . I tried Chilblains, Rheumatism, Gout, tight Boots, nothing of that sort would do, so this is, as I was going to say, the thing.

The sick obviously claimed plenty of minor exemptions, such as the right to be lazy correspondents. 'I ought to have written sooner', Crabbe told his son in 1824, 'but I . . . take the Privilege of an Invalid.'[20] When sick, the gentry expected to be pampered. When Lady Holland grumbles to the Duchess of Leinster, 'how one misses somebody to nurse one and read to one in those illnesses', we see her expectations about the perks of the sick.[21] And on the wider social stage, sickness also received its privileges. One lay in the law courts. It became standard practice for felons guilty of capital crimes to receive mercy if mental illness was judged responsible for the deed – as also with epilepsy, or puerperal derangement in the case of infanticidal women.[22]

Yet, to balance these indulgences, society insisted that it was bad form to ostentate one's sickness unnecessarily. Court etiquette, for example, would not allow sickness to intrude. 'Illness here – till of late – has been so unknown, that it is commonly supposed it must be wilful, and therefore meets little notice', wrote Fanny Burney from Windsor in 1789, soon after George III's first bout of insanity. In her early career as a lady-in-waiting, she had found this very difficult to bear, drawing up in exasperation her own sardonic protocol:[23]

> *Directions for Coughing, Sneezing or Moving, Before the King and Queen.*
> In the first place you must not cough. If you find a cough tickling in your throat, you must arrest it from making any sound; if you find yourself choking with the forbearance, you must choke – but not cough.
> In the second place you must not sneeze. If you have a vehement cold, you must take no notice of it; if your nose-membranes feel a great irritation, you must hold your breath; if a sneeze still insists upon making its way, you must oppose it, by keeping your teeth grinding together; if the violence of the repulse breaks some blood-vessel you must break the blood vessel – but not sneeze.
> In the third place, you must not, upon any account, stir either hand or foot. If, by chance, a black pin runs into your head, you must not take it out. If the pain is very great, you must be sure to bear it without wincing; if it brings the tears into your eyes, you must not wipe them off; if they give you a tingling by running down your cheeks, you must look as if nothing was the matter. If the blood should gush from your head by means of the black pin, you must let it gush; if you are uneasy to think of making such a blurred appearance, you must be uneasy, but you must say nothing about it. If, however, the agony is very great, you may, privately, bite the inside of your cheek, or of your lips, for a little relief taking care, meanwhile, to do it so cautiously with that precaution, if you even gnaw a piece out, it will not be minded, only be sure either to swallow it, or commit it to a corner of the inside of your mouth till they are gone – for you must not spit.

Thus, though a certain tolerance was shown towards the sick, it had strict limits, and some vented their resentment. It took a bear such as Samuel Johnson to complain straight out. 'Mr Johnson has such an Aversion to the Liberties taken by sick People with their surrounding Friends', recorded Hester Thrale:[24]

> that it has greatly blunted his Compassion – it is so difficult says he for a sick Man *not to be a Scoundrel*: Oh! set in the Pillows soft – Mr Grumbler is coming – Oh! let no Air in for the World, Mr Grumbler will catch Cold;

this perpetual Preference is so offensive, where the Privileges of Illness are supported by Wealth; and nourished by Dependence; that one cannot wonder a rough mind is revolted by them.

The drollery is, that being habitually watchful against such behaviour, he is sometimes ready to suspect it in himself, & when one asks him how he does – will often reply – "ready to become a Scoundrel dear Madam, with a little more spoiling you will make *me* a Rascal very soon'.

Jane Austen deplored the 'Egotism of an Invalid' (though never so disloyal as to say so, she surely watched it daily in her mother);[25] Elizabeth Montagu directed the accusation against herself ('there is not so ugly a monster as a woman in vapours');[26] and Lady Mary Wortley Montagu – staunchly Augustan in her advocacy of the social virtues – distrusted the self-absorption of the sick:[27]

> I hate complaining; 'tis no sign I am easy that I do not trouble you with my head-aches, and my spleen; to be reasonable one should never complain but when one hopes for redress. A physician should be the only confidant of bodily pains; and for those of the mind, they should never be spoke of but to them that can and will relieve 'em.

In their mild way, these barbs seem to anticipate Nietzschian disgust at the sick as enemies of society. As Lady Holland grumbled, 'the people that die are those whom one least expects, and complaining sick folks go on for ever.'[28]

Sickness thus wore a disturbing double face and was an anarch, replacing order with a certain confusion. Sterne invited his readers to conjecture an upside-down world:[29]

> In the foreground of this picture, a statesman turning the political wheel, like a brute, the wrong way round – against the stream of corruption, – by heaven! – instead of with it.
>
> In this corner, a son of the divine Esculapius, writing a book against predestination; perhaps worse, – feeling his patient's pulse, instead of his apothecary's – brother of the faculty in the background upon his knees in tears, – drawing the curtains of a mangled victim to beg his forgiveness; – offering a fee, – instead of taking one.

In sickness, parents waited upon the children they normally commanded, servants were treated by the physicians who normally treated them with disdain, and the powerful even sometimes submitted to doctors' orders. Sickness dissolved old, and created new obligations, new rituals of its own.

The Medical Grapevine

Sickness was a very public event; it was news. A glance at the newspapers of the day, at letters and diaries, and at the jottings of those like Horace Walpole who treasured the daily tittle-tattle, proves that the *beau monde* was riveted by news of people falling sick, summoning doctors, undergoing this or that treatment, worsening, dismissing their physician, relapsing, recovering, dying.

In some ways, it seems yet another mark of the sheer avidity of the Georgians to know what was going on. Newspapers, improvements in the post, faster travel, and the like roused a thirst for news.[30] Some of the circulation of medical gossip smacks of ghoulishness. The newspapers liked to inform their readers of famous personages who were about to die. 'Dr Johnson is so dangerously relapsed', noted the *Public Advertiser* on 8 December 1784, 'that there are little hopes of his getting over the winter. His disorder is dropsy . . . to men of his time of life . . . generally fatal.'[31] 'I don't hear much news', Mary Curzon told her friend, Mary Heber, 'but see by the papers that the Duchess of Devonshire is so ill as to be given over by her Physicians.'[32] Eighteenth-century obituary columns are uncommonly detailed on last sufferings.[33]

Sickness and death set local tongues wagging. Soon after his wife died, Thomas Turner's antennae picked up a whispering campaign:[34]

This day I was informed of the ill-natured and cruel treatment I have privately received from malevolent tongues, who have made, propagated and spread with indefatigable industry and diligence a report that Mr. Snelling [the surgeon] at my request (and by force) castrated my wife, which operation was the immediate cause of her death.

Turner was scandalized at how such an irresponsible, groundless rumour had spread like wildfire through the locality:[35]

there is hardly a child of four years old or any old woman of four score within ten miles of the place but has it at their tongue's end, and even so credulous as to give sanction to it; that is, if they do not directly believe it they will by no means let it die with them, but still continue to circulate it about, so vile and envious is man to man. Now from what occasion this palpable falsehood could take its rise I am quite at a loss to guess; as to my own part I know myself thoroughly innocent, therefore I defy and despise the malice of the vulgar multitude.

He concluded, with hardly convincing compassion, 'if I know my own heart I sincerely forgive them; neither have I in the least any anger against them for it.'[36]

Mercenary motives played their part in broadcasting and harvesting medical news. Every death meant wills and widows, inheritances, sinecures and vacant places. The correspondence of Prebendary Pyle reads like a non-stop sickness bulletin on the wheezing lungs and slippery bowels of the deans and bishops of the Church of England, all with a view to prospects of advancement in the clerical parlour-game of upwardly mobile musical thrones.[37]

But, of course, this eagerness to hear all about everyone's health also marked profound feeling for the sufferings of friends, relations, acquaintances, and even public figures. It was also valuable to find out what sorts of treatments were in or out of favour, who were the fashionable and successful doctors, which patent medicines were being puffed by whom. In a world of patient choice, knowledge was vital for decision-making.[38]

Not least, it was important to know the geographical drift of epidemics – whether they were encroaching or receding, worsening or waning. Action depended on information. In the case of smallpox, for example, visiting would be restrained to those who had already had the disease and acquired immunity. Thus, Elizabeth Purefoy informed her nephew in 1737 that smallpox was rampant in Buckinghamshire: 'When our fears are over, shall be glad to see you and Mrs Porter'.[39]

Perhaps most significantly of all, the world of talk surrounding the sick activated help on their behalf. People were always exchanging information and advice about health and remedies. When Samuel Johnson heard that his acquaintance, John Perkins, was going travelling, he sent him lengthy health advice:[40]

I am pleased that You are going on a very long Journey, which may by proper conduct restore your health and prolong your life.
Observe these rules
1. Turn all care out of your head as soon as you mount the chaise.
2. Do not think about frugality, your health is worth more than it can cost.
3. Do not continue any day's journey to fatigue.
4. Take now and then a day's rest.
5. Get a smart seasickness if you can.
6. Cast away all anxiety, and keep your mind easy.

Similarly, there was an effective grapevine in ideas about cures. Those from aristocratic sources were particularly in demand. Joseph Spence copied down 'Lord Northumberland's cure for an ague':[41]

Gromwell seed, pounded quite fine, the weight of 18d in silver a dose, to be taken in half a pint of ale, blood warm, when the fit is coming on. Lord Northumberland says three doses never fail of curing.

Succouring the Sick

The sick needed to be nursed. Home nursing was energetically pursued and well-organized, conducted by family and friends, and, above all, by regular domestics. Certain villagers had reputations as good nurses; they would be called in, perhaps to 'watch' – to keep attendance in the sick-room, especially overnight, particularly if death were feared. Sometimes, watching was an act of charity; sometimes, payment would change hands. When the Wells physician, Claver Morris, fell sick early in the eighteenth century, he paid relays of watchers to sit around his bedside.[42]

Slightly more formal was sick-visiting. This was treated as a Christian office of great gravity by the early Methodists; for George Whitefield, there was 'nothing more useful than visiting a sick bed!'[43] From the late eighteenth century onwards, visiting the sick also became significant amongst evangelical female charities, and with friendly societies that offered to help members in times of illness.[44] Sick-visits were not always welcome. They might be seen as intrusive, particularly when conducted by those of higher rank, intent upon religious proselytization, moral reform, and cleanliness crusades. The Rev. William Jones discovered parishioners distrusted his efforts, suspecting that he was calling only because the prognosis was grave:[45]

When I first came into the parish, I called upon the sick, without waiting to be sent for; & I am sorry to add that, in some instances, my visits were ill-received, & even rejected. After tapping, for some time, at dame Peake's door, old nurse Hobbs opened it just enough to put her head out, & to tell me that I was not to enter. "She is not bad enough for you, Sir!" I asked her what she supposed me to be? perhaps she mistook me for *a carrion-crow*; & that I ought not to call upon any of the sick in my parish, until I could sniff or smell death.

Despite such setbacks, sick-visiting was an active tradition. For the seventeenth-century Nonconformist, Philip Henry, it was a religious office. He was, we are told, 'very industrious in visiting the Sick, instructing them and praying with them; and in this he would say, he aimed at the good, not only of those that were *Sick*, but also of their *Friends* and *Relations* that were about them.'[46] More pragmatic, Parson Woodforde usually regaled the sick with joints of meat. Of one parishioner he visited, he recorded a good death. 'The poor Woman whom I sent some Veal to Sunday died yesterday morning – She eat nothing afterwards till she died. But she eat hearty of the Veal I sent her.'[47] Quakers were notably active in this pious act. Of Mary Hall, her son said that[48]

Her charity began at home, but did not end there. She was diligent in seeking out the sick and the poor in their squalid abodes. Often have I trudged by her side when on these errands she would carry a basket with some little comforts, and then would read and pray with the sufferers.

Visiting the sick was no light responsibility. When his friend, Mr Chute, succumbed to gout, Thomas Gray stayed with him for five weeks, as he was on his own.[49]

In the end, however, care of the sick was the family's responsibility. Here again, sickness was meant to bring moral transformation. 'If any of the Family happen to be sick', servants were told,[50]

> let all Animosity, all former Displeasure they may have given you be
> forgot: Visit, attend, and comfort them all you can, whether you are
> ordered by your Mistress to do so or not; you have a superior Authority
> for this Act of Compassion, 'tis a Duty enjoined by God, and owing to
> Humanity, and which you know not how soon you may stand in need of
> yourself. . . . A tender Assiduity about a sick Person is half a Cure.

One would like to know more about the socio-dynamics of the sick bed. Would we mainly have witnessed micro-manoeuvrings for power between family factions, alien perhaps to the elementary needs of the sick themselves? Certainly, Harriet Martineau made a long and impassioned plea to well-wishers to let the sick be. She viewed being sick almost as a state of being sick of other people. Sufferers, she argued, needed privacy. 'Though the cases are numerous of sufferers who prefer, and earnestly endeavour to procure solitude', she wrote,[51]

> they are, if not resisted, wondered at, and humoured for a supposed
> peculiarity, rather than seen to be reasonable; whereas, if they are
> listened to as the best judges of their own comforts, it may be found that
> they have reason on their side.

In thus contending, she was largely echoing Samuel Johnson's sentiments:[52]

> Visitors are no proper companions in the chamber of sickness. They
> come when I could sleep, or read, they stay till I am weary, they force me
> to attend, when my mind calls for relaxation, and to speak when my
> powers will hardly actuate my tongue. The amusements and consola-
> tions of languor and depression are conferred by familiar and domestick
> companions, which can be visited or called at will, and can occasionally
> be quitted or dismissed, who do not obstruct accommodation by cere-
> mony, or destroy indolence by awakening effort.

The Public Face of Sickness
Relative to many societies, early modern England was not noted for collective healing rituals. Catholic nations still had thriving healing shrines, holy wells, processions behind the Cross in time of pestilence, and so forth.[53] Healing and holiness really were of a piece, from the churching of women through to extreme unction. As Lady Mary Wortley Montagu and others perceived, most formal Christian ceremonials of healing had disappeared, or been abolished, in England. To a small degree, they had been supplanted by the theatrical razzmatazz of professional quackery, and by public lectures on health.[54]

The main focus of public gestures towards sickness became the hospitals, founded in a growing stream from the 1730s in London and the provinces. Hospitals had created many fund-raising rituals: dinners, sermons, race-meetings, concerts, etc. We know very little, however, about the patterns of life within the hospital, beyond what the rule books stipulate. According to Joseph Wilde, an actor who became a patient in the Devon and Exeter Hospital early in the nineteenth century, patients essentially ran their own sub-culture: cooking, cleaning, running errands for each other, and maintaining ward-discipline. This impression is confirmed by the slightly later account of another patient, Henry White, for whom the central feature of collective hospital life was the preparation of food.[55]

The main public healing place in Georgian England was the spa, and increasingly, the seaside resort.[56] By contrast to their equivalents in France or Germany,[57] the largest – Bath, Buxton, Scarborough, Cheltenham, Weymouth, Brighton, etc. – were thoroughly commercialized, and were resorts of pleasure no less than of healing. Many disapproved of this apparent trivialization; John Byng complained that Weymouth attracted 'the giddy and the gay' – all he could find were misses 'expecting to drown their nervous fears, and hysteric wanderings, in the sea, assisted by the use of gentle dancing with soft speeches from beaus, and the indulgence of polite conversation.'[58]

This is not the place to explore spa culture. What is important, however, from the viewpoint of this book, is that the sick clamoured to visit spas in great numbers, and with serious intent, often quite independently of professional advice. It was a practical and positive activity for the preservation or restoration of health. The spa or the seaside gave the sick an opportunity to care for their health in public. It might even be a measure of the earnestness with which people turned to health resorts that they attracted droves of hypochondriacs, as Jane Austen satirically observed in *Sanditon*.

Certain other small-scale collective health activities developed. From the mid-eighteenth century, parish authorities commonly organized mass smallpox inoculation. Entrepreneurs set up rest homes where the better-off could prepare and recover.[59] Late in the century, there was a vogue for mesmeric seances.

Nevertheless, all the signs are that the health culture of early modern England was, by most standards, essentially private.[60] The individual or the family unit was the typical nexus of self-help. People had to cope on their own, or by privately contracting with medical practitioners. The strain could be trying. Eliza Pierce thus apologized to Thomas Taylor in the 1760s:[61]

I should have answer'd your Letter sooner had I not been pretty well employ'd last week on account of one of our Maids having the small Pox, who died Friday Evening, and unluckily at the same time the House-keeper was confin'd to her Bed in an inflamation; so that both myself & my Wise Maid have had enough to do. I call her my Wise Maid, because since the Girls death, she has taken it into her Head that she should have the disorder, tho' she was inocculated about three years ago, and had them very thick. This has provoked me & done me more harm then any

thing else, as she wou'd sit like a dead thing, and no reasons had any
effect on her, – however she now begins to find nothing really ails her &
to move about again as usual – I declare I began to fear what effect the
force of imagination wou'd have on her, & am convinced that had she
had the least real complaint, or any feverish disorder that the College of
Physicians could not have saved her Life, so strongly was she prepos-
sessed she would have the small Pox – it is a most provoking thing that
when there is so much trouble in a family people should add to it by such
whimseys.

And for those who could afford it, the desideratum of medical treatment was
the practitioner who came to visit one's own home: the 'family practitioner'
became the norm.[62]
    This privatization of health corresponded with commonly-held beliefs.
Sickness was seen as an essentially individual matter. Few saw it as the
responsibility of the state. Though doctors such as William Buchan fulmi-
nated against the wickedness of knowingly communicating infections, especially venereal disease, such actions were never criminalized.[63] Plans had been
advanced in the seventeenth century by reformers such as William Petty and
John Bellers, and later by Defoe and others, for the public policing of health,
and for state sickness provision. But such projects made no headway, in great
contrast with the extensive 'medical police' movement in Germany.[64]. Those
who felt threatened had to act on their own initiative, as, for instance, Charles
Henry Coote, seventh Earl of Mountrath, who so profoundly feared smallpox
that he permitted his house in Devon to be approached only through a series of
five relays.[65] Dealing with sickness was left largely to private initiative.

Notes

[1]   Christie (ed.), *Diary of the Revd William Jones*, 190–1. Jones has a similar story of a
      Pope: 189.
[2]   Ibid., 191.
[3]   Parsons, *Social System*. Discussed in Turner, *Body and Society*, 85f.; and *idem*,
      Medical Power and Social Knowledge.
[4]   Castle (ed.), *Jerningham Letters*, I, 270.
[5]   Ibid.
[6]   Taylor, *Montaigne*, 7.
[7]   Adam Smith, *Theory of Moral Sentiments*, 38.
[8]   Porter, *Mind Forg'd Manacles*, chs. 1 and 2.
[9]   Porter, 'Making Faces'; Shortland, 'Body in Question'; *idem*, 'Skin Deep', *idem*,
      'Figure of the Hypocrite'.
[10] Pottle (ed.), *Boswell's London Journal*, 164.
[11] Bonnard (ed.), *Edward Gibbon. Memoirs*.
[12] [Martineau], *Life in the Sick-Room*, 120.
[13] Thomas, 'Old Poor Law and Medicine'; Himmelfarb, *Idea of Poverty*.
[14] Woodward, *To Do the Sick No Harm*; Porter, 'Gift Relationship'.
[15] Fischer-Homberger, 'Hypochondriasis'.

16   Verney (ed.), *Memoirs*, II, 308.

17   Quennell (ed.), *Private Letters of Princess Lieven*, 48.

18   Little and Kahrl (eds), *Letters of David Garrick*, III, 935.

19   Gittings (ed.), *Letters of John Keats*, 71.

20   Faulkner (ed.), *Letters and Journals of George Crabbe*, 297.

21   Fitzgerald (ed.), *Correspondence of Emily, Duchess of Leinster*, I, 493.

22   R. Smith, *Trial by Medicine*; Falconer, *Dissertation on the Influence of the Passions*; Haygarth, *Of the Imagination*.

23   Barrett (ed.), *Diary of Fanny Burney*, II, 407.

24   Ingrams (ed.), *Dr Johnson by Mrs Thrale*, 118. It was a theme often repeated by Johnson: 'Disease produces much selfishness; a man in pain is looking after ease, and lets most other things go': Chapman (ed.), *Letters of Samuel Johnson*, III, 71; 'a sick man's thoughts soon turn back upon himself': ibid., III, 155; 'the first talk of the sick is commonly of themselves': ibid., III, 123.

25   Chapman (ed.), *Jane Austen's Letters*, 495. During her last illness, she was forced to prop herself up on a couple of chairs as a makeshift bed, because her mother hogged the sofa.

26   Climenson (ed.), *Elizabeth Montagu*, II, 26.

27   Johnson (ed.), *Letters from Lady Mary Wortley Montagu*, 42.

28   Fitzgerald (ed.), *Correspondence of Emily, Duchess of Leinster*, I, 416.

29   Sterne, *Tristram Shandy*, 207.

30   Porter, 'Newspapers as Resources for Social History'.

31   See Porter and Porter (eds), *Patient's Progress*.

32   Bamford (ed.), *Dear Miss Heber*, 11.

33   Porter, 'Lay Medical Knowledge in the Eighteenth Century'; *idem*, 'Laymen, Doctors and Medical Knowledge'.

34   Vaisey (ed.), *Diary of Thomas Turner*, 230.

35   Ibid.

36   Ibid.

37   Hartshorne, *Memoirs of a Royal Chaplain*, 303:

Dean Lynch, after a previous illness of irregular gout, & bilious cholic, has had a paralytic stroke; which has sorely shattered half his vast carcass. He is not yet well enough to go to Bath.

He is possessed of the best thing the bishop of Winton has in his gift, viz. the Mastership of the Hospital of St. Cross near Winchester: (£500 a year; called 700).

If He dies, Dr. Hoadly's ill state may embarras the bishop sadly. That Hospital may be held by any man, lay or clerk: And to be sure the Dr. would be the man. But he will not live ¼ of a year; I fear, perhaps not half so long.

How far it may be propper for Chancellor Hoadly to have it thrown upon the heap of his preferment, which is £1,500 a year already; will, I am sure, be well considered. He has no child; &, I believe, cares not a farthing about mere money. For my part, I will not ask for; if Dr. Lynch should vacate it, & Dr. B. Hoadly be dead. And if it should be offered me, on condition of resigning my prebend, I should consider of it a little.

38   Porter and Porter, *Patient's Progress*, ch. 7.

39   Mitchell (ed.), *Purefoy Letters*, 99.

40   Chapman (ed.), *Letters of Samuel Johnson*, III, 498.

41   Spence, *Observations*, I, 438.

42   Hobhouse (ed.), *Diary of a West Country Physician*, 38.

43   Whitefield, *Journals*, 143. Whitefield called sick-beds 'improving sights'. Cf. Mant, *The Order for the Visitation of the Sick*.

44   Gray (ed.), *Papers and Diaries of a York Family*, 67.
45   Christie (ed.), *Diary of William Jones*, 276.
46   Henry, *Life and Death of Philip Henry*, 42.
47   Beresford (ed.), *Diary of a Country Parson*.
48   Hack (ed.), *Christian Womanhood*, 89, Cf. Allen, *A Beloved Mother*, 34.
49   Toynbee and Whibley (eds), *Correspondence of Thomas Gray*, III, 482.
50   *Present for a Servant Maid*, 35.
51   [Martineau], *Life in the Sick-Room*, 30, 90, 197.
52   Chapman (ed.), *Letters of Samuel Johnson*, III, 118.
53   Devlin, *Superstitious Mind*, 43f.
54   Porter, *Health for Sale*.
55   Porter, 'Gift Relation'; Wilde, *Hospital*; White, *Record of My Life*, 85ff.
56   Barbeau, *Bath*; Schnorrenberg, 'Medical Men of Bath'; Neale, *Bath 1680–1850*.
57   Brockliss, 'Taking the Waters'.
58   Andrews (ed.), *Torrington Diaries*, I, 88. After a bad time at Cheltenham spa, Byng
     wrote, 'Cheltenham, I quit thee with pleasure, and hope never more to revisit thee!':
     I, 38.
59   J. R. Smith, *Speckled Monster*; Miller, *Adoption of Inoculation*; Zwanenberg, 'The
     Suttons and the Business of Inoculation'.
60   Compare Macfarlane, *Origins of English Individualism*.
61   Macdonald (ed.), *Letters of Eliza Pierce*, 89.
62   Loudon, *Medical Care and the General Practitioner*.
63   Buchan, *Observations on the Venereal Disease*, xviii.
64   Rosen, *From Medical Police to Social Medicine*; Porter and Porter, 'What Was Social
     Medicine?'.
65   Greig (ed.), *Farington Diary*, IV, 193n.

Chapter 12:
Creating Identity

Georgian culture thus recognized that the pains of sickness were, at bottom, intensely private. This chapter further explores the social construction of this interior experience. We have already examined the resources available to the sick: a lore of healthy living, maps of the body and its diseases, explanatory models giving physical causes and higher meanings for falling sick. We have seen, through individual cases, how those shattered by sickness responded.

Now we move to the deeper consequences of pain. We will assess how the experience of illness – acute or chronic – became integral to a sense of self and to interpersonal dynamics. Illness often defined both the scene of tears for life's drama and an individual's role in it.[1] Alexander Pope's phrase, 'this long disease my life', evokes just this dialectics of sickness and selfhood.[2]

Susan Sontag has deplored today's tendency to see sickness as a projection of the self.[3] The legacy of Freud, in such thinkers as Groddeck and Norman O. Brown, treats body styles, dysfunctions, and even diseases as embodiments of unconscious conflicts.[4] Wilhelm Reich viewed 'organic' sickness as the somatization of 'sick' personality traits and types.[5] We need not formally subscribe to such-like outlooks to accept their postulate that the dualistic notion of a person as an autonomous *cogito* chained to a purely biological body will not hold water. Self and soma are at least synergistically united, if not the same. Their mutual interplay, through experience, results in their mutual transformation.

But isn't it anachronistic to apply a (post-Freudian) dynamic interactionist model of embodied existence to earlier centuries? Far from it! For there is nothing essentially new in the notion that consciousness, character, and body form a trinity. After all, traditional humoral theory saw temperament, physique, and health all determined by the same fluctuating equilibrium of internal fluids, spirits, appetites, and 'souls'. Furthermore, when humoralism crumbled, it was replaced in Enlightenment England by Locke's theory of the person, which restated the synthesis of body and consciousness via the notions of sensation and the nervous system. In a way especially relevant here, Locke stressed that personality was made not born, was the factitious product of experience, and thus of habits developed from the *tabula rasa* of early childhood: beliefs, morals, value-systems, of course, but basic physical dispositions, such as bowel control, no less. The implied equivalence between shitting and thinking offended Swift and tickled Sterne but provided David Hume – as we shall see – with a springboard for philosophical scepticism, and a supple language for analysing the games psyche and soma play.[6] Lockians advanced highly interactionist views of the self as the product of its life-experiences.[7] Those accustomed to 'imagine' their own selves within such a tradition – and that means many well-educated, reflective Georgians – would be specially receptive to the view that sickness shaped the self, while, conversely, that everyone got the sicknesses they deserved.[8]

Two further brain-children of Lockian empiricism proved crucial in fixing such perceptions. One was the increasing importance accorded, from the late Enlightenment into the Romantic era, to sensibility.[9] Increasingly, the real hallmark of the superior person became his – or, in particular, *her* – capacity for exquisite feeling (while yet a teenager, Fanny Burney was known as '*feeling Fanny*').[10] This could take many forms; one, obviously, could be the ability to sustain and even nourish intense suffering, emotional or physical, to radiate as a man or woman of feeling. The sensitive soul was the suffering soul, and suffering was, after all, ennobling. Consider this affecting scene, sketched by Lady Jerningham in 1809, of her father at death's door:[11]

> Last Thursday, My Uncle Ed who appears very light and thoughtless, considering the present circumstances of things, went up to my Father's room after Dinner (he appeared a little elevated) but when he saw my Mother sitting by the bed side suffering with the gout, and his Brother lying as he does, silent and weak – he was suddenly so struck with the melancholy of the scene, that he burst into violent and loud weeping. Edward, who was in the outward room with Frederic, rushed in dreadfully alarmed supposing my Father was gone and that the screams came from my Mother. He dragged my Uncle out, who was in a perfect hysteric.

Perhaps Uncle Ed was subsequently overcome by what James Vere called the 'regret and reproach' of such finer souls, which created 'a sort of internal war, which divides the man against himself; and hence a large share of disquiet and restlessness will be the unavoidable consequence.'[12] Trembling with pain forged a particular socio-cultural identity.

The other cultural nuance was the tribute Lockians paid to imagination. 'Nothing is more full than the imagination of man', wrote Locke.[13] Modern scholarship has destroyed the Romantic and Victorian myth of the Georgians as so regimented by reason and facts as to be indifferent to imagination.[14] Assuredly, empiricism by no means wholly approved of the imagination unbound, which, unrestrained by judgement, would fly to misconceptions, delusions, sickness, and madness. But the sheer power of that associating and sympathetic faculty in shaping consciousness was generously acknowledged.

The result was a vision of the organism as prey to intense suggestibility: imagination could 'make you sick', but it could also make you better. 'I am not well to day', begins a not uncharacteristic letter from that mimosa, Mary Wollstonecraft, to William Godwin in late 1798, 'a lowness of spirits, which I cannot conquer, leaves me at the mercy of my imagination, and only painful recollections and expectations assail me.'[15] Many, such as the Scottish physician, John Moore, complained about epidemics of 'imaginary complaints', experienced by such suspects as the 'old lady [who] cannot dine with comfort till [the physician] has felt her pulse, looked at her tongue, and told her whether her chicken should be roasted or boiled.'[16]

Hypochondria

This delicacy, of course, crystallized in the figure of the hypochondriac. From Classical times to the turn of the eighteenth century, 'hypochondria' was primarily defined as a somatic abdominal disorder accompanied by a mystifying multiplicity of symptoms migrating around the body. Increasingly, however, these secondary syndromes moved stage-centre; emphasis switched to the non-specific pains, and their relations to the ever-fecund imagination. The hypochondriac mutated into the *malade imaginaire*.[17]

Clearly, hypochondria could be a joke, as in Peacock's creation, the morbid 'Mr Hippy' of Hypocon House.[18] Having the 'hyp' could be stigmatizing, implying at best that the sufferer's mind and body were all askew, at worst that he was indulging his feelings, even malingering. Whether or not the sufferer had a physical disease, he might have a mental one.[19] Hence, many waxed indignant were it suggested that their sufferings were, at bottom, merely hypochondriacal.

Hypochondriacs were thus ripe for sport, as those (as Dr Adair put it) 'sick by way of amusement, and melancholy to keep up their spirits'.[20] In the Victorian age, one of Charles Darwin's nieces was so badly smitten that she was[21]

always going away to rest, in case she might be tired later on in the day, or even the next day . . .. And when there were colds about she often wore a kind of gas-mask of her own invention. It was an ordinary wire kitchen strainer, stuffed with antiseptic cotton-wool, and tied on like a snout, with elastic over her ears. In this she would receive her visitors and discuss politics in a hollow voice out of her eucalyptus-scented seclusion.

Crabbe condemned valetudinarians of this ilk for their fantastical self-indulgence:[22]

Say ye, oppress'd by some fantastic woes,
Some jarring nerve that baffles your repose;

Who press the downy couch, while slaves advance
With timid eye, to read the distant glance;
Who with sad prayers the weary doctor tease,
To name the nameless ever-new disease.

Nevertheless, ridicule aside, the hypochondriac also became a figure of fascination, precisely because he represented that strange self, defined – perfected even – by sickness. There were plenty of self-confessed hypochondriacs. Boswell – no stranger himself! – went around collecting them. 'I should have mentioned', he wrote,[23]

> that one day last week I paid a visit to Lady Diana Beauclerk . . .. She was exceedingly agreeable; and she owned herself a true hypochondriac. She said she was sometimes quite miserable, and could paint nothing but what was hideous. She said she believed she should die mad, melancholy mad. Our conversation was fine raving.

Boswell's friend, Seward, also confessed the habit to him. When they breakfasted together, 'we hypochondrized mutually'.[24] And things, of course, had come to a pretty pass when doctors themselves turned hypochondriacs. Mrs Offley complained to Farington that the eminent Dr Reynolds 'talked more abt. Himself and His own complaints, than abt. His Patients'.[25]

What brought this situation about? Samuel Johnson grumbled that people had become too self-absorbed, too nervously introspective. This excited undue attention to trivia, convincing worriers that every least twinge required treatment. The result was habitual physicking, not least self-physicking, often by way of prophylaxis, reinforcing mental morbidity while weakening the body. 'Dr Taylor's nose fell a bleeding tonight', recorded Boswell:[26]

> He said it was because he had omitted four days to have himself blooded after a quarter of a year's interval. Dr. Johnson, who is a great physician, disapproved much of periodical bleeding. "For", said he, "you accustom yourself to an evacuation which Nature cannot perform of herself, and therefore she cannot help you, should you, from forgetfulness or any other cause, omit it; and you may be suddenly suffocated".

Such habitual brooding over health was doubly dangerous, it was argued, if the sufferer had a vivid imagination. Mandeville's *Treatise of the Hypochondriack and Hysterick Diseases* (1730) considered the fictional case of a man of leisure ('Misomedon') with nothing to do but dwell upon his aches and pains, and cursed with sufficient book-learning to be adept at fantasizing the effects of drugs and regimens upon his organs. Partly thanks to unscrupulous physicians and apothecaries, 'Misomedon's' entire life became a battle with 'diseases' which were initially purely imaginary, but which, in time, actually materialized, as needless physicking took its toll.[27] Some might scoff,

Mandeville argued, but hypochondria could be the death of people and deserved both sympathy and – here lay the Mandevillian paradox! – expert doctoring.

Hypochondria seemed epidemic. How had it come about? Doctors such as James McKittrick Adair tended to blame the laity for meddling with a matter – their health – upon which professional doctors alone could speak with authority. Far too many books were appearing in the 'Every Man his own Doctor' mould, which proferred that 'little learning' that was such a dangerous thing.[28] Ignorant self-examination (chid the doctors) led to groundless fears. Sickness-talk became almost obsessive. 'The mutual communication of their ailments is often a topic of conversation', complained Adair; 'the imagination frequently suggests a similarity of disease, though none such really exists.'[29] 'Lady and Gentlemen Doctors' preened themselves on their expertise, and the medicine bore emerged. Mrs Piozzi had to promise not to turn into the typical valetudinarian correspondent. 'My health is growing very bad, to be sure', she admitted to Johnson:[30]

> I will starve still more rigidly for a while, and watch myself carefully; but more than six months will I not bestow upon that subject; you shall not have in me a valetudinary correspondent, who is always writing such letters, that to read the labels tied on bottles by an apothecary's boy would be more eligible and amusing; nor will I live, like Flavia in Law's 'Serious Call', who spends half her time and money on herself, with sleeping draughts, and waking draughts, and cordials and broths . . . you will not suspect me of wearing blisters, and living wholly upon vegetables for sport . . . but if health is gone, and gone for ever, we will act as Zachary Pearce the famous bishop of Rochester did, when he lost the wife he loved so – call for one glass to the health of her who is departed, never more to return and so go quietly back to the usual duties of life, and forbear to mention her again from that time till the last day of it.

She was almost true to her word, but many correspondents lacked the bishop's nerve. One consequence, it was noted, was a growing tendency for every man to suppose his complaint unique, and to find a special name for it. The wise clinician, William Heberden, deplored this anarchic, sufferer-led linguistic fantasia characteristic of an age of sensibility:[31]

> The gout, formerly a regular but uncommon disease, which attacked only the external parts of persons advanced in years, has now become a constitutional indisposition, a juvenile complaint, torturing the patient in a thousand different forms . . . instead of the gout in the *feet* or *hands* we hear every day of the nervous gout, the gout of the *head*, and even the fatal gout in the *stomach*. No rank, age, or mode of life seems to be exempt from this fashionable enemy.

The very language of hypochondria proved volatile. The *Gentleman's Magazine* suggested that hypochondria was itself mutating rapidly:[32]

> Mr Stencastle having in his younger Days learnt something of Physick finds it of great Use to him among his good Neighbours in Northumberland. When, says he, I first dabbled in this Art, the old Distemper call'd Melancholy, was exchang'd for the Vapours, and afterwards for the Hypp, and at last took up the new current Appellation the Spleen, which it still retains tho' a learned Doctor of the West, in a little Tract he hath written, divides the Spleen and Vapours, not only into the Hypp, the Hyppos, and the Hypocons; but subdivides these Divisions into the markambles, the Moon palls, the Strong-Fives and the Hockogrokles.

Not content to talk itself into hitherto unheard-of conditions, fashionable society then had to cure itself with a proliferation of favourite reliefs, shop-bought nostrums, and family recipes, many of them powerful or poisonous. They installed medicine chests, swapped remedies ('we received your basket of medicines', Cowper thanked his poet friend, William Hayley),[33] and inaugurated daily self-dosing habits, downing purges, vomits, emulsions, infusions, juleps, and tonics. These, in turn, destroyed the stomach, producing serious side-effects, whose symptoms triggered further fears and medication.

Hypochondria was thus a dangerous malady in a culture that gave abundant opportunities for lay self-dosing. 'Your brother's complaint seems to me hypochondriasis', explained Erasmus Darwin to one of his patients:[34]

> It is very apt to last long and is but very little under the influence of medicine. He should endeavour as much as he can to amuse his mind among objects which are new and interesting & by travelling in foreign countries.

As thus implied, hypochondria was thought particularly obdurate, because the malady was (as it were) constitutional. 'No disease is more troublesome', pronounced Adair,[35]

> either to the Patient or Physician, than hypochondriac Disorders; and it often happens, that, thro' the Fault of both, the Cure is either unnecessarily protracted, or totally frustrated; for the Patients are so delighted, not only with a Variety of Medicines, but also of Physicians.

The difficulty was that hypochondria was largely immune to the interventions of the doctors. For as John Hill stressed: 'Though the physician can do something toward the cure, much more depends upon the patient; and here his constancy of mind will be employed most happily.'[36] Medicines could achieve little without a change of heart in the patient himself: 'But prior to the course of any medicine, and as an essential to any good hope from it, the patient must prescribe himself a proper course of life, and a well chosen diet.'[37] This was evident when Matthew Baillie was called in to treat Tom Wedgwood. Baillie responded:[38]

> In all chronic ill health, there is a great deal of sympathy or action & reaction between different parts of the system. As your disorder affects your mind, let your mind affect your disorder, try travelling, change of climate, & collect circumstances that amuse your mind . . .

Baillie attempted to wean the patient off doctors, for the doctor's intervention would, all too easily, merely bind him more securely in that dependence from which the hypochondriac needed to escape. Didn't the sufferer actually enjoy his condition? Consciously or not, the hypochondriac did not want to be cured at all. All in all, as John Hill emphasized, to overcome hypochondria, 'the patient must do a great deal for himself'.[39]

Perhaps the creation of this stereotype sounds like an artificial 'scare' launched by the medical profession, to excite morbid fears about hypochondria, blame the victims, and cash in upon a lucrative trade. Nevertheless, in a sensitivity-valuing culture, sufferers themselves needed little encouragement to spin dramas of their own health, making it their emotional lifeline. Shelley fits the lurid stereotype only too well.

Shelley had constant health worries. It is possible that the youthful poet picked up some kind of venereal infection while still at Eton, or, more likely, while a student at Oxford; perhaps he merely believed he did.[40] He consulted numerous doctors, following their prescriptions and regimens. But he also dosed himself heavily with violent drugs, including arsenic and vitriol.[41] The urge to purge himself of poisons and to recoup his constitution probably accounts for his switch to vegetarianism, and, at a later stage, to his travelling south.[42]

Energetic self-dosing produced serious and chronic side-effects, particularly in weakening his stomach.[43] He interpreted minor bodily changes, such as premature greying, as symptomatic of underlying venereal malady.[44] Over the years, he experienced increasing fatigue, listlessness, irritability, and depression – most probably exacerbated by his dread of premature decay.[45]

Shelley did not see himself as a *malade imaginaire*; nor did his friends level the accusation (contrast, say, Thomas Carlyle's circle, ever distrustful over his complaints).[46] Yet his absorption with his disintegrating health stirred that profound vision of disaster, degeneration, and death which watermarks his poetic philosophy.[47] The suspected venereal infection also coloured his ambivalence towards women, seen as exterminating angels.[48] Within Romanticism, disease contributed to a mythology of love, death, and blighted youth.[49]

If Shelley would have denied hypochondria, others owned it. James Boswell wrote his newspaper column under the pseudonym of 'The Hypochondriac'.[50] He had no great need to imagine ailments. His hangover headaches and biliousness were real enough, as were his twenty-odd doses of the clap and the urino-genitary condition that hastened his death.[51] Yet he was undoubtedly prone to wider health anxieties; he suffered guilt about indulging his sexual desires; and was eaten by a dread of death, which dissipation hardly held at bay. The profound gloom all these induced he called 'hypochondria', as endless diary entries record ('Friday 12 November [1784] . . . Was quite hypochondriac').[52] Boswell recognized that many of his fits of what he called 'the English malady' were psychological in origin.[53]

Why was Boswell so eager to don the hypochondriac mask? It was an identity that authorized him to hold forth on subjects such as death, suicide, drinking, and the like.[54] It also gratified a sense of self-importance, distinctiveness ('I'm a singular man'),[55] and indeed of élitism: 'We *Hypochondriacks* may console ourselves in the hour of gloomy distress, by thinking that our sufferings mark our superiority'.[56] Boswell liked to identify with great-souled melancholics. 'Read a good part of *Hamlet*', he wrote, 'to interest me in a melancholy character.'[57]

And yet he was not uncritical of this identity. Johnson repeatedly warned him against its egotism and presumption.[58] Cheyne's equation of nervous suffering with superiority was dangerous nonsense, a descent towards downright mental illness, even madness. 'Do not let him teach you a foolish notion that melancholy is a proof of acuteness', warned Johnson.[59] Boswell deflected these warnings, yet he acknowledged in print the dangers of luxuriating in morbid introspection.

Boswell's older contemporary, Thomas Gray, likewise built his persona as a poet upon a perception of frail health, seeing himself as one whose '*Verve*' did not 'stir out of its chamber above three days in a year'.[60] Gray celebrated a refined, eligible depression, while recognizing its dangers:[61]

> Mine, you are to know, is a white Melancholy, or rather Leucocholy for the most part; which though it seldom laughs or dances, nor ever amounts to what one calls Joy or Pleasure, yet is a good easy sort of a state, and *ca ne laisse que de s'amuser*. The only fault of it is insipidity; which is apt now and then to give a sort of Ennui.

Hinting at the contrast between white and black (good and bad) magic, Gray hoped to keep his melancholy 'white':[62]

> But there is another sort, black indeed, which I have now and then felt [which] excludes and shuts its eyes to the most possible hopes, and every thing that is pleasurable; from this the Lord deliver us! for none but he and sunshiny weather can do it.

Sickliness seemed the poet's stamp, and led to elegaic verse.

The hypochondriac thus represented one in whom being sick bred a sickly sensibility, pleasurable as a way of life. Others indulged precarious health in similar ways. One was the hysteric.[63] Often hypochondria and hysteria were represented as brother and sister. Hysteria had classically been defined as an authentic female somatic malady, a disease of the womb. The womb was traditionally believed to be mobile, hence capable of producing unpredictable symptoms all over the body. As it 'rose', it constricted the internal organs, finally producing the '*globus hystericus*' effect in the throat.

By the eighteenth century, the term was breaking free from its somatic and etymological moorings, being used to classify the volatile physical symptoms associated with hypersensitivity. This lability was believed especially common in women. But it was not exclusive to them – Joseph Farington reported how his friend, Hone, had 'been in a very nervous Hysterical state, the effect of anxiety of mind'.[64] In hybrid idioms such as 'hysteric cholic', the adjective signalled status superiority (top people couldn't be suffering from vulgar, common-or-garden, wind), while also marking a mysterious *je ne sais quoi* – something intermittent, unpredictable, without tangible physical cause, a disorder following not from specific lesions but from general indisposition.

Hypochondria and hysteria – alongside the vapours, spleen, biliousness, and the like – become part and parcel of the faddish language of 'nervous disease'.[65] The terms conveyed allure and mystique; a nervous condition was a prize bloom. 'My cough began to alarm me', Garrick told George Colman, 'a Nervous One.'[66] 'I have had a little nervous fever lately', confessed the ever-delicate William Cowper to Lady Hesketh, 'that has somewhat abridged my sleep . . . I feel my head lightish.' For relief, he took bark, Hoffman's compound, Daffy's Elixir, 'and now and then a very small quantity of Magnesia'.[67]

This 'coming-out' of the hypochondriac as a cultural type marks an important moment. It signals a stage in medicine itself, with lay desires generating a medical consumerism integral to the wider development of market society. But it also had deeper cultural affinities. Polite society encouraged social individualism. People in the fast lane were expected to be different, special, interesting, prima donna-ish, albeit within the permitted degrees of conventional polish. Yet such a freedom exacted its price. The tensions between individual brilliance and polite conformity bred anxieties, in turn somatized into physical complaints, which could be partly owned and partly disowned. Sickliness provides social alibis while suffering purchased the right to be different, to be oneself. Pain commanded a certain social bargaining power.[68]

And yet not without ambiguities. For the valetudinarian, as we have seen, by no means met universal sympathy. 'My Sister Pounsett poorly, is continually complaining and does not bear up against it at all, but gives way to her Disorder, which is nervous': Woodforde's sting in the tail is quite clear.[69] Indeed, there was widespread hostility towards the practice of resorting to 'illness' for attention. William Law painted a portrait of one such, the character 'Caelia', in a book to which we have already seen Mrs Piozzi referring:[70]

When Cross accidents have so disordered her spirits that she is forced to send for a doctor to make her able to eat, she tells him in great anger at Providence that she never was well since she was born, and that she envies every beggar that she sees in health.

We have argued that a new language was popularized in the eighteenth century registering a heightened interplay of self and sickness, and thereby enculturing sickness. Sickness, in certain of its modes, became eligible. As James McKittrick Adair put it, 'people of fashion claim an exclusive privilege of having always something to complain of.'[71]

The remainder of this chapter will explore nuances of these developments as they appeared in particular sufferers. These are all, in their various ways, studies of 'the sick role', i.e., that conscious or unconscious psychological strategy and social permission according to the sick a package of responsibilities and privileges: disabling them (temporarily at least) from normal life; exempting them from responsibilities, and granting them immunities.[72] Playing the sick role made its mark – indeed, generally took its toll – upon the self. Thus George Crabbe remarked upon 'the engrossing Selfishness of pain', while Samuel Johnson insisted, 'Disease produces much selfishness; a man in pain is looking after ease, and lets most other things go, as chance shall dispose them'.[73] Sickness as a catalyst for personality change is our concern.

David Hume and the Nervous Breakdown
If anyone should have a mind immune to, and soaring above, the toils of the body, surely it must be the philosopher. After all, hadn't the very act of philosophizing, in the Stoic great tradition from Marcus Aurelius onwards, been the declaration of rational independence, the quest for true 'apathy'? What, then, happens to a philosopher who falls sick in such a way as not to liberate, but to disorient, his mind.

In his late twenties, the Scotsman David Hume – already recognized for intellectual talent and philosophical promise – slithered into a career crisis. He abandoned the legal studies, full of security, into which he had been channelled, and launched on to the troubled waters of philosophy. For a while, he studied at fever-pitch, but then succumbed to fatigue and ennui: 'I could no longer raise my Mind to that pitch, which formerly gave me such excessive Pleasure'.[74]

He tried to work, but by the Spring of 1730 was experiencing severe physical and mental pains. He grew rawboned and looked consumptive, and developed a scorbutic condition of the skin. He was inclined to blame his studies for his sickness, for he had plunged into the philosophy of the Ancients, and this, being abstract and metaphysical, had entrapped him in the suggestive fantasies of the imagination. Not least, those doughty 'Reflections against Death, & Poverty, & Shame & Pain', which he read amongst the Stoics, had the clean contrary effect on him; for far from enabling him to transcend his malaise, they merely accentuated the fact that he was sick.[75] All this time, he was wrestling with his daring experimental science of the self, abandoning the philosophy of first principles and *a priori* reason for the unremitting examination of every scratch of sensation upon the consciousness, under a ruthless and sceptical honesty – studies that were to lead to the *Treatise of Human Nature*.

Hume grew both physically and mentally disordered. He was unwilling to believe his condition was purely in the head, due, say, to 'vapours'; for that would have implied a disturbing loss of self-control. He surmised something organic was amiss, and a physician 'prescribed anti-scorbutic juices'. These, however, were only partly successful, and the doctor was not deceived: 'he laught at me, & told me I was now a Brother, for that I had fairly got the Disease of the Learned.' He was prescribed 'a Course of Bitters, & Anti-hysteric Pills', claret, and riding. His nerves and spirits needed reinvigorating.[76]

Over eighteen months, Hume's health went up and down. A regime demanding moderation and balance seemed beneficial:[77]

I now began to take some Indulgence to myself; studied moderately, & only when I found my Spirits at their highest Pitch, leaving off before I was weary, & trifling away the rest of my Time in the best manner I could. In this way, I liv'd with Satisfaction enough; and on my return to Town next Winter found my Spirits very much recruited, so that, tho they sunk under me in the higher Flights of Genius, yet I was able to make considerable Progress in my former Designs. I was very regular in my Diet & way of Life from the beginning, & all that Winter, made it a constant Rule to ride twice or thrice a week, & walk every day. For these Reasons, I expected when I return'd to the Countrey, & cou'd renew my Exercise with less Interruption, that I wou'd perfectly recover.

But he was wrong. In May 1731, he began to suffer from palpitations and wind, and rode out daily to a spa. He found concentration difficult and lacked stamina. Conscious of fatigue, he could work only with frequent diversions. Still he wished to believe it was no authentic – or, indeed, no *mere* – personality disorder, for that would have implied either mental disorder or malingering. He saw it as rather due to organic 'weakness' than to 'lowness of spirits'.[78]

This was a comforting excuse, yet he could not disguise that his condition had some psychic tinge. The best parallel to his condition, Hume noted, lay in the strange sicknesses of religious mystics:[79]

I have notic'd in the Writings of the French Mysticks, & in those of our Fanatics here, that, when they give a History of the Situation of their Souls, they mention a Coldness and Desertion of the Spirit, which frequently returns, & some of them, at the beginning, have been tormented with it many Years. As this kind of Devotion depends entirely on the Force of Passion, & consequently of the Animal Spirits, I have often thought that their Case & mine were pretty parallel, & that their rapturous Admirations might discompose the Fabric of the Nerves & Brain, as much as profound Reflections, & that warmth or Enthusiasm, which is inseparable from them.

Hume thus paints a self-deprecating portrait of the philosopher as a young enthusiast. He can hardly have felt flattered by his fate.

He was in a cleft stick. Study prostrated him, but an easy life left him down. By 1734, he had had enough. 'I began to rouze up myself; & being encourag'd by Instances of Recovery from worse degrees of this Distemper, as well as by the Assurances of my Physicians, I began to think of something more effectual, than I had hitherto try'd.'[80] His recourse was to open the history of his complaints in a long, and profoundly revealing letter to a physician. He states in this letter that it will be anonymous. There is no certainty to whom it was addressed, though it may have been either George Cheyne, the great expert on such maladies, or John Arbuthnot, both London-domiciled Scotsmen. Hume poured forth his troubles.[81]

Was the letter ever sent? Probably not. It is at least possible that the very act of composing it composed his malady – indeed, was *intended* to do so – allowing Hume, through taking his own 'history', to master his condition. Thus, he may have effected a kind of self-cure, using the 'doctor' as a surrogate, and discovering in the process the true power of mind over matter – not in the Stoic sense of detached mastery, but through the psychology of 'belief'. Hume found himself, and thereafter managed his temper perfectly, enjoying sunny health through the remainder of his career.

Arguably this acutely self-monitored sickness episode was critical in shaping Hume's philosophical temper and credo. For it was living proof of the frailty of pure reason, a demonstration of the all-pervasive anthropomorphism – indeed, somatomorphism – of consciousness: thinking could not divorce itself from sensation, and sensation was rooted in the body. Nervous collapse surely convinced Hume that his own special philosophical project – to delve into sensations to resolve the problem of identity – entailed the kind of morbid introspection that was making him sick. Philosophy was autobiography.

Yet, out of his sickness he emerged a new breed of philosopher, in ways notably paralleled nearly a century later in the outcome of John Stuart Mill's nervous breakdown, which transformed a scientific utilitarian into a libertarian individualist.[82] Those who wallowed in morbid introspection remained religious enthusiasts; understanding and overcoming the condition led to Humean philosophy.

Harriet Martineau

Hume's inquiry into human nature was profoundly shaped by having to master a single particularly perplexing bout of sickness – nothing life-threatening, but an experience precipitating anxiety about the springs of belief and action. A century later, the philosophy of Harriet Martineau (1802–76), political economist and essayist, evolved through the pressure of successive episodes of incapacity. Struggling with sickness, she ploughed her own lonely furrow, aiming at independence and self-definition. Hers was a very personal experience, yet it also drew upon a highly conventional Victorian conception of suffering as the seedbed of personal development and the emancipator of the self. The 'pains and penalties of life', she argued, had an 'intimate connexion with the formation of character.'[83]

Autobiography must be the spring of such an outlook on life, and sickness is woven into the very fabric of hers. Martineau wrote her life in her early fifties, convinced by her physicians that she was suffering from an incurable heart complaint that might at any time prove fatal. Writing under this death sentence, she composed the testament of one who had found herself through illness.

Sickness impinged upon her in two main formative phases. One was her early childhood spent amongst strict and respectable Unitarians, first in Norfolk, then in the North-East. Even her earliest days had been soured by illness, due, she recalled, to a negligent wet-nurse who had no milk. She grew up sick, ugly, and awkward. She recollected little affection from her parents ('no body cared for me');[84] childhood was a 'bondage',[85] for 'never did pass a day without crying'.[86] To cope with isolation and desolation, she took refuge in the stern stoical philosophy which her elders and betters intoned at her, and she echoed back, sanctimoniously telling others 'never ky for tyfles'.[87] 'Fortitude' became 'my favourite virtue'; the lonely girl contemplated death and planned an infant suicide (aware, she tells us, it would be an act of vengeance), and admired the Christian martyrs, because their sufferings had assumed such triumphal meaning.[88] With a compliant friend, she would play at being dead, creeping into a hole in the ground and lying doggo.[89] She gloried in her trials:[90]

> My youthful vanity took the direction which might be expected in the case of a pious child. I was patient in illness and pain because I was proud of distinction, and of being taken into such special pupilage by God; and I hoped for, and expected early death till it was too late to die early.

What made her singularity so stark was her progressive deafness. Adults would not believe it was real; 'none so deaf', her parents rebuked, 'as those that won't hear.'[91] So she became known as obstinate. But deafness enabled her to be a Robinson Crusoe of the interior, free from the petty goings-on all around, while also legitimating escape into solitude. Deafness brought shame, not guilt.[92] 'Deafness is about the best thing that ever happened to me.'[93]

Thus, childhood sickness thrust her back upon herself. Harriet grew up with a blend of independence and fortitude that proved her lifeline. To recruit her health, she was, fortunately, sent away from home. On her father's death, family poverty then required her to return, to work at home, writing for a living. This proved a further emancipation, from what would otherwise have been an empty life, genteel idleness. The strains of writing while looking after her mother and elderly aunt proved taxing, however. She developed agonizing internal pains, which she attributed to emotional anxiety.[94] 'Of pain of body and mind it was truly a terrible year', was her recollection of being twenty-five.[95]

Her friends advised that her malady stemmed from overwork and stress. Work and writing, she countered, were tonics. In her eyes, intellectual work should not be romanticized as an activity requiring inspired genius or, even worse, such artificial stimulants as coffee, alcohol, or opium. A physician pressed her to keep a bottle by her side as she wrote.[96] Pernicious prescription! The pains of composition were best overcome by discipline and grit, not sloppy self-indulgence with its mythology of writer's block. Thus, a writing career was raised upon the foundations of independence laid by childhood sickness and deafness.

In 1838, Harriet fell seriously sick, as a result, she interpreted it, of the strains of coping with her mother.[97] Drawing upon the thoroughly psycho-somatic medical lore of the day, she concluded 'a tumour was forming of a kind which usually originates in mental suffering' (her doctors diagnosed an ovarian cyst).[98] After being tended by relatives, she decamped to live on her own – bar a maid – in a lodging-house in Tynemouth, where she lay on her bed for five years.

While prostrate, Harriet framed her thoughts on being sick. Between September and November 1843, she wrote them down, publishing them in an anonymous volume titled *Life in the Sick-Room*, aiming to be 'a sort of pioneer in the regions of pain'.[99]

The *Life* told readers to think positively about pain. It was the duty of a patient – above all, a Christian – to face illness squarely as a trial of life. Sickness would prove the parent of honesty. The ultimate realities – pain, suffering, and death – should strip the normal defences, evasions, and hypocrisies: 'everything but truth becomes loathed in a sick-room'. Thus, illness stimulated that candour, that earnestness, which animated Harriet's ideals. Moreover, it would also train up true individualism. For it forced the sufferer back upon his mental and spiritual resources.

Above all, it provided confirmation of the ultimate sovereignty of the spirit. Harriet conceived of suffering as probation, a minor martyrdom. The greater the pain suffered by the flesh, the more assured the reality of the spirit: 'It may look like a paradox to say that a condition of permanent pain is that which, above all, proves to one the transient nature of pain; but this is what I do affirm, and can testify.'[100] Thus, illness was ennobling, uplifting, instructive, useful. It built character.[101]

After five years of prostration with her 'tumour', Harriet felt better and resumed a normal life. She owed her recovery, she claimed, not to the ministrations of the doctors but to undergoing mesmeric therapy on her own initiative (much to the derision of the medical profession). Thus, sickness proved a positive experience, and health was regained through self-help.[102]

Thereafter she herself practised mesmeric healing.[103]

At long last, she believed, 'I had got out of the prison of my own self.'[104] Having confronted dying, she was ready to live.[105] Her early life had been a 'winter'; now she could enjoy its late summer and autumn.

When the autobiographer looked back upon the self who had penned the *Life in the Sick-Room*, she knew how far she had travelled in a decade and a half. For the intervening years, and the subsequent 'fatal' heart complaint, served to emancipate her from the mawkish celebration of pain and dying which her earlier Christian creed had inculcated. She had become a Positivist and a free-thinker, disparaging her earlier rapture over sickness as a morbidity which had cloaked, but not dispelled, a fear of living:[106]

> Tracts and religious books swarm among us, and are thrust into the hands of every body else, which describe the sufferings of illness, and generate vanity and egotism about bodily pain and early death, rendering these disgraces of our ignorance and barbarism attractive to the foolish and the vain, and actually shaming the wholesome, natural desire for a 'sound mind in a sound body'.

Luxuriating upon sickness had been so much time wasted.[107] It was culpable egoism to cocoon oneself in one's own petty complaints; rather one must give oneself to life as a cosmic whole, a system of necessary natural laws animating all.[108]

Thus sickness once made Harriet make sense of herself in Christian terms: life was a cross one should be proud to bear. But it then led her to reject what she subsequently regarded as its mawkish cult of suffering and its degenerate emotionality about death. In the *Autobiography*, she explained her patient's progress in a discussion worth quoting at length:[109]

> I am aware that the religious world, proud of its Christian faith as the 'Worship of Sorrow,' thinks it a duty and a privilege to dwell on the morbid conditions of human life; but my experience of wide extremes of health and sickness, of happiness and misery, leads me to a very different conclusion. For pathological purposes, there must be a study of morbid conditions; but that the study should be general, – that it should be enforced as a duty, and held up as a pleasure – seems to me one of those mistakes in morals which are aggravated and protracted by the mischievous influence of superstition.

Here, she was coming quite close to indicating her own earlier writings amongst those 'mistakes' tainted by 'superstition'.[110]

> The Christian superstition, now at last giving way before science, of the contemptible nature of the body, and its antagonism to the soul, has shockingly perverted our morals, as well as injured the health of

Christendom and every book, tract, and narrative which sets forth a
sick-room as a condition of honour, blessing and moral safety, helps to
sustain a delusion and corruption which have already cost the world too
dear.

This great champion of honesty was, at least, honest enough to admit to her
own former heresies:[111]

> I know too much of all this from my own experience to choose to do any
> thing towards encouragement of the morbid appetite for pathological
> contemplation, – physical or moral . . . It is grievous to me now to think
> what an amount of time and thought I have wasted in thinking of dying,
> – really believing as I did for many years that life was a mere preparation
> for dying: and now, after a pretty long life, when I find myself really
> about to die, the event seems to me so simple, natural, and, as I may say,
> negative in comparison with life and its interests, that I cannot but
> marvel at the quantity of attention and solicitude I lavished upon it while
> it was yet so far off as to require no attention at all. To think no more of
> death than is necessary for the winding up of the business of life, and to
> dwell no more upon sickness than is necessary for its treatment, or to
> learn to prevent it, seems to me the simple wisdom of the case, – totally
> opposite as this is to the sentiment and method of the religious world.

Writing this in 1855, Martineau expected to die very soon (in fact, she had a
further twenty years to run).[112] She disclaimed all the fancy wrapping in which
Christianity mystified death; she could now face its certainty with
equanimity:[113]

> When I learned what my state is, it was my wish (as far as I wish
> anything, which is indeed very slightly and superficially) that my death
> might take place before long, and by the quicker process . . . I do not
> want to deteriorate and get spoiled in the final stage of my life, be ceasing
> to hear the truth, and the whole truth: . . . I should wish, as she knows,
> to live under complete and healthy moral conditions to the last.

Whether or not the *body* was healthy, it was thus vital that 'healthy' *attitudes*
triumph over morbid ones. Above all, she now felt finally emancipated, by
once again facing death, from her earlier immature attitudes:[114]

> I have now had three months' experience of the fact of constant
> expectation of death: and the result is, as much regret as a rational
> person can admit at the absurd waste of time, thought, and energy that I
> have been guilty of in the course of my life in dwelling on the subject of
> death . . . I romanced internally about early death till it was too late to
> die early; and, even in the midst of work and the busiest engagements of

my life, I used to be always thinking about death, – partly from taste, and partly as a duty. And now that I am waiting it at any hour, the whole thing seems so easy, simple and natural that I cannot but wonder how I could keep my thoughts fixed upon it when it was far off.

Harriet Martineau possessed that intuitive grasp of our unacknowledged motives common to the pre-Freudians. We could well say she 'used' sickness to great effect; she might have admitted it served her well. Early invalidism – deafness, in particular – provided her with the perfect guilt-free escape from the dreaded trivial round: here she was of a piece with Elizabeth Barrett, Florence Nightingale, and the other classic female invalids. It also spared her from men, marriage, and children – all lethal to a self-defining career. But if illness liberated her, she went on to liberate herself, in due course, from illness. Harriet Martineau schooled herself through sickness.

Sickness Culture as Addiction: Coleridge
In the introductory section of this chapter, we sketched how sickness became implanted in Georgian culture, directing attention to the extreme case of the hypochondriac. Faced with what Samuel Johnson called the 'choice of life', some found the 'sick role' so eligible as to play it not, like most, for brief periods, but as their star part.

The two examples just analysed show intellectuals with a needle-sharp awareness of how the course of their lives involved adjusting to the threats sickness posed to their well-being, survival even. What has come down to us of the consciousness of David Hume and Harriet Martineau – and that is, of course, carefully 'doctored' – shows individuals tossed upon the stormy waters of sickness eventually attaining the bank of health, and seeing the world anew from that vantage-point.

Many sufferers underwent a different crisis. They adopted – or found themselves engulfed in – a life-course, the effect, though not the intention, of which was chronic suffering. There was, of course, nothing whatsoever new about people neglecting their well-being, drinking or eating themselves to death. What many thought was novel in the Georgian age was the growing tendency of people to *medicate* themselves into a decline or even death; or at least to consume a newly-available cornucopia of *soi-disant* stimulants and pain-killers to relieve their distempers, only to become habituated to their use, with the direst consequences. The century is seminal for both the perception, and the actuality, of addiction.

Mainstream traditional Christian Humanist values asserted the ideal of free will, ontologically undetermined by physical reality, external or internal. Many currents in Enlightenment culture – its scientific bent, its sentimentalism, its sociological claims – by contrast encourage the paradigm of the *determined* self: he who is passive, the patient. Any *philosophe* would have agreed with Marx that although man makes his own history, he does not do it under conditions of his own making.[115] This notion of man creating himself, and *thereby* determining his future, was well expressed by the physician, Thomas Trotter:[116]

> For as the ambition or ingenuity of man finds out for him new employ-
> ments; these, while they draw forth latent talents, call forth also new
> passions and desires: so that however much he may be styled the *creature
> of habit*, he is in many respects the *creator* of his own *temperament*.

Product no less than producer, man was the result of all the stimuli surrounding and determining him, and, via the physical senses, consciousness was itself a consequence no less than a cause. Utilitarianism proclaimed pleasures and pains were infinitely manipulable. Medicine, broadly understood as one of the 'extensions' of man, had it within its power to deploy substances to quell pain and induce pleasure.

Moreover, with the mobilization of the market society, Georgian man also increasingly became a consumer. More made-up goods were more readily, more cheaply, available. Every economic index confirms the voice of apologists and Jeremiahs alike that consumption was rapidly rising of a whole range of substances – tea, coffee, tobacco, sugar, ardent spirits (especially cheap gin between the 1730s and the 1750s), fortified liquors (above all, port and brandy), bitters, tonics, quack, patent and proprietary medicines, and so forth – all of which were widely believed to be at best deleterious, at worst, poisonous and destructive. In many nostrums, the alcohol or narcotic content was high. Man the consumer was thus prey to the diseases of civilization earlier discussed.[117]

Hard-drinking was endemic. Farington told the chilling story of the drunkard wife of a certain Hodges:[118]

> He then told me His wife was in a very bad way; that she drank, &
> finding that the habit *was inveterate in Her, He had given orders to supply
> her with as much liquor as she requested.* – This the Doctor disapproved, &
> calling upon Hodges the next day had farther conversations with Him
> respecting it. On His conduct being condemned Hodges became warm
> & insisted that Gretton should see Her & He took Him to Her Bedside &
> addressing Her said 'Lydia, do you know who this?' – She took little
> notice, and only said 'Umpgh' and then put Her hand to a pot & drank. –
> This the Doctor said was *Brandy* which was supplied as often as wanted.
> The next morning she died.

Drink, of course, had always been the death of people. The Georgian age, however, is spectacular for its growing use of opium and its derivatives, often in vast quantities. Some opiate use in Georgian England was recreational. Philip Thicknesse, a confirmed user, valued its mood-influencing efforts as well as needing to deaden the pain of the stone. Somewhat later, the circles around Thomas Beddoes, Humphry Davy, and Coleridge were eager to experiment with all sorts of narcotics, from nitrous oxide (laughing gas) to opiates. Tom Wedgwood – Lamb called him 'an amateur in narcotics' – swapped drugs and experiences with Coleridge, who obtained drugs through John Wordsworth, the poet's sea-captain brother. 'We will have a fair trial of Bang', Coleridge avowed to Tom on one occasion, 'Do bring down some of the Hyoscyamine pills, and I will give a fair trial of Opium, Henbane, and Nepenthe.'[119] Wedgwood often attempted to ween himself off the drug but to no avail:[120]

> I am very low at present [he wrote] having had constant fever & headache since I have been here & have lost 4lbs. of flesh. This is the third attempt I have lately made to reduce my opium. I cannot do it – my spirits become dreadful – the dullness of my life is absolutely unsupportable without it.

Yet the opium habit was predominantly medicinal in origin. As Thomas De Quincey stressed, 'it was not for the purpose of creating pleasure, but of mitigating pain in the severest degree, that I first began to use opium as an article of daily diet.'[121] Tom Wedgwood's addiction began with his treatment by Erasmus Darwin, who, to rectify his nervous troubles and his consumptive tendency, recommended 'About five grains of rhubarb, and 3/4 of a grain, or a grain, of opium, taken every night for many months, perhaps during the whole winter.'[122] The reason was simple. Opiates were by far the most effective pain-killers. It is debatable whether the 'age of feeling' had a lower pain threshold than previous centuries;[123] what is clear is that the Georgians eagerly seized upon opiates for their anaesthetizing properties. George Cheyne praised the poppy to the skies:[124]

> Providence has been kind and gracious to us beyond all Expression, in furnishing us with a certain *Relief*, if not a Remedy, even to our most *intense Pains* and *extreme Miseries*. When our Patience can hold out no longer, and our Pains are at last come to be *insupportable*, we have always ready at Hand a Medicine, which is not only a present Relief, but, I may say, a standing and *constant Miracle*.

Doctors had but a dim awareness of the possible harmful consequences – Sir Richard Blackmore specifically discounted addiction – and hence prescribed freely. Erasmus Darwin tells the 'true story' of the fate of his own first wife, Mary, who succumbed to a combination of alcohol and opiates (which he himself surely prescribed):[125]

> She was siezed with pain on the right side about the lower edge of the liver, this pain was follow'd in about an hour by violent convulsions, and these sometimes relieved by great doses of opium, which induced intoxication.

Presumably this sufficed to induce a long-term disposition, leading to fatal consequences:[126]

> This kind of disease had several returns in the course of 4 or 6 years and she then took to drinking spirit and water to relieve the pain, and I found (when it was too late) that she had done this in great quantity, the liver became swelled and she gradually sunk.

Dozens of eminent Georgians were notorious in their own day for their heavy and habitual recourse to narcotics (often combined with alcohol), to ward off the pains of illness and the tribulations of life. Robert Clive, Samuel Johnson's wife, Tetty,[127] Johnson's close friend, Topham Beauclerc,[128] the Scottish natural philosopher, John Robison,[129] William Wilberforce, and William Gladstone's sister, Helen,[130] and to various degrees most of Tennyson's brothers,[131] are all well-recorded cases of those whose habit either wrecked their lives, or (in some cases) kept them going in the face of great pain.

Pessimists argued that the English, indulging in affluent consumerism, were enslaving themselves to stimulants. Tell-tale evidence of this, confirmed Cheyne, lay in the pattern whereby powerful substances, once primarily medicines, taken at the physicians' direction, had become items of everyday consumption, indeed household necessities:[132]

> Strong Liquors were never designed for common Use: They were formerly kept (here in *England*) as other Medicines are, in *Apothecaries Shops* and prescribed by *Physicians*, as they do *Diascordium* and *Venice Treacle*; to refresh the *Weary*, to strengthen the *Weak*, to give Courage to the *Faint-hearted* and raise the Low-spirited. And it were as just and reasonable, to see Men (and, if they go on, it is not impossible I may hear of it, since *Laudanum* is already taken into *Feasts* and *Entertainments*) sit down to a Dish of *Venice Treacle* or Sir *Walter Raleigh's Confection*, with a Bottle of *Hysteric Cordial*, as to a Dish of *Crawfish Soop*, and *Ox Cheek*, or *Venison Pasty*, with a Bottle of *Hermitage*, or *Tockay*, or, which some prefer to either of them, a Bowl of PUNCH.

Such a fear was articulated most fully by Thomas Trotter in his *View of the Nervous Temperament*. Trotter claimed that high-stress city life weakened the nerves; the constitution then needed the artificial support of drugs and stimulants, creating a treadmill of deteriorating health. Proof of this process lay in the fact that coffee, tea, tobacco, etc., had once been used as medicines, but had become reduced to 'necessities'; the same had recently happened to soda water ('a medicine converted into a tavern beverage').[133] The problem was greatly exacerbated by dosing with proprietary medicines stowed in the family medicine chest. Trotter thought self-medication a menace. Dr James's Fever Powders, for example, were abused, because people started swallowing them as preventives.[134]

At the time that James's Powders were in general use, and when families were in the practice of taking medicine as a preventive of fever, at stated periods, weakness of stomach and indigestion were often traced to this cause.

Overall, Trotter pessimistically surveyed a 'nervous society' in the making – a drugging culture, in which the mental habits of civilization itself became a disease:[135]

All nervous persons are uncommonly fond of drugs; and they are the chief consumers of advertised remedies, which they conceal from their medical friends. Among some well-meaning people, this inordinate desire for medicine has frequently become of itself a disease.

Under such conditions, the putatively clear distinction between disease and medicine broke down. Medicating habits became sources of pain, and the craving for artificial regulators of sensation was viewed (as Trotter saw it) as a form of 'disease of the mind'. Cases appeared whose consciousness was defined by self-spun cocoons of sensation-creating and sensation-killing narcotics.

Samuel Taylor Coleridge blighted his life through such a habit. That prophet of mental autonomy gradually enslaved himself, and thus became the walking contradiction of his own philosophy, before finally undergoing rescue. He somatized the Christian process of spiritual perdition and salvation.

Coleridge's opium habits were no secret, and for many he became a bogey figure, a symbol of moral weakness. Not surprisingly, Harriet Martineau, so insistent upon defining self against sickness, did not approve. 'If Coleridge should be remembered, it will be as a warning.'[136]

Coleridge was the superfine sensibility seeking sensation. His ache for experiments towards the better life – morally, spiritually, artistically, politically, physically – precipitated him to indulge in narcotic substances, inducing a bondage of opium-addiction, or what he termed 'the desire of a desire'.[137] Through habituation, sickness appropriated the self, and once the self succumbed, salvation had to supervene through the agency of the doctor.[138]

Coleridge perhaps first made medicinal use of opium while still a pupil at Christ's Hospital; he certainly took large quantities for rheumatic fever in 1791 while a student at Jesus College, Cambridge. He probably graduated to using it for pleasure during the 1790s, unaware of, or oblivious to, its side-effects; he records sweet dreams and feelings of release:[139] 'Thou has the keys of Paradise, O just, subtle, and mighty opium!'

Yet the young poet was soon to feel the pains of opium too – undergoing that terrible epiphany experienced later by De Quincey:[140]

Farewell, a long farewell to happiness . . . Farewell to smiles and laughter! farewell to peace of mind, to tranquil dreams, and to the blessed consolation of sleep! . . . Here opens upon me an Iliad of woes: for now I enter upon THE PAINS OF OPIUM.

Coleridge seems to have begun substantial opium consumption on a regular basis from around 1801, soon after he discovered a potent, opium-based, propietary medicine, Kendal Black Drop. He initially dosed himself to quell neuralgia, associated with 'gout' and nervous shooting pains in the knees and head, unable to bear the agonies these complaints produced on what Davy was to call his 'excessive sensibility'.[141]

Coleridge's dosing brought its own emotional and physical sequelae. His letters of the early 1800s testify to appalling insomnia – Coleridge feared sleep, since his nightmares were intolerable. Above all, a paralysing dread of death seized him. Organically, the habit led to 'the weakly Bowels of Disease' – the chronic constipation typical of opium.[142] Drugging also ruined his digestion; he could keep the opium down only by first settling his stomach with tumblers of brandy. Many other stimulants, including ginger, camphor, and rhubarb, were required to counter the constipation.[143] Letter after letter bears sad witness to the shipwreck of his health:[144]

street-damp struck up from my Shoes to my Bowels, and passed like a poison-flash thro' my nervous system – A violent Inflamation of the Bowels ensued, the Stomach became inflamed by Sympathy, and for four and twenty hours I suffered from acrid scalding evacuations, and if possible worse Vomitings (for the latter were accompanied with more than mere bodily torture) as much suffering as could well, I think, be compressed into that space of Time. – At length Symptoms of Convulsion threatened me.

While affirming that 'my state of Health is a Riddle',[145] Coleridge continued to convince himself that his maladies were essentially organic (Wordsworth, by contrast, was, he thought, an arrant hypochondriac). He insisted to his wife that he used opium purely medicinally, to counter 'the exquisite Affectibility of my Skin, & the instant sympathy of my Stomach and mesenteries with the Affections of the Skin':[146]

– & once in the 24 hours (but not always at the same hour) I take half a grain of purified opium, equal to 12 drops of Laudanum – which is not more than [an] 8th part of what I took at Keswick, exclusively of B[eer,] Brandy, & Tea, which last is undoubtedly a pernicious S[timulant –] all which I have left off – & will give this Regimen a *fair, compleat* Trial of the month . . .. But I am fully convinced, & so is T. Wedgwood, that to a person, with such a Stomach & Bowels as mine, if any stimulus is needful, Opium in the small quantities, I now take it, is incomparably better in every respect better than Beer, Wine, Spirits, or any *fermented Liquor* – nay, far less pernicious than even Tea.

This convoluted vindication concluded with a pathetic coda asking after the health of his sons: *'It is my particular Wish, that Hartley & Derwent should have as little Tea as possible – & always very weak, with more than half milk.'*

During his thirties, Coleridge's frequent bouts of sickness and deepening addiction began to stamp themselves upon his consciousness. On the one hand, he continued to exonerate himself: opium was purely a medicament. On the other, wracked by 'loneliness, continued Pain, accessory Irritations, and a sense of morbid Despondency', he increasingly became the man of sorrows, victim and martyr – indeed, the Ancient Mariner – destined for 'self suffering', an innocent destroyed.[147] Eventually his agonies grew unbearable:[148]

> For many weeks with only two Intervals, and those but day-long, I have been ill – very ill – confined mostly to my Bed, altogether to my bedroom. In my pain I earnestly wish to die – and in my best hours the only odour of Hope, that remains at the bottom of my Pandora Casket, is a relaxation of that wish – a passiveness of Life – the continuance of which to any useful purpose I have as little reason to expect, as, for any pleasurable end, to desire.

Thus, unlike most people analysed in this book, Coleridge did not seek to transcend, and distance himself from, his physical sufferings by recourse to religion or philosophy. He lived them out, at the nerve-ends. Yet he also remained acutely self-aware, and, no less importantly, guilt-ridden, about the self-indulgence of the suffering soul, who had trespassed so greedily upon the goodwill of friends and family alike. From about 1808, he began to force himself to confront a self that was sick. Long-deteriorating health made this urgent:[149]

> I have been very ill during the whole Week – For seven days I have had no passage from my Bowels, tho' night after night I have taken strong aperient medicines . . . . I am in hopes therefore, that the obstruction, wherever it may be, or perhaps inflammation, is on it's departure – It has happened very unluc[kily].

At last he acknowledged openly the damaging effects of 'that accursed drug', into which he had been 'seduced' by 'the Horrors of Sleep' and 'the Dread of sudden Death'.[150] He continued, nevertheless, to insist that he had taken it up purely for medicinal reasons:[151]

> I was seduced into the ACCURSED Habit ignorantly. – I have been almost bed-ridden for many months with swellings in my knees – in a medical Journal I unhappily met with an account of a cure performed in

a similar case (or what to me appeared so) by rubbing of Laudanum, at
the same time taking a given dose internally – It acted like a charm, like a
miracle!

Thus, 'I was seduced into the use of narcotics, . . . & saw not the truth, till my
Body had contracted a habit & a necessity.'[152] How had this happened? As
ever, Coleridge presented himself as passive: he had allowed himself to
become habituated because of his '*Terror & Cowardice* of PAIN & Sudden
Death, not (so help me God!) by any temptation of Pleasure, or expectation or
desire of exciting pleasurable Sensations'. Nevertheless, the effects had been
catastrophic, for addiction had produced a bondage of the will, a mental
disease. The true evil of opium was that it produced alienation of mind:[153]

> By the long long Habit of the accursed Poison my Volition (by which I
> mean the faculty *instrumental* to the Will, and by which alone the Will
> can realize itself – it's Hands, Legs, & Feet, as it were) was compleatly
> deranged, at times frenzied, disseverd itself from the Will, & become an
> independent faculty: so that I was perpetually in the state, in which you
> may have seen paralytic Persons, who attempting to push a step forward
> in one direction are violently forced round to the opposite.

Coleridge thus saw himself, rhetorically at least, as reduced to a kind of
lunacy:[154]

> O God! how willingly would I place myself under Dr Fox in his
> Establishment – for my Case is a species of madness . . . You bid me
> rouse myself – go, bid a man paralytic in both arms rub them briskly
> together, & that will cure him. Alas! (he would reply) that I cannot move
> my arms in my Complaint & my misery. –

Here is a remarkable perception, of a kind not hitherto seen in this volume: a
man acknowledging he had been possessed, to the point of paralysis, by a
sickness, which in his guilty moments he sees to be self-induced, indeed, an
expression of the self:[155]

> In truth, I have been for years almost paralytic in mind from self-
> dissatisfaction – brooding in secret anguish over what from so many
> baffled agonies of Effort I had thought and felt to be inevitable.

Thus enslaved to this '*free-agency-annihilating* Poison', Coleridge underwent
what he described as 'a continued act of thirty years' Self-poisoning thro'
cowardice of pain'.[156] For the 'tyranny of habit', the 'slavery to opium' – at
rock bottom he had been consuming some five ounces of laudanum a day –
wrecked self-destruction:[157]'Deteriora sequor – was the motto of my Life – as
far as this process of slow self-destruction was concerned'. Eventually, from

the depths, Coleridge solicited the advice of physicians. It was something, he said, he had long wished to do but had shrunk from, doubting he had the will-power to achieve it:[158]

> I have however done it at last – and tho' the result after a severe Trial proved what I had anticipated, yet such is the Blessedness of walking altogether in Light, that my Health & Spirits are better [than] I have known them for years.

A slave to self, Coleridge could not effect a self-cure; it was totally appropriate that, whereas Harriet Martineau could wave her doctors aside and cure herself through mesmeric will, Coleridge could be restored only through the agency of a physician, Dr James Gilman, who boarded him at Highgate for the remaining sixteen years of his life.

We have not broached the vexed question of the relations – real or mythical – between Coleridge's opium habit and his poetic creativity. Rather, our concern has been to show how that habit catalysed sickness and self. Despite his reflex protestations, Coleridge's maladies were not external afflictions, but were expressions of a self ever pained, and traumatized by inability to act. Illness was an objective correlative to inner weakness, enabling him to deflect spiritual conflicts while expressing them: 'I am a starling self-incaged . . . and my whole Note is, Tomorrow, & Tomorrow, & Tomorrow.'[159]

Ada Byron: Hysteria or Fatal Disease?

Illness can thus be a force transforming people's very sense of themselves. The instances examined so far have principally shown an individual mapping out his own destiny in relative isolation. Both Hume and Martineau endorsed epistemological individualism; Coleridge, as we have seen, characterized himself as 'lonely'. Our last example moves from the individual to social dynamics. What happens when illness becomes the arena and idiom through which family tensions are expressed and battles fought? The life of Byron's daughter, Ada, shows sickness and health, indeed the power to *define* them, being used as weapons in family politics.

It is difficult to decide whether Ada Byron had more problems growing up as the daughter of the Romantic poet (absent, and soon to be dead), or of her very present mother, Annabella, who, after her separation, played the perdur-able role of wronged woman and martyr, and saw it as her mission to 'save' her only daughter. Lady Byron – an ardent phrenologist and medical dabbler – made much of her own bouts of illness, ostentatiously demonstrating her fortitude in the teeth of great sufferings ('I am rather better for a horrid *mouthful* of leeches this morning').[160] Thus Ada, born in 1815, grew up in surroundings in which sickness had powerful, yet paradoxical cultural reso-nances. Authenticated illness could excuse, winning sympathy and power. Yet sickness, if suspect, lost credit, and rendered one subject to the power – or, indeed, contempt – of others. Lady Byron and her daughter struggled for years, the mother for dominion, the daughter for autonomy. In that epic battle, the symbols of sickness were crucial pawns.

Having been a sickly child, Ada suffered an attack of paralysis at the age of thirteen and a half, after a bout of measles. In bed for a year, on crutches for another, it was three years before she fully recovered.[161] Her recovery was arguably delayed by the protracted bed-rest to which her mother subjected her; for Lady Byron, that was surely the most effective way of keeping her handful of a teenage daughter under control – the mother did not want the daughter to stand on her own two feet. Once recovered and mobile, Ada immediately tried to fly, eloping with her tutor (she was caught).[162]

Ada's late teens were occupied with efforts (in which she and her mother rarely saw eye-to-eye) to find her an identity as a young lady. She channelled her intellectual ambitions into mathematics – a lasting passion; and she married the wealthy and courtly William King, later Lord Lovelace. They had two children who survived youth, Byron and Annabella, though she confessed that she 'should never have desired a child', but merely wanted heirs.[163]

In her mid-twenties, she became involved with the mathematical genius, Charles Babbage, assisting his attempts to develop a calculating engine. Once more, symptoms of physical and mental strangeness appeared, accompanied by heightened consciousness and grandiosity. By March 1841, she was writing:[164]

> I believe myself to possess a most singular combination of qualities exactly fitted to make me *pre-eminently* a discoverer of the *hidden realities* of nature . . . the belief has been *forced* upon me . . . I have *perceptions* of some things which no one else has.

It was all, she explained, 'owing to some peculiarity of my nervous system'. Soon, she was contemplating the possibility that she was the 'rising star' who might become 'the Elijah of Science'.[165]

Increasingly suffering from 'gastritis', she recorded her 'sufferings and peculiarities'.[166] In many respects, her physical pains fascinated her, making her feel special. Thus her stomach or, as she called it, her '*Molecular Laboratory*', became painful, yet she liked the thought that this spurred a further development of her scientific bent:[167]

> Do you know it is to me quite delightful to have a frame so susceptible that it is an *experimental laboratory* always about me, & inseperable from me. I walk about, not in a Snail-Shell, but in a *Molecular Laboratory*. This is a new view to take of one's physical frame; & amply compensates me for all sufferings, had they been even greater.

To some degree, she subscribed to the Romantic mythology that physical torments were the price of genius: 'it is the growth of my Ideality and Causality that has made me ill, & that the excitement of writing all this has *swelled* one side of my face.'[168] Now expansive and ebullient, now depressed, she could confide, 'You know I am a d——d ODD animal.'[169]

By the mid-1840s, her life was whirling in a vortex. She grew dangerously intimate with her science tutor, John Crosse; her mania for gambling on the turf became a ruinously costly addiction, and led to an estrangement from her mother; alongside euphoria, she felt increasingly desolate and desperate; her pains and sufferings worsened, not least heart 'spasms' and palpitations. Ada was careful to attribute her condition to external causes, especially 'the miserable East Winds'. Her physician, the fashionable Dr Locock, thought it *sui generis*: 'there is no giving a name to it . . . [it is] not at all according to any precedents.'[170]

A swelling appeared in the cervix. Locock was optimistic (as always): there was a 'sore', but it was 'healthy'. By contrast, Lady Byron seized the opportunity to disparage her daughter, branding her troubles as hypochondriacal and hysterical. Lady Byron had always disapproved of her daughter's scientific and mathematical pretensions, believing she had a duty to avoid 'stimulants with a brain like yours'. Now, once again, she had been proved right all along. 'I have long anticipated some illness in you from overexciting habits.'[171]

Increasingly, Ada had recourse to laudanum. This produced extraordinary sensations, creating an aura of great artistic and aesthetic powers. 'I am indebted tonight to Laudanum for such sense and tranquility as is really creeping over me this evening', she wrote at one point; and at another:[172]

> The Opium has a remarkable effect on my eyes, seeming to *free* them, & make them *open & cool*. Then it makes me so philosophical, & so takes off all *fretting* eagerness & anxieties. It appears to harmonize the whole constitution, to make each function act in a *just proportion*; (with *judgment, discretion, moderation*).

Yet her cervix continued to worsen. At times she attributed it to a '*current drawn off from* the Brain' – evidence of an interest, shared with Crosse, in electricity, and perhaps echoing her mother's fascination – one she did not share – with mesmerism.[173] Eventually, Locock recognized that Ada had not a healthy sore but a tumour. Yet he still believed (she reported) that it formed part of a 'curative' process; Ada herself had to confess that this 'curative' stage was more painful than when the disease had been 'gaining ground'. Nevertheless, she was relieved that she was not, after all, 'dying by inches'.[174] Mother and daughter battled over therapies. Ada restored to opium in ever larger doses, and then to chloroform; Lady Byron disapproved, seeing it as a soft surrender, and recommended mesmerism instead.

As the sickness worsened, Ada began to contemplate her very being as invaded by sickness and defined by pain: 'If my wits & feelings were not *crushed* as they certainly are by great illness & pain, I could hope that there is some ulterior object in individual existence.'[175] Above all – and the contrast with Harriet Martineau is so striking – Ada found that worsening physical pain actually attenuated her perception of spiritual vitality: 'But alas! everything spiritual & human *goes* with some miserable alteration in the material tissues. The more one suffers, the more appalling is it to feel that it may all be in order to *"die like a dog"*.'[176] As Ada's pains worsened, she found her mother growing ever more overbearing and demanding; Lady Byron still believed that the true enormity of Ada's gambling debts, and other dark secrets, had been hidden from her. She proposed to visit her estranged, bed-ridden daughter, clearly to force out the truth ('I am conscious of the power to destroy', she warned). Ada appealed to Locock's authority, arguing a visit might be counterproductive. Lady Byron insisted, self-righteously determined to use her daughter's prostration to extract the whole truth. Under torturing pressure, and perhaps beginning to interpret her illness as a judgement, Ada revealed to her mother her affair with Crosse and the pawning of the family diamonds. It is an ironical illustration of Martineau's view that sickness brings forth truth.

Lady Byron appropriated Ada's illness. For long she defined the complaint as mere 'Imagination', and thought a mesmerist would cure.[177] Meanwhile, Ada herself continued to worsen: 'I begin to understand DEATH, which is going on quietly & gradually every minute, & will never be a thing of one particular *moment*.'[178] Nevertheless, she had an intuitive notion of the requirements of the art of dying and the self-management of death, and began to plan her funeral. Lapsing into incoherence, she told her husband that 'the suffering she was to undergo would last 1,000,000 years'. According to Lady Byron, Ada confessed that she believed that 'her *father* had sent her this disease, & doomed her to an early death!'.[179] If she truly said that, it must have gratified her mother. Lady Byron battled to induce a true belief in God's loving mercy: and to turn her against her friends such as Crosse. She enjoyed her full triumph before Ada finally died on 27 November 1852.

The tormented life of Ada Byron is interesting here for two principal reasons. Partly because we see pain, sickness, genius, and ideals fused together in her consciousness, in ways powerfully resonant, and deeply confused. Experience of sickness alerted her particularly sharply to the strange sympathies between body and mind, sparked her interest in mental electricity, and allowed her to cast herself as a genius. It was when she recognized that she was dying, that her ambition blossomed to produce great poetry (back to her father).

Second, it demonstrates how, for every party, sickness was inseparable from the assertion of power. Invalidism was both weakness and strength; a deathbed a place from which to command, yet, above all, a bed of nails. Once Ada was dying, Lady Byron was able to enforce moral suzerainty over her on a scale such as had eluded her since Ada had been a child. For Lady Byron, the deathbed counted mainly as a site of purgation, repentance (by her daughter), and gracious forgiveness (by herself). Lady Byron battled with William Lovelace and with the doctors to dominate her dying daughter. Whereas, in their various ways, for Hume, Martineau, and Coleridge, sickness had provided a story of their life's development, for Ada it was a Trojan horse, weakening her defences and laying her vulnerable.

Through this book we have been examining how people were affected by, and coped with, pain. This chapter has taken the argument one stage further, contending that, in certain cases, it was pain that created people: and, indeed, that the Georgian mind, with its culture of feeling and its concept of man as a creature of habit, was highly receptive to the notion that a person was what pained him.

NOTES

[1] It may be worth reiterating that our intention here is not to practise psycho-history, using the supposed insights of post-Freudian dynamic psychiatry to find answers to dead people's problems in their unconscious. It is rather to explore the consciousness of sufferers in its socio-cultural setting.

[2] See the excellent study by Nicolson and Rousseau, *This Long Disease*.

[3] Sontag, *Illness as Metaphor*.

[4] Groddeck, *Meaning of Illness*; Brown, *Love's Body*, 4f.

[5] Reich, *Character Analysis*.

[6] Yolton, *John Locke and the Way of Ideas*.

[7] This is well brought out in Passmore, *Perfectibility of Man*, 191.

[8] Tuveson, *Imagination as a Means of Grace*.

[9] Todd, *Sensibility*, 20f.; Hagstrum, *Sex and Sensibility*.

[10] Ellis (ed.), *Early Diary of Frances Burney*, 7.

[11] Castle (ed.), *Jerningham Letters*, I, 353.

[12] Quoted in Hunter and Macalpine, *Three Hundred Years of Psychiatry*, 466.

[13] Locke, *Essay Concerning Human Understanding*, sect V pt 2; Tuveson, *Imagination as a Means of Grace*.

[14] Engell, *Creative Imagination*.

[15] Wardle (ed.), *Letters of Mary Wollstonecraft*, 370.

[16] Quoted in Hunter and Macalpine, *Three Hundred Years of Psychiatry*, 496.

[17] Jackson, *Melancholia and Depression*; Moore, 'English Malady'; Doughty, 'English Malady'; Fischer-Homberger, 'Hypochondriasis'.

[18] In Melincourt, Garnett (ed.), *Novels of Peacock*, 144:

The name of this old gentleman was Hippy: Humphry Hippy, Esquire, of Hypocon House, in the county of Durham. He was a bachelor, and his character exhibited a singular compound of kind-heartedness, spleen, and melancholy, which governed him by turns and sometimes in such rapid succession that they seemed almost co-existent.

[19] Porter, *Mind-Forg'd Manacles*, ch. 2.

[20] Adair, *Essays on Fashionable Diseases*, 95. There is a good characterization of a hypochondriac in Buchan, *Observations Concerning the Prevention and Treatment of the Venereal Diseases*, 202, especially with respect to syphilophobia.

[21] Wedgwood and Wedgwood, *Wedgwood Circle*, 339.

[22] Mills (ed.), *Crabbe, Tales and Poems*, 7: 'The Village', lines 250–61. Cf. Baird and Ryskamp (eds), *William Cowper, Poems*, 362:

In making known how oft they have been sick,
And give us in recitals of disease
A doctor's trouble, but without the fees:

Relate how many weeks they kept their bed,
How an emetic or cathartic sped,
Nothing is slightly touched, much less forgot,
Nose, ears and eyes seem present on the spot.
Now the distemper spite of draught or pill
Victorious seem'd, and now the doctor's skill;
And now – alas for unforeseen mishaps!
They put on a damp night-cap and relapse;
They thought they must have died they were so bad,
Their peevish hearers almost wish they had.

23 Lustig and Pottle (eds), *Boswell: Applause of the Jury*, 89.
24 Ibid., 122.
25 Cave (ed.), *Diary of Joseph Farington*, X, 3704.
26 Weis and Pottle (eds), *Boswell in Extremes*, 154.
27 Mandeville, *Treatise on the Hypochondriack and Hysterick Diseases*.
28 Heberden, *Commentaries*, 22–3; Willich, *Lectures on Diet and Regimen*, 2. Willich argued that people were increasingly making themselves ill by thinking about their health.
29 Adair, quoted in Hunter and Macalpine, *Three Hundred Years of Psychiatry*, 490.
30 Hayward (ed.), *Life and Writings of Mrs Piozzi*, 210.
31 Heberden, *Commentaries*, 32f.
32 *Gentleman's Magazine*, 2 (1732), 1062.
33 King and Ryskamp (eds), *Letters and Prose Writings of William Cowper*, IV, 101.
34 King-Hele (ed.), *Letters of Erasmus Darwin*, 273.
35 Adair, *Essays on Fashionable Diseases*.
36 Hill, *Hypochondriasis*, 24.
37 Ibid.
38 Wedgwood and Wedgwood, *Wedgwood Circle*, 124.
39 Hill, *Hypochondriasis*, 9. 'Sometimes the patient's own resolution has set him free': 22.
40 Crook and Guiton, *Shelley's Venomed Melody*, 21.
41 Ibid., 39.
42 Ibid., 69.
43 Ibid., 85.
44 Ibid., 119.
45 Ibid., 136.
46 Marrs (ed.), *Letters of Thomas Carlyle*.
47 Crook and Guiton, *Shelley's Venomed Melody*, 208.
48 Ibid., 181.
49 Praz, *Romantic Agony*.
50 Bailey (ed.), *Boswell's Column*, xiii.
51 Ober, *Boswell's Clap*.
52 Lustig and Pottle (eds), *Boswell: Applause of the Jury*, 263. Two days later, he read Hamlet: Ingram, *Boswell's Creative Gloom*, 8–10.
53 Ryskamp and Pottle (eds), *Boswell. The Ominous Years*, 300; cf. ibid., 240.
54 Bailey (ed.), *Boswell's Column*.
55 Brady and Pottle (eds), *Boswell in Search of a Wife*, 41.
56 Bailey (ed.), *Boswell's Column*, 42-3.
57 Lustig and Pottle (eds), *Boswell: Applause of the Jury*, 263.
58 Porter, *Mind-Forg'd Manacles*, ch. 2.
59 Chapman (ed.), *The Letters of Samuel Johnson*, II, 145.
60 Ketton-Cremer, *Thomas Gray*, 146.

61 Ibid., 65.
62 Ibid.
63 Veith, *Hysteria*; Trillat, *Hystérie*.
64 Cave (ed.), *Diary of Joseph Farington*, X, 3705. Hone added that he 'had been relieved by medicines prescribed by Doctor Reynolds who He had known 35 years'. For the gender specificity of hysteria, note that when Edward Jenner had the symptoms, he wrote that 'in a female I should call it Hysterical – but in myself I know not what to call it, but by the old sweeping term nervous': Miller (ed.), *Letters of Edward Jenner*, 109.
65 Rousseau, 'Nerves, Fibres and Spirits'; *idem*, 'Psychology'.
66 Little and Kahrl (eds), *Letters of David Garrick*, II, 553.
67 King and Ryskamp (eds), *Letters and Prose Writings of William Cowper*, III, 6.
68 Adair, quoted in Hunter and Macalpine, *Three Hundred Years of Psychiatry*, 490.
69 Beresford (ed.), *Diary of a Country Parson*, IV, 227.
70 Law, *A Serious Call*, 262.
71 Adair, *Essays on Fashionable Diseases*.
72 Parsons, *The Social System*; Turner, *Medical Power and Social Knowledge*.
73 Faulkner (ed.), *Letters and Journals of George Crabbe*, 118. Chapman (ed.), *Letters of Samuel Johnson*, III, 71.
74 Mossner, *Life of David Hume*, 66.
75 Ibid., 67.
76 Ibid.
77 Greig (ed.), *Letters of Hume*, I, 15.
78 Mossner, *Life of David Hume*, 70.
79 Ibid.
80 Ibid., 80.
81 Ibid., 85.
82 Mazlish, *James and John Stuart Mill*, 207f.
83 Martineau, *Autobiography*, I, 180.
84 Ibid., 19.
85 Ibid., 133.
86 Ibid., 43.
87 Ibid., 12.
88 Ibid., 45.
89 Ibid., 59.
90 Ibid.
91 Ibid., 76.
92 Ibid., 124.
93 Ibid., 78.
94 Ibid., 174.
95 Ibid., 134.
96 Ibid., 192.
97 Ibid., II, 150.
98 Ibid., 151.
99 Ibid., 147f. See Webb, *Martineau*, 206.
100 [Martineau], *Life in the Sick-Room*, 2.
101 Cf. the interesting chapter 'Tynemouth: The Uses of Suffering', in Webb, *Martineau*, 193ff.
102 Martineau, *Autobiography*, II, 214.
103 Ibid., 248. Cf. Webb, *Martineau*, 236ff.
104 Martineau, *Autobiography*, II, 333.
105 Ibid., 207.

[106] Ibid., 148.

[107] Ibid., 149.

[108] Ibid., 187.

[109] Ibid., 147.

[110] Ibid.

[111] Ibid.

[112] Ibid.

[113] Ibid., 433–4.

[114] Ibid., 435–6.

[115] Passmore, *Perfectibility of Man*.

[116] Trotter, *View of the Nervous Temperament*, 33; cf. Willich, *Lectures on Diet*, 422.

[117] Note *inter alia* the growing importance of sugar; Mintz, *Sweetness and Power*, 108ff.

[118] Cave (ed.), *Diary of Joseph Farington*, VII, 2862–3.

[119] Quoted in Wedgwood and Wedgwood, *Wedgwood Circle*, 127.

[120] Quoted in ibid., 129.

[121] De Quincey, *Confessions of an English Opium Eater*, 35.

[122] King-Hele (ed.), *Erasmus Darwin*, 248. Darwin was very free in his recommendation of opium. For James Watt's daughter, he suggested, 'In some I have seen a great benefit by beginning with a pill of half a grain of opium taken at breakfast, and at going to bed . . . every day as a habit'. King-Hele (ed.), *Letters of Erasmus Darwin*, 245.

[123] De Moulin, 'Historical-Phenomenological Study of Bodily Pain'.

[124] Cheyne, *Essay on Health and Long Life*, 213. Cheyne claimed this could all be achieved 'without any Fear of *Over-dosing*': 219. Trotter, *View of the Nervous Temperament*, called opium 'the noblest attribute of medicine': 135.

[125] King-Hele (ed.), *Letters of Erasmus Darwin*, 218. On alcoholism see Trotter, *Essay on Drunkenness*. It is noteworthy that Trotter particularly emphasizes how habitual drunkenness is a *mental* disorder. Compare the story of the alcoholic rector and schoolmaster, Mr Purdie, in Burton (ed.), *Autobiography of Alexander Carlyle*, 101ff. Much of the diary of William Jones is taken up with attempts – which in the end failed – to cure himself of his snuff habit.

[126] King-Hele, *Erasmus Darwin*, 218.

[127] Quoted in Maddan, 'Johnson's Alcohol Problem'. Mrs Thrale records Robert Levett as saying 'she was always drunk and reading Romances in her Bed, where She killed herself by taking Opium': ibid., 145.

[128] Garlick and MacIntyre (eds), *Diary of Joseph Farington*, I, 221: 'He took laudanum regularly in vast quantities'. There is plenty of evidence of very heavy consumption of opium for medical purposes back in the seventeenth century. E.g., see the letters between John Locke and Benjamin Furly, in De Beer (ed.), *Correspondence of John Locke*, IV, 214, 226, 244, 245.

[129] Cockburn, *Memorials of his Time*, 56.

[130] Checkland, *Gladstones*, 288. Helen's deteriorating physical health, her bowel problems and spasms, were probably due to medically-originated opium use. Checkland writes of the Gladstone 'family circle of invalidism': 168.

[131] Martin, *Tennyson*.

[132] Cheyne, *Essay on Health and Long Life*, 43.

[133] Trotter, *Essay on Drunkenness*, 319.

[134] Ibid., 107.

[135] Trotter, *View of the Nervous Temperament*, 105.

[136] Martineau, *Autobiography*, I, 397.

[137] Discussed in Lefebure, *Coleridge. Bondage of Opium*, 375.

[138] Discussed in Porter and Porter, *Patient's Progress*, ch. 10.

[139]   Lefebure, *Bondage of Love*, 131. See also Lefebure, *Coleridge. Bondage of Opium*; Fruman, *Coleridge, the Damaged Archangel*.

[140]   Lefebure, *Bondage of Love*, 132.

[141]   Cottle, *Reminiscences of Coleridge and Southey*, 293.

[142]   Griggs (ed.), *Collected Letters of Samuel Taylor Coleridge*, II, 399.

[143]   Ibid., II, nos 475, 483, where he talks of his 'nervous rheumatism'.

[144]   Ibid., III, 51.

[145]   Ibid., II, 1035–6.

[146]   Ibid., 844. See discussion in Lefebure, *Coleridge. Bondage of Opium*, 379.

[147]   Griggs (ed.), *Collected Letters of Samuel Taylor Coleridge*, III, 63, 64.

[148]   Ibid., 74.

[149]   Ibid., 346.

[150]   Ibid., 212.

[151]   Ibid., 476.

[152]   Ibid.

[153]   Ibid., III, 489.

[154]   Ibid., 476.

[155]   Ibid., 131.

[156]   Ibid., VI, 894.

[157]   Ibid., 626.

[158]   Ibid.

[159]   Quoted in Lefebure, *Coleridge. Bondage of Opium*, 340.

[160]   Stein, *Ada, A Life and Legacy*, 27.

[161]   Ibid., 29.

[162]   Ibid., 35.

[163]   Ibid., 64.

[164]   Ibid., 86.

[165]   Ibid., 139.

[166]   Ibid., 144.

[167]   Ibid., 139.

[168]   Ibid., 164.

[169]   Ibid., 174.

[170]   Ibid., 217, 285.

[171]   Ibid., 218.

[172]   Ibid., 288.

[173]   Ibid., 221.

[174]   Ibid., 223.

[175]   Ibid., 224.

[176]   Ibid., 229.

[177]   Ibid.

[178]   Ibid., 239.

[179]   Ibid., 244.

Chapter 13:
Coping and Resignation

In his *Familiar Letters*, Samuel Richardson showed how to congratulate a friend on recovery from a dangerous illness:[1]

> Dear Sir,
>   Give me leave to mingle my joy with that of all your friends and relations, in the recovery of your health, and to join with them to bless God for continuing to your numerous well-wishers the benefit of your useful and valuable life. May God Almighty long preserve you in health, and prosper all your undertakings, for the good of your worthy family, and the pleasure of all your friends and acquaintance, is the hearty prayer of sir,
>   Your faithful friend, and humble Servant

Recuperation was, of course, the devoutly desired outcome of all sickness experiences. But as seen, what so often ensued was protracted distress, disablement, and even death.

Shortly before her death in 1817 from a painful wasting condition – we now call it Addison's Disease – Jane Austen thanked her cousin, Fanny Knight, for her solicitude:[2]

> I certainly have not been well for many weeks, and about a week ago I was very Poorly, I have had a good deal of fever at times, & indifferent nights, but considerably better now & recovering my looks a little, which have been bad enough, black & white & every wrong colour. I must not depend upon being ever very blooming again.

She concluded with a mordant reflection: 'Sickness is a dangerous Indulgence at my time of Life.' The detachment is courageous. The true gravity of the matter is not masked – as, indeed, one would expect from that supreme ironist who, in her last, unfinished, novel, *Sanditon*, dissected the morbid growth of invalidism. Was that resolve unique to the novelist? Or was it common?

We have so far investigated the sting of pain, the attempts made to identify, understand, and explain disease, and the dialectic between self and sickness. We turn to examine the cultural resources to hand for coping, in a world without effective drugs, in which surgery was performed upon fully-conscious patients. How, for example, did Sir Nathaniel Dance-Holland cope with this operation, reported by Farington?[3]

> Dance told me that Sir N. Dance-Holland had remained in town to have two Wens cut out, one on His Breast, – the other on His Back. – Horne performed the operation, which was very painful, as it was necessary to go to the bottom & to preserve the skin, which took more time. Horne sd. Sir Nathaniel suffered the pain witht. flinching.

One possible response, as suggested in the previous chapter, was to make sense of sickness by embracing its high drama, making one's sufferings unique, and flaunting them. Yet hypochondriacism gained only limited tolerance in a society entertaining no mean suspicion of the sick. The unwell were expected to bear affliction with fortitude, in return for their exemptions and privileges. So how did individuals respond? The idioms are standard, the accents are individual.

God's Will

'He was never inclined to make use of doctors or phisick', wrote William Stout, approvingly, of his late father, 'but, as he had lived temperately, to resign himself to the will of God. He was endowed with much patience, and went off gradually.'[4] Christian protocols made sense of enduring suffering, as discussed earlier, by looking piously upwards to Providence, and viewing it as what the early Harriet Martineau called 'the chastisement of a Father . . . in some way or other, ordained for, or instrumental to good',[5] thus ensuring one had not 'suffered in vain'.[6] And the divine stab of pain could pave the way for a joyous acceptance of death itself. Facing a dying friend, Sir Thomas Browne enunciated this uniquely Christian attitude to death: 'not to fear death, nor to desire it [i.e., the characteristic pagan, Stoic formula] was short of his Resolution: to be dissolved, and be with Christ, was his dying ditty':[7]

> But to be content with Death may be better than to desire it: a miserable Life may make us wish for Death, but a virtuous one to rest in it: which is the Advantage of those resolved Christians, who looking on Death not only as the sting, but the period and end of Sin, the Horison and Isthmus between this Life and a better, and the Death of this World but as Nativity of another, do contentedly submit unto the common Necessity, and envy not Enoch or Elias.

In the eighteenth century, this Christian assent to suffering was filtered through theodicies rationalizing the evils of pain, suffering, and death as apparent only. William Paley argued in his celebrated *Natural Theology* (1802) – a work written while undergoing treatment at Buxton for a severe kidney complaint – that Christians must see pain as subordinate to higher purposes. For one thing, it should serve as a 'monitor, to alert us to danger and disease'.[8] For another, pain made us appreciate pleasure more. Suffering shed 'a satisfaction over intervals of ease', and remissions produced more gratitude towards God than did the routine benefits of existence. Moreover:[9]

> pain also itself is not without its alleviations. It may be violent and frequent; but is seldom continued: and its pauses and intermissions become positive pleasures. It has the power of shedding a satisfaction over intervals of ease, which, I believe, few enjoyments exceed. A man resting from a fit of the stone or gout, is, for the time, in possession of feelings which undisturbed health cannot impart. They may be dearly bought, but still they are to be set against the price.

Along similar lines, Anna Seward tells us that Mary Howard, Erasmus Darwin's first wife, confessed, 'Pain taught me the value of ease, and I enjoyed it with a glow of spirit, seldom, perhaps, felt by the habitually healthy.'[10] With a pinch more casuistry, Paley further argues that afflictions had higher meanings in respect to the hidden purposes of an all-loving God, acting providentially for the good of each individual sufferer.

In these circumstances, it was every Christian's duty to embrace his fate. Yet it was not expected that this could be struggle-free. Achieving full mastery of mind over the body was an agonizing process, 'I am sixty-seven years of age and it is yet a warfare', wrote the Quaker, Anna Braithwaite:[11]

> I often think of Fenelon's remark to this effect, that he found it more difficult to be patient with himself than with other people. The effects of physical symptoms afford strong temptation to impatience, and the spasmodic feelings on the chest together with muscular weakness especially require me continually to recollect that quiet submission; not striving against them by active exertion, is the watchword to both mind and body, naturally quick of apprehension to surrounding circumstances, and ardent in feeling . . . O lord God! Thou alone knowest all my weakness and the sins that most easily beset me. Be with me now in the evening of life.

However difficult, resignation was the Christian's duty. Therein lay wisdom, according to the Quaker, Isabella Harris. For when He, 'in infinite wisdom', killed off her son with scarlet fever in 1796, she could reflect 'that my dear children are taken from a world of sorrow and suffering to a place of inconceivable happiness' – a thought that 'enables me to be resigned to the will of my Heavenly Father'.[12] This gave her further comfort in the next year, for when her mother fell mortally sick she 'was enabled calmly to resign herself as being in the Lord's Hand.[13] Faith in the Lord overcame human pangs:[14]

> When nature was tried with overwhelming pain, [her mother] never expressed a murmuring word, but appeared quite resigned to the disposal of unerring Wisdom, believing all things which happened to her would be for the best.

Elizabeth Fry's journals show a similar striving for resignation when tested with illness. In 1802, one of her babies sickened with a cough. 'I felt much tired', she wrote, 'and longed for resignation and patience':[15]

> 20th – I felt our dearest child in great danger, as did many besides me, indeed I believe all of us. This was indeed a trial, but I was supported with some resignation of soul, feeling the weight of that part of the prayer, "Thy will and not mine be done"
> 21st – As the morning advanced, my little infant began to change from a very feverish state to an almost deadly languid one, that I believe most present, thought might be the beginning of a more awful change. She sat on my lap . . . I think I may say, I felt resigned to the all-wise dispensations of Providence, which was a great blessing; my mind felt depending on that Power that alone can support in the day of trial. I desire to feel that of myself I can do nothing, and that I may remember the blessing of being able to say, "Thy will and not mine be done".

Not least, Christians were taught neither to see, nor to expect, prolongation of life at all costs. When Isabella Harris's mother was dying, her words were, 'Do not pray for my life, pray that the Lord may release me'.[16] Indeed, while assenting to divine will, it was proper to wish for release under certain circumstances. When the sixty-seven-year-old John Arbuthnot fell badly sick, it was release he craved:[17]

> A Recovery in my Case, and at my Age is impossible; the kindest Wish of my Friends is Euthanasia [i.e., an easy death]. Living or dying, I shall always be Your most faithful Friend.

Ralph Verney noted his cousin Leeke was 'wearing apace but not so fast as she desires', for 'this terrible disease commonly takes times & leasure in its execution'. Providentially, she soon died, and 'as fit for Heaven as Cousin Leeke' became the family phrase for patient soul.[18]

Fortitude
When pain is unavoidable, bravery is best. People imbibed that elementary truth with their mothers' milk. Miss Berry went to visit Mrs Dundas:[19]

her daughter, whose foot had been cut off exactly six weeks before, was sitting cheerful and happy upon the sofa, a different creature both in appearance and in spirits, from what we had seen her in the summer. The operation has been performed at her own earnest request, and her behaviour was so heroic as quite to overcome Home, the surgeon who performed it.

Fortitude was enjoined on everyone, Christians, Deists, and those of no fixed religion too. Pragmatism and idealism both appreciated the benefits of establishing the dominion of the mind over the unruly flesh. Tristram Shandy admired the Pythagoreans for 'their *getting out of the body in order to think well*'.[20] Appreciating the virtues of Stoicism, some adopted such a 'philosophical' programme for coping with pain. Thus, Edward Fitzgerald stressed, 'I use my reason as much as I can'. One of its benefits lay in helping him to grasp 'how much better bodily pain is than mental'.[21]

Locke commended hardening. Many who never heard of Locke had an intuitive sense of the wisdom of bearing tribulation unflinchingly. Thomas Bewick wrote of a Dalesman who suffered terribly 'from the breast to the shoulders': 'Upon my mentioning medical assistance, he rejected it, and told me, if I sent him any drugs, I might depend upon it he would throw them all behind the fire.'[22] The hypochondriacal Boswell was similarly impressed with the courage of his friend Malone when sick: 'He looked ill but had such a manly fortitude that he did not trouble the company with melancholy complaints.'[23]

As implied here, Stoicism amounted to more than a personal life-raft; it was a reaffirmation of social duties. One ought to mask one's maladies and carry on regardless. Ralph Verney wrote about the heroic Leeke, 'though she walkes about the house, yet I may say many and great Paines and a lingering Death with a thousand other inconveniences are visible uppon her . . . I beleeve she conceales the worst from you, well knowing how sensible your Ladyshipp would be of her distresses.' Another member of the household was deeply impressed by her 'magnanimity & Truly Christian patience'.[24]

It was good to smile at misfortune. 'My pain is lively, my weakness excessive, the season cold', Gibbon reflected: 'I shall be well satisfied if I am on my legs the 20th in the medical sense of the word. At present I am a Corpse carried about by four arms which do not belong to me. Yet I try to smile.'[25] Gibbon made light of gout, by turning it into a joke. 'Laid up with the gout in both feet, I suffer like one of the first Martyrs, and possibly have provoked my punishment as much.'[26]

Reinforcing Stoicism was the manliness of the true gentleman. The stiff upper lip was not the discovery of the Victorians; it had been implicit in codes of chivalry and courtesy for centuries. Bearing pain satisfied macho vanity. Lord Uxbridge was wounded at the battle of Waterloo:[27]

He told me immediately he must lose his leg & then began conversing about the action & seemed to forget his wound in the exultation for the

Victory. When the Surgeons examined it, they are agreed that it would be at the imminent danger of his life to attempt to save the limb. He only said 'Well Gentlemen I thought so myself and if amputation is to take place the sooner it is done the better' . . . During the operation, he never moved or complained, no one even held his hands. He said once it was over his nerves did not appear the least shaken, and the Surgeon observed his pulse was not altered. He said smiling 'I have had a pretty long run, I have been a Beau these 47 years and it would not be fair to cut the young men out any longer'; and then asked us if we did not admire his vanity. I have seen many operations, but this neither Lord Greenock nor myself could bear. We were obliged to go to the other end of the room. I thank God he is doing as well as possible. There has been no fever and the Surgeons say nothing can be going on more favourably.

Crucial to the philosophy of bearing suffering was the conviction of the sovereign value of truth. The sick person must not flinch from the worst. The question of the obligation of a physician to strict and complete veracity was much disputed. Astute clinicians rightly perceived that not all patients wanted to hear the whole truth, arguing that optimistic white lies were often, in any case, therapeutic. But certain sufferers entertained lofty conceptions of their own moral integrity, and of the duties implicit in the doctor/patient relationship, which required utter veracity.

During his first bout of insanity, George III resented the evasive euphemisms of the court physicians. Samuel Johnson was adamant on the same point, arguing that if a patient could not trust his physician to tell the truth, he could not trust him in other respects.[28] Not surprisingly, truthfulness in sickness became one of Harriet Martineau's commandments. Facing facts improved the bracing moral challenge of being a patient: contrary to the 'popular method of consolation', 'the strong find it irritating to be medicined with soft fictions, or presented with anything but sound truth'.[29] One of the cardinal 'lessons of the sick room', she contended, is to 'avoid every shadow of falsehood':[30]

> Let the nurse avow that the medicine is nauseous. Let the physician declare that the treatment will be painful. Let sister, or brother, or friend, tell me that I must never look to be well. When the time approaches that I am to die, let me be told that I am to die, and when. If I encroach thoughtlessly on the time or strength of those about me, let me be reminded; if selfishly, let me be remonstrated with. Thus to speak the truth in love is in the power of all.

Brave words. Yet not all could agree, believing that such Stoicism could not be true to human nature. For grief and the need for consolation could be overwhelming. Erasmus Darwin lost his son, Charles, to a dissecting-room infection. Shortly after, he had to send condolences to Richard Lovell

Edgeworth on the death of *his* son. Darwin's message was that, in the end, the
Stoic formulae could not quell the feelings of flesh and blood:[31]

> I much console with you on your late loss, I know how to feel for your
> misfortune! . . . nil admirari may be a means to escape misery, but not
> to procure happiness – there is not much to be had in this world, we
> *expect* too much. – I have had my loss also! – – the letter of Sulpitius to
> Cicero, Melmoth's trans. V.III. p. 6, is fine eloquence, but comes not to
> the heart, it tugs but does not draw the arrow – pains and diseases of the
> mind are only cured by Forgetfulness; – Reason but skins the wound,
> which is perpetually liable to fester again.

Reality taught the limits of the consolations of philosophy.

Hope and Despair

Faced with crippling pain, Christian resignation and Stoic fortitude were not
always enough. Sufferers were also urged to cultivate hope. It was, of course, a
religious and moral virtue, but its practical therapeutic value was also
appreciated. Eliza Pierce was nursing her aunt, whose health was in sorry
state:[32]

> We have been oblig'd to send for Dr. Glass who says that she must have
> caught a fresh Cold . . . but I am sure she is much worse than she has
> been yet having been confin'd to her bed for these three days and when
> she will get out of it nobody knows but we all hope it will be soon.

This led her to ruminate on the cardinal importance of hope, in particular for
those without 'Phylosophy':[33]

> if it was not that thing call'd *hope* we should certainly be most Miserable
> Creatures and since the return of my Aunts disorder I begin to lose that
> happiness which Sweetens most of the Anxietys of Life for I own after a
> Confinement of three Months without seeing any Creatures except
> Doctors & Apothecarys and a probability of its continueing as much
> longer I have not Phylosophy enough to keep up my spirits – indeed if it
> was only to see what pain my Aunt is in (and what Affects me still more)
> the Anxiety my Uncle is under upon her Account it is enough to depress
> peoples Spirits who are possess'd of them in a much higher degree then I
> am.

Others, perhaps, did not respond to the trials of sickness with the fortitude
enjoined upon them. Just the reverse. Sickness may have sapped, rather than
reinforced, standards of personal conduct. It is quite possible that living in the
shadow of death in London in the plague year, Pepys turned more hedonistic,
more promiscuous, than before. Preachers had traditionally wrung their

hands when epidemics failed to revolt men from their abominations: and such attitudes underlie Edward Young's reflections upon a 'pleuretic fever' outbreak in mid-eighteenth-century Hertfordshire:[34]

> Few escape it, & many Die. And yet ye Survivors are as Gay as ever, & as free from Apprehensions of Death, as if they were Immortal. This is so strange & yet so True that it naturally excites mere wordly Curiosity to enquire into ye Cause of it. Can You conceive, Madam, ye Cause of so astonishing a Truth? I take it to be This. The shortness, & Casualty of Life, & ye Certainty of Death, are such obvious, & quite Indisputable Points, yt it seems nonsense to talk about them And from not Talking, they come to not Thinking, about them too.

For Young, it was the hedonism of despair – laying down the arms of reason and religion in the face of a terrible foe. Many deplored this as symptomatic of the age, seeing its temper as especially brittle, effeminate, lacking backbone. Proof of this seemed to lie in the extraordinary English propensity to suicide.[35]

Statistics are too rudimentary to resolve whether the 'suicide epidemic' contemporaries sensed was real, or merely a projection of cultural pessimism, fanned by the publicity given to notorious cases. Yet it was widely feared that people were resorting to suicide almost as the 'done thing' when sickness (not to mention gambling debts, etc.) became too severe. George Cheyne, explained: 'the Frequency of *Self-murders* here, in *England* especially, beyond any other Country':[36]

> For few have *Grace* and *Resignation* enough, to suffer patiently the lasting Pains of a *chronical* Distemper, or the yet more *torturing* and *crucifying Anguish* of a perpetual *Dispiritedness*: though I have observed *generally*, That all *Self-murderers* are *distracted* and distemper'd in their *intellectual* Faculties.

There may be some plausibility to this. Oliver Anderson has recently intimated that suicide might be viewed as self-medication taken to extremes.[37] He who has access to therapeutic means to give relief in sickness may well be inclined, when pain becomes unbearable, to take such self-help further in search of escape. He who is used to open a vein in phlebotomy, may ultimately slash his wrists or cut his throat; he who doses himself with opiates may also overdose – as apparently with Lord Crawford, whose death was reported by Horace Walpole:[38]

> Last week, Lord Crawford died too, as is supposed, by taking a large quantity of laudanum, under impatience at the badness of his circumstances, and at the seventeenth opening of the wound which he got in Hungary, in a battle with the Turks.

The Georgian household was certainly well-stocked with sedatives and poisons, not to mention razors and lancets: how much of a temptation were they? – particularly as the signs are that physicians themselves were making increased use of strong narcotics to induce peaceful and painless deaths ('euthanasia' in the strict sense). The evidence is fragmentary, but it may be indicative that one of the best recorded cases of resort to 'medical' means for suicide is that of a physician, Samuel Garth. Garth found himself decaying, and life became burdensome:[39]

> When Dr. Garth had been for a good while in a bad state of health, he sent one day for a physician with whom he was particularly intimate, and conjured him by their friendship and by everything that was more sacred (if there was anything more sacred) to tell him sincerely whether he thought he should ever be able to get rid of his illness or not. His friend, thus conjured, told him that 'he thought he might struggle on with it perhaps for some years, but that he much feared he could never get the better of it entirely'. Dr. Garth thanked him for his dealing so fairly with him, turned the discourse to other things, and talked very cheerfully all the rest of the time he stayed with him.
>
> As soon as he was gone, he called for his servant, said he was a good deal out of order and would go to bed, and then sent him for a surgeon to bleed him. Soon after, he sent for a second surgeon by a different servant, and was bled in the other arm, He then said he wanted rest, and when everybody had quitted the room he took off the bandages and lay down with a design of bleeding to death. His loss of blood made him faint away and that stopped the bleeding. He afterwards sunk into a sound sleep, slept all the night, waked in the morning without usual pains, and said that 'if it would continue so, he could be content to live on'.

If suicide was widely regarded as a cowardly evasion, Stoicism nevertheless provided a model for heroic death by one's own hand, proof of that nobility of soul that could transcend paltry concerns of self-preservation, through embracing a lofty 'contempt'. One such heroic end was recorded by the youthful David Hume (himself a defender of suicide) – the last days of Alexander Forbes, during preparations for the battle of Quiberon:[40]

> He express's vast Anxiety that he shou'd be oblig'd to leave his Duty, & Fear, least his Honour shou'd suffer by it. I endeavoured to quiet his Mind as much as possible, & thought I had left him tolerably compos'd at Night; but returning to his Room early next Morning, I found him with small Remains of Life, wallowing in his own Blood, with the Arteries of his Arm cut asunder. I immediately sent for a Surgeon, got a Bandage ty'd to his Arm, & recovered him entirely to his Senses & Understanding. He liv'd above four & twenty hours after, & I had

several conversations with him. Never a man exprest a more steady Contempt of Life nor more determined philosophical Principles, suitable to his Exit. He beg'd of me to unloosen his Bandage & hasten his Death, as the last Act of Friendship I could show him: But alas! we live not in Greek or Roman times. He told me, that he knew, he could not live a few Days: But if he did, as soon as he became his own Master, he wou'd take a more expeditious Method, which none of his Friends cou'd prevent.

The overwhelming majority of the sick did not, of course, take their own lives. They had to inure themselves to suffering. It was one of the pains of living, whose child was wisdom. 'I have swallowed the weight of an Apothecary in medicine', pondered Elizabeth Montagu:[41]

and what I am better for it, except more patient and less credulous I know not. I have learnt to bear my infirmities and not to trust to the skill of Physicians for curing them. I endeavour to drink deeply of Philosophy, and to be wise when I cannot be merry, easy when I cannot be glad, content with what cannot be mended, and patient where there can be no redress. The mighty can do no more, and the wise seldom do as much.

Pain taught patience.

NOTES

1 Richardson, *Familiar Letters*, 57.
2 Chapman (ed.), *Letters of Jane Austen*, 487.
3 Greig (ed.), *Farington Diaries*, V, 199.
4 Marshall (ed.), *Autobiography of William Stout*, 74.
5 [Martineau], *Life in the Sick-Room*, 7. Christian pieties were well set out in *The Spectator*, see Bond (ed.), *Spectator*, IV, 320-4 (18 October 1712, no. 513).
6 [Martineau], *Life in the Sick-Room*, ix.
7 Browne, 'To a Friend', 189.
8 Paley, *Works*, I, 243.
9 Ibid.
10 King-Hele, *Doctor of Revolution*, 82.
11 Braithwaite (ed.), *Memoirs of Anna Braithwaite*, 189.
12 Harris, *Family Memorials*, 22. The year is 1796.
13 Ibid., 23.
14 Ibid.
15 Fry and Cresswell (eds), *Memoirs of Elizabeth Fry*, I, 111.
16 Harris (ed.), *Family Memorials*, 25.
17 Quoted in Mack, *Alexander Pope*, 635.
18 Verney, *Memoirs*, IV, 133.
19 Lewis (ed.), *Journals and Correspondence of Miss Berry*, II, 333-4.
20 Sterne, *Tristram Shandy*, 472.

21   Fitzgerald (ed.), *The Correspondence of Emily, Duchess of Leinster*, II, 68.
22   Weekley (ed.), *Memoir of Thomas Bewick*, 98.
23   Lustig and Pottle (eds), *Boswell, The Applause of the Jury*.
24   Verney, *Memoirs*, IV, 131-2.
25   Norton (ed.), *Letters of Edward Gibbon*, II, 164-5. 'Writing is really painful'
     concluded Gibbon.
26   Ibid., 163.
27   Anglesey (ed.), *Capel Letters*, 116.
28   Chapman (ed.), *Letters of Samuel Johnson*, II, 304.
29   [Martineau], *Life in the Sick-Room*, 18.
30   Ibid., 26.
31   King-Hele (ed.), *Letters of Erasmus Darwin*, 201.
32   Macdonald (ed.), *Letters of Eliza Pierce*, 66-7.
33   Ibid.
34   Pettit (ed.), *Correspondence of Edward Young*, 249.
35   Sprott, *English Debate on Suicide*.
36   Cheyne, *Essay on Health and Long Life*, 181.
37   Anderson, *Suicide in Victorian and Edwardian England*.
38   Toynbee (ed.), *Letters of Horace Walpole*, II, 421.
39   Spence, *Observations*, I, 325-6.
40   Greig (ed.), *Letters of David Hume*, I, 97.
41   Climenson (ed.), *Elizabeth Montagu*, I, 36.

Chapter 14:
Reconciliation with Death

Patience or not, pain often heralded death. 'DEATH himself knocked on my door', Tristram Shandy tells us, conveying the terrifying immediacy of mortality.[1] No wonder. At times, so many seemed to be dying that households resembled the denouement of a Shakespearean tragedy, corpses outnumbering the living. Elizabeth Fry reported on 29 August 1844:[2]

> Sorrow upon sorrow! Since I last wrote, we have lost by death, first, my beloved sister, Elizabeth Fry; second, Gurney Reynolds, our sweet, good grandson; third Julian Fry, my dearest William and Julia's second daughter; and fourth, above all, our most beloved son, William Storrs Fry, who appeared to catch the infection of his little girl, and died on Third-day of scarlet fever, the 27th of this month . . . The trial is almost inexpressible. Oh! may the Lord sustain us in this time of deep distress.

Contemplating their complaints, sufferers were brought face-to-face with the prospect of dying. 'I have such a numbedness and *what I can't express* all over my thighs, Knees and legs as seems tending to a total deprivation of the use of them and even of life itself, which I have a strong suspicion is advancing fast on me', John Baker recorded in his diary, like so many finding himself lost for words when describing pain; the inevitable reflections followed:[3]

> it palpably grows worse and worse every day and I think must soon end in death; surely it can be nothing else – As for a cure, 'tis the utmost impossibility, so fast am I wasting away with a kind of benumbed irritation or tingling all over the parts mentioned – Yes, I must be plainly wasting away with great rapidity; this is certainly what is commonly called the hand of death itself, grasping me daily closer.

He concluded, unconvincingly, 'I submit without murmuring'. When Harriet Martineau asked, 'What subject is so interesting . . . as that of death?', she was being neither morbid, nor even particularly philosophical, but merely reflecting on the fact that through the ruck of life strutted death, and that no one could suffer twinges without fearing this might be the time to join the ranks of the great departed.[4] Would one pull through? Claver Morris recorded the knife-edge early in the eighteenth century:[5]

Aug 2   I lay a bed, out of order in a Cold till near 11.
3   So sick of a Fever with a violent Pain Head, Stomach & Limbs that I could not get out of bed till past 2 in afternoon. About 4 I took, in small Car – [MS indecipherable] which worked upward 7 times & downward near as often beginning to do so about the 3d vomit. Twas all over in 2 hours or less. And took a dose twice of an Alterative Electuary and went to bed.
4   It being our Mutual Entertainment at Colonel Berkeley's though I continued very sick, I went thither; I eat nothing but a little Tench & a Glass of Jelley of Harts-horn, sip'd once or twice of a Glass of October & drank in the middle of ye Afternoon half a glass of Punch. All the rest of the day sometime (to near the quantity of a pint in all) I drank fresh small drink: But sitting in complasance to Colonel Horner, Mr. Cummin of Trinity College, his friend Mr Pope, Mr Whitehand, Mr White, Mr Mills, Mr Aris, & Mr Bayley in Garden Summer-House, though windows were shut, I came away about 6 worse than I came.
5   I sweat in the Sweating Chair & continued it for 3 hours after.
6   I was let blood to 16 ounces by Mr Lucas in the right arm.
10   All doubted my recovery.
11   My Disease appeard to be Spotted Fever.

Typhus – if that was what he thought he had – was commonly fatal. This time, however, there was a happy ending. He turned the corner:[6]

17   I left off Watchers.
18   I began to eat Flesh.
20   I writ a Letter to my Daughter Betty in the first I was able to write.
23   I went to Church, & first abroad after my Sickness. I had Jackson's Anthem for my Recovery sung by Mr Wiltshire.
Sept 6   Receiv'd 10 Gallons of White Lisbone Wine from Mr. Mitchel.

Pre-modern culture was defined by death. *Et plurima mortis imago* – the face of death is everywhere – reads the caption in Hogarth's engraving, 'The Company of Undertakers', with its mugshot montage of leading quacks and physicians,[7] and its none-too-subtle hint that the medical profession, far from being death's enemy, was in reality its oldest ally ('a young doctor fattens the churchyard' ran the proverb). 'About 4 o'clock yester Evening', the Rev. William Jones recorded, 'a putrid Fever, seconded by a blunderer in physic, carried off the poor Major.'[8]

People got used early to the Grim Reaper. William Hutton's mother died while he was still a lad. Her friend told him, 'your mother's gone'. He burst into tears. 'Don't cry, you will soon go yourself', she rebuked.[9] Human vulnerability seemingly knew no bounds, and the slightest cause could have the most fatal effects.[10] As the Verney letters dolefully record, in 1699, the Queen of Portugal 'dyed with only making a holl in her yeare for to wear pendants' ('gangrene' set in).[11] So dwelling on death was thus not a morbid fixation but an honest realism. 'As sure as Death' retained its proverbial truth; nothing was certain, insisted Ben Franklin, 'except death and taxes'. Gazing around his parish of Broxbourne at the close of the eighteenth century, the Rev. William Jones reflected upon the universal mortality:[12]

I have been *reading* the parish & hamlet; & cannot remark any one house tenanted by the same mortals with whom I conversed thirty-six years ago. Most of the houses have frequently changed their tenants. The houses, gardens, grounds & have been, to their utmost 'capability', improved & beautified: – & then Death has, without ceremony, or much previous notice, ejected the occupiers.

Traditional Death

Christianity personified Death as the Terror of Terrors, the Great Leveller.[13] The Black Death had cast its long shadow, creating the culture of the *danse macabre*, the wormy cadaver, the skull and crossbones, and the charnel house. Orthodox theology saw death as the wages of sin, and stressed that for untold millions, dying literally meant plunging into the boiling oil of Hellfire. Protestantism was particularly severe, because it repudiated the comforts of efficacious Catholic deathbed repentance and of salvation through sacraments or, even, after purgatory.[14] Indeed, Protestant voluntarism typically portrayed the providential hand of God smiting man with sudden death. The pious Christian must be prepared.[15] As Cotton Mather put it, 'A prudent man will *Dy Daily*'; 'I know not when I shall die', recorded Robert Horne in similar vein, and therefore, 'every day shall be as my dying day', and Bishop Ken's hymn taught Christians to 'Live ev'ry day as if 'twere thy last'.[16] Indeed, seventeenth-century handbooks of the *ars moriendi*, such as Jeremy Taylor's *Holy Dying*, treated life itself as but propaedeutic to death. It 'must be the business of our whole Lives to prepare for Death', proclaimed William Sherlock's influential *A Practical Discourse Concerning Death* (1690).[17] The Puritan, Philip Henry, was praised by his biographer, because 'he made Death very familiar to himself'; 'such is the comfort of dying daily, when we come to dye indeed'.[18]

Thus, a multitude of cultural emblems – from the macabre icons of Jacobean funeral tablets, with their grinning deaths' heads, to the testimony of Puritan diaries – fuse to confirm that in post-Reformation society, death was the unique trauma. A man's duty – his interest too – was positively to confront it. The ultimate test for a Protestant was to engage in single-handed combat with Death and vanquish it. An eighteenth-century medical self-help manual,

Every Patient His Own Doctor, significantly subtitles itself as: *The Sick Man's Triumph Over Death and the Grave.*[19]

Death was the Terror. Its sting was drawn by religious rituals girding the living against its threat. Family prayers, fasting, repentance, devotions, Bible-reading, and so forth, both before and at the deathbed, fortified the faithful as they died the good death. For what dying predominantly meant amongst the articulate elite in Stuart England was a religious rite, the liberation of the soul from its carnal prison, and its escape into the blissful. Philip Henry's deathbed offers a paradigm of the charged drama of this rite of passage. Sensing death, Henry took his farewells of his family, bestowing upon them blessings and warnings, and uttering pious ejaculations, prayers, and Scripture texts. His biographer concludes:[20]

> His Understanding and Speech continued almost to the last Breath, and he was still in his dying Agonies calling upon God, and committing himself to him. One of the last words he said, when found himself just ready to depart, was *O Death, where is thy*—with that his speech falter'd

– and he quickly expired.

Within such religious dramas, medical procedure for treating prospectively fatal illness typically remained in the shadows, secondary, almost irrelevant. Medical theory and practice acknowledged the fact that life and death lay in the hands of Nature (as Classical medicine stipulated) or of Providence. The art of physic from the Hippocratics onwards was the business more of diagnosis and prognosis than of cure, and certainly not of 'miracle cure', snatching people from death's jaws.[21] Doctors and laymen alike accepted that death was inexorable, implacable. Hence – with few exceptions, such as the lives of sovereigns – doctors did not attempt heroic intervention to delay or defy death. Indeed, the excruciating deathbed of Charles II – who, of course, civilly apologized to his physicians for being an unconscionable time a-dying – perhaps indicates why the faculty was wise to steer clear of futile heroics.[22]

The New Death in the Eighteenth Century

The coming of the eighteenth century brought no sudden change of mind or practice. Death's blow remained fell, mysterious, fatal, and Christians squeezed their moral pieties from it.

Thus John Woolman, the Quaker, dramatized what he thought was his own imminent death.[23]

> In this swift race it pleased God to visit me with sickness, so that I doubted of recovery; then did darkness, horror, and amazement with full force seize me, even when my pain and distress of body were very great. I thought it would have been better for me never to have had being, than to see the day which I now saw. I was filled with confusion, and in great affliction, both of mind and body, I lay and bewailed myself.

I had not confidence to lift up my cries to God, whom I had thus offended.

In similarly reverential tones, William Cowper, in his evangelical phase in 1767, admired the pious death of a Bristol boy who:[24]

> during his whole illness, which lasted little more than 48 hours . . . would pray with great Fervency. To his Nurse on Monday morning early, he said, 'Nanny, I have nothing more to do with Books and Learning now – I have laid 'em all aside'. Even in his Rovings which were frequent, he was either talking of his Books, or praying earnestly & Singing Hymns. On Monday he desir'd his Mother to read to him the 21st. Psalm, or rather, said He let Me read it. He took the Book in hand, but his Eyes were already dim – He then desired his Mother again to read it, & afterwards to pray with him. She did so, & he Joined with Fervor. On Tuesday Night about 2 hours before he died, his Mother was for applying fresh warm Flannels to his Bowels; upon touching him, he said, Oh you disturb me in my Journey. 2 Hours after he died, without a Struggle or a Groan, in the Midst of a Hymn. –

Certain eighteenth-century developments, such as the emergence of actuarialism and life assurance,[25] betoken more secular attitudes to life's chances. Yet even in the polished obituary columns of the *Gentleman's Magazine*, death was still seen as awful, arbitrary, and absolute. Occasionally, the dying man himself even spared the obituarist the need to point the moral. One entry reads:[26]

> Suddenly, at Oswestry, Mr. Harrison, supervisor of excise in that town. Just before he fell, he exclaimed, 'O Lord! how suddenly I am struck! All medical skill and assistance are useless!'

Protestant Dissenters, above all, continued to regard dying as the ultimate duty of meeting one's Maker face-to face. But the vision of Death as the supreme ordeal was not exclusive to them. Samuel Johnson's dread of death as a judgement was not unusual amongst Anglicans, especially those schooled, like him, upon the pietist, William Law.[27] Boswell shared Johnson's fears – hence his fascination with execution – seeing it as a fearsome 'evil'.[28]

In 1712, Nathaniel Spinckes, an Anglican clergyman, penned his *The Sick Man Visited*, for the benefit of those undergoing their 'last conflict with Death'. Spinckes said hardly a word about routine medicine, but elaborated on 'spiritual physic', exercises in penitence and humiliation which the dying person ought, like Job, to undergo, under the 'correction' of disease and the 'usefulness' of sickness, to win a glorious 'victory over Death'.[29] And a generation later, the pious physician, James Stonhouse, wrote a handbook for the gravely ill, *Friendly Advice to a Patient*, in which cleansing the conscience took priority over any last-ditch measures of the physician. The 'smarting rod' and the 'afflicting hand of God' should render the patient 'chastened', since they were the 'effects of sin', albeit designed to prepare man for Death's 'awful sight'.[30]

We see much the same sorts of attitudes in the writings of the Dissenting doctor, Richard Kay, towards mid-century. Kay, above all, stresses the Divine mystery of death, its suddenness, and the need to attend to it, lest it overtake us unprepared. 'Lord, Help me to make Death very familiar to me'; 'by these Decays in Nature may I learn to die daily'.[31] He knew its suddenness from direct sick-round experience:[32]

> In my Return I call'd at Brother Joseph Baron's in Bury, where they told me yt Coz. John Hamer at Bucksden was dead, when I came Home Father likewise gave me the same Account, and that he dyed this Morning. O what need we have always to be ready lest Death shou'd find us unprepared, we know neither, the day nor the Hour wherein the Son of Man cometh, he many Times cometh as a Thief in the Night, at an Hour when we think not of, but yet whenever Death comes we must go prepared or unprepared. Lord therefore help us to redeem our Time because our days are few and evil.

Such experiences made him, as a pious Dissenter, anticipate his own departure:[33]

> We live here in a very uncertain World, in a World full of Changes; yet one Event happeneth to all. It must not always be with me as at present, that I must go out and come in, No; a Time will come and God knows how soon when the Powers of my Nature must be tied and blocked up from Working, when I must think, speak, act or move no more; the Time will come when Afflictions and Death will seize me, when I must be laid speechless and motionless by the cold Wall, when I must have my Winding-Sheet thrown over me and be laid in the dark and silent Grave, not withstanding my present Health, Strength and Capacity yet Death the Kings of Terrours will overcome; there is no Discharge in that War; O Death, where is thy Sting; O Grave where is thy Victory.

Throughout the Georgian age, people thus continued to manage their own deaths in the time-honoured ways. George Williamson described his father's preparations in 1821:[34]

> He gave me directions how his coffin was to be put into the grave, and told me that, after the grave was dug, the headstone which I had erected to the memory of my mother should be taken carefully out of its place and laid upon two poles to prevent its being injured, and that, after the coffin had been put in and the earth well pressed round it, the stone was

to be replaced. I gave implicit obedience to these directions. When I last took leave of him he said, by next Saturday all would be over, and he feared he would die hard, as he was very tough.

Nevertheless, outlooks on death did modulate in polite society, particularly those touched by the Enlightenment suspicion of 'enthusiasm'. Amongst the elite, rationalist, philosophical and Stoic attitudes grew more conspicuous. Making a *manly* end counted. Lady Mary Wortley Montagu admired the exit of a certain Dr J––:[35]

Who died at Rome with as much stoicism as Cato at Utica, and less desperation, leaving a world he was weary of with the cool indifference you quit a dirty inn, to continue your journey to a place where you hope for better accommodation. He took part of a bowl of punch with some Englishmen of my acquaintance the day before his death, and told them with a firm tone of voice, 'by G – he was going'.

The potentially providence-challenging concept of 'natural death' became more widely accepted,[36] as by the Deist, Erasmus Darwin, who confided, 'when I think of dying it is always without pain or fear'.[37] Similarly, the doctor philosopher, David Hartley, offered a purely rational account of why Death was so awesome – it being both unknown, yet also associated with horrifying events.[38] A few *esprits forts*, such as David Hume, openly questioned the afterlife, accepted oblivion, and met their ends calmly, neither fired with hope nor racked with fear. Boswell 'asked him if the thought of Annihilation never gave him any uneasiness. He said not the least'.[39] Hume notoriously bantered with Adam Smith on his deathbed about his lack of excuse for delaying embarcation upon Charon's ferry across the Styx:[40]

I thought I might say to him 'Good Charon, I have been correcting my works for a new edition. Allow me a little time that I may see how the public received the alterations'. But Charon would answer, 'When you have seen the effect of these, you will be making other alterations. There will be no end of such . . . '

Such attitudes scandalized Boswell and Johnson, terrified of damnation or oblivion. Boswell wanted to see people meeting death fighting bravely, to set him an example. When Lord Kames shuffled off without such a gladiatorial performance, he was disappointed: 'I regretted that he did not say one word as a dying man. Nothing edifying, nothing pious'.[41]

Hume, however, remained one of a tiny minority, though many others, while not denying the Christian message, distanced themselves from its liturgical forms. A few protested that the horror holy dying induced was artificial and unnecessary. Lady Elizabeth Holland, for example, argued that 'the worst part of the Christian dispensation is the terror it inculcates upon a deathbed. The wisest dread it; no person who is strictly brought up in the principles of Christianity can ever thoroughly shake off the fear of dying.'[42]

As part of this trend, burials in a pagan style became not uncommon; at the funeral of John Underwood of Whittlesea, reported in the *Gentleman's Magazine* in 1733, the requiem involved singing the 31st Ode of Horace, and the mourners were instructed to forget the departed.[43] And paralleling this, new attitudes towards suicide gained ground, dispelling the traditional cannon law characterization of it as a vice, sin, and crime, and treating it with sympathy and tolerance.[44]

Indeed, Ariès, Illich, and others have pinpointed a transformation in the protocols of dying during the Enlightenment.[45] It would be misleading to depict it as a dramatic reversal – as it were, abandoning expectation of the world to come, and focusing instead on the parting from this. Rather, as belief in eternal hellfire collapsed,[46] much greater confidence was expressed in the assurance of future bliss. Death thus ceased to be the ultimate foe, requiring heroic acts of will, faith, purgation, and penitence. Instead, it became seen as an easy transition to a happier state, a natural metamorphosis to be accepted, even welcomed. The dying Joseph Addison grasped his son's hand and declared, 'See in what peace a Christian can die'.[47] Death could be a gentle friend. As the surgeon, John Hunter, reported on his deathbed, 'If I had a pen in my hand now, and were able to write, I could tell how easy and pleasant a thing it is to die.'[48] Henry Cockburn similarly recorded Joseph Black's end: 'He died seated, with a bowl of milk on his knee, of which his ceasing to live did not spill a drop; a departure which seemed, after the event happened, might have been foretold of this attenuated philosophical gentleman.'[49]

Of course, to many, such an approach was impossible, repulsive, even perverse. Brought up on Scottish Calvinism, Boswell continued to personify Death as the final foe – though he himself passed away in a coma.[50] But in polished circles, the macabre associations of death became minimized, and dying could be imagined to be as easy as sleeping. Angels replaced traditional deaths-heads on tombs, funeral tablets testified earthly virtues, and the Gothic paraphernalia of yew trees and screech owls – the ambience of Gray's *Elegy*[51] – transformed death from transcendental trauma into a human morality drama, teaching that the paths of glory lead but to the grave. Thus for many, dying ceased to be a joust with death, or a trial before a hanging judge, or even a leap in the dark. The idea of natural death became more acceptable, and conversely, uncontrollable terror when contemplating that quintessentially natural process became stigmatized as morbid: the dreaded hypochondria.[52]

During the eighteenth century, the family assumed pride of place in the procedures of dying, as in so many other scenes of life. When the Rev. William Jones contemplated his own death, his family crowded into this thoughts:[53]

> *Dulce domum*! I feel that I can neither live, nor die, anywhere, so comfortably, as in my own nest. I must not attempt to fly far from it! I am often much inconvenienced, when only a few hours, or a few miles from my home. I shall very much like to have my Old Mate, and my dear

children, around my death-bed, and to utter a few (*novissima verba*) last words of farewell to them.

Our records of Georgian deathbeds suggest they were rarely great public enactments, with clergymen prominent and doors flung open to the world, as in traditional Catholicism.[54] Rather, they reveal a sombre private sadness, involving concentrated quiet emotion, expressed largely through person-to person contact, amongst the circles of kith and kin.

Peaceful Death

The new keynotes, thus, were intimacy, sweetness, and peace. Early in the nineteenth century, the seventeen-year-old Lucy Warren, a clergyman's daughter from Edmonton, was wasting away. The family physician diagnosed 'nervous rheumatism', presumably a form of consumption. He played a supportive role in her last weeks, and the family desired that 'no relief which medicine could afford might be neglected'. But what buoyed up the dying girl were the ministrations of her nuclear family, as is evident from the elaborate journal they kept of her last days.[55]

It is easy to find such scenes mawkish or morbid – Victorianism before the Victorians – and certainly, their governing assumptions are through and through *Christian*. But what principally transpired on that deathbed was an epitome of regular family relations; a dutiful daughter, who, above all 'wished to avoid giving trouble', sustained with 'patience and submission', obeying doting parents who nursed, fed, and watched over her. In that family, there was no question of wrestling with death. Indeed, death itself had become unspeakable (her mother wrote of Lucy, 'she never mentioned the subject in express terms'). But death was now exemplarily embraced 'with serenity and calmness' as a sweet release. The Quaker, Isabella Harris's, father went much the same way:[56]

About half an hour before his close he requested us to pray, after which we inquired if he felt his mind comfortable. He replied, 'Yes; very happy', and as long as he could articulate, his words were, 'Happy, Happy'. He appeared perfectly sensible to the last; and after bestowing an inexpressible look of affection on us all, we stood around his bed, he quietly fell asleep in Jesus, without sigh or groan, or any apparent suffering, which was a favour he had often in health ardently desired might be granted him.

In his turn, Isabella's husband followed in the same way:[57]

There was no struggle, no appearance of death, not even a sigh escaped him, but he appeared like one falling asleep. Thus departed my dearest one, spared all conflict bodily and mental; it was more like a translation than a death.

Jane Austen's death, as recorded by her sister, matched these ideals (albeit with the aid of medicines applied by her doctor 'to give her ease'):[58]

> There was nothing convulsed or which gave the idea of pain in her look, on the contrary, but for the continual motion of the head, she gave me the idea of a beautiful statue, & even now in her coffin, there is such a sweet serene air over her countenance as is quite pleasant to contemplate.

These examples illustrate that the emergent Georgian goal was a peaceful death, free of pain. The Georgians wished to die in peace. In the nineteenth century, they also had to turn into angels, partly because they were too good for the world. In the 1841, Mrs Stanley wrote to her mother-in-law, Lady Maria Josepha Holroyd Stanley, about the ailing Catherine Thomas, her husband's cousin, Lady Stanley's niece:[59]

> We are all prepared to part with dear Catherine but it is hard to bear the fluctuations of hope & fear – *she* is better for having us . . . She is so tender & has often said she was so glad I was here; when all together she said, 'pray talk of me always when I am gone & never say poor Catherine'. She desired to be buried in the North Transept, gave all directions. I cannot feel she is for this world she is too heavenly minded & Dr Lubbock says tho' her symptoms are not so bad he never saw a patient recover who had such a strong feeling of death.

A later letter to Lady Stanley from Mary, Catherine's sister, tells us 'the Soul seems already winged for flight – she is lying in the most heavenly state, speaking a word of comfort to each, quite alive to everything that passes'.[60] We are brought down to earth, however, by the elderly Lady Stanley's no-nonsense response:[61]

> I have longed for a letter from you for some days – I want to hear more of the dear Child's bodily state & less of her mental or spiritual . . . I really think you have all lost your wits – have got into the seventh heaven of enthusiasm & forgot everything sublunary. You gave her over . . . & have fancied her under inspiration almost, forgetting that the greatest criminals & villains frequently go out of the world exulting at the gallows in their assurances of eternal happiness & really, I have no doubt, feel what they say . . . I could not say all this or ask for these *medical* particulars if I was not very sanguine of her recovery.

Over two centuries, there were thus massive shifts in how people armed themselves against death. The traditional Christian confrontation eventually gave way to a Victorian sentimentality concerned mainly to mask its reality. What was the part of medicine in this changing model of dying? Did the profession play any part in establishing it? The answer is 'yes', but that part is not quite that as depicted by recent historians. Illich, in particular, has argued that, puffed up by Enlightenment pride, doctors began to nurse the illusion that they could prolong life and conquer death.[62] There is some truth in Illich's interpretation of death-denying doctors, for in hospital foundations, in smallpox inoculation, and in the rise of public health, medicine undeniably went on to the offensive against disease. Certain developments – above all, the Humane Movement, designed to resuscitate the apparently drowned – mark medical campaigns to snatch people back from the jaws of death.[63]

Nevertheless, in 1800 no less than in 1650, dying the 'good death' was critically important; but how precisely one died well, was changing. In the seventeenth century, the good death meant vigilance, being at every instant prepared to meet your Maker. Death was fearful, courage essential and Victory the prize. Increasingly, such a vision of Death's torments seemed incompatible with a loving and even a just God, and with humanity towards the dying themselves. Under a benevolent Deity, surely death was not to be feared; it was, after all, only like a sleep. And if like a sleep, surely it could be encountered with all of sleep's serenity. If, then, dying were no great trauma, its management by the medical profession seemed merely a logical extension of the routine care they offered. Death's sting had indeed been drawn.

NOTES

1   Sterne, *Tristram Shandy*, 459. The substance of this chapter is dealt with more fully in Porter, 'Death and the Doctors'.
2   Fry and Cresswell (eds), *Memoir of the Life of Elizabeth Fry*, II, 488.
3   Yorke (ed.), *Diary of John Baker*, 419.
4   [Martineau], *Life in the Sick-Room*,104.
5   Hobhouse (ed.), *Diary of a West Country Physician*, 55.
6   Ibid.
7   For discussion see Jarrett, *England in the Age of Hogarth*, 210f.,228.
8   Christie (ed.), *Diary of the Revd William Jones*, 63.
9   Jewitt (ed.), *Life of William Hutton*, 115.
10 Oliver Heywood chronicles thousands of sudden deaths, as did the seventeenth-century Puritan, Nehemiah Wallington (see Seaver, *Wallington's World*); Clarkson *Death, Disease and Famine*.
11 Verney (ed.), *Verney Letters*, I, 44.
12 Christie (ed.), *Diary of the Revd William Jones*, 267.
13 Ariès, *Western Attitudes Towards Death*; idem, *Hour of Our Death*; McManners, *Death and the Enlightenment*; Gittings, *Death, Burial and the Individual*; Lebrun, *Les Hommes et la Mort en Anjou*.
14 Huizinga, *Waning of the Middle Ages*; Kurtz, *Dance of Death*; Clark, *Dance of Death*; Boase, *Death in the Middle Ages*; Vovelle and Vovelle, *La Vision de la Mort*.
15 See Stannard, *Puritan Way of Death*. There are some valuable pages in Wear, 'Interfaces'.
16 Quoted in Wear, 'Puritan Perceptions of Illness', 64; cf. Stannard, *Puritan Way of Death*, 77.
17 Sherlock, *Practical Discourse Concerning Death*, 351.

[18] Henry, *Account of the Life and Death of Philip Henry*, 129.
[19] Robinson, *Every Patient His Own Doctor*. See also O'Connor, *Art of Dying Well*.
[20] Henry, *Account of the Life and Death of Philip Henry*, 11.
[21] Temkin, *Galenism*.
[22] Crawfurd, *Last Days of Charles II*.
[23] Whittier (ed.), *Journal of John Woolman*, 55.
[24] King and Ryskamp (eds), *Letters and Prose Writings of William Cowper*, I, 177.
[25] Supple, *Royal Exchange Assurance*.
[26] *Gentleman's Magazine*, 62 (1792), 869.
[27] For Johnson, see Porter, ' "Hunger of Imagination" '; Hagstrum, 'Dr Johnson's Fear of Death'.
[28] Bailey (ed.), *Boswell's Column*, 83-102, esp. 91, 98 (death is 'immediately an evil').
[29] Spinckes, *Sick Man Visited*, 93, 102, 132, 190, 344.
[30] Stonhouse, *Friendly Advice to a Patient*, 3, 12, 13, 24, 25, 30.
[31] Brockbank and Kenworthy (eds), *Diary of Richard Kay*, 46.
[32] Ibid., cf. 157f.
[33] Ibid., 145.
[34] Williamson, *Autobiography*, 50.
[35] Johnson (ed.), *Letters from Lady Mary Wortley Montagu*, 525.
[36] Illuminating is Illich, *Limits to Medicine*, 186.
[37] King-Hele, *Life of Erasmus Darwin*, 252. The occasion for writing is the death of Josiah Wedgwood.
[38] Hartley, *Observations on Man*, 293. Hazlitt reflected on such issues in his 'On the Fear of Death': see Blythe (ed.), *William Hazlitt Selected Writings*, 47-81.
[39] Mossner, *Life of David Hume*, 598.
[40] Ibid., 589f.
[41] Lustig and Pottle (eds), *Boswell: Applause of the Jury*, 45.
[42] Ilchester (ed.), *Lady Holland's Journal*, I, 156. She did not believe death final, ibid., 195.
[43] Quoted in Williams, *Age of Agony*, 277.
[44] See above all Sprott, *English Debate on Suicide*; Noon, 'On Suicide'; MacDonald, 'The Secularization of Suicide in England'.
[45] Ariès, *Hour of our Death*; Illich, *Limits to Medicine*, 174f.
[46] Walker, *Decline of Hell*.
[47] Smithers, *Life of Joseph Addison*, 560.
[48] Quoted in Ferriar, *Medical Histories*, 9.
[49] Cockburn, *Memorials*, 51.
[50] Brady, *James Boswell: The Later Years*, 490. His son reported, 'he is ignorant of the dangerous situation in which he was, and, I am sorry to say, still continues to be'.
[51] Cf. Sells and Sells, *Thomas Gray*.
[52] Rush, *Medical Inquiries*, 326.
[53] Christie (ed.), *Diary of the Rev'd William Jones*, 271, cf. Stone, *Family, Sex and Marriage*; Trumbach, *Rise of the Egalitarian Family*.
[54] McManners, *Death and the Enlightenment*; Ariès, *Images of Man and Death*, 100.
[55] Journal of Lucy Warren, Wellcome Manuscript Collection. There is much illuminating in Morley, *Death, Heaven and the Victorians*; Curl, *The Victorian Celebration of Death*.
[56] Harris (ed.), *Family Memorials*, 56-7.
[57] Ibid.
[58] Chapman (ed.), *Jane Austen's Letters*, 513.
[59] Mitford (ed.), *Ladies of Alderley*, 16.
[60] Ibid., 17.

61 Ibid., 18. Lady Stanley was the teenage Maria Josepha Holroyd, the daughter of Gibbon's friend, Lord Sheffield, and had charmed the great historian.

62 Illich, *Limits to Medicine*, 189f.

63 Hawkins, 'History of Resuscitation'; Payne, 'On the Resuscitation of the Apparently Dead'; Bishop, *Short History of the Royal Humane Society*.

Chapter 15:
Fighting Back

Besieged on all sides by threats to their health, people often succumbed. We have surveyed them falling ill, trying to make sense of sickness, inuring themselves to suffering, and finally, going under and dying (or, perhaps, achieving blessed release). Yet another course was open: fighting back. Threatened with disease, people, of course, tried to ward it off, or, were that too late, to conquer it. Self-defence was a positive duty, for, as George Cheyne remarked, 'It is a common Saying, That every Man past Forty, is either a *Fool* or *Physician*.'[1]

'Prevention is easier than cure' ran the proverb, and everyone believed in going forearmed. Thus, when the Hon. John Byng set off on his travels round England, he made sure he took his own sheets (dry and bugless) and medicine chest. 'I am also stock'd with James's powder; so should a fever overtake me, I will hope that by taking some of his doses and being well wrapp'd up in blankets I shall chase away sickness, without consulting the medical country blockheads, who kill, or cure, by chance.'[2]

It was hoped, of course, that sickness bouts would prove temporary, and end with recovery, or at least, relief. Confidence in this outcome was instilled partly through experience; partly through the Christian faith in a guiding Providence; partly through the ministrations of doctors; and, last but not least, because of a widespread trust in the healing powers of Nature. From Hippocratic times onwards, medicine itself had subscribed, sometimes more, sometimes less, to the *vis medicatrix naturae*. It had plenty of advocates amongst the faculty in Georgian times, particularly those honest – or cynical – enough, to recognize that so many medical 'cures' merely masked spontaneous remissions. As John Moore put it:[3]

> This *vis medicatrix naturae*, this constant tendency in nature to overcome disease and restore health, was observed by the father of medicine; and a sentiment to the same purpose is the very first expressed by Sydenham in his inestimable work, and is acknowledged by all candid and discerning practitioners, to have a powerful influence in the cure of diseases. Indeed

I am inclined to believe that physicians, in proportion to their candour and discernment, acknowledge and rely upon this power in nature; and in proportion to their selfishness and weakness, impute every recovery to their own prescriptions.

Doubting the healing power of doctors, the laity, not surprisingly, found the doctrine inviting. Philip Thicknesse, that bumptious amateur physician, tirelessly advocated 'DR NATURE', 'that first of all physicians'.[4] 'Let well alone' – another adage often quoted – was adjudged by Maria Edgeworth an 'excellent proverb', noting the black humour of the Italian epitaph *'stavo ben, ma per star meglio, sto qui'*.[5] When people fell sick, they did, indeed, frequently leave recovery to nature, and with confidence.[6] Thus the Quaker William Stout:[7]

> In the 2nd month this year, I was seized with great paine in my bowels and violent purging and other distempers. Which much weakened me, and was advised to doctors, which I had not hitherto done for thirty years last past; but always let nature and time worke a cure, as it has hitherto done, and now did, with patience and resignation.

When Stout's sister, Ellen, grew old, she developed serious pains in her breast, but trusted to God and Nature, and:[8]

> by Divine Providence she got over it, although for some weeks she was very weake, faint and thirsty: was advised to apply to a doctor, but was allways averse to it, and freely gave up to let nature have its course in life or death, which considering her infirmities, I think has rather prolonged her life.

But the idea did not appeal solely to canny outsiders like Stout. People of all walks and ranks of life believed that Nature often knew best. Lady Caroline Fox subjected her son, Stephen, to a hefty barrage of medication. She then changed tack, finally writing in April 1759 that, on the advice of Dr Duncan, she would 'let him alone for some time and leave nature to work'.[9]

'The healing power of nature' was a phrase with a rationale. Sicknesses were commonly seen as Nature's way of coping with imbalances or poisons in the system; hence, a malady was self-limiting and possessed its own 'wisdom'. Yet trusting to nature rarely amounted to a dogmatic embargo upon doctoring. For most people when sick *acted*. Action was indicated by a normal sense of everyday practical responsibilities: the need to be well enough to cope, carry on, earn a living, and sustain self-respect. Protestantism underwrote the duty of self-help. Enlightenment optimism instilled confidence in man's power, right, and duty even, to control his own destiny.[10]

Hand-me-down wisdom was brimful of saws telling what should be done to ward off sickness (magic, of course, still had its charms for the masses).[11] It is worth reiterating a point made in Chapter 2: prevention was the first priority, and within prevention, cleanliness gained increasing prominence as the prophylactic against sickness. Domestic improvements set personal hygiene within the sights of the affluent bourgeoisie. John Evelyn wrote in 1653:[12]

> I first began a Course of yearely washing my head with Warme Water, mingld with a decoction of Sweete herbs, & immediately, with cold Spring water, which much refreshd me, & succeeded very well with me divers yeares:

Pepys was no less cleanliness-conscious. 'Had Sarah to comb my head clean, which I find so foul with poudering and other troubles', he wrote in 1662.[13] He grew fussy about dirt:[14]

> So to my wife's chamber, and there supped and got her cut my hair and look my shirt, for I have itched mightily these six or seven days; and when all came to all, she finds that I am louzy, having found in my head and body above 20 lice, little and great.

The diarist was appalled, 'being more than I have had I believe almost these 20 years.'

Incidents such as these show a concerted attempt by go-ahead people to regulate their lives for health's sake within a safer environment. John Byrom's letters to his wife reveal immense solicitude over the particulars of health care for his children. He enquires after his daughter, Beppy, who had been sick. 'If she is not better I suppose there may be occasion', he suggests, 'to have her bled.'[15] These thoughts released a welter of health advice for the rest of his family. The children must not 'go too bare about the neck for coughs and cold weather'. For diet, they were to be restricted to 'herbs, roots and fruits in season, good house-bread, water porridge, milk fresh, etc.', rather than being fed artificial concoctions such as dumplings, for to 'take bread and crumble it and sugar it and plum it and boil it, is to take much pains to turn wholesome nourishment into unwholesome.' Anyway, it is bad to accustom children to sugar, as distinct from the 'proper nourishing sweetness' naturally contained in 'green gooseberries, apricots, etc.'. Mention of sugar prompted the question of tea. This could prove medicinal: 'I believe a good dish of bohea of a good reasonable strength sweetened and creamed to her palate must be as good a thing for Beppy's cough as one can devise any how else.' Nevertheless caution was needed. 'When the children have tea they had better drink it while it is good, and not the last dregs of it only.' Byrom was apologetically insistent over his health-advice minutiae: 'Thou must excuse me for talking thus rambling about their food, etc.; since I have lost one of my young folks it makes me more impertinent about the rest.'

People thus were alert to the rules of prevention. But these were often not enough, and sickness supervened. What did they do then?

This final chapter clearly cannot begin to spell out by chapter-and-verse the regimens and treatments deployed by the sick for all that ailed them. Rather, we shall sketch the options. Taking medicines was by no means the universal resort – though it probably became an increasingly normal choice.[16] Even more so, summoning or visiting a regular medical practitioner was certainly not the immediate and automatic response of the sick. On falling sick, most pre-moderns first had recourse to a spectrum of remedies, treatments, and help supplied by self, family, and/or friends. In many cases, this was thought quite sufficient. Professional doctors were often far away, their charges grated even on those who could perfectly well afford them, and putting oneself in their care all too readily represented a further health hazard. The *habitué* of the doctor was either the fop with time, at least, to kill, or the hardened hypochondriac, addicted to being doctored.[17]

So people commonly kept 'primary care' in their own hands. What did they do? Obviously much depended upon myriad variables – their capacity to put family and business responsibilities on ice while seeking remedy, their financial situation, and a host of other practical factors, to say nothing of the gravity of the complaint in question. For some troubles, the remedy was obvious. The constipated reached for the jar of rhubarb or senna.[18] In other cases, diagnosis was more difficult, and the range of possibilities greater. The sick person might well solicit the advice of those around him; he would frequently also pursue – simultaneously or *seriatim* – more than one avenue of cure. The more lethal (or 'incurable') the condition, the greater the number of recipes in the family recipe books and on the grapevine. Everything had its 'cure'. When plague was rife in 1665, Aunt Asham knew just what Sir Ralph Verney needed: 'Ware a quill as is filed up with quicsilver', she recommended:[19]

and sealed up with hard waxe & soed up in a silke thinge with a string to ware aabout your neck, this is as sartine as any thinge is to keep one from taking of the Plage if one is in the house with them . . . iff you let your Horse ware it about his head he will never have the desese. This is a slite bisness if itt does presarve one from this sad desese, as the lady Bemone tells me she hath worn it herselfe & intends to have some for all her sarvants, & Sir Tho: Bemone hunted with his nabores Hounes as thate Horses ware infected & his horse nevor choed the desese . . .

Regimen
On falling sick, people commonly intensified (or remembered all too late) those regimens designed to keep them healthy, especially the non-naturals.[20] 'Dr Merryman, Dr Diet, Dr Quiet, . . . cure all diseases', instructed Robert Burton, in a jingle which had echoed down the centuries.[21] When Dr John North, later Master of Trinity College, Cambridge, was flattened by illness, he was recommended 'for doctors, to use only the famous three, Diet, Quiet, and Merriman'.[22]

No less frequently urged were change and diversion. Sick bodies and brooding minds needed distraction. Gibbon was a great believer in change of air. When the wife of his friend, John Holroyd, fell sick, he made known his concern about her 'health, her spirits and her thinness'. A doctor might do some good:[23]

> I wish she may receive benefit from Dr. Pepys's prescription but am of opinion that change of air and amusements would prove the best Physician. Recollect the service our little tour did to her, consider that the evenings are growing long and Sheffield place affords no variety of objects or company. You *know she loves Bath*, which is now in season, and I should think that place would fill up the gloomy vacuity between this time and Christmas.

(Did Gibbon suspect what was really behind Mrs Holroyd's indisposition, or did he merely have massive faith in the therapeutics of imagination?) Change of air seemed of capital importance to Thomas Gray. Enquiring of his friend, Mason, about his consumptive wife, Gray typically poohpoohed the 'Physicians' and 'the inutility of their applications', recommending instead instant removal:[24]

> I am told, that Ld H: offers you the use of Walmer-Castle, but that you wait till the spring is more advanced to put this in execution. I think, I should by no means delay at all. The air of the coast is at all seasons warmer, than that of the inland-country: the weather is now mild & open, & (unless the rains increase) fit for travelling. Remember, how well she bore the journey to London; & it is certain, that sort of motion in her case instead of fatigue often brings an accession of strength.

Alongside travelling, change of diet was a popular panacea. Thomas Turner grew worried about his perennially inflamed eyes: a new eating pattern was the solution:[25]

> Sat. 17 Sept. . . . I am come to a resolution, as I am so continually almost troubled with the inflamation in my eyes, to leave off during life (unless anything very material should intervene) eating any sort of meat, unless sometimes a bit of boiled lamb, mutton, or veal, of chick, or any such harmless diet; as also to refrain from all sorts of strong liquor; and to continue not eating any supper, from eating of which I have debarred myself for the general part this 12 months.
> Sun. 18 Sept. My whole family at church in the morn, that is, myself, wife, maid and 2 boys . . . . We dined on a piece of boiled beef, a currant suet pudding and carrots . . . .

As the old adage had it, a 'good cook is half physician'. Ever full of tips for the self-medicator, the *Gentleman's Magazine* printed in 1751 a self-cure for asthma, which drew attention to the primary need to rectify one's diet:[26]

RECIPE FOR AN ASTHMA

My good old friend! accept from me
The following rules without a fee . . .
An asthma is your case, I think;
[He recommended abstinence from sharp foods:]
I mean of meat preserv'd in salt,
Or any liquor made of malt.
From season'd sauce avert your eyes,
From hams, and tongues, and pigeon pies.
If ven'son pasty's set before ye,
Each bit you eat memento mori.

No less important than air and diet for combating sickness was exercise. 'I must be on horseback for life, if I would be healthy', claimed John Wesley.[27] In 1773, John Baker went down with 'shivering fits', and the great Dr Fothergill was called in. He declined to prescribe, sending Baker 'out for airing'.[28] On one occasion, Garrick attributed his own recovery to 'that excellent *physician*, a *horse*';[29] and Betsy Sheridan said of her sick father that 'Riding is to him of more service than all the Phisicians can do for him'.[30] Richard Radcliffe hoped to be of use to a friend's father, 'to banish for ever that same gout':[31]

A sedentary life is evidently hurtful to you, and yet you are resolved to persist in it. Give me leave, therefore, to send you the following prescription: Ride more, sit less, and don't confine yourself so much to your nasty school.

Leigh Hunt developed frightening symptoms: 'a palpitation of the heart', associated with a 'visitation of hypochondria': 'The palpitation was so strong and incessant, that I was forced for some nights, to sleep in a reclining posture, and I expected sudden death.' He drove out all his hypochondriacal tendencies by 'riding':[32]

when I began the horseback, I soon found that the more I rode, and (I used to think) the harder I rode, the less of the palpitation became. Galloping one day up a sloping piece of ground, the horse suddenly came to a stand, by a chalk-pit, and I was agreeably surprised to find myself not only unprecipitated over his head (for though a decent, I was not a skilful rider), but in a state of singular calmness and self-possession – a right proper masculine state of nerves.

Rather more heroic was his contemporary, Colonel Hawker, who had a short way with the 'shivers', i.e., ague. Strenuous exercise was the answer:[33]

> in order to shake off the shivers that I've had for a week I slipped my
> long water boots and waded up the river. I killed in good style all that I
> shot at viz 3 jack snipes, 2 of them a brilliant double shot to front and
> rear with 9 moorhens and 3 divers. I then shifted my boots and beat all
> the woods and the rows and the only head of game I set eyes on was 1
> rabbit which I bagged.

But exercise could benefit the delicate, too. When his friend, Mrs King, was
poorly William Cowper offered these words of advice: 'I know not why, but I
rather suspect that you do not allow yourself sufficient air and exercise'.[34]
Exercise was thought especially valuable for mental maladies, or those caused
by excessive study or introspection. Boswell 'complained to Mr Johnson that I
was much afflicted with melancholy, which was hereditary in our family.'
Johnson knew the answer: 'He advised me to have constant occupation of
mind, to take a great deal of exercise, and to live moderately; especially to
shun drinking at night.'[35] Like many others, Johnson thought it was one of the
very few consolations of the poor that they escaped such disorders: 'labouring
men who work much and live sparingly are seldom or never troubled with low
spirits.'
    Boswell never took that advice to heart, but even he was occasionally willing
to believe that physical jerks would prove beneficial. On 6 May 1763, he
'awaked as usual, heavy, confused, and splenetic. Every morning this is the
case with me.' What *was* to be done? A friend had the answer:[36]

> Dempster prescribed to me to cut two or three brisk capers round the
> room, which I did, and found attended with most agreeable effects. It
> expelled the phlegm from my heart, gave my blood a free circulation,
> and my spirits a brisk flow; so that I was all at once made happy. I must
> remember this and practise it.

Being sick was being dispirited. Hence, it was important that the ailing had
opportunities for company and diversion. Solitude was thought bad for the
sick, whereas, as Dr Andrew Borde had argued back in the sixteenth century,
'mirth is one of the chiefest things of physic'. Eliza Pierce had an uncle who
was sick:[37]

> we have had the pleasure of Miss Sydenhams company for three or four
> days this week and I don't know if their enlivening conversation has not
> been the means of restoring my Uncle to his former health sooner then it
> might have been otherwise. I assure it is a sovereign remedy.

All these practical actions had an immense hold on the lay mind. Many
thought that pursuit of the non-naturals was much more promising than

taking physick. As Henry More wrote to Anne Conway:[38]

> I do not at all mislike your resolution in giving over Physick if there be
> no better effect of it. Ease of minde, fresh ayr and diet, may leasurely do
> that, which Physick could not effect so suddenly. And you must absteine
> not onely from reading but from thinking too intensely.

Therapeutics

As has just been suggested, many responses in sickness necessitated neither
consulting a doctor nor taking physick (that is perhaps what explains their
popularity). People also commonly tried a standard repertoire of therapeutic
interventions, indicated for a great variety of conditions. These were, above
all, purging, vomiting, sweating, and blood-letting. A common rationale
underlies them all. Believing that sickness marked the build-up in the body of
an imbalance of 'peccant humours' (toxic fluids), the obvious remedy was to
encourage the body's own attempts to expel bad blood, vile bile, or indurated
faeces. Recommendations to purge, bleed, etc., often issued from a consultation with a practitioner; commonly, he prescribed the preferred laxative or
sudorific, or the surgeon actually let blood. Thus, Garrick reported to his
physician, Messenger Monsey, on the great success of the purge he had
prescribed to his wife:[39]

> My dear Doctor,
> Your patient took the prescription on Sunday night; she fancies that she
> felt queerly all night, and about five in the morning she was a little sick,
> and had some little propensity to puke, but did not. At six, she
> swallowed the four other pills, which agreed well with her; and now she
> finds herself much better for the operation. On Wednesday she intends
> taking the three pills, as directed, and four of the others, as before, in the
> morning. They were sufficiently strong for her; and, unless you would
> have her manure the whole parish, she shall leave the other two for
> another opportunity. She has such faith in you, that she is sure, and
> swears, that you will restore her status quo.

Or take vomiting. On 31 August, Nicholas Blundell recorded in his diary,
'Mary Wogden being extreamly ill Apothecary Livsey came to see her & gave
her a vomit'; on 12 September, it was Blundell's own turn for the same
treatment; Dr Lancaster puked his wife on 18 September, and four days later,
he both bled and purged her.[40]

But all these were spheres of action which it was perfectly proper for the sick
to administer on their own initiative, to themselves or their households.
Parson Woodforde was forever physicking his dependants. His maid, Nancy,
had a bad stomach:[41]

I gave her a Vomit about Noon and it kept down near an Hour and then it operated very briskly indeed, brought off a great Quantity of nasty green thick stuff from her Stomach. She was soon after better, but very much swelled in the face by reaching and very weak. She had a Glass of warm red Wine and Water with some Sugar and a bit of Toasted bread with it, after the Vomit had done operating, she kept her Bed all the Day after and in the Evening gave her a small Dose of Rhubarb with a little Ginger.

Doctors do not seem to have objected; if they had, their objections would have been futile, since self-medicating was almost an Englishman's birthright. Some doctors expressed concern, however, that self-purging was getting out of hand. What had once been used for occasional relief was turning into a ritual, almost a nightcap, designed to keep the system in order. James McKittrick Adair was one of many doctors who condemned as deleterious habits of indiscriminate and automatic use of laxatives and emetics.

These modes of therapy often had drastic results. Lord Herbert informed the Rev. William Cole in 1782 that he had been sick:[42]

On Monday last, I was seized with this cursed infection to a violent degree & sufficed as much martyrdom for 24 hours as if all my bones had been broken. Bleeding, purging and sweating has cleared me compleatly of all ailing, but has left me very weak.

All the same, it is easy to understand their attraction to the pre-moderns. They were treatments over which the sick person himself could clearly exercise control. They often relieved the immediate symptoms – and quickly. And they produced tangible results, thus satisfying the psychological need for action and effects.

This is revealed in a comment of Caroline Holland's. She told her sister, Emily, she had had yet more of her 'miserable sick fits': 'I never was worse than this last time. I hope it was the crisis of my distemper, for my spirits had been bad, and I not quite well for some time before, as I told you.' But she knew the answer: 'So I hope in God now I shall be better after bleeding and other prodigious evacuations I always have when I'm in that sick way.'[43]

Self-Medicating

Sick people exercised their prerogative to evacuate their bodies through standard procedures. But self-therapeutics went far beyond this. The laity had knowledge of and access to a galaxy of individual medicines that they administered to themselves and their dependants. The gentry still shared with their cooks, gardeners, and farriers a copious herbal lore. Pre-modern manuscript recipe books show kitchen physick cures set down in vast array alongside recipes for made dishes, glue, polish, starch, and the like.[44]

The rationales underlying such cures often stemmed from occult doctrines of signatures, or from magic – forms of knowledge discredited by the élite.

Thus, wood sorrel was a cordial, because its leaves were heart-shaped; liverwort was for disorders of the liver; the yellow juice of the celandine was used as a medicine against jaundice; and so forth.[45] Yet polite society seems to have been willing to give them a trial on an empirical basis, though maybe with some embarrassment. In 1758, Mrs Delany recommended two or three snails should be boiled in barley-water tea, for someone suffering from a dreadful night cough: 'taken in time they have done wonderful cures'. She added it was important to keep the ingredients *secret*. 'She must know nothing of it. They give no manner of taste. It would be best nobody should know it but yourself.'[46]

Pre-modern herbal lore needs further study. As Mary Fissell has emphasized, recipes presupposed that the sick, or at least lay physicians, would have a first-hand knowledge for identifying many herbs and knowing their preparation;[47] yet it is no less clear that an increasing proportion of ingredients – e.g., exotic spices – could only have been shop-bought. Some recipes obviously pride themselves on simplicity, yet others display what *prima facie* seems like the most Byzantine conspicuous waste. For example, the Orlebar family recipe book, dating from the seventeenth century, gives a recipe for Mrs Lake's Plague Water:[48]

> Take Angelico, Cardus, Turmetill, Marygold flowers, Rue, Egremonyh, Wormwood, Sallendin, Sage, Balme, Rosemary, Mugworte, Dragon, Pimpernell, Featherfeve, nett sorrell, of each one handful: of Rosemary two handfulls, and a few Elicompany roots scraped: steep all these in three quarts of the best wine, or if you will, halfe Canary, six dayes and six nights: then put it into a simple still and so still it: you may take three spoonfuls at a time with as much Methredate as a beane. Dissolve your Methredate very well in a spoonful of the water before you take it. It will remove any disease that lyeth at the heart or stomache.

That mix was certainly cost- and labour-intensive. What then is one to make of the recipe for Lady Hewet's Water, printed by Eliza Smith in her popular *Compleat Housewife*? This was made of:[49]

> Red Sage, betony, spearmint unset, hyssop, thyme, balm, pennyroyal, celandine, water-cresses, hearts-ease, lavender, angelica, germander, calamint, tamarisk, coltsfoot, avens, valerian, saxifrage, pimpernel, vervain, parsely, rosemary, savory, scabious, agrimony, mother-thyme, wild marjoram, roman wormwood, carduus benedictus, pellitory of the wall, field daisies, flowers and leaves, of each a handful, after they are pick'd and wash'd; of rue, yarrow, comfry, plantane, camomile, maidenhair, sweet morjoram, and dragns, of each a handful, before they are wash'd or pick'd; red rose leaves and cowslip flowers, of each half a peck, rosemary flowers a quarter of a peck, hartsthorn two ounces, juniper-berries one drachm, china roots an ounce, compfry-roots slic'd,

aniseeds, fennel-seeds, carraway-seeds, nutmegs, ginger, cinamon, peper, spikenard, parsley-seeds, cloves and mace, of each three drachms, sassafras slic'd half and ounce, elecampane roots, melilot-flowers, calamus-aromaticus, cardamums, lignum-aloes, rhubarb sliced thin, galingal, veronica, and cubebs, of each two drachms, musk twenty-four grains, ambergrease twenty grains, powder of coral two drachms, powder of amber one drachm, powder of pearl two drachms, white sugar-candy one pound.

Of this water, Smith wrote, 'there never was a better cordial in cases of the greatest illness, two or three spoonfuls almost revive from death.' One hopes so. Her book contained kitchen physic recipes against all known diseases under the sun, including plague, smallpox, and cancers.

Of course, a recipe book is not in itself a proof of use, but entries are frequently 'authorized' by a phrase such as 'probat' (tried) or 'on the recommendation of' such a person, suggesting that the kitchen physick tradition remained a living and growing one. Household recipe books were augmented over the generations.

Lay therapeutic lore was often thus put down on paper. But it circulated and snowballed in many other ways. Much passed by word of mouth, or through letters. Thomas Hearne, the Oxford antiquary, was always jotting down cures. He recorded a fatality following a viper bite. 'It may here be noted', he added, 'that in such accidents as this, sallad oil applied warm to the wound is an effectual cure.'[50] On another occasion, a cure for the gravel caught his eye:[51]

Feb. 25. Such as are inclined to gravel must use themselves to such white wine and oily medicines, which tho' they will not effect an absolute cure, will render the distemper less painfull. Syrrup of marsh mallow and parsley water, when the fit is upon you, with warm broth, will give you the greatest ease.

Countless such remedies were exchanged through correspondence or published in newspapers and magazines. Readers were inundated with advice as to how they could take curing themselves into their own hands. Worried about the endlessly sick son Stephen, Lady Caroline Holland wrote in 1759 to say that 'he now takes Mr Compton's medicine' – i.e., one recommended to her by the (later) 8th Earl of Northampton; it was made of the plant Lady's Smock 'which Mr Compton's family seem positive cured him, and which all assure me can't possibly hurt him if it does him no good.'[52]

Self-drugging was always, however, tinged with controversy, because drugging itself was. Many were perturbed at what seemed the cascade of medicines gushing down gullible gullets. 'My plague is physic, which teases my poor stomach', complained Lady Holland.[53] As we have seen, some doctors thought indiscriminate self-drugging was creating sickness, hypochondria, and addiction; these the laity tended to blame on the doctors.

New Treatments

It might be assumed that self-physicking was on the wane, rendered obsolete by real or spurious advances in professional medicine. Were not the remedies of kitchen physick being steadily consigned to the antiquarian, and to those too poor to call on professional aid? The answer seems to be no. All the signs point to the continued vitality of lay healing traditions. This is visible in various ways. One is the active and enthusiatic willingness to experiment with novel or different therapies. When sick, Parson Woodforde, for example, used folk remedies without much sign of embarrassment:[54]

> Mar. 11, Friday. The Stiony on my right Eye-lid still swelled and inflamed very much. As it is commonly said that the Eye-lid being rubbed by the tail of a black Cat would do it much good if not entirely cure it, and having a black Cat, a little before dinner I made a trial of it, and very soon after dinner almost free from Pain. I cannot therefore but conclude it to be of the greatest service to a Stiony on the Eye-lid. Any other Cats Tail may have the above effect in all probability – but I did my Eye-lid with my own black Tom Cat's Tail.

He was willing to try out folk cures on others, as when his servant Jack had a fit of the ague: 'My boy Jack had another touch of the Ague about noon. I gave him a dram of gin at the beginning of the fit and pushed him headlong into one of my ponds and ordered him to bed.' The heroic remedy worked: 'and he was better after it and had nothing of the cold fit after, but was very hot.'[55] Equally drastic, but less successful, was an ague cure tried out in the Fens, as came to light in the trial of a soldier at Huntingdon in 1736, 'who pretended to cure a boy of the Ague; and thinking to frighten it away, by firing his Piece over the Boy's Head, levell'd it too low, and shot his brains out.'[56]

The public was eager to try new remedies and therapies, such as medical electricity. Early in the eighteenth century, the Virginian, William Byrd, discovered ginseng and praised it to the skies:[57]

> This kept up my Spirits, and made me trip away as nimbly in my Jack-Boots as younger men cou'd in their shoes . . . Its vertues are, Spirits beyond any other Cordial. It chears the Heart even of a Man that has a bad Wife, and makes him look down with great Composure on the crosses and Viscous Humours, that are apt to obstruct the Narrow channels of the Nerves. It helps the Memory, and would quicken even Helvetial dullness. 'Tis friendly to the Lungs, much more than Scolding itself. It comforts the one Word, it will make a Man live a great while, and very well while he does live. And what is more, it will even make Old Age amiable, by rendering it lively, chearful, and good-humour'd. However 'tis of little use in the Feats of Love, as a great prince once

found, who hearing of its invigorating Quality, sent as far as China for some of it, though his ladys could not boast of any Advantage thereby.

Educated lay people were, of course, eager to be inoculated (indeed, the initial introduction of the practice into England owed nothing to doctors). And they were no less enthusiastic about other forms of medication which they could control, such as taking the waters. It was, of course, the done thing to grumble. '*Watering Places*', scoffed John Byng:[58]

> – a mighty soft name truly for a parcel of Pest-houses, which you visit for the express convenience of being ducked, like a thief, a dozen times in a week; and then, by way of recovering your breath, toiling up one perpendicular cliff, and down another, like Bunyan's Pilgrim.

Yet, as Walpole noted, the English were always waddling like ducks to waters and actually submitted themselves to the considerable unpleasantness of bathing, pumping, and drinking. Many had faith in them. The Rev. John Penrose came to Bath from Cornwall for his gout and breathing problems, followed the medical advice strictly, and believed he benefited. He urged such treatments upon his friends:

> Mr. Pender must come to Bath: I hate for gouty folks to lie at home grunting when so cheap a Remedy as Water is within 200 miles of them.[59]

People took the waters seriously. As Edward Young confided to his friend, Samuel Richardson,[60] 'I bless God I at last find benefit from the waters – as to appetite, rest and spirits. I have now, for three nights, had pretty good rest; after two sleepless months; and I believe that persevering in the waters is the point; at least, in my complaint.' Compare the experiment with cold-bathing that Dudley Ryder forced on himself while in London. He thought it would work wonders:[61]

> Rose between 6 and 7. Went to the cold bath and agreed with the mistress of it for a whole year, for which I gave her two guineas and entered my name in her book. I intend to go in often. The reason of my design is that I think it will strengthen my body, purge it of ill humours, fence me against cold, prevent convulsions which I have sometimes been afraid of by reason of those sudden startings which I have sometimes. I have heard also it is good against the stone and gravel, which I have been afraid of upon the account of those sharp pains I have had about my belly. I expect also it will cure me those rheumatic pains which I sometimes feel and secure me against the gout, which I believe I have felt something of in my health. It will also cure the laxity of the nerves which is the occasion of what they call the vapours.

In short, fatalism in the face of sickness was not required by the Englishman's faith or moral code; nor was it part of the temper of the times. No one underestimated sickness as a foe. But, especially because being sick was seen largely as a personal affair, associated with inner failings, it triggered a combative response. In the consumer society, people did, indeed, flock to the medical profession for help. But in no way did that sap sturdy traditions of therapeutic self-help.

NOTES

[1] Cheyne, *Essay on Health and Long Life*, i.
[2] Andrews (ed.), *Torrington Diaries*, IV, 8.
[3] Moore, quoted in Hunter and Macalpine, *Three Hundred Years of Psychiatry*, 497.
[4] Thicknesse, *Valetudinarian's Bath Guide*, 29.
[5] Colvin (ed.), *Correspondence of Maria Edgeworth*, 317.
[6] Whorton, *Crusaders for Fitness*, 5f.
[7] Marshall (ed.), *Autobiography of William Stout*, 178.
[8] Ibid.
[9] Fitzgerald (ed.), *Correspondence of Emily, Duchess of Leinster*, I, 214-15.
[10] Porter, 'Enlightenment in England'; Macfarlane, *Origins of English Individualism*.
[11] Porter, 'Medicine and the Decline of Magic'.
[12] De Beer (ed.), *Diary of John Evelyn*, III, 8 (13 August 1653).
[13] Latham and Matthews (eds), *Diary of Samuel Pepys*, II, 96.
[14] Ibid., IX, 424.
[15] Talon (ed.), *Selections from the Journals and Papers of John Byrom*, 116.
[16] See Porter and Porter, *Patient's Progress*, *passim*.
[17] Porter, 'The Patient in the Eighteenth Century'.
[18] Buchan, *Domestic Medicine*, 101f. deals with simple home medicaments.
[19] Verney, *Memoirs*, IV, 118. Many more Verney recipes are reproduced in the following pages, including the use of tobacco for the plague, and 'Meatreadat', i.e. Mithridate.
[20] Niebyl, 'Non-Naturals'.
[21] Burton, *Anatomy of Melancholy*, 481.
[22] North, *Life of John North*, 152.
[23] Norton (ed.), *Letters of Edward Gibbon*, I, 343.
[24] Toynbee and Whibley (eds), *Correspondence of Thomas Gray*, letter 951.
[25] Vaisey (ed.), *Diary of Thomas Turner*, 111.
[26] *Gentleman's Magazine*, 20 (1751), 84.
[27] Knox, *Enthusiasm*, 425. Wesley was, for some years, a vegetarian. Knox comments as follows on Wesley's attempts to develop a regimen for himself:

Wesley himself was content with five hours' sleep, and formed the habit at Oxford, never discontinued, of rising at four in the morning. On the voyage to Georgia, just when he left Oxford, he and his companions gave up flesh and wine, and afterwards left off taking supper, in Georgia itself he and Delamotte tried, successfully, the experiment of living on nothing but bread. We are not told how long these austerities continued; he returned to vegetarianism after an interval of 'several years' in 1747, but gave it up two years later owing to a flux. Meanwhile, in 1746, he had given up drinking tea, though admittedly with the primary intention of setting the poor an example of thrift; and he records that it cost him only three days of headache. (Ibid., p.431.)

28   Yorke (ed.), *Diary of John Baker*, 254. Fothergill would not take a fee for his services; soon after, he ordered Baker to Bath.
29   Little and Kahrl (eds), *Letters of David Garrick*, I, 236.
30   LeFanu (ed.), *Betsy Sheridan's Journal*, 95.
31   Evans (ed.), *Letters of Richard Radcliffe and John James*, 36-7.
32   Hunt, *Autobiography of Leigh Hunt*, 169.
33   Ponsonby, *More English Diaries*, 166.
34   King and Ryskamp (eds), *Letters and Prose Writings of William Cowper*, III, 181.
35   Pottle (ed.), *Boswell's London Journal*, 319.
36   Ibid., 253.
37   Macdonald (ed.), *Letters of Eliza Pierce*, 38-9.
38   Nicolson (ed.), *Conway Letters*, 80.
39   Little and Kahrl (ed.), *Letters of David Garrick*, I, 164-5.
40   Bagley (ed.), *Great Diurnal of Nicholas Blundell*, III, 222, 223.
41   Beresford (ed.), *Diary of a Country Parson*, II, 275.
42   Herbert (ed.), *Pembroke Papers*, 199.
43   Fitzgerald (ed.), *Correspondence of Emily, Duchess of Leinster*, I, 361.
44   Porter, 'Medicine and the Decline of Magic'; Chamberlain, *Old Wives' Tales*.
45   As John Clare recorded of the gypsies:

They had pretentions to a knowledge of medicine but their receipts turned more on mystic charms and spells yet they had a knowledge of Plants – which they gave names too themselves as I had a knowledge of wild plants I used to be amusd with the names they calld them by a little plant with a hard stem that grows in villages and waste places one sort bearing minute yellow flowers and another purple ones they calld burvine and reckond famous for the scurvey. (Robinson (ed.), *John Clare's Autobiographical Writings*, 71.)

46   Paston (ed.), *Mrs Delany*, 39.
47   Fissell, 'Physic of Charity'; Black, *Folk Medicine*, 157. This and many others quoted in Gomme, *Gentleman's Magazine Library: Popular Superstitions*, 127ff.
48   Orlebar (cd.), *Orlebar Chronicles*, 68.
49   Eliza Smith, *Compleat Housewife*, 257.
50   Bliss (ed.), *Reliquiae Hearnianae*, III, 148.
51   Ibid., 171.
52   Fitzgerald (ed.), *Correspondence of Emily, Duchess of Leinster*, I, 215.
53   Ibid., 492.
54   Beresford (ed.), *Diary of a Country Parson*, III, 253.
55   Ibid., I, 252. Within a few days, two other servants also fell ill and were dosed by Woodforde. Both Nanny the maid and Ben the man-servant had stomach upsets and Woodforde gave them his most trusted remedy, a dose of rhubarb. Ibid., I, 252-3.
56   Grange, 'Cambridgeshire Country Cures'.
57   Blandton, *Medicine in Virginia*, 183.
58   Andrews (ed.), *Torrington Diaries*, I, 18. See also Beresford, *Miseries of Human Life*, 10.
59   Mitchell and Penrose (eds), *Letters from Bath*, 51.
60   Pettit (ed.), *Correspondence of Edward Young*, 467. Young concludes the letter, 'May the new year, dear sir, make you a present of health, spirits and peace.' Others found that the waters failed to do them much good. 'Bath might give me the gout, but cannot cure it', opined Walpole, see Toynbee (ed.), *Letters of Horace Walpole*, XI, 87. Walpole said his 'management' of himself was based 'on the best observations I can make on my own constitution after long experience.'
61   Matthews (ed.), *Diary of Dudley Ryder*, 196. Alas, he found it did him little good.

Chapter 16:
Conclusion

It is worth reiterating the limitations of this study, and restating what it does and does not aim to achieve. Our goal in this book has not been to analyse either the bio-medical or even the social history of sickness in the 'long eighteenth century'. Nor have we said much about *collective* responses to disease. Above all, we have not discussed the medical profession or doctor-patient relations. These omissions do not, of course, mean that we think such aspects unimportant. Rather, we have simply chosen to orient this investigation around how individual people made sense of sickness in general and of their own episodes of being ill. We have examined attitudes more than actions, but have sought to interpret those attitudes in the contexts of changing beliefs and values, both religious and secular, public and private.

The individuals whose beliefs and feelings we have analysed derive from that socio-intellectual élite that characteristically kept diaries, exchanged letters, etc. That primarily means the urban bourgeoisie – amongst whom Dissenters are disproportionately represented – and the Quality. The sickness culture profile drawn in the foregoing chapters must be understood as referring solely to this minority. It would take different research strategies to determine how far, or how little, this 'great' or 'patrician' sickness culture was coterminous with, or differentiated from, distinct 'little' or 'plebeian' cultures. Recent studies of the relations between polite and popular culture in Georgian England have tended to emphasize that the links between them remained strong, complex, and two-way. Popular attitudes to sickness await research; intelligent use of the vast folklore collections compiled by Victorian antiquarians could change this.[1]

Even amongst the élite, our researches are evidently impressionistic rather than definitive. This is a new field, and we believe a bold survey is called for. We hope, however, that our picture will not be found wildly unrepresentative. Subsequent consideration of additional evidence will, of course, add light and shade, but we do not believe it will utterly transform the picture.

Not least, we regret that for reasons of space we have not been able to scrutinize particular cases in great analytical depth, or to discuss in detail the hermeneutical problems posed by particular texts. Our readings are brisk and assertive: we fully recognize, however, that many alternative approaches are possible. Above all, it would be highly desirable to give far more explicit consideration both to the intricate fabric of sickness language, and to say more about the lives of those discussed as a whole.

Such disclaimers notwithstanding, we believe some substantial conclusions emerge from this study. For one thing, we have shown just how rich and vital was the culture of sickness amongst the vocal laity. It will come as no surprise that matters so overwhelming as disease and death commanded great attention, and assumed tremendous symbolic significance. But the care with which the pre-moderns attempted to manage their precarious health has hitherto been little noticed. And it is important to see in operation here something akin to a medical equivalent of Protestantism – a priesthood of all sufferers, coterminous with the existence of a 'church', i.e., the medical profession. The Georgians did not resign their health to the doctors. Nor did they rebel against medical theory or the medical profession, going off in search of alternatives. The evidence adduced in this book suggests, rather, that sick people pursued health much as Protestants pursued salvation: medicos, like ministers, were auxiliaries not charismatic miracle-workers.

But if lay people cultivated their health with sturdy independence, that is not to say that they nursed medical knowledge radically distinct from that of the faculty. It remains an open issue how far Georgian England boasted a 'folk medicine' that was genuinely 'plebeian', ancestral, and oral, deriving from magic and the occult. What is patent, however, is that polite society did not subscribe – at least overtly – to such a set of alternative medical beliefs and practices. All the signs are that the educated eagerly assimilated those bodies of orthodox medical knowledge that were increasingly in circulation in a print-dominated market society.

Such a convergence between lay and professional outlooks should hardly be surprising. After all, in pre-modern medicine, the sick person's account of what was wrong remained the basis of the doctor's knowledge. Likewise, therapeutics – travelling, exercising, changing diets, etc. – remained substantially in the patient's hands. Not least, before the emergence of stricter professionalization in the Victorian era, doctors remained socially and economically highly dependent upon lay patronage. Thus, everything conspired to make lay and professional knowledge and attitudes mutually compatible.

Nevertheless, certain important distinctions do appear between lay and professional outlooks. Explanation and theory mark one divide. Lay medical knowledge was practical experience-based know-how upon which to make diagnoses and activate remedies. We rarely see medical-theoretical underpinnings spelt out or disputed. Doctors, by contrast, commonly made a show of the theories behind their medical systems. Unlike the sick, they had a stake in establishing intellectual authority over patients and colleagues alike.

And above all, what lay writings *do* express – and here the doctors are far more muted – is a phenomenology of sickness, the intimate experience of being ill. Of course, this was sometimes deliberately played down; so many Georgians cultivated a deadpan Stoicism that enabled them to cope with the omnipresence of pain and the precariousness of life. Georgians were active in their attempts to prevent and relieve; but they coped with unavoidable sufferings by making sense of them within wider conceptions of living and dying, of the nature of the self, of the relations between soul and body, person and society. Sufferers engaged in dialogues with their bodies . If the essentially *medical* dimensions of sickness do not often spark lengthy involved dispute amongst the sick, *illness* poses major and unsolved problems for the interpretation of the career of the self, and for the integration of the individual into the social web. Sickness both jeopardizes and commands sympathy. It produces a distance and a difference, while requiring support. Being sick means having one's position disturbed; it generates new forms of power and dependence.

> The Capture of Vandamme was the consequence of a bellyache, and the metropolitan representation depended on a headache. If the truth could be ascertained, perhaps many of the greatest events in history turned upon aches of one sort or another. Montaigne might have written an essay on it.

In that reflection of Charles Greville's,[2] we see the moral vision passed down from antiquity of the cosmic accident of disease.

In the next, we have a foretaste of the new, personal, introverted sickness culture of Georgian England:[3]

> 'I hope you will eat some of this toast', said he, . . . 'I hope you like dry toast'.
> 'With a reasonable quantity of butter spread over it, very much –' said Charlotte – 'but not otherwise –'.
> 'No more do I' – said he exceedingly pleased – 'We think quite alike there. – So far from dry toast being wholesome, I think it is a very bad thing for the stomach. Without a little butter to soften it, it hurts the coats of the stomach. I am sure it does. – I will have the pleasure of spreading some for you directly – and afterwards I will spread some for myself. – Very bad indeed for the coats of the stomach – but there is no convincing *some* people. – It irritates and acts like a nutmeg grater. –'
> He could not get command of the butter however, without a struggle; his sisters accusing him of eating a great deal too much, and declaring he was not to be trusted; – he maintaining that he only eat enough to secure the coats of his stomach; – and besides, he only wanted it now for Miss Heywood. . . .
> Mr Arthur Parker's enjoyments in invalidism were very different from his sisters' – by no means so spiritualized. – A good deal of earthly dross hung about him. Charlotte could not but suspect him of adopting that line of life, principally for the indulgence of an indolent temper –

and to be determined on having no disorders but such as called for warm rooms and good nourishments.

In one particular however, she soon found that he had caught something from *them*. – 'What! said he – 'Do you venture upon two dishes of strong green tea in one evening? – What nerves you must have! – How I envy you. – Now, if I were to swallow only one such dish – what do you think its effect would be upon me? –'

'Keep you awake perhaps all night' – replied Charlotte, meaning to overthrow his attempts at surprise, by the grandeur of her own conceptions.

'Oh! if that were all!' – he exclaimed. – 'No – it acts on me like poison'.

NOTES

[1] For a pioneering attempt to probe at the interface of high and low medical cultures, see Fissell, 'Physick of Charity'.
[2] Reeve (ed.), *Greville Memoirs*, II, 274.
[3] Austen, *Sanditon*, 202-3.

Bibliography

Ackerknecht, E. H., 'Anticontagionism between 1821 and 1867', *Bulletin of the History of Medicine*, 22 (1948), 562–93.

Adair, J. M., *Essays on Fashionable Diseases* . . . (London, Bateman, 1790).

Allen, J. B., *A Beloved Mother. Life of Hannah S. Allen by Her Daughter* (London, Samuel Harris, 1884).

Altick, R., *The Shows of London: A Panoramic History of Exhibitions, 1600–1862* (Cambridge, Mass., Belknap Press, 1978).

Amory, T., *Life of John Buncle*, ed. by E. A. Baker (London, Routledge, 1901).

Anderson, H. B., 'Robert Burns, His Medical Friends, Attendants, and Biographer', *Annals of Medical History*, 1st Series, 10 (1928), 48–58.

Anderson, O., *Suicide in Victorian and Edwardian England* (Oxford, Clarendon Press, 1987).

Andrews, C. B. (ed.), *The Torrington Diaries*, 4 vols (London, Eyre & Spottiswoode, 1954).

Anglesey, The Marquess of (ed.), *Capel Letters* (London, Jonathan Cape, 1955).

Appleby, A., *Famine in Tudor and Stuart England* (Stanford, Stanford University Press, 1978).

Arbuthnot, J., *An Essay Concerning the Nature of Aliments* (London, J. & R. Tonson, 1731).

————, *An Essay Concerning the Effects of Air on Human Bodies* (London, J. & R. Tonson & S. Draper, 1733).

Archer, J., *Every Man His Own Doctor* (London, for the Author, 1671).

Ariès, P., *Centuries of Childhood: A Social History of Family Life* (London, Jonathan Cape, 1962).

————, *Western Attitudes Towards Death: from the Middle Ages to the Present* (Baltimore, Johns Hopkins University Press, 1974; London, Marion Boyars, 1976).

————, *The Hour of Our Death*, trans. by H. Weaver (London, Allen Lane, 1981).

————, *Images of Man and Death*, trans. Janet Lloyd (Cambridge, Cambridge University Press, 1985).

Aronson, J. K., *An Account of the Foxglove & its Medicinal Uses, 1785–1985* (London, Oxford University Press, 1985).

Aspinall, A. (ed.), *Letters of the Princess Charlotte, 1811–1817* (London, Home & Van Thal, 1949).

Astruc, J., *A Treatise on all the Diseases Incident to Women* (London, Cooper, 1743).

Aubrey, J., *Aubrey's Brief Lives*, ed. Oliver Lawson Dick (Harmondsworth, Penguin Books, 1972).
————, *Miscellanies* (London, Edward Castle, 1696).
Austen, J., *Emma*, ed. R. Blythe (Harmondsworth, Penguin, 1966).
————, *Sanditon*, ed. M. Drabble (Harmondsworth, Penguin, 1974).
Axtell, J. L. (ed.), *The Educational Writings of John Locke* (London, Cambridge University Press, 1968).
Ayres, J. (ed.), *Paupers and Pig Killers. The Diary of William Holland. A Somerset Parson 1799–1818* (Gloucester, Alan Sutton, 1984).
Bagley, J. J. (ed.), *The Great Diurnal of Nicholas Blundell*, transcr. and annot. by F. Tyrer, 3 vols (Record Society of Lancashire and Cheshire, 110 (1968); 112 (1970); 114 (1972)).
Bailey, M. (ed.), *Boswell's Column* (London, Martin Kimber, 1951).
Baird, J. D., and Ryskamp, C. (eds), *The Poems of William Cowper*, vol. I, (Oxford, Clarendon Press, 1980).
Bakan, D., *Disease, Pain and Sacrifice: Towards a Psychology of Suffering* (Chicago & Boston, Beacon Publications, 1971).
Baker, H., *The Dignity of Man. Studies in the Persistence of an Idea* (Cambridge, Mass., Harvard University Press, 1947).
Bambrough, J. B., *The Little World of Man* (London, Longman, Green, 1952).
Bamford, F. (ed.), *Dear Miss Heber* (London, Constable, 1936).
Barbeau, A. (ed.), *Life and Letters at Bath in the Eighteenth Century*, ed. by A. Dobson (London, Heinemann, 1904).
Barkan, L., *Nature's Work of Art: the Human Body as Image of the World* (New Haven, Yale University Press, 1975).
Barker, F., *The Tremulous Private Body* (London, Methuen, 1984).
Barnes, B., and Shapin, S. (eds), *Natural Order: Historical Studies of Scientific Culture* (London, Sage, 1979).
Barrett, C. F. (ed.), *The Diary and Letters of Madame d'Arblay, Author of Evelina, Cecilia, etc. 1778–1840*, 7 vols (London, H. Colburn, 1842–1846).
Barrett, M., and Roberts, H., 'Doctors and their Patients: The Social Control of Women in General Practice', in C. Smart and B. Smart (eds), *Women, Sexuality and Social Control* (London, Routledge & Kegan Paul, 1978), 41–52.
Barrow, A., *The Flesh is Weak: an Intimate History of the Church of England* (London, Hamilton, 1980).
Barry, J., 'Piety and the Patient: Medicine and Religion in Eighteenth-Century Bristol', in R. Porter (ed.), *Patients and Practitioners* (Cambridge, Cambridge University Press, 1985), 145–76.
Baur, S., *Hypochondria: Woeful Imaginings* (Princeton, Princeton University Press, 1988).
Bayne-Powell, R., *The English Child in the Eighteenth-Century* (London, John Murray, 1939).
Beall, O. T., jr, 'Aristotle's Masterpiece in America: a Landmark in the Folklore of Medicine', *William and Mary Quarterly*, 20 (1963), 207–22.
Beddoes, T., *Hygeia*, 3 vols (Bristol, Phillips, 1802–3).
Beekman, D., *The Mechanical Baby. A Popular History of the Theory and Practice of Child-Raising* (London, Dennis Dobson, 1977).
Beier, L. M., 'In Sickness and in Health: a Seventeenth-Century Family

Experience', in R. Porter (ed.), *Patients and Practitioners* (Cambridge, Cambridge University Press, 1985), 101–28.

————, *Sufferers and Healers. The Experience of Illness in Seventeenth-Century England* (London, Routledge & Kegan Paul, 1987).

Bell, R. M., *Holy Anorexia* (London, University of Chicago Press, 1985).

Benthall, J., and Polhemus, T. (eds), *The Body as a Medium of Expression* (London, Allen Lane, 1975).

Beresford, J., *The Miseries of Human Life: or the Last Groans of Timothy Testy and Samuel Sensitive; with a Few Supplementary Sighs from Mrs Testy . . .*, 2 vols (London, William Miller, 1807).

Beresford, J. (ed.), *The Diary of a Country Parson: the Rev. James Woodforde, 1758–1802*, 5 vols (reprinted Oxford, Oxford University Press, 1978–81).

Berman, A., 'The Heroic Approach to Nineteenth-Century Therapeutics', *Bulletin of the American Society of Hospital Pharmacists*, 11 (1954), 320–7.

Berman, M., *The Re-enchantment of the World* (Ithaca, Cornell University Press, 1981).

Berridge, V., and Edwards, G., *Opium and the People* (London, Allen Lane, 1981).

Bessborough, Earl of, and Aspinall, A. (eds), *Lady Bessborough and Her Family Circle* (London, Murray, 1940).

Bigelow, J. (ed.), *The Life of Benjamin Franklin by Himself* (London, Oxford University Press, 1924).

Bishop, P. J., *A Short History of the Royal Humane Society* (London, The Society, 1974).

Bishop, W. J., 'The Evolution of the General Practitioner in England', in E. Ashworth Underwood (ed.), *Science, Medicine and History: Essays on the Evolution of Scientific Thought and Medical Practice*, 2 vols (London, Oxford University Press, 1953), II, 351–7.

Black, W. G., *Folk Medicine: A Chapter in the History of Culture* (London, Folklore Society, 1883).

Blacking, J. (ed.), *The Anthropology of the Body* (London and New York, Academic Press, 1977).

Blackman, J., 'Popular Theories of Generation: the Evolution of *Aristotle's Works*. The Study of an Anachronism', in J. Woodward and D. Richards (eds), *Health Care and Popular Medicine in Nineteenth-Century England* (London, Croom Helm, 1977), 56–88.

Blandton, W. B., *Medicine in Virginia in the Eighteenth Century* (Richmond, Garrett & Massie, 1931).

Bliss, P. (ed.), *Reliquiae Hearnianae: The Remains of Thomas Hearne, M. A. of Edmund Hall . . .*, 3 vols (London, John Russell Smith, 1869).

Bloom, E. A., and Bloom, L. D., '"This Fragment of Life": From Process to Mortality', in V. Grosvenor-Myer (ed.), *Laurence Sterne: Riddles and Mysteries* (London, Vision and Barnes & Noble, 1984), 57–72.

Blunden, E. (ed.), *The Life of George Crabbe: By His Son* (London, Cresset Press, 1947).

Blythe, R. (ed.), *William Hazlitt. Selected Writings* (Harmondsworth, Penguin, 1970).

Boase, T. S. R., *Death in the Middle Ages: Mortality, Judgement and Remembrance* (New York, McGraw-Hill, 1972).

Bond, D. (ed.), *The Spectator*, 5 vols (Oxford, Clarendon Press, 1965).

Bond, J., *An Essay on the Incubus, or Night-Mare* (London, Wilson & Durham, 1753).

Bonnard, G. A. (ed.), *Edward Gibbon. Memoirs of My Life*, (London, Nelson, 1966).

Boorde, A., *Dyetary of Health* (London, T. Colwel, 1562).

————, *The Breviary of Health* (London, T. East, 1587).

Boswell, J., *The Life of Samuel Johnson*, ed. G. B. Hill, 6 vols (Oxford, Clarendon Press, 1934).

Bottomley, F., *Attitudes to the Body in Western Christendom* (London, Lepus Books, 1979).

Bottrall, M., *Every Man a Phoenix. Studies in Seventeenth-Century Autobiography* (London, John Murray, 1958).

Boucé, P.-G., 'Some Sexual Beliefs and Myths in Eighteenth-Century Britain', *British Journal for Eighteenth-Century Studies*, 3 (1980), 28–46.

————, 'Aspects of Sexual Tolerance and Intolerance in Eighteenth-Century England', ibid., 173–89.

———— (ed.), *Sexuality in Eighteenth-Century England* (Manchester, Manchester University Press, 1982).

————, 'Les Jeux Interdits de l'Imaginaire: Onanism et Culpabilisation Sexuelle au XVIIIe Siècle', in J. Céard (ed.), *La Folie et le Corps* (Paris, Presses de l'Ecole Normale Supérieure, 1985), 223–43.

————, 'Imagination, Pregnant Women, and Monsters in Eighteenth-Century England and France', in G. S. Rousseau and Roy Porter (eds), *Sexual Underworlds of the Enlightenment* (Manchester, Manchester University Press, 1988), 86–100.

Bourne, K. (ed.), *The Letters of the Third Viscount Palmerston to Laurence and Elizabeth Sulivan 1804–1863* (London, Royal Historical Society, 1979).

Bovill, E., *Country Life in England 1780–1830* (London, Oxford University Press, 1962).

Brady, F., and Pottle, F. A. (eds), *Boswell in Search of a Wife 1766–1769* (London, Heinemann, 1957).

————, *James Boswell: the Later Years* (London, Heinemann, 1984).

Braithwaite, J. B. (ed.), *Memoirs of Anna Braithwaite, Being a Sketch of Her Early Life and Ministry and Extracts from Her Private Memoranda, 1830–59* (London, Headley Brothers, 1905).

Brett, R. C. (ed.), *Barclay Fox's Journal* (New Jersey, Rowman & Littlefield, 1929).

Brett, S. (ed.), *The Faber Book of Diaries* (London, Faber, 1987).

Brian, T., *The Piss-Prophet, or Certain Piss-Pot Lectures* (London, R. Thrale, 1637).

Bristow, E., *Vice and Vigilance, Purity Movements in Britain since 1700* (Dublin, Gill & Macmillan, 1977).

Broadbent, J., 'The Image of God or Two Yards of Skin', in J. Benthall and T. Polhemus (eds), *The Body as a Medium of Expression* (London, Allen Lane, 1975), 305–26.

Broadhurst, J., 'Peeps with Pepys at Hygiene and Medicine', *Annals of Medical History*, 1st Series, 10 (1928), 165–72.

Brockbank, W., and Kenworthy, F. (eds), *The Diary of Richard Kay (1716–51) of Baldingstone, Near Bury* (Manchester, Chetham Society, 1968).

Brockliss, L. W. B., 'Taking the Waters in Early Modern France: Some

Thoughts on a Commercial Racket', *Bulletin of the Society for the Social History of Medicine*, 40 (1987), 74–7.

Brodum, W., *A Guide to Old Age or a Cure for the Indiscretions of Youth* (London, J. W. Myers, 1795).

Brody, H., *Stories of Sickness* (New Haven, Yale University Press, 1987).

Brown, N. O., *Love's Body* (New York, Vintage Books, 1966).

————, *Life Against Death. The Psychoanalytical Meaning of History* (London, Routledge & Kegan Paul, 1957).

Browne, Sir T., 'To a Friend upon the Occasion of the Death of his Intimate Friend', in L. C. Martin (ed.), *Religio Medici and Other Works* (Oxford, Clarendon Press, 1964), 170–96.

Browning, A. (ed.), *The Memoirs of Sir John Reresby* (Glasgow, Jackson, 1936).

Bryant, G. E., and Baker, G. P. (eds), *A Quaker Journal, Being the Diary and Reminiscences of William Lucas* (London, Hutchinson, 1934).

Bryder, L., *Below the Magic Mountain. A Social History of Tuberculosis in Twentieth-Century Britain* (Oxford, Clarendon Press, 1988).

Bryson, G., *Man and Society* (Princeton, Princeton University Press, 1945).

Buchan, W., *Domestic Medicine, or a Treatise on the Prevention and Cure of Diseases by Regimen and Simple Medicines* (Edinburgh, Balfour, Auld & Smellie, 1769).

————, *Observations Concerning the Prevention and Cure of the Venereal Disease* (London, Chapman, 1796).

Buchanan-Brown, J. (ed.), *John Aubrey, Three Prose Works* (Sussex, Centaur Press, 1972).

Burke, P., *Popular Culture in Early Modern Europe* (New York, Harper & Row, 1978).

————, 'Revolution in Popular Culture', in R. Porter and M. Teich (eds), *Revolution in History* (Cambridge, Cambridge University Press, 1986), 206–25.

————, *The Historical Anthropology of Early Modern Italy: Essays on Perception and Communication* (Cambridge, Cambridge University Press, 1987).

————, (ed.), *New Perspectives on Historical Writing* (Cambridge, Polity Press, 1988).

Burton, E., *The Early Tudors at Home* (London, Allen Lane, 1976).

Burton, J., *A Treatise on the Non-Naturals. In Which the Great Influence They Have on Human Bodies is Set Forth and Mechanically Accounted For* (York, A. Staples & J. Hildyard etc., 1738).

Burton, J. H. (ed.), *The Autobiography of Alexander Carlyle* (Edinburgh and London, W. Blackwood, 1860).

Burton, R., *The Anatomy of Melancholy*, ed. by D. Floyd and P. Jordan-Smith (New York, Tudor Publishing Company, 1948; 1st edn, London, H. Cripps, 1621).

Byles, C. E. (ed.), *Reminiscences of the Ministry of the Revd John Hawker, With a Brief Memoir of his Life by one of His Congregation* (London, Bodley Head, 1906).

Bynum, W. F., 'Health, Disease and Medical Care', in G. S. Rousseau and R. Porter (eds), *The Ferment of Knowledge* (Cambridge, Cambridge University Press, 1980), 211–54.

————, 'Cullen and the Study of Fevers in Britain 1760–1820', in W. F.

Bynum and V. Nutton (eds), *Theories of Fever from Antiquity to the Enlightenment* (*Medical History*, Supplement no. 1, London, Wellcome Institute for the History of Medicine, 1981), 135–48.

————, 'Treating the Wages of Sin: Venereal Disease and Specialism in Eighteenth-Century Britain', in W. F. Bynum and R. Porter (eds), *Medical Fringe and Medical Orthodoxy, 1750–1850* (London, Croom Helm, 1987), 5–28.

Bynum, W. F., and Nutton, V. (eds), *Theories of Fever from Antiquity to the Enlightenment* (*Medical History*, Supplement no. 1, London, Wellcome Institute for the History of Medicine, 1981).

————, and Porter, R. (eds), *William Hunter and the Eighteenth-Century Medical World* (Cambridge, Cambridge University Press, 1985).

————, *Medical Fringe and Medical Orthodoxy* (London, Croom Helm, 1987).

————, *Medicine and the Five Senses* (Cambridge, Cambridge University Press, forthcoming).

Cadogan, W., *A Dissertation on the Gout* (London, Dodsley, 1771).

Calder-Marshall, A., *The Great Age of the Lady, Regency and Georgian Elegance in the Age of Romance and Revolution 1720–1820* (London, Gordon Cremonesi, 1979).

Camporesi, P., *Bread of Dreams. Food and Fantasy in Early Modern Europe* (Cambridge, Polity Press, 1988).

————, *The Incorruptible Flesh. Bodily Mutation and Mortification in Religion and Folklore* (Cambridge, Cambridge University Press, 1988).

Capp, B., *Astrology and the Popular Press. English Almanacs, 1500–1800* (London and Boston, Faber & Faber, 1979).

Capra, F., *The Turning Point: Science, Society and the Rising Culture* (New York, Simon & Schuster, 1982).

Carlton, C., 'The Dream Life of Archbishop Laud', *History Today* (Dec. 1986), 9–14.

Carpenter, K. J., *The History of Scurvy and Vitamin C* (Cambridge, Cambridge University Press, 1986).

Cartwright, A., *Patients and Their Doctors: A Study of General Practice* (London, Routledge & Kegan Paul, 1967).

Cash, A., *Laurence Sterne: the Early and Middle Years* (London, Methuen, 1975).

————, 'The Birth of Tristram Shandy: Sterne and Dr Burton', in P. -G. Boucé (ed.), *Sexuality in Eighteenth-Century Britain* (Manchester, Manchester University Press, 1982), 198–224.

Castle, E. (ed.), *The Jerningham Letters (1780–1843)*, 2 vols (London, Bentley, 1896).

Cave, K. (ed.), *The Diary of Joseph Farington*, vols VII–XVI (New Haven, Yale University Press, 1982–4).

Chamberlain, M., *Old Wives' Tales: Their History, Remedies and Spells* (London, Virago, 1981).

Chambers, J. D., *Population, Economy, and Society in Pre-Industrial England* (Oxford, Oxford University Press, 1972).

Chaplin, A., *Medicine in England during the Reign of George III* (London, Henry Kimpton, 1919).

Chapman, R. W. (ed.), *The Letters of Samuel Johnson*, 3 vols (Oxford, Clarendon Press, 1984).

———— (ed.), *Jane Austen's Letters to Her Sister Cassandra & Others* (London, Oxford University Press, 1952).

Checkland, S. G., *The Gladstones. A Family Biography 1764–1851* (Cambridge, Cambridge University Press, 1971).

Cherno, M., 'Feuerbach's "Man is What He Eats"; A Rectification', *Journal of the History of Ideas*, 23 (1962), 397–406.

Cheyne, G., *An Essay on the True Nature and Due Method of Treating the Gout* (London, G. Strahan, 1722).

————, *An Essay on Health and Long Life* (8th edn, London, Strahan and Leake, 1734, 1st edn, 1724).

————, *The English Malady; or, A Treatise of Nervous Diseases* (London, G. Strahan, 1733).

————, *An Essay on Regimen* (London, C. Rivington, 1740).

————, *Account of Himself* (London, J. Wilford, 1743).

————, *Rules and Observations for the Enjoyment of Health and Long Life* (Leeds, G. Wright, 1770).

————, *The Natural Method of Cureing Diseases of the Body and the Disorders of the Mind* (London, G. Strahan, 1742).

Childs, F., 'Prescriptions for Manners in Eighteenth-Century Courtesy Literature' (University of Oxford, D. Phil. Thesis, 1984).

Christie, O. F. (ed.), *The Diary of the Rev'd William Jones, 1777–1821, Curate and Vicar of Broxbourne and the Hamlet of Hoddesdon 1781–1821* (London, Brentano's, 1929).

Clark, J. M., *The Dance of Death in the Middle Ages and the Renaissance* (Glasgow, Jackson, 1950).

Clark, R. W., *Benjamin Franklin* (London, Weidenfeld & Nicolson, 1983).

Clarkson, L., *Death, Disease and Famine in Pre-Industrial England* (Dublin, Gill & Macmillan, 1975).

Clifford, J. L. (ed.), *Dr. Campbell's Diary of a Visit to England in 1775* (Cambridge, Cambridge University Press, 1947).

Clifford, S., *The Signs and Causes of Melancholy with Directions Suited to the Case of Those Who Are Afflicted with It. Collected Out of the Works of Mr Richard Baxter* (London, S. Cruttenden & T. Cox, 1716).

Climenson, E. J. (ed.), *Passages from the Diary of Mrs Philip Lybbe Powys, 1756–1808* (London, Longmans, 1899).

————, *Elizabeth Montagu, The Queen of the Blue Stockings. Her Correspondence from 1720–1761*, 2 vols (London, John Murray, 1906).

Cobbett, W., *Advice to Young Men, and (Incidentally) to Young Women in the Middle and Higher Ranks of Life*, ed. by G. Spater (Oxford, Oxford University Press, 1980; 1st edn, 1830).

Coburn, K. (ed.), *The Letters of Sara Hutchinson from 1800–1835* (London, Routledge & Kegan Paul, 1954).

Cockburn, H., *Memorials of His Time* (Edinburgh, Mercat Press, 1971).

Cockshutt, A. O. J., *The Art of Autobiography in Nineteenth and Twentieth Century England* (New Haven, Conn., Yale University Press, 1984).

Coleridge, E. (ed.), *Memoir and Letters of Sara Coleridge*, 2 vols (London, Henry S. King, 1873).

Coleridge, S. T., *Table Talk* (London, John Murray, 1835; G. Routledge, 1874).

Collier, J. (ed.), *The Scandal and Credulities of John Aubrey* (London, Peter Davies, 1931).

Collins, K. E., 'Two Jewish Quacks in Eighteenth-Century Glasgow and How
    They Advertised Their Cures in the *Glasgow Advertiser*', *Jewish Echo* (27
    January 1984), 5.
Collison, R. L. W., *The Story of Street Literature: The Forerunner of the Popular
    Press* (London, Dent, 1973).
Colp, R., *To Be an Invalid: The Illness of Charles Darwin* (Chicago, Chicago
    University Press, 1977).
Coltheart, P., *The Quacks Unmasked* (London, The Author, 1727).
Colvin, C. (ed.), *The Correspondence of Maria Edgeworth* (Oxford, Clarendon
    Press, 1974).
Comaroff, J., 'Medicine, Symbol and Ideology', in P. Wright and A. Treacher
    (eds), *The Problem of Medical Knowledge* (Edinburgh, Edinburgh
    University Press, 1982), 49–68.
Comfort, A., *The Anxiety Makers* (London, Nelson, 1967)
Coope, R., *The Quiet Art: A Doctor's Anthology* (Edinburgh, Livingstone, 1952).
Cooter, R., 'The Power of the Body: The Early Nineteenth Century', in B.
    Barnes and S. Shapin (eds), *Natural Order: Historical Studies of Scientific
    Culture* (London and Beverly Hills, Sage Publications, 1979), 73–92.
————, 'Anticontagionism and History's Medical Record', in P. Wright and
    A. Treacher (eds), *The Problem of Medical Knowledge* (Edinburgh,
    Edinburgh University Press, 1982), 87–108.
————, 'Bones of Contention? Orthodox Medicine and the Mystery of the
    Bone-Setter's Craft', in W. F. Bynum and R. Porter (eds), *Medical Fringe
    and Medical Orthodoxy, 1750–1850* (London, Croom Helm, 1986), 158–73.
Corbin, A., *The Foul and the Fragrant: Odour and the French Social Imagination*
    (Cambridge, Mass., Harvard University Press, 1986).
Corsi, P., and Weindling, P. (eds), *Information Sources in the History of Science
    and Medicine* (London, Butterworth Scientific, 1983).
Cottle, J., *Reminiscences of Samuel Taylor Coleridge and Robert Southey*
    (Highgate, Lime Tree Bower Press, 1970; 1st edn, London, Houlston &
    Stoneman, 1847).
Cousins, N., *The Physician in Literature* (Philadelphia, Saunders Press, 1982).
Cox, S. D., *'The Stranger Within Thee': The Concept of the Self in Late
    Eighteenth-Century Literature* (Pittsburgh, University of Pittsburgh Press,
    1980).
Cozens-Hardy, B. (ed.), *The Diary of Sylas Neville 1767–1788* (London, Oxford
    University Press, 1950).
Crawford, P., 'Attitudes to Pregnancy from a Woman's Spiritual Diary,
    1687–88', *Local Population Studies*, 21 (1978), 43–5.
————, '"The Sucking Child": Adult Attitudes to Child Care in the First
    Year of Life in Seventeenth-Century England', *Continuity and Change*, 1
    (1986), 23–51.
————, 'Attitudes to Menstruation in Seventeenth-Century England', *Past
    and Present*, 91 (1981), 47–73.
Crawfurd, Sir R. H. P., *The Last Days of Charles II* (Oxford, Clarendon Press,
    1909).
Crellin, J. K., and Scott, J. R., 'Lionel Lockyer and his Pills', *Proceedings of the
    XXIII Congress of the History of Medicine*, 2 (1972) (London, Wellcome
    Institute for the History of Medicine, 1974), 1182–6.
Crook, N., and Guiton, D., *Shelley's Venomed Melody* (Cambridge, Cambridge

University Press, 1986).

Cross, W., *The Life and Times of Laurence Sterne* (New York, Macmillan, 1930).

Curl, J. S., *The Victorian Celebration of Death* (Newton Abbot, David & Charles, 1972).

Curtis, L. P. (ed.), *Letters of Laurence Sterne* (Oxford, Clarendon Press, 1935).

Curwen, E. C. (ed.), *The Journal of Gideon Mantell, Surgeon and Geologist* (London, Oxford University Press, 1940).

Darlington, A., 'The Teaching of Anatomy and the Royal Academy of Arts 1768–1782', *Journal of Art and Design Education*, 5 (1986), 263.

Darwin, E., *Zoonomia*, 4 vols (London, J. Johnson, 1801).

————, *The Temple of Nature or the Origin of Society: A Poem with Philosophical Notes* (London, J. Johnson, 1803).

Davidoff, L., and Hall, C., *Family Fortunes. Men and Women of the English Middle Classes* (London, Hutchinson, 1987).

Davis, W. (ed.), *George Whitefield's Journals, 1737–1741* (Florida, Scholars Facsimiles and Reprints, 1969).

Day, S., 'Puerperal Insanity: The Historical Sociology of a Disease' (University of Cambridge, Ph.D. Thesis, 1985).

De Beer, E. S. (ed.), *The Diary of John Evelyn*, 6 vols (Oxford, Oxford University Press, 1955).

————, (ed.), *The Correspondence of John Locke*, 8 vols (Oxford, Clarendon Press, 1976–1981).

Defoe, D., *A Journal of the Plague Year* (London, E. Nutt etc., 1722; Harmondsworth, Penguin, 1986).

Delany, M. P., *Autobiography* (London, Richard Bentley, 1861–2).

Delany, P., *British Autobiography in the Seventeenth-Century* (London, Routledge & Kegan Paul, 1969).

Delumeau, J., *La Peur en Occident (14e–18e Siècles)* (Paris, Fayard, 1978).

DeMause, L. (ed.), *History of Childhood* (London, Harper Torchbooks, 1975).

De Moulin, D., 'A Historical-Phenomenological Study of Bodily Pain in Western Medicine', *Bulletin of the History of Medicine*, 48 (1974), 540–70.

De Quincey, T., *Confessions of an English Opium Eater* (Harmondsworth, Penguin, 1971).

Devlin, J., *The Superstitious Mind. French Peasants and the Supernatural in the Nineteenth-Century* (New Haven, Yale University Press, 1987).

Dewhurst, K., *John Locke (1632–1704), Physician and Philosopher* (London, Wellcome Historical Medical Library, 1963).

Dick, O. L. (ed.), *Aubrey's Brief Lives* (Harmondsworth, Penguin, 1972).

Dirckx, J. H., *The Language of Medicine. Its Evolution, Structure, and Dynamics* (New York, Praeger, 1983).

Doble, C. E. (ed.), *Remarks and Collections of Thomas Hearne*, 3 vols (Oxford, Clarendon Press, 1888–9).

Dobson, M. J. 'Population, Disease and Mortality in Southeast England, 1600–1800' (University of Oxford, D.Phil. Thesis, 1982).

————, 'A Chronology of Epidemic Disease and Mortality in Southeast England, 1601–1800' (Historical Research Series, 19, 1987).

————, *From Old England to New England: Changing Patterns of Mortality* (Oxford, School of Geography University of Oxford Research Paper 38, 1987).

[Dodsley, J.], *A Collection of Poems In Four Volumes by Several Hands* (London, J. Dodsley, 1783).

Doe, V. S. (ed.), *The Diary of James Clegg of Chapel-en-le-Frith, 1708–55*, 3 vols (Chesterfield, Derby, Derbyshire Record Society, 1978–81).

Donnison, J., *Midwives and Medical Men. A History of Interprofessional Rivalries and Women's Rights* (London, Heinemann Educational, 1977).

Doughty, O., 'The English Malady of the Eighteenth Century', *Review of English Studies*, 2 (1929), 257–69.

Douglas, M., *Purity and Danger* (London, Routledge & Kegan Paul, 1966).

Drinka, G. F., *The Birth of Neurosis. Myth, Malady, and the Victorians* (New York, Simon & Schuster, 1985).

Drummond, J. C., and Wilbraham, A., *The Englishman's Food: A History of Five Centuries of English Diet* (London, Jonathan Cape, 1957).

Duden, B., *Geschichte unter der Haut. Ein Eisenacher Arzt und seine Patientinnen um 1730* (Stuttgart, Klett-Cotta, 1987).

Duffy, M., *The Englishman and the Foreigner* (Cambridge Chadwyck-Healey, 1986).

———— (series ed.), *The English Satirical Print 1600–1832*, 7 vols (Cambridge, Chadwyck-Healey, 1986).

Durey, M., *The Return of the Plague: British Society and the Cholera 1831–2* (Dublin, Gill & Macmillan, 1979).

Eland, G. (ed.), *Purefoy Letters*, 2 vols (London, Sidgwick & Jackson, 1931).

Elias, N., *The Civilizing Process* (Oxford, Basil Blackwell, 1983).

Ellenberger, H. F., *The Discovery of the Unconscious* (London, Allen Lane, 1970).

Ellis, A. R. (ed.), *The Early Diary of Frances Burney, 1768–1778*, 2 vols (London, George Bell, 1889).

Ellis, J. H. (ed.), *The Works of Anne Bradstreet in Prose and Verse* (Gloucester, Mass., Peter Smith, 1962).

Engelhardt, H. T., 'The Concepts of Health and Disease', in H. T. Engelhardt and S. Spiker (eds), *Evaluation and Explanation in the Biomedical Sciences* (Dordrecht and Boston, D. Reidel Publishing Company, 1975), 125–41.

Engell, J., *The Creative Imagination* (Cambridge, Mass., Harvard University Press, 1981).

Esher, Viscount (ed.), *The Girlhood of Queen Victoria. A Selection from her Majesty's Diaries between the Years 1832–1840*, 2 vols (London, John Murray, 1912).

Evans, M. (ed.), *The Letters of Richard Radcliffe and John James of Queen's College, Oxford, 1755–83* (Oxford, Oxford Historical Society, vol. 9, 1887).

Everard, M., *The Method and Means of Enjoying Health* (London, D. Newman, 1683).

Ewing, E., *Dress and Undress. A History of Women's Underwear* (London, Batsford, 1978).

Falconer, W., *An Essay on the Bath Waters* (London, G. G. J. & J. Robinson, 1770).

————, *A Dissertation on the Influence of the Passions Upon Disorders of the Body* (London, C. Dilly, 1788).

Family Companion for Health (London, F. Fayram & Leake, 1729).

Family Guide to Health (London, J. Fletcher, 1767).

Family Receipt-Book (London, Oddy & C. La Grange, 1810–17).

Farr, A. D., 'Medical Developments and Religious Belief, with Special

Reference to the Eighteenth and Nineteenth Centuries' (Open University Ph.D. Thesis, 1977).

Faulkner, T. C. (ed.), *Selected Letters and Journals of George Crabbe* (Oxford, Clarendon Press, 1985).

Faust, B. C., *The Catechism of Health* (London, C. Dilly, 1794; Edinburgh, W. Creech, 1797).

Fellman, A. C., and Fellman, M., *Making Sense of Self. Medical Advice Literature in Late Nineteenth-Century America* (Philadelphia, University of Pennsylvania Press, 1981).

Ferriar, J., *Medical Histories and Reflections*, 3 vols (London, Cadell & Davies, 1792–8).

Ferrier, S., *Marriage, a Novel*, ed. by H. Foltinek (Oxford, Oxford University Press, 1977).

Fessler, A., and France, R. S., 'Syphilis in Seventeenth-Century Lancashire', *British Journal of Venereal Disease*, 2 (1945), 177–8.

———, 'The Official Attitude Towards the Sick Poor in Seventeenth-Century Lancashire', *Transactions of the Historic Society of Lancashire and Cheshire*, 102 (1950) , 85–113.

Fiedler, L., *Freaks* (Harmondsworth, Penguin, 1978).

Fielding, H., *Journal of a Voyage to Lisbon* (London, Dent, 1901).

Figlio, K., 'Chlorosis and Chronic Disease in Nineteenth-Century Britain: The Social Constitution of Somatic Illness in a Capitalist Society', *Social History*, 3 (1978), 167–97.

———, 'Sinister Medicine? A Critique of Left Approaches to Medicine', *Radical Science Journal*, 9 (1979), 14–68.

Fildes, V., *Breasts, Bottles and Babies: a History of Infant Feeding* (Edinburgh, Edinburgh University Press, 1985).

Finer, A., and Savage, G. (eds), *The Selected Letters of Josiah Wedgwood* (London, Cory, Adams & Mackay, 1965).

Fischer-Homberger, E., 'Hypochondriasis of the Eighteenth Century – Neurosis of the Present Century', *Bulletin of the History of Medicine*, 46 (1972), 391–401.

Fissell, M. E., 'The Physic of Charity: Health and Welfare in the West Country, 1690–1834' (Philadelphia, University of Pennyslvania Ph.D. Thesis, 1988).

Fitzgerald, B. (ed.), *Correspondence of Emily, Duchess of Leinster*, 3 vols (Dublin, Irish Manuscripts Commission, 1949–57).

Flinn, M., 'The Stabilization of Mortality in Pre-Industrial Western Europe', *Journal of European Economic History*, 3 (1974), 285–318.

———, *The European Demographic System 1500–1820* (Brighton, Harvester Press, 1981).

Ford, J. M. T. (ed.), *A Medical Student at St Thomas's Hospital, 1801–1802. The Weekes Family Letters* (*Medical History* Supplement no. 7, London, Wellcome Institute for the History of Medicine, 1987).

Foucault, M., *The History of Sexuality*, vol. 1, Introduction (London, Allen Lane, 1978).

———, *Discipline and Punish. The Birth of the Prison* (London, Allen Lane, 1979).

Franklin, B., *The Life of Benjamin Franklin, Written by Himself*, ed. J. Bigelow (Oxford, Oxford University Press, 1924).

————, *Poor Richard's Almanack* (New York, Paddington Press, 1976; 1st edn, 1735–58).

Fraser, A., *The Weaker Vessel* (London, Weidenfeld & Nicolson, 1984).

Freidson, E., *Profession of Medicine: A Study of the Sociology of Applied Knowledge* (New York, Dodd, Mead, 1970).

Fremantle, A. (ed.), *The Wynne Diaries*, 3 vols (London, Oxford University Press, 1935–40).

Friedli, L., ' "Passing Women": A Study of Gender Boundaries in the Eighteenth-Century', in G. S. Rousseau and Porter (eds), *Sexual Underworlds of the Enlightenment* (Manchester, Manchester University Press, 1988), 234–60.

Fruman, N., *Coleridge, the Damaged Archangel* (London, Allen & Unwin, 1971).

Fry, K., and Cresswell, R. E. (eds), *Memoir of the Life of Elizabeth Fry*, 2 vols (London, Gilpin, 1847).

Fuller, F., *Medicina Gymnastica; or, Every Man His Own Physician*, 7th ed. (London, E. Curll, 1740).

Furst, D., 'Sterne and Physick: Images of Health and Disease in *Tristram Shandy*' (Ph.D. Dissertation, Columbia University, 1974).

Fyfe, J. G. (ed.), *Scottish Diaries 1550–1746* (Stirling, Eneas-Mackay, 1928).

Gabbay, J., 'Asthma Attacked? Tactics for the Reconstruction of a Disease Concept', in P. Wright and A. Treacher (eds), *The Problem of Medical Knowledge* (Edinburgh, Edinburgh University Press, 1982).

Gallagher, C. and Laqueur, T. (eds), *The Making of the Modern Body. Sexuality and Society in the Nineteenth-Century* (Berkeley, University of California Press, 1987).

Garlick, K., and Macintyre, A. (eds), *The Diary of Joseph Farington*, vols I–VI (New Haven, Yale University Press, 1978–9).

Garnett, D. (ed.), *The Novels of Thomas Love Peacock* (London, Rupert Hart-Davis, 1948).

Garrison, Fielding H., 'Medicine in *The Tatler, Spectator* and *Guardian*', *Bulletin of the History of Medicine*, 2 (1934), 477–503.

Garth, Sir S., *The Dispensary, a Poem*, 5th ed. (London, J. Nutt, 1703).

Gay, P., 'The Enlightenment as Medicine and as Cure', in W. H. Barber (ed.), *The Age of the Enlightenment. Studies Presented to Theodore Besterman* (Edinburgh, St Andrews University Publications, 1967), 375–86.

————, *The Enlightenment: an Interpretation*, 2 vols (New York, Knopf, 1967–9).

Gazley, J. G., *The Life of Arthur Young* (Philadelphia, American Philosophical Society, 1973).

Gelfand, T., 'The *Annales* and Medical Historiography: *Bilan et Perspective*', in R. Porter and A. Wear (eds), *Problems and Methods in the History of Medicine* (London, Croom Helm, 1987), 15–39.

Gentleman's Magazine (London, Edward Cave, 1731–1907).

Geyer-Kordesch, J., 'The Cultural Habits of Illness: the Enlightened and the Pious in Eighteenth-Century Germany', in R. Porter (ed.), *Patients and Practitioners* (Cambridge, Cambridge University Press, 1985), 177–204.

Gibbs, L. (ed.), *The Admirable Lady Mary. The Life and Times of Lady Mary Wortley Montagu (1689–1762)* (London, Dent, 1949).

Gillow, J., and Hewitson A. (eds), *The Tyldesley Diary* (Preston, A. Hewitson, 1873).

Gilman, S., 'Touch, Sexuality and Disease', in W. F. Bynum and R. Porter (eds), *Medicine and the Five Senses* (Cambridge, Cambridge University Press, forthcoming).

————, *Disease and Representation: Images of Illness from Madness to Aids* (Ithaca, Cornell University Press, 1988).

Ginzburg, C., *The Cheese and the Worms: the Cosmos of a Sixteenth-Century Miller* (London, Routledge & Kegan Paul, 1980).

Gittings, C., *Death, Burial and the Individual in Early Modern England* (London, Croom Helm, 1984).

Gittings, R. (ed.), *Letters of John Keats: A Selection* (Oxford, Oxford University Press, 1979).

Goellnicht, D. C., *The Poet-Physician. Keats and Medical Science* (Pittsburgh, University of Pittsburgh Press, 1984).

Goffman, E., *The Presentation of Self in Everyday Life* (Harmondsworth, Penguin, 1969).

Gomme, G. L., *The Gentleman's Magazine Library: Popular Superstitions* (London, Elliot Stock, 1884).

Goodwyn, E. A. (ed.), *Selections from Norwich Newspapers* (Ipswich, East Anglian Magazine, 1972).

Gosse, P., *Dr. Viper. The Querulous Life of Philip Thicknesse* (London, Cassell, 1952).

Goubert, J.-P., *Malades et Médecins en Bretagne 1770–1790* (Rennes, Institut Armoricain de Recherches Historiques, 1974).

———— (ed.), *La Médicalisation de la Société Française 1770–1830* (Waterloo, Ontario, Historical Reflections Press, 1982).

————, 'Twenty Years On: Problems of Historical Methodology in the History of Health', in R. Porter and A. Wear (eds), *Problems and Methods in the History of Medicine* (London, Croom Helm, 1987), 40–56.

Grange, J., 'Cambridgeshire Country Cures', *Cambridgeshire Life Magazine* (May 1985), 29.

Granville, M., *Autobiography and Correspondence* (London, Richard Bentley, 1861).

Gray, E. (ed.), *Papers and Diaries of a York Family* (London, Sheldon Press, 1927).

Greig, J. (ed.), *Diaries of a Duchess. Extracts from the Diaries of the First Duchess of Northumberland (1716–1776)* (London, Hodder & Stoughton, 1926).

Greig, J. Y. T. (ed.), *The Letters of David Hume*, 2 vols (Oxford, Clarendon Press, 1969).

Griggs, E. L. (ed.), *Collected Letters of Samuel Taylor Coleridge*, 6 vols (Oxford, Clarendon Press, 1956–1968).

Groddeck, G., *The Meaning of Illness*, trans. G. Mander (London, Hogarth Press, 1977).

Grosskurth, P. (ed.), *The Memoirs of John Addington Symonds* (London, Hutchinson, 1984).

Grosvenor, B., *Health. An Essay* (Boston, J. Winter, 1761).

Gunn, F., *The Artificial Face* (Newton Abbot, David & Charles, 1973).

Gunn, P. (ed.), *Byron: Selected Prose* (Harmondsworth, Penguin, 1972).

Guthrie, D., 'The Patient: A Neglected Factor in the History of Medicine', *Proceedings of the Royal Society of Medicine*, 37 (1945), 490–4.

Hack, M. Pryor, *Christian Womanhood* (London, Hodder & Stoughton, 1882).

Hagstrum, J. H., 'On Dr Johnson's Fear of Death', *E. L. H. A Journal of English Literary History*, 14 (1947), 308–19.

————, *Sex and Sensibility: Erotic Ideal and Erotic Love from Milton to Mozart* (London & Chicago, University of Chicago Press, 1980).

Hair, P. E. H., 'Deaths from Violence in Britain; A Tentative Secular Survey', *Population Studies*, 25 (1971), 5–24.

Hale-White, Sir W., *Keats as Doctor and Patient* (London, Oxford University Press, 1936).

Halévy, E., *The Growth of Philosophical Radicalism* (London, Faber & Faber, 1924).

Haley, B., *The Healthy Body and Victorian Culture* (Cambridge, Mass., Harvard University Press, 1978).

Hall, E. (ed.), *Miss Weeton. Journal of a Governess 1807–11*, 2 vols (London, Oxford University Press, 1936).

Halsband, R., *The Life of Lady Mary Wortley Montagu* (Oxford, Clarendon Press, 1956).

Hambridge, R. A., 'Empiricomany, or an Infatuation in Favour of Empiricism, or Quackery: the Socio-Economics of Eighteenth Century Quackery', in S. Soupel and R. A. Hambridge (eds), *Literature, Science and Medicine* (W. A. Clark Memorial Library, University of California, Los Angeles, 1982), 47–102.

Hamilton, B., 'The Medical Professions in the Eighteenth Century', *Economic History Review*, 4 (1951), 141–69.

Hamilton, D., *The Healers: A History of Medicine in Scotland* (Edinburgh, Canongate, 1981).

Hand, W. O., 'The Folk-Healer: Calling and Endowment', *Journal of the History of Medicine*, 26 (1971), 263–75.

Hankin, C. C. (ed.), *The Life of Mary Anne Schimmelpenninck*, 2 vols (London, Longmans, 1858).

Hardstaff, R. E., and Lyth, P., *Georgian Southwell* (Newark, Newark District Council, n.d.).

Hardy, A., 'Water and the Search for Public Health in London in the Eighteenth and Nineteenth Centuries', *Medical History*, 28 (1984), 250–82.

Hardyment, C., *Dream Babies. Child Care from Locke to Spock* (London, Jonathan Cape, 1983).

Hare, E. H., 'Masturbatory Insanity: the History of an Idea', *Journal of Mental Science*, 108 (1962), 1–25.

Harris, I., *Family Memorials: Chiefly The Memoranda left by Isabella Harris with Some Extracts From the Journal of Her Mother* (privately printed, n.p., 1869).

Harris, W., *Treatise on the Acute Diseases of Infants*, trans. by J. Martyn (London, T. Astley, 1742).

Harrison, B., *Drink and the Victorians: The Temperance Question in England, 1815–1872* (London, Faber & Faber, 1971).

Hartley, D., *Observations on Man, his Frame, his Duty, and his Expectations*, 2 vols (London, J. Leake & W. Frederick, 1749).

Hartshorne, A. (ed.), *Memoirs of a Royal Chaplain, 1729–1763. The Correspondence of Edmund Pyle, D.D. Chaplain in Ordinary to George II, With Samuel Kerrich D.D., Vicar of Dersingham, Rector of West Newton*

(London, John Lane: Bodley Head, 1905).

Hawkins, L. H., 'The History of Resuscitation', *British Journal of Hospital Medicine*, 4 (1970), 495–500.

Haygarth, J., *Of the Imagination, as a Cause and as a Cure of Disorders of the Body* (Bath, Cadell & Davies, 1800).

Hayter, A., *Opium and the Romantic Imagination* (California, University of California Press, 1970).

Hayward, A. (ed.), *Life and Writings of Mrs. Piozzi* (London, Longmans, Green and Roberts, 1861).

Heberden, W. (the elder), *Medical Commentaries* (London, T. Payne, 1802).

Hell Upon Earth or the Town in an Uproar (London, Roberts and Dodd, 1729).

Helman, C., '"Feed a Cold, Starve a Fever": Folk Models of Infection in an English Suburban Community, and Their Relation to Medical Treatment', *Culture, Medicine and Psychiatry*, 2 (1978), 107–37.

————, *Culture, Health and Illness* (Bristol, Wright, 1984).

Hemlow, J. (ed.), *The Journals and Letters of Fanny Burney (Madame D'Arblay)*, 12 vols (Oxford, Clarendon Press, 1972–84).

Henry, M., *An Account of the Life and Death of Philip Henry by his Son* (London, John Lawrence, 1699).

Herbert, Lord (ed.), *Pembroke Papers (1790–1794). Letters and Diaries of Henry, Tenth Earl of Pembroke and his Circle* (London, Jonathan Cape, 1950).

Herzlich, C., and Pierret, J., *Illness and Self in Society*, trans. E. Forster (Baltimore, Johns Hopkins University Press, 1987).

Heywood, T. (ed.), *The Diary of the Rev. Henry Newcome Sepr 30 1661 to Sepr 29 1663* (Manchester, Chetham Society, 1849).

Highmore, A., *Pietas Londinensis: The History, Design and Present State of the Various Public Charities in and near London* (London, Phillips, 1810).

Hill, A. W., *John Wesley Among the Physicians* (London, Epworth Press, 1958).

Hill, B., 'Scavenger of the Faculty. Joshua Ward (1685–1761)', *Practitioner* (1970), 820–25.

Hill, Sir J., *The Old Man's Guide to Health and Longer Life*, 6th edition (London, E. & C. Dilly, 1771.

————, *Hypochondriasis. A Practical Treatise on the Nature and Cure of That Disorder* (London, for the Author, 1756).

Hill, Sir John, *see also* Seymour, Juliana–Susannah.

Hillam, F. C., 'The Development of Dental Practice in the Provinces from the Late Eighteenth Century to 1855' (Ph.D. Thesis, University of Liverpool, 1986).

Himmelfarb, G., *The Idea of Poverty* (London, Faber; New York, Knopf, 1984).

Hobhouse, E. (ed.), *The Diary of a West Country Physician, AD 1684–1726. Extracts from Dr. Claver Morris' Diary* (London, Simpkin Marshall, 1934).

Holcroft, T., *The Adventures of Hugh Trevor* (Oxford, Oxford University Press, 1928).

Holmes, G., *Augustan England: Professions, State and Society, 1680–1730* (London, George Allen & Unwin, 1982).

Home, J. A. (ed.), *Letters and Journals of Lady Mary Coke*, 4 vols (Bath, Kingsmead Reprints, 1970; 1st edn, privately printed, 1889–96).

Hone, C. R., *The Life of Dr. John Radcliffe 1652–1714. Benefactor of the University of Oxford* (London, Faber & Faber, 1950).

Hopkins, D., *Princes and Peasants: Smallpox in History* (London and Chicago, University of Chicago Press, 1983).

Howe, G. M., *Man, Environment and Disease in Britain. A Medical Geography Through the Ages* (New York, Barnes & Noble Books, 1972).

Hufeland, C. W., *The Art of Prolonging Life* (London, J. Bell, 1797; reprinted, 1852).

Hughes, E., *North Country Life in the Eighteenth Century*, 2 vols (London, Oxford University Press, 1965–1969).

Huizinga, J., *The Waning of the Middle Ages* (Harmondsworth, Pelican, 1972).

Hultin, N. C., 'Medicine and Magic in the Eighteenth Century: the Diaries of James Woodforde', *Journal of the History of Medicine and Allied Sciences*, 30 (1975), 349–66.

Hunt, J. H. L., *The Autobiography of Leigh Hunt with Reminiscences of his Friends and Contemporaries* (London, Smith & Elder, 1850).

Hunter, M., *John Aubrey and the Realm of Learning* (London, Duckworth, 1975).

————, and Gregory, A. (eds), *An Astrological Diary of the Seventeenth Century. Samuel Jeake of Rye 1652–1699* (Oxford, Clarendon Press, 1988).

Hunter, R., and Macalpine, I., *Three Hundred Years of Psychiatry, 1535–1860* (London, Oxford University Press, 1963).

Ignatieff, M., *A Just Measure of Pain (the Penitentiary in the Industrial Revolution 1750–1850)* (London, Macmillan, 1978).

Ilchester, The Earl of (ed.), *Lady Holland's Journal*, 2 vols (London, Longmans & Green, 1908).

Illich, I., *Limits to Medicine. The Expropriation of Health* (Harmondsworth, Penguin, 1977).

Imhof, A. E., 'Methodological Problems in Modern Urban History Writing: Twenty Graphic Presentations of Urban Mortality 1750–1850', in R. Porter and A. Wear (eds), *Problems and Methods in the History of Medicine* (London, Croom Helm, 1987), 101–32.

Inglis, B., *Fringe Medicine* (London, Faber & Faber, 1964).

————, *Natural Medicine* (London, Collins, 1979).

————, *The Diseases of Civilisation* (London, Hodder & Stoughton, 1981).

Ingram, A. M., *Boswell's Creative Gloom* (London, Macmillan, 1982).

Ingram, R., *The Gout* (London, P. Vaillant, 1767).

Ingrams, R. (ed.), *Dr. Johnson by Mrs Thrale* (London, Chatto & Windus, 1984).

J. M., *Letters to a Sick Friend Containing Such Observations as may Render the Use of Remedies Effectual towards the Removal of Sickness and Preservation of Health* (London, T. Parkhurst, 1682).

Jackson, S., *Melancholia and Depression from Hippocratic Times to Modern Times* (New Haven, Yale University Press, 1986).

Jackson, T. (ed.), *The Journal of the Rev. Charles Wesley* (London, John Mason, 1849).

Jaeger, M., *Before Victoria: Changing Standards and Behaviour, 1787–1837* (London, Chatto & Windus, 1956).

James, R., *A Medicinal Dictionary*, 3 vols (London, T. Osborne, 1743–5).

James, W., *Varieties of Religious Experience* (London, Longmans, 1902).

Janeway, J., *A Token for Children* (London, n.p., 1720).

Jarrett, D., *England in the Age of Hogarth* (London, Hart Davis, 1974).

Jeaffreson, J. C., *A Book About Doctors* (London, Hurst & Blackett, n.d.).

Jewitt, L. (ed.), *The Life of William Hutton* (London, Frederick Warne, 1872).
Jewson, N., 'Medical Knowledge and the Patronage System in Eighteenth Century England', *Sociology*, 8 (1974), 369–85.
————, 'The Disappearance of the Sick Man from Medical Cosmology, 1770–1870', ibid., 10 (1976), 225–44.
Johnson, R. B. (ed.), *Letters from the Right Honourable Lady Mary Wortley Montagu, 1709–1762* (London, Dent, 1906).
Jones, J., *The Mysteries of Opium Reveal'd* (London, R. Smith, 1701).
Josten, C. H. (ed.), *Elias Ashmole (1617–1692). His Autobiographical and Historical Notes, His Correspondence*, 5 vols (Oxford, Clarendon Press, 1966).
Kanner, L., *Folklore of Teeth* (New York, Macmillan, 1928).
Kaplan, B. B., 'Greatrakes the Stroker: the Interpretations of his Contemporaries', *Isis*, 73 (1982), 178–85.
Kassler, J. C., 'Breaking Wind', *New Journal of Chemistry*, 11 (1987), 451–3.
Keele, K., *Anatomies of Pain* (Oxford, Blackwell Scientific Publications, 1957).
Ketton-Cremer, R. W., *Thomas Gray: A Biography* (Cambridge, Cambridge University Press, 1955).
Kiefer, J. H., 'Uroscopy: The Clinical Laboratory of the Past', *Transactions of the American Association of Genito-Urinary Surgeons*, 50 (1958), 161–72.
King, J., and Ryskamp, C. A. (eds), *The Letters and Prose Writings of William Cowper*, 4 vols (Oxford, Clarendon Press, 1979–84).
King, L. S., *The Medical World of the Eighteenth Century* (Chicago, University of Chicago Press, 1958).
————, *The Road to Medical Enlightenment, 1650–1695* (London, Macdonald, 1970).
————, *The Philosophy of Medicine: The Early Eighteenth Century* (Cambridge, Mass., Harvard University Press, 1978).
King-Hele, D. (ed.), *Erasmus Darwin* (London, Macmillan, 1963).
————, (ed.), *The Essential Writings of Erasmus Darwin* (London, MacGibbon & Kee, 1968).
————, *Doctor of Revolution: The Life and Genius of Erasmus Darwin* (London, Faber, 1977).
————, (ed.), *The Letters of Erasmus Darwin* (Cambridge, Cambridge University Press, 1981).
Kingsley, F. E. (ed.), *Charles Kingsley: His Letters and Memories of His Life*, 2 vols (London, Macmillan, 1910).
Kleinman, A., *Patients and Healers in the Context of Culture: An Exploration of the Borderline between Anthropology, Medicine, and Psychiatry* (Berkeley, University of California Press, 1980).
————, *Social Origins of Distress and Disease. Depression, Neurasthenia, and Pain in Modern China* (New Haven, Yale University Press, 1986).
————, and Good, B. (eds), *Culture and Depression. Studies in the Anthropology and Cross-Cultural Psychiatry of Affect and Disorder* (Berkeley, University of California Press, 1985).
Knapp, L. M., *Tobias Smollett: Doctor of Men and Manners* (Princeton, New Jersey, Princeton University Press, 1949).
Knibiehler, Y. and Fouquet, C., *La Femme et Les Médecins. Analyse Historique* (Paris, Hachette, 1983).
Knox, R. A., *Enthusiasm* (London, Oxford University Press, 1950).

Kurtz, L. P., *The Dance of Death and the Macabre Spirit in European Literature* (New York, Institute of French Studies, 1934).

L. F. C. (ed.), *Extracts from the Diary of a Living Physician* (London, Saunders & Otley, 1851).

Lain Entralgo, P., *Mind and Body. Psychosomatic Pathology: A Short History of the Evolution of Medical Thought* (London, Harvill, 1955).

———, *Doctor and Patient*, trans. Frances Partridge (London, Weidenfeld & Nicolson, 1969).

Lane, J., 'The Provincial Practitioner and his Services to the Poor 1750–1800', *Society for the Social History of Medicine Bulletin*, 28 (1981), 10–14.

———, 'The Medical Practitioners of Provincial England in 1783', *Medical History*, 28 (1984), 353–71.

———, '"The Doctor Scolds Me": The Diaries and Correspondence of Patients in Eighteenth-Century England', in R. Porter (ed.), *Patients and Practitioners* (Cambridge, Cambridge University Press, 1985), 207–47.

———, 'The Role of Apprenticeship in Eighteenth-Century Medical Education in England', in W. F. Bynum and R. Porter (eds), *William Hunter and the Eighteenth-Century Medical World* (Cambridge, Cambridge University Press, 1985), 57–104.

———, 'A Provincial Surgeon and his Obstetric Practice: Thomas W. Jones of Henley-in-Arden, 1764–1846', *Medical History*, 31 (1987), 333–48.

Laqueur, T., 'Orgasm, Generation, and the Politics of Reproductive Biology', *Representations*, 14 (1986), 1–14.

Latham, R., and Matthews, W. (eds), *The Diary of Samuel Pepys*, 11 vols (London, Bell & Hyman, 1970–83).

Law, W., *A Serious Call to a Devout and Holy Life* (London, Longmans, 1907).

Lawrence, C., 'William Buchan: Medicine Laid Open', *Medical History*, 19 (1975), 20–35.

———, 'The Nervous System and Society in the Scottish Enlightenment', in B. Barnes and S. Shapin (eds), *Natural Order* (Beverly Hills & London, Sage Publications, 1980), 19–40.

———, 'Medicine as Culture: Edinburgh and the Scottish Enlightenment' (University of London, Ph.D. Thesis, 1984).

———, 'Incommunicable Knowledge: Science, Technology and the Clinical Art in Britain, 1850–1914', *Journal of Contemporary History*, 20 (1985), 503–20.

Lawrence, S., 'Science and Medicine at the London Hospitals. The Development of Teaching and Research 1750–1815' (Ph.D. Thesis, University of Toronto, 1985).

———, 'Educating the Senses. Students, Teachers and Medical Rhetoric in Eighteenth-Century London', in W. F. Bynum and R. Porter (eds), *Medicine and the Five Senses* (Cambridge, Cambridge University Press, forthcoming).

Le Brun, F., *Les Hommes et la Mort en Anjou aux 17e et 18e Siècles* (Paris, Mouton, 1977).

Leder, D., 'Medicine and Paradigms of Embodiment', *Journal of Medicine and Philosophy*, 9 (1984), 29–43.

LeFanu, W. (ed.), *Betsy Sheridan's Journal* (London, Eyre & Spottiswoode, 1960).

———, 'The Lost Half Century in English Medicine, 1700–1750', *Bulletin of the History of Medicine*, 46 (1972), 319–48.

————, *British Periodicals of Medicine: A Chronological List* (Oxford, Oxford Wellcome Unit for the History of Medicine, 1984).

Lefebure, M., *Samuel Taylor Coleridge: A Bondage of Opium* (London, Victor Gollancz, 1974).

————, *A Bondage of Love* (London, Victor Gollancz, 1986).

Leventhal, H., *In the Shadow of the Enlightenment. Occultism and Renaissance Science in Eighteenth-Century America* (New York, New York University Press, 1976).

Lever, T. (ed.), *The Letters of Lady Palmerston* (London, Murray, 1957).

Levine, J., *Dr Woodward's Shield* (Berkeley, University of California Press, 1977).

Lewis, C. S., *The Problem of Pain* (London, Centenary Press, 1940).

Lewis, J. S., *In the Family Way. Childbearing in the British Aristocracy 1760–1860* (New Brunswick, N. J., Rutgers University Press, 1986).

Lewis, Lady T. (ed.), *Extracts of the Journals and Correspondence of Miss Berry from the Year 1763–1852* (London, Longmans, 1865).

Lewis, T. T. (ed.), *Letters of The Lady Brilliana Harley, Wife of Sir Robert Harley* (London, Camden Society, 1854).

Lilly, W., *Christian Astrology Modestly Treated of in Three Books* (London, Partridge & Blunden, 1647).

Linebaugh, P., 'The Tyburn Riot Against the Surgeons', in E. P. Thompson *et al.* (eds), *Albion's Fatal Tree* (London, Allen Lane, 1975), 65–118.

Little, D., and Kahrl, G. (eds), *The Letters of David Garrick*, 3 vols (London, Oxford University Press, 1963).

Littlewood, S. R., *Elizabeth Inchbald, a Charming Old Lady* (London, Daniel O'Connor, 1921).

Livingstone, D. N., 'Human Acclimatization: Perspectives on a Contested Field of Inquiry in Science, Medicine and Geography', *History of Science*, 25 (1987), 359–94.

Llanover, Lady (ed.), *The Life and Correspondence of Mary Granville, Mrs Delaney*, 6 vols (London, Richard Bentley, 1862).

Locke, J., *An Essay Concerning Human Understanding*, 2 vols, ed. by J. Yolton (London, Dent, 1965).

Loudon, I. S. L., 'Chlorosis, Anaemia and Anorexia Nervosa', *Journal of the Royal College of General Practitioners* (1980), 30, 1669–87.

————, 'Leg Ulcers in the Eighteenth and Early Nineteenth Century', ibid., 31 (1981), 263–73, and 32 (1982), 301–9.

————, 'The Concept of the Family Doctor', *Bulletin of the History of Medicine*, 58 (1984), 347–62.

————, 'The Nature of Provincial Medical Practice in Eighteenth-Century England', *Medical History*, 29 (1985), 1–32.

————, *Medical Care and the General Practitioner 1750–1850* (Oxford, Clarendon Press, 1986).

Loudon, J. B. (ed.), *Social Anthropology and Medicine* (London and New York, Academic Press, 1976).

Loux, F., 'Présentation: Langages et Images du Corps', *Ethnologie Française*, 6 (1976), 215–18.

————, *Sagesse du Corps, Santé et Maladie dans les Proverbes Régionaux Français* (Paris, Maisonneuve et Larose, 1978).

————, *Pratiques et Savoirs Populaires: Le Corps dans la Societé Traditionelle* (Paris, Berger-Levrault, 1979).

————, 'Popular Culture and Knowledge of the Body: Infancy and the Medical Anthropologists', in R. Porter and A. Wear (eds), *Problems and Methods in the History of Medicine* (London, Croom Helm, 1987), 81–97.

Lustig, J. S., and Pottle, F. A. (eds), *Boswell: The Applause of the Jury, 1782–85* (London, Heinemann, 1982).

Lynch, B., *A Guide to Health Through the Various Stages of Life* (London, the author, 1744).

Lyons, J. O., *The Invention of the Self* (Carbondale, Southern Illinois University Press; London, Feffer & Simons, 1978).

Maccubbin, R. P. (ed.), *'Tis Nature's Fault. Unauthorized Sexuality during the Enlightenment* (Cambridge, Cambridge University Press, 1987).

MacDonald, M., 'The Inner Side of Wisdom: Suicide in Early Modern England', *Psychological Medicine*, 7 (1977), 565–82.

————, 'Insanity and the Realities of History in Early Modern England', ibid., 11 (1981), 11–25.

————, *Mystical Bedlam; Madness, Anxiety and Healing in Seventeenth-Century England* (Cambridge, Cambridge University Press, 1981).

————, 'Anthropological Perspectives on the History of Science and Medicine', in P. Corsi and P. Weindling (eds), *Information Sources in the History of Science and Medicine* (London, Butterworth, 1983), 61–96.

————, 'The Secularization of Suicide in England, 1660–1800', *Past and Present*, 111 (1986), 50–100.

————, 'Madness, Suicide, and the Computer', in R. Porter and A. Wear (eds), *Problems and Methods in the History of Medicine, 1750–1850* (London, Croom Helm, 1987), 207–29.

MacDonald, R. H., 'The Frightful Consequences of Onanism', *Journal of the History of Ideas*, 28 (1967), 423–41.

Macdonald, V. M. (ed.), *The Letters of Eliza Pierce (Eliza Taylor) 1751–1775* (London, F. Etchells & H. Macdonald, 1927).

Macfarlane, A., *The Family Life of Ralph Josselin* (Cambridge, Cambridge University Press, 1970).

————, (ed.), *The Diary of Ralph Josselin, 1616–1683* (Oxford, Oxford University Press, 1976).

————, *The Origins of English Individualism* (Oxford, Basil Blackwell, 1978).

————, *Marriage and Love in England* (Oxford, Basil Blackwell, 1986).

MacGregor, H., 'Eighteenth-Century V.D. Publicity', *British Journal of Venereal Disease*, 31 (1955), 117–18.

Mack, M., *Alexander Pope* (London, W. W. Norton, 1985).

McKendrick, N., Brewer J., and Plumb J. H. (eds), *The Birth of a Consumer Society: The Commercialization of Eighteenth Century England* (London, Europa, 1982).

MacKenzie, J., *History of Health* (Edinburgh, W. Gordon, 1758).

McManners, J., *Death and the Enlightenment: Changing Attitudes Towards Death Among Christians and Unbelievers in Eighteenth-Century France* (Oxford, Clarendon Press, 1981).

MacNeil, M., *Under the Banner of Science* (Manchester, Manchester University Press, 1987).

McNeill, W. H., *Plagues and Peoples* (Oxford, Anchor Press, 1976).

Maddan, J. S., 'Samuel Johnson's Alcohol Problem', *Medical History*, 11 (1976), 141–5.

Malthus, T. R., *Essay on Population* (London, Macmillan, 1966; 1st edn, 1798).

Mandeville, B., *A Treatise of the Hypochondriack and Hysterick Diseases* (London, Tonson, 2nd edn., 1730; reprinted by George Olms Verlag, Hildesheim, 1981).

————, *The Virgin Unmask'd* (London, J. Morphew & J. Woodward, 1709).

Mant, R., *The Order For the Visitation of the Sick* (London, F. C. & J. Rivington, 1806).

Manuel, M., *The Eighteenth Century Confronts the Gods* (Cambridge Mass., Harvard University Press, 1959).

Marchand, L. A. (ed.), *Byron's Letters and Journals*, 12 vols (London, John Murray, 1973–81).

Marcovich, A., 'Concerning the Continuity between Image of Society and the Image of the Human Body: An Examination of the Work of the English Physician J. C. Lettsom (1746–1815)', in P. Wright and A. Teacher (eds), *The Problem of Medical Knowledge* (Edinburgh, Edinburgh University Press, 1982), 69–87.

Marrs, E. W. (ed.), *Letters of Charles and Mary Lamb*, 3 vols (Ithaca, Cornell University Press, 1975–8).

————, (ed.), *The Letters of Thomas Carlyle to His Brother Alexander with Related Family Letters* (Cambridge, Mass., Harvard University Press, 1968).

Marshall, J. D. (ed.), *The Autobiography of William Stout of Lancaster 1665–1752* (Manchester, Chetham Society Publications, 3rd series, vol. 4; and New York, Barnes & Noble, 1967).

Marten, J., *A Treatise of All The Degrees and Symptoms of the Venereal Disease*, 6th ed. (London, S. Crouch, 1708).

Martin, R. B., *Tennyson: The Unquiet Heart* (Oxford, Clarendon Press, 1980).

[Martineau, H.], *Life in the Sick-Room. Essays by an Invalid* (2nd edn, London, Moxon, 1854).

————, *Autobiography*, 2 vols (London, Virago, 1983; 1st ed., 1877).

Matthews H. (ed.), *Diary of An Invalid* (London, John Murray, 1835).

Matthews, L. G., *History of Pharmacy in Britain* (Edinburgh & London, E. & S. Livingstone, 1962).

Matthews, W. (ed.), *The Diary of Dudley Ryder* (London, Methuen, 1939).

———— (ed.), *British Diaries. An Annotated Bibliography of British Diaries Written Between 1442–1942* (Gloucester, Mass., Peter Smith, 1967).

————, (ed.), *British Autobiographies. Annotated Bibliography of British Autobiographies Published or Written Before 1975* (London, Archon Books, 1968).

Mauriceau, F., *The Diseases of Women with Child* (London, Andrew Bell, 1710).

Maynwaring, E., *The Method and Means of Enjoying Health, Vigour and Long Life* (London, Dorman Newman, 1683).

Mazlish, B., *James and John Stuart Mill, Father and Son in the Nineteenth Century* (London, Hutchinson, 1975).

Mead, R., *Medica Sacra; or, A Commentary on the Most Remarkable Diseases, Mentioned in the Holy Scriptures* (London, J. Brindley, 1755).

Mechanic, D., 'The Concept of Illness Behaviour', *Journal of Chronic Disease*, 15 (1962), 189–94.

Melville, L. (ed.), *The Berry Papers: Being the Correspondence Hitherto Unpublished of Mary Agnes Berry, 1763–1852* (London, John Lane, 1914).

Mennell, S., *All Manner of Foods* (Oxford, Basil Blackwell, 1985).

Miller, C. K. (ed.), *The Memoirs of Martinus Scriblerus* (New Haven, Yale University Press, 1950).

Miller, G., *The Adoption of Inoculation for Smallpox in England and France* (London, Oxford University Press, 1957).

———, 'Airs, Waters, and Places in History', *Journal of the History of Medicine*, 17 (1962), 129–38.

——— (ed.), *Letters of Edward Jenner* (Baltimore, Johns Hopkins University Press, 1983).

Miller, J., *The Body in Question* (London, Cape, 1978).

Mills, H. (ed.), *George Crabbe, Tales, 1812, and Other Poems* (Cambridge, Cambridge University Press, 1967).

Mintz, S., *Sweetness and Power* (New York, Viking, 1985).

Mitchell, B., and Penrose, H. (eds), *Letters from Bath 1766–1767 by the Rev. John Penrose* (London, Alan Sutton, 1983).

Mitchell, L. G., *The Purefoy Letters, 1735–53* (London, Sidgwick & Jackson, 1973).

Mitford, N. F. (ed.), *The Ladies of Alderley* (London, Chapman & Hall, 1967).

Moore, C. A., 'The English Malady', in C. A. Moore (ed.), *Backgrounds of English Literature 1700–1760* (Minneapolis, University of Minnesota Press, 1953), 179–235.

Morley, H., *Memoirs of Bartholomew Fair* (London, Chapman Hall, 1859).

Morley, J., *Death, Heaven and the Victorians* (London, Studio Vista, 1971).

Morris, R. J., *Cholera, 1832. The Social Response to an Epidemic* (London, Croom Helm, 1976).

———, 'Religion and Medicine: The Cholera Pamphlets of Oxford 1832, 1849 and 1854', *Medical History*, 19 (1975), 256–70.

Morsley, C., *News From the English Countryside* (London, Harrap, 1977).

Mossner, E. C., *The Life of David Hume* (Oxford, Clarendon Press, 1970).

Muchembled, R., *Popular Culture and Elite Culture in France 1400–1750*, trans. by Lydia Cochrane (Baton Rouge, Louisiana State University Press, 1985).

Mulhallen, J., and Wright, D. J. M., 'Samuel Johnson: Amateur Physician', *Journal of the Royal Society of Medicine*, 76 (1983), 217–22.

Mullett, C., 'The Lay Outlook on Medicine in England, circa 1800–1850', *Bulletin of the History of Medicine*, 25 (1951), 168–84.

Murray, J. M. (ed.), *The Newfoundland Journal of Aaron Thomas, Able Seaman in H.M.S. Boston* (London, Longmans, 1968).

Myer, V. G. (ed.), *Laurence Sterne: Riddles and Mysteries* (London, Vision Press, 1984).

———, 'Tristram and the Animal Spirits', in Valerie Grosvenor Myer (ed.), *Laurence Sterne: Riddles and Mysteries* (London, Vision Press, 1984).

Neale, R. S., *Bath 1680–1850. A Social History* (London, Routledge & Kegan Paul, 1981).

Nelson, J., *Essay on the Government of Children Under Three General Heads: Health, Manners and Education* (London, R. & J. Dodsley, 1756).

Nichols, J., *Literary Anecdotes of the Eighteenth Century*, ed. by C. Clair (Sussex, Centaur Press, 1967).

Nicolson, M., 'The Metastatic Theory of Pathogenesis and the Professional

Interests of the Eighteenth-Century Physician', *Medical History*, 32 (1988), 47-70.

Nicolson, M. H. (ed.), *The Conway Letters* (New Haven, Yale University Press, 1930).

——, and Rousseau, G. S., *This Long Disease My Life. Alexander Pope and the Sciences* (Princeton, Princeton University Press, 1968).

Niebyl, P., 'The Non-Naturals', *Bulletin of the History of Medicine*, 45 (1971), 486–92.

——, 'Old Age, Fever, and the Lamp Metaphor', *Journal of the History of Medicine*, 26 (1971), 351–68.

Nokes, D., *Jonathan Swift: A Hypocrite Reversed. A Critical Biography* (Oxford, Oxford University Press, 1985).

Noon, C., 'On Suicide', *Journal of the History of Ideas*, 39 (1978), 371–86.

North, R., *General Preface and Life of Dr John North*, ed. by P. Millard (Toronto, Univerity of Toronto Press, 1984).

Norton, J. E. (ed.), *The Letters of Edward Gibbon*, 3 vols (London, Cassell, 1956).

Ober, W. B., *'Boswell's Clap' and other Essays: Medical Analyses of Literary Men's Afflictions* (Carbondale, Southern Illinois University Press; London and Amsterdam, Feffer & Simons, 1979).

O'Brian, P., *Joseph Banks: A Life* (London, Collins, 1987).

O'Connor, M. C., *The Art of Dying Well: The Development of the Ars Moriendi* (New York, AMS Press, 1981).

Oddy, D. J., *The Making of the Modern British Diet* (London, Croom Helm, 1976).

——, *Diet and Health in Modern Britain* (London, Croom Helm, 1985).

Old Cornutor of Seventy-five. Being a Genuine Narrative of the Life, Adventures, and Amours, of Don Ricardo Honeywater (London, 1748).

Onania; or, the Heinous Sin of Self-Pollution, and All Its Frightful Consequences, 15th ed. (London, J. Isted, 1730).

O'Neill, J., *Five Bodies, The Human Shape of Modern Society* (Ithaca, Cornell University Press, 1985).

Oppenheimer, J., *New Aspects of John and of William Hunter* (London, Heinemann, 1946).

Orlebar, F. St. John (ed.), *The Orbelar Chronicles* (London, Mitchell Hughes & Clarke, 1930).

O'Rourke, D. T., 'John Houghton (1645–1705), Journalist, Apothecary and F.R.S.', *Pharmaceutical Historian*, 9, 1 (1979), unpaginated.

Osborn, J. M. (ed.), *Joseph Spence. Observations, Anecdotes and Characters of Books and Men*, 2 vols (Oxford, Clarendon Press, 1966).

Paley, W., *The Works of William Paley, D. D. and an Account of the Life and Writings of the Author, by the Rev. Edmund Paley, A.M., vicar of Easingwold*, 4 vols (London, Longman, etc., 1838).

Park, K., and Daston, L., 'Unnatural Conceptions: The Study of Monsters in Sixteenth-Century France and England', *Past and Present*, 92 (1981), 20–54.

Parkinson, R. (ed.), *The Autobiography of Henry Newcome* (Manchester, Chetham Society Publications, 1852).

Parry, E. A. (ed.), *Letters of Dorothy Osborne to Sir William Temple 1652-4* (London, Griffith, Farran, 1888 and Dent, Wayfarer's Library, 1914).

Parsons T., *The Social System* (London, Routledge & Kegan Paul, 1951).

Passmore, J. A., *The Perfectibility of Man* (London, Duckworth, 1972).

Paston, G. (ed.), *Mrs Delany (Mary Granville) A Memoir, 1700–1788* (London, Grant Richards, 1900).

Payne, J. P., 'On the Resuscitation of the Apparently Dead: A Historical Account', *Annals of the Royal College of Surgeons*, 45 (1969), 98–107.

Pelling, M., *Cholera, Fever and English Medicine 1825–1865* (Oxford, Oxford University Press, 1978).

———, and Webster, C., 'Medical Practitioners', in C. Webster (ed.), *Health, Medicine and Mortality in the Sixteenth-Century* (Cambridge, Cambridge University Press, 1979), 165–235.

———, 'Medicine Since 1500', in P. Corsi and P. Weindling (eds), *Information Sources in the History of Science and Medicine* (London, Butterworth Scientific, 1983), 379–407.

———, 'Old People and Poverty in Early Modern Towns', *Bulletin of the Society for the Social History of Medicine*, 34 (1984), 42–7.

———, 'Healing the Sick Poor: Social Policy and Disability in Norwich, 1500–1640', *Medical History*, 29 (1985), 115–37.

———, 'Appearance and Reality: Barber-Surgeons, the Body and Disease', in A. L. Beier and R. Finlay (eds), *London 1500–1700: The Making of the Metropolis* (New York, Longman, 1986), 82–112.

———, 'Medical Practice in Early Modern England: Trade or Profession?', in W. Prest (ed.), *The Professions in Early Modern England* (London, Croom Helm, 1987), 90–128.

Penn, W., *Letter to His Wife and Children* (London, Tract Association of the Society of Friends, 1882).

Perrin, Noel, *Dr Bowdler's Legacy* (New York, Atheneum, 1969).

Peterson, D., 'Literature of Madness: Autobiographical Writings by Mad People and Mental Patients in England and America from 1436–1975' (Stanford University, Ph.D. Thesis, 1977).

Pettit, H. (ed.), *The Correspondence of Edward Young, 1683–1765* (Oxford, Clarendon Press, 1971).

Plot, R., *The Natural History of Oxfordshire, Being An Essay Towards Natural History of England* (London, Millers, 1677).

Polhemus, T. (ed.), *Social Aspects of the Human Body* (Harmondsworth, Penguin, 1978).

Pollock, L. A., *Forgotten Children. Parent-Child Relations from 1500 to 1900* (Cambridge, Cambridge University Press, 1983).

———, *A Lasting Relationship. Parents and Children Over Three Centuries* (London, Fourth Estate, 1987).

Ponsonby, A. (ed.), *More English Diaries* (London, Methuen, 1927).

Ponsonby, D. A., *Call a Dog Hervey* (London, Hutchinson, 1949).

Porter, D. (See also Watkins, D.).

Porter, D., and Porter R., 'What Was Social Medicine? A Historiographical Essay', *Journal of Historical Sociology*, 1 (1988), 90–106.

———, and Porter, R., *Patient's Progress. The Dialectics of Doctoring in Eighteenth-Century England* (Cambridge, Polity Press, 1989).

Porter, R., 'The Enlightenment in England', in R. Porter and M. Teich (eds), *The Enlightenment in National Context* (Cambridge, Cambridge University Press, 1981), 1–18.

————, 'Was There a Medical Enlightenment in Eighteenth-Century England?', *British Journal for Eighteenth-Century Studies*, 5 (1982), 46–63.

————, *English Society in the Eighteenth Century* (Harmondsworth, Penguin, 1982).

————, 'The Sexual Politics of James Graham', *British Journal for Eighteenth-Century Studies*, 5 (1982), 201–6.

————, 'Sex and the Singular Man: the Seminal Ideas of James Graham', *Studies on Voltaire and the Eighteenth-Century*, 228 (1984), 1–24.

————, 'Spreading Carnal Knowledge or Selling Dirt Cheap? Nicholas Venette's *Conjugal Love* in the Eighteenth-Century', *Journal of European Studies*, 14 (1984), 233–55.

————, 'Against the Spleen', in V. G. Myer (ed.), *Laurence Sterne: Riddles and Mysteries* (London and New York, Vision Press, 1984), 84–99.

————, 'Lay Medical Knowledge in the Eighteenth Century: the Evidence of the *Gentleman's Magazine*', *Medical History*, 29 (1985), 138–68.

————, 'The Patient's View: Doing Medical History from Below', *Theory and Society*, 14 (1985), 175–98.

————, 'The Hunger of Imagination: Approaching Samuel Johnson's Melancholy', in W. F. Bynum, R. Porter and M. Shepherd (eds), *The Anatomy of Madness*, 2 vols (London, Tavistock, 1985), I, 63–88.

————, 'The Drinking Man's Disease:' 'The Prehistory of Alcoholism in Georgian Britain', *British Journal of Addiction*, 80 (1985), 384–96.

————, ' "Under the Influence": Mesmerism in England', *History Today* (September 1985), 22–9.

————, 'Laymen, Doctors and Medical Knowledge in the Eighteenth Century: The Evidence of the *Gentleman's Magazine*', in R. Porter (ed.), *Patients and Practitioners* (Cambridge, Cambridge University Press, 1985), 283–314.

————, (ed.), *Patients and Practitioners. Lay Perceptions of Medicine in Pre-Industrial Society* (Cambridge, Cambridge University Press, 1985).

————, 'Making Faces: Physiognomy and Fashion in Eighteenth-Century England', *Etudes Anglaises*, 38 (1985), 385–96.

————, 'Medicine and the Decline of Magic', *Strawberry Fayre* (Autumn, 1986), 88–94.

————, 'Love, Sex and Madness in Eighteenth-Century England', *Social Research*, 53 (1986), 212–42.

————, ' "I Think Ye Both Quacks": The Controversy Between Dr Theodor Myersbach and Dr John Coakley Lettsom', in W. F. Bynum and R. Porter (eds), *Medical Fringe and Medical Orthodoxy 1750–1850* (London, Croom Helm, 1987), 56–78.

————, 'Monsters and Madmen in Eighteenth-Century France', in D. Fletcher (ed.), *The Monstrous* (Durham, Durham French Colloquies, Number 1, 1987), 83–103.

———— 'Medicine and Religion in Eighteenth-Century England: A Case of Conflict?', *Ideas and Production*, 7 (1987), 4–17.

————, ' "The Secrets of Generation Display'd": *Aristotle's Masterpiece* in Eighteenth-Century England', in R. P. Maccubbin (ed.), *'Tis Nature's Fault. Unauthorised Sexuality During the Enlightenment* (Cambridge, Cambridge University Press, 1987), 7–21.

————, 'The Language of Quackery in England, 1660–1800', in P. Burke and R. Porter (eds), *The Social History of Language* (Cambridge, Cambridge University Press, 1987), 73–103.

————, *Mind-Forg'd Manacles. A History of Madness from the Restoration to the Regency* (London, Athlone, 1987).

————, *A Social History of Madness. Stories of the Insane* (London, Weidenfeld & Nicolson, 1987).

————, 'A Touch of Danger: The Man-Midwife as Sexual Predator', in G. S. Rousseau and R. Porter (eds), *Sexual Underworlds of the Enlightenment* (Manchester, Manchester University Press, 1988), 206–32.

————, 'Seeing the Past', *Past and Present*, 118 (1988), 186–205.

————, 'Newspapers as Resources for Social Historians', in E. Johansson (ed.), *Newspapers and the Press* (London, British Library, 1988).

————, *Edward Gibbon* (London, Weidenfeld & Nicolson, 1988).

————, 'Libertinism in the Enlightenment', in J. Miller (ed.), *Don Giovanni* (London, Faber, forthcoming).

————, 'Body Politics: Approaches to the Cultural History of the Body', in P. Burke (ed.), *Historiography Today* (Cambridge, Polity Press, forthcoming).

————, 'Bodies of Thought: Thoughts About the Body in Eighteenth Century England', in J. Pittock and A. Wear (eds), *Interpretations in Cultural History* (Princeton, Princeton University Press, forthcoming).

————, 'Barely Touching', in G. Rousseau (ed.), *Mind and Body in the Enlightenment* (Los Angeles, University of California Press, forthcoming).

————, 'The Gift Relation: Philanthropy and Provincial Hospitals in Eighteenth Century England', in L. Granshaw and R. Porter (eds), *Hospitals in History* (London, Routledge, forthcoming).

————, 'The Patient in Eighteenth-Century England', in A. Wear (ed.), *History of Medicine in Society* (Cambridge, Cambridge University Press, forthcoming).

————, 'Quacks at Court', in W. F. Bynum and V. Nutton (eds), *Medicine at the Royal Court* (London, Routledge, forthcoming).

————, 'Death and the Doctors in Georgian England', in R. Houlbrook (ed.), *The Social History of Death* (London, Longmans, forthcoming).

————, *Health for Sale: Quack Medicine in Eighteenth-Century England* (Manchester, Manchester University Press, forthcoming).

————, 'Brunonian Psychiatry', in W. F. Bynum and R. Porter (eds), *John Brown and Brunonianism* (*Medical History*, Supplement No. 8, forthcoming).

————, 'The Rise of the Physical Examination', in W. F. Bynum and R. Porter (eds), *Medicine and the Five Senses* (Cambridge, Cambridge University Press, forthcoming).

————, 'Cleaning up the Great Wen', in W. F. Bynum (ed.), *Living and Dying in London* (London, Routledge, forthcoming).

———— (ed.), 'Introduction' to Thomas Trotter, *An Essay on Drunkenness* (London, Routledge Reprint, forthcoming; 1st edition, 1804).

———— (ed.), 'Introduction' to George Cheyne, *The English Malady* (London, Routledge Reprint, forthcoming; 1st edition, 1734).

———— (ed.), 'Introduction' to John Haslam, *Illustrations of Madness* (London, Routledge Reprint, forthcoming; 1st edition, 1810).

Pottle, F. A. (ed.), *Boswell's London Journal* (London, Heineman, 1951).

————, *James Boswell; The Earlier Years 1740–1769* (London, Heinemann, 1966).

Poynter, F. N. L. (ed.), *The Journal of James Yonge [1647–1721] Plymouth Surgeon* (London, Longmans, 1963).

Poynter, J. R. *Society and Pauperism* (London, Routledge & Kegan Paul, 1969).

Praz, M., *The Romantic Agony* (London, Oxford University Press, 1951).

Prentiss, E., *The Life and Letters of Elizabeth Prentiss* (London, Hodder & Stoughton, 1882).

Present for a Servant-Maid (Dublin, George Faulkner, 1743).

Price, S. R. F., 'The Future of Dreams: From Freud to Artemidorus', *Past and Present*, 113 (1986), 3–37.

Prior, M., *Women in English Society* (London, Methuen, 1985).

Quennell, P. (ed.), *The Private Letters of Princess Lieven to Prince Metternich, 1820–1826* (London, John Murray, 1937).

Quincy, J., *Lexicon Physico-Medicum; or A New Physical Dictionary* (London, A. Bell, 1719).

Quinton, J., *A Treatise of Warm Bath Water* (London, n.p., 1733).

Rainnie, D. W. (ed.), *Remarks and Collections of Thomas Hearne*, vol. IV (Oxford, Clarendon Press, 1898).

Randolph, S. N. (ed.), *The Domestic Life of Thomas Jefferson Compiled from Family Letters and Reminiscences* (Cambridge, Mass., Harvard University Press, 1939).

Raphael, F., *Byron* (London, Thames & Hudson, 1982).

Rathborne, Mrs Ambrose (ed.), *The Letters of Lady Jane Coke to Her Friend Mrs Eyre at Derby 1747–1758* (London, Swan Sonnenschein, 1899).

Rather, L., 'Old and New Views of the Emotions and Bodily Changes', *Clio Medica*, 1 (1965), 1–25.

————, *Mind and Body in Eighteenth-Century Medicine* (London, Wellcome Historical Medical Library, 1965).

————, 'The "Six Things Non-Natural": a Note on the Origins and Fate of a Doctrine and a Phrase', *Clio Medica*, 3 (1968), 337–47.

Ray, J., *The Deaths of the Kings of England* (London, Sherratt & Hughes, 1913).

Raymond, J. (ed.), *The Reminiscences of Captain Gronow. Being Anecdotes of the Camp, Court, Clubs and Society, 1810–1860* (London, Bodley Head, 1964).

Razzell, P., *The Conquest of Smallpox* (Firle, Caliban Books, 1977).

Rees, G., *Francis Bacon's Natural Philosophy: A New Source* (Chalfont St Giles, British Society for the History of Science, 1984).

Reeve, H. (ed.), *The Greville Memoirs: a Journal of the Reigns of King George IV and King William IV by the Late Charles C. F. Greville*, 3 vols (London, Longmans, Green, 1875).

Reich, W., *Character Analysis* (London, Vision, 1958).

Reiser, S. J., *Medicine and the Reign of Technology* (Cambridge, Cambridge University Press, 1978).

Richardson, R., 'Old People's Attitudes to Death in the Twentieth Century', *Bulletin of the Society for the Social History of Medicine*, 34 (1984), 48–51.

————, *Death, Dissection and the Destitute: A Political History of the Human Corpse* (London, Routledge & Kegan Paul, 1987).

————, and Hurwitz, B., 'Jeremy Bentham's Self Image: an Exemplary Bequest for Dissection', *British Medical Journal*, 18 July 1987, 195–7.

Richardson, S., *Familiar Letters on Important Occasions*, ed. B. W. Downs (London, Routledge, 1928, 1st edn, 1741).

Riesse, W., *The Conception of Disease. Its History, Its Versions and Its Nature* (New York, Philosophical Library, 1953).

Riley, J. C., *The Eighteenth Century Campaign to Avoid Disease* (Basingstoke, Macmillan, 1987).

Risse, G., 'Doctor William Cullen, Physician, Edinburgh: A Consultation Practice in the Eighteenth Century', *Bulletin of the History of Medicine*, 48 (1974), 338–51.

———, 'Health and Disease: History of the Concepts', in W. T. Reich (ed.), *Encyclopedia of Bioethics*, 2 vols (New York, Free Press, 1978), 579–85.

———, '"Typhus" Fever in Eighteenth-Century Hospitals: New Approaches to Medical Treatment', *Bulletin of the History of Medicine*, 59 (1985), 176–95.

———, *Hospital Life in Enlightenment Scotland: Care and Teaching at the Royal Infirmary of Edinburgh* (Cambridge, Cambridge University Press, 1986).

———, 'Hospital History: New Sources and Methods', in R. Porter and A. Wear (eds), *Problems and Methods in the History of Medicine, 1750–1850* (London, Croom Helm, 1987), 175–203.

Robinson, E. (ed.), *John Clare's Autobiographical Writings* (Oxford, Oxford University Press, 1983).

———, and McKie, D. (eds), *Partners in Science. Letters of James Watt and Joseph Black* (London, Constable, 1970).

Robinson, H. W., and Adams, W. (eds), *The Diary of Robert Hooke (1672–1680)* (London, Taylor & Francis, 1935).

Robinson, L., *Every Patient His Own Doctor; or, The Sick Man's Triumph Over Death and the Grave* (London, J. Cooke, 1778).

Robinson, N., *The Theory of Physick* (London, Betteworth, 1729).

Rodgers, J., 'Ideas of Life in "Tristram Shandy"' (University of East Anglia, Ph.D. Thesis, 1978).

Roe. F. G. *The Georgian Child* (London, Phoenix House, 1961).

Rogers, P., 'The Rise and Fall of Gout', *Times Literary Supplement* (20 March 1981), 315–6.

———, *Eighteenth Century Encounters* (Brighton, Harvester Press, 1985).

Rolleston, Sir H. D., 'Samuel Johnson's Medical Experiences', *Annals of Medical History*, New Series, 1 (1929), 540–52.

———, *The Cambridge Medical School. A Biographical History* (Cambridge, Cambridge University Press, 1932).

[Rolleston, S.], *A Philosophical Dialogue Concerning Decency* (London, James Fletcher and J. and J. Rivington, 1751).

Romanell, P., *John Locke and Medicine: A New Key to Locke* (New York, Prometheus Books, 1984).

Rosen, G., 'An Eighteenth-Century Plan for a National Health Service', *Bulletin of the History of Medicine*, 16 (1944), 429–36.

———, 'What is Social Medicine? A Genetic Analysis of the Concept', ibid., 21 (1947), 674–733.

———, *A History of Public Health* (New York, MD Publications, 1958).

———, *From Medical Police to Social Medicine* (New York, Science History Publications, 1974).

Rosenberg, C., 'The Therapeutic Revolution: Medicine, Meaning and Social Change in Nineteenth-Century America', in C. Rosenberg and M. J. Vogel (eds), *The Therapeutic Revolution: Essays in the Social History of American Medicine* (Philadelphia, University of Pennsylvania Press, 1979), 3–25.

————, 'Medical Text and Medical Context; Explaining William Buchan's *Domestic Medicine*', *Bulletin of the History of Medicine*, 57 (1983), 22–24.

Rousseau, G. S., 'John Wesley's *Primitive Physick* (1747)', *Harvard Library Bulletin*, 16 (1968), 242–56.

————, 'Science and the Discovery of the Imagination in Enlightenment England', *Eighteenth-Century Studies*, 3 (1969–70), 108–35.

————, 'Nerves, Spirits and Fibres: Towards Defining the Origins of Sensibility; with a Postscript', *The Blue Guitar*, 2 (1976), 125–53.

————, 'Science and Literature, the State of the Art', *Isis*, 69 (1978), 583–91.

————, 'Psychology', in G. S. Rousseau and R. Porter (eds), *The Ferment of Knowledge* (Cambridge, Cambridge University Press, 1980), 143–210.

————, 'Literature and Medicine: the State of the Field', *Isis*, 72 (1981), 406–24.

————, *Tobias Smollett. Essays of Two Decades* (Edinburgh, T. & T. Clark, 1982).

————, and Porter, R. (eds), *Sexual Underworlds of the Enlightenment* (Manchester, Manchester University Press, 1988).

Rush, B., *Medical Inquiries and Observations upon Diseases of the Mind* (New York, Hafner Reprint, 1962; 1st edn, 1812).

Ryskamp, C., and Pottle, F. A.(eds), *Boswell. The Ominous Years* (London, Heinemann, 1963).

Sacks, O., *A Leg to Stand On* (London, Duckworth, 1984).

————, *The Man Who Mistook His Wife for a Hat* (London, Duckworth, 1985).

Sampson, A. and Sampson, S., *The Oxford Book of Ages* (Oxford, Oxford University Press, 1985).

Saunders, P. L. L., *Edward Jenner; The Cheltenham Years, 1795–1823* (London, University Press of New England, 1982).

Sawyer, R. C., 'Health, Disease, and Healing in the Southeast Midlands, 1597–1634' (University of Wisconsin, Madison, Ph.D. Thesis, 1986).

Scarry, E., *The Body in Pain* (Oxford, Oxford University Press, 1985).

Schnorrenberg, B. B., 'Is Childbirth any Place for a Woman? The Decline of Midwifery in Eighteenth Century England', *Studies in Eighteenth Century Culture*, 10 (1981), 393–408.

————, 'Medical Men of Bath', *Studies in Eighteenth Century Culture*, 13 (1984), 189–203.

Schrank, B. G. and Supino, D. (eds), *The Famous Miss Burney* (New York, John Day, 1976).

Schwarz, W., *Daily Life in Johnson's London* (Madison, University of Wisconsin Press, 1983).

Sears, E., *The Ages of Man. Medieval Interpretations of the Life Cycle* (Princeton, Princeton University Press, 1986).

Seaton, T., *The Conduct of Servants in Great Families* (London, Tim Goodwin, 1720).

Seaver, P. S., *Wallington's World: A Puritan Artisan in Seventeenth-Century London* (London, Methuen, 1985).

Sedgwick, R. (ed.), *Lord Hervey's Memoirs* (London, Kimber, 1952).

Sekora, J., *Luxury: The Concept in Western Thought, Eden to Smollett* (Baltimore and London, Johns Hopkins University Press, 1977).

Sells, A. L., and Sells, I. L., *Thomas Gray: His Life and Works* (London, Allen & Unwin, 1980).

Senate, E., *The Medical Monitor* (London, the author, 1810).

Severn, C. (ed.), *Diary of the Rev. John Ward* (London, Colburn, 1839).

Seymour, J.-S. [i.e., John Hill], *On the Management and Education of Children* (London, Baldwin, 1754).

Sheils, W. (ed.), *The Church and Healing* (Oxford, Basil Blackwell, 1982).

Sherlock, W., *A Practical Discourse Concerning Death* (London, W. Rogers, 1690).

Sherson, E., *The Lively Lady Townshend and Her Friends* (London, William Heinemann, 1926).

Shorter, E., *A History of Women's Bodies* (Harmondsworth, Penguin, 1983).

——, *Bedside Manners: The Troubled History of Doctors and Patients* (New York, Simon & Schuster, 1986).

——, 'Paralysis: The Rise and Fall of a "Hysterical Symptom"', *Journal of Social History*, 19 (1986), 549–82.

Shortland, M., 'The Body in Question; Some Perceptions, Problems and Perspectives of the Body in Relation to Character, c. 1750–1850' (Ph.D. thesis, University of Leeds, 1985).

——, 'Skin Deep: Barthes, Lavater and the Visible Body', *Economy and Society*, 14 (1985), 273–312.

——, 'The Figure of the Hypocrite: Some Contours of an Historical Problem', *Studies in the History of Psychology and the Social Sciences*, 4 (1987), 256–74.

Showalter, E., *The Female Malady: Women, Madness, and English Culture, 1830–1980* (New York, Pantheon Press, 1986).

Sibly, E., *The Medical Mirror; or, Treatise on the Impregnation of the Human Female. Shewing the Origin of Diseases, and the Principles of Life and Death* (London, n.p., 1794).

Siebert, D. T., 'Swift's Fiat Odor: The Excremental Re-Vision', *Eighteenth-Century Studies*, 19 (1985), 21–38.

Silverman, K., *The Life and Times of Cotton Mather* (New York, Harper & Row, 1984).

Simpson, J., *The Journal of Dr John Simpson of Bradford, 1825* (Bradford, Metropolitan Bradford Libraries, 1981).

Skultans, V., *Madness and Morals: Ideas on Insanity in the Nineteenth Century* (London and Boston, Routledge & Kegan Paul, 1975).

——, *English Madness. Ideas on Insanity 1580–1890* (London, Routledge & Kegan Paul, 1979).

Slack, P., 'Mirrors of Health and Treasures of Poor Men: Uses of the Vernacular Medical Literature of Tudor England', in C. Webster (ed.), *Health, Medicine and Mortality in the Sixteenth Century* (Cambridge, Cambridge University Press, 1979), 237–74.

——, 'Books of Orders: The Making of English Social Policy, 1577–1631', *Transactions of the Royal Historical Society*, 5th series, 30 (1980), 1–22.

——, *The Impact of Plague in Tudor and Stuart England* (London, Routledge & Kegan Paul, 1985).

Smith, A., *The Theory of Moral Sentiments* (London, H. G. Bohn, 1853).

Smith, D. C., 'Medical Science, Medical Practice, and the Emerging Concept of Typhus in Mid-Eighteenth-Century Britain', in W. F. Bynum and V. Nutton (eds), *Theories of Fever from Antiquity to the Enlightenment* (London, Medical History Supplement no. 1, London Wellcome Institute for the History of Medicine, 1981), 121–34.

Smith, E., *The Compleat Housewife*, 3rd ed. (London, J. Pemberton, 1729).

Smith, F. B., *The Retreat of Tuberculosis 1850–1950* (London, Croom Helm, 1988).

Smith, G., 'Thomas Tryon's Regimen for Women: Sectarian Health in the Seventeenth Century', in London Feminist History Group (eds), *The Sexual Dynamics of History* (London, Pluto Press, 1983), 47–65.

————, 'The Physiology of Air: Eighteenth-Century Fever Therapy in the Advice Literature', *Bulletin of the Society for the Social History of Medicine*, 35 (1984), 21.

————, 'Prescribing the Rules of Health: Self-Help and Advice in the Late Eighteenth-Century England', in Roy Porter (ed.), *Patients and Practitioners: Lay Perceptions of Medicine in Pre-industrial Society* (Cambridge and New York, Cambridge University Press, 1985), 249–82.

————, *see also*: V. S. Smith.

Smith, G. C. Moore (ed.), *The Letters of Dorothy Osborne to Sir William Temple* (Oxford, Clarendon Press, 1968).

Smith, H., *The Family Physician* (London, J. Harrison, 1770).

Smith, J. R., *The Speckled Monster. Smallpox in England 1670–1970, with Particular Reference to Essex* (Chelmsford, Essex Record Office, 1987).

Smith, N. C. (ed.), *Selected Letters of Sydney Smith* (Oxford, Oxford University Press, 1981).

Smith, R., *Trial by Medicine. Insanity and Responsibility in Victorian Trials* (Edinburgh, Edinburgh University Press, 1981).

Smith, V. S., 'Cleanliness: the Development of an Idea and Practice in Britain 1770–1850' (University of London, Ph.D. Thesis, 1985).

————, 'Physical Puritanism and Sanitary Science: Material and Immaterial Beliefs in Popular Physiology 1650–1840', in W. F. Bynum and R. Porter (eds), *Medical Fringe and Medical Orthodoxy* (London, Croom Helm, 1986), 174–97.

Smith, W., *A Dissertation Upon the Nerves* (London, W. Owen, 1768).

————, *Nature Studied with a View to Preserve and Restore Health* (London, W. Owen, 1774).

————, *A Sure Guide in Sickness and Health* (London, J. Bew & J. Walter, 1776).

Smithers, P., *The Life of Joseph Addison* (Oxford, Clarendon Press, 1968).

Smollett, T., *The Life and Adventures of Sir Launcelot Greaves*, ed. by D. Evans (London, Oxford University Press, 1973).

————, *The Expedition of Humphry Clinker*, ed. by A. Ross (Harmondsworth, Penguin, 1982).

Smythson, H., *The Compleat Family Physician* (London, Harrison, 1781).

Solomon, S., *Guide and Health, or, Advice to Both Sexes in a Variety of Complaints*, 2nd ed. (Stockport, the author, c. 1800).

Sontag, S., *Illness as Metaphor* (New York, Farrar, Straus & Giroux, 1978; London, Allen Lane, 1979).

Sorlien, R. P. (ed.), *The Diary of John Manningham* (New Hampshire, University Press of New England, 1976).

Spacks, P. M., *Imagining a Self* (Cambridge, Mass., Harvard University Press, 1976).

————, *The Adolescent Idea* (London, Faber & Faber, 1982).

Spillane, J., *The Doctrine of the Nerves* (London, Oxford University Press, 1981).

————, *Medical Travellers* (Oxford, Oxford University Press, 1984).

Spinckes, N., *The Sick Man Visited; or Meditations and Prayers for the Sick Room* (London, Freeman, 1712).

Sprigge, T. L. S. (ed.), *The Correspondence of Jeremy Bentham*, 5 vols (London, Athlone, 1968–81).

Sprott, D. (ed.), *1784* (London, Allen & Unwin, 1984).

Sprott, S. E., *The English Debate on Suicide from Donne to Hume* (La Salle, Illinois, Open Court, 1961).

Squirrell, R., *Maxims of Health or an Abridgement of an Essay on Indigestion* (London, Murray & Highley, 1798).

Stanhope, Earl, *Life of the Right Honourable William Pitt*, 4 vols (London, John Murray, 1867).

Stannard, D. E., *The Puritan Way of Death: A Study in Religion, Culture and Social Change* (New York and Oxford, Oxford University Press, 1977).

Stansfield, D. A., *Thomas Beddoes M. D. 1760–1808, Chemist, Physician, Democrat* (Lancaster, Reidel, 1984).

Starobinski, J., 'The Body's Moment', *Montaigne: Essays in Reading* (Yale French Studies, no. 64, 1983), 273–305.

Staum, M. S., and Larsen, D. E. (eds), *Doctors, Patients and Society: Power and Authority in Medical Care* (Ontario, Waterloo, The Calgary Institute of the Humanities, 1981).

Stedman, J., *The Journal of John Gabriel Stedman*, ed. by T. Stanbury, (London, Mitre Press, 1962).

Stein, D., *Ada. A Life and Legacy* (Cambridge Mass., M.I.T. Press, 1985).

Steneck, N., 'Greatrakes the Stroker: The Interpretations of Historians', *Isis*, 73 (1982), 160–77.

Stengers, J., and Van Neck, A., *Histoire d'une Grande Peur: La Masturbation* (Brussels, University of Brussels Press, 1984).

Sterne, L., *The Life and Opinions of Tristram Shandy*, ed. C. Ricks (Harmondsworth, Penguin, 1967).

————, *Journal to Eliza*, ed. E. Rhys (London, Dent, 1937).

Stevenson, L., '"New Diseases" in the Seventeenth Century', *Bulletin of the History of Medicine*, 39 (1965), 1–21.

Stock, R. D., *The Holy and the Daemonic from Sir Thomas Browne to William Blake* (Princeton, N. J., Princeton University Press, 1982).

Stone, L., *The Family, Sex and Marriage in England 1500–1800* (London, Weidenfeld & Nicolson, 1977).

Stonhouse G., *Friendly Advice to a Patient* (London, C. Rivington, 1769).

Stott, R., 'The Medical Practice of George Chalmers, M.D.', *Archivaria*, 10 (1980), 51–67.

Supple, B., *The Royal Exchange Assurance: A History of British Insurance 1720–1970* (Cambridge, Cambridge University Press, 1970).

Swift, J., *Journal to Stella, see* Williams, H. (ed.).

Szasz, T., *Pain and Pleasure. A Study of Bodily Feelings* (London, Tavistock Publications, 1957).
————, *The Myth of Mental Illness* (New York, Paladin, 1961).
Talon, H. (ed.), *Selections from the Journals and Papers of John Byrom, Poet – Diarist – Shorthand Writer* (London, Rockliff, 1950).
Taylor, James Spottiswoode, *Montaigne and Medicine* (London, Humphrey Milford, 1922).
Taylor, John, *Records of My Life* (New York, J. & J. Harper, 1833).
Temkin, O., *The Falling Sickness; a History of Epilepsy from the Greeks to the Beginnings of Modern Neurology* (Baltimore, Johns Hopkins University Press, 1945).
————, *Galenism: Rise and Decline of Medical Philosophy* (Ithaca, Cornell University Press, 1973).
————, 'Health and Disease', in P. Wiener (ed.), *Dictionary of the History of Ideas* (New York, Scribner's, 1973), II, 395–407.
————, 'An Historical Analysis of the Concept of Infection', in *The Double Face of Janus and Other Essays in the History of Medicine* (Baltimore and London, Johns Hopkins University Press, 1977), 456–71.
Thale, M. (ed.), *The Autobiography of Francis Place (1771–1854)* (Cambridge, Cambridge University Press, 1972).
Thane, P., 'The Perception and Experience of Old Age 1945–1965', *Bulletin of the Society for the Social History of Medicine*, 34 (1984), 52–5.
Thicknesse, P., *Valetudinarian's Bath Guide* (London, Dodsley, 1780).
Thomas, E. G., 'The Old Poor Law and Medicine', *Medical History*, 24 (1980), 1–19.
Thomas, K., *Religion and the Decline of Magic: Studies in Popular Beliefs in Sixteenth- and Seventeenth-Century England* (London, Weidenfeld & Nicolson, 1971; reprinted, Harmondsworth/New York, Penguin, 1978).
————, *Man and the Natural World* (Harmondsworth, Penguin, 1984).
Thompson, S. (ed.), *Stedman's Journal, 1744–1797* (London, Mitre Press, 1962).
Thompson, W., *Sickness* (London, R. Dodsley, 1745).
Thomson, G. S. (ed.), *Letters of a Grandmother 1732–1735: Being the Correspondence of Sarah Duchess of Marlborough with her Granddaughter Diana, Duchess of Bedford* (London, Jonathan Cape, 1943).
Tibble, J. W., and Tibble, A. (eds), *The Prose of John Clare* (London, Routledge & Kegan Paul, 1951).
Tilley, M. P. (ed.), *Dictionary of Proverbs in England* (Ann Arbor, University of Michigan Press, 1950).
Timbs, J., *Doctors and Patients; or Anecdotes of the Medical World and Curiosities of Medicine* (London, Bentley, 1876).
Tissot, S-A. A. D., *Onanism or a Treatise Upon the Disorders Produced by Masturbation*, trans. by A. Hume (London, n.p., 1766).
Todd, J., *Sensibility* (London, Methuen, 1986).
Tomalin, C. (ed.), *Life and Death of Mary Wollstonecraft* (London, Weidenfield & Nicolson, 1974).
Tomaselli, S., 'The First Person: Descartes, Locke and Mind-Body Dualism', *History of Science*, 22 (1984), 185–205.
Townsend, J., *Guide to Health* (London, Cox, etc., 1795).
Toynbee, P., and Whibley, L. (eds.), *Correspondence of Thomas Gray*, 3 vols

(Oxford, Clarendon Press, 1971).

Toynbee, Mrs Paget (ed.), *The Letters of Horace Walpole*, 16 vols (Oxford, Clarendon Press, 1903–25).

Toynbee, W. (ed.), *Diaries of William Charles Macready* (London, Chapman & Hall, 1912).

Trials for Adultery: or the History of Divorces. Being Select Trials at Doctors Commons for Adultery, Cruelty, Fornication, Impotence etc., 7 vols (London, Bladon, 1774–80).

Trillat, E., *Histoire de l'Hystérie* (Paris, Seghers, 1986).

Trimmer, E. J., 'Medical Folklore and Quackery', *Folklore*, 20 (1965), 161–75.

————, *Rejuvenation: The History of An Idea* (London, Hale, 1967).

Trotter, T., *An Essay, Medical, Philosophical and Chemical on Drunkenness* (London, Longmans, 1804).

————, *A View of the Nervous Temperament* (London, Longman, Hurst, Rees & Owen, 1807).

Trumbach, R., *The Rise of the Egalitarian Family* (London and New York, Academic Press, 1978).

Turner, B. S., *The Body and Society: Explorations in Social Theory* (Oxford and New York, Blackwell, 1984).

————, *Medical Power and Social Knowledge* (London, Sage Publications, 1987).

Turner, E. S., *Call The Doctor, A Social History of Medical Men* (London, Michael Joseph, 1958).

————, *Taking The Cure* (London, Quality Book Club, 1967).

Turner, J. H. (ed.), *The Rev. Oliver Heywood B. A. 1630–1702. His Autobiographical Diaries, Anecdote and Event Books*, 4 vols (Brighouse and Bingley, T. Harrison, 1881–5).

Tuveson, E. L., *Imagination as a Means of Grace* (Berkeley, University of California Press, 1960).

Tytler, G., *Physiognomy in the European Novel* (Princeton, Princeton University Press, 1982).

Vaisey, D. (ed.), *The Diary of Thomas Turner* (Oxford, Oxford University Press, 1984).

Veith, I., *Hysteria* (Chicago, Chicago University Press, 1965).

Verney, Lady F. P., and Verney Lady M. M., *Memoirs of The Verney Family*, 4 vols (London, Tabard, 1970).

Verney, Lady M. M. (ed.), *Verney Letters of the Eighteenth Century from the MSS at Clayton House*, 2 vols (London, Ernest Benn, 1930).

Versluysen, M. C., 'Midwives, Medical Men and "Poor Women Labouring of Child": Lying-in Hospitals in Eighteenth Century London', in H. Roberts (ed.), *Women, Health and Reproduction* (London, Routledge & Kegan Paul, 1981), 18–49.

Viets, H. R. 'George Cheyne, 1673–1743', *Bulletin of the Institute for the History of Medicine*, 23 (1949), 435–52.

Vigarello, G., *Le Corps Redressé: Histoire d'un Pouvoir Pédagogique* (Paris, J. P. Delarge, 1978).

Vovelle, M., *Piété Baroque et Déchristianisation au XVIIIe Siècle: Les Attitudes Devant la Mort d'après les Clauses des Testaments* (Paris, Editions du Seuil, 1978).

————, *La Mort et l'Occident de 1300 à Nos Jours* (Paris, Editions Gallimard, 1983).

————, and Vovelle, G., *La Vision de la Mort et de l'Au-delà en Provence Après les Autels des Ames du Purgatoire XVe – XXe Siècles* (Paris, A. Colin, 1970).

Wagner, P., 'The Veil of Science and Morality: Some Pornographic Aspects of the ONANIA', *British Journal for Eighteenth-Century Studies*, 4 (1983), 179–84.

————, *Eros Revived: Erotica of the Enlightenment in England and America* (London, Secker & Warburg, 1988).

Wain, J., *Samuel Johnson* (London, Macmillan, 1980).

Walker, D. P., *The Decline of Hell: Seventeenth-Century Discussions of Eternal Torment* (London, Routledge & Kegan Paul, 1964).

————, *Unclean Spirits* (London, Scolar Press, 1980).

Walker, S., *A Treatise on Nervous Diseases* (London, J. Philips, 1796).

Walpole, H., *Memoirs of George II, 1751–1754*, ed. by J. Brooke (New Haven, Yale University Press, 1985).

Ward, N., *The London Spy*, ed. by K. Fenwick (London, Folio Society, 1955).

Wardle, R. M. (ed.), *Collected Letters of Mary Wollstonecraft* (Ithaca, Cornell University Press, 1979).

Warter, J. W. (ed.), *Southey's Common-Place Book* (London, Longman, Brown, Green & Longmans, 1831).

Waterson, M., *The Servants' Hall, a Domestic History of Erddig* (London, Routledge & Kegan Paul, 1980).

Watkins, D. E., 'The English Revolution in Social Medicine, 1889–1911' (University of London, Ph.D. Thesis, 1984).

————, 'Problems and Methods in the History of Medicine', *Bulletin of the Society for the Social History of Medicine*, 36 (1985), 61.

Wear, A., 'Perceptions of Health and the Environment in the Settlement of North America in the Early Seventeenth Century', ibid., 35 (1984), 11–13.

————, 'Puritan Perceptions of Illness in Seventeenth-Century England', in R. Porter (ed.), *Patients and Practitioners* (Cambridge, Cambridge University Press, 1985), 55–99.

————, 'Historical and Cultural Aspects of Pain', *Bulletin of the Society for the Social History of Medicine*, 36 (1985), 7–21.

————, 'Interfaces: Perceptions of Health and Illness in Early Modern England', in R. Porter and A. Wear (eds), *Problems and Methods in the History of Medicine, 1750–1850* (London, Croom Helm, 1987), 230–55.

Webb, R. K., *Harriet Martineau, A Radical Victorian* (London, Heinemann, 1960).

Weber, F. P., *Aspects of Death in Art, Epigram and Poetry* (London, Fisher, Unwin, 1918).

Webster, C. (ed.), *Health, Medicine and Mortality in the Sixteenth Century* (Cambridge, Cambridge University Press, 1979).

Wedgwood, B. and Wedgwood, H., *The Wedgwood Circle* (London, Studio Vista, 1980).

Weekley, M. (ed.), *A Memoir of Thomas Bewick Written by Himself* (London, Cresset Press, 1961).

Weidhorn, M., *Dreams in Seventeenth-Century Literature* (The Hague, Mouton, 1970).

Weis, C. McC., and Pottle, F. A. (eds), *Boswell in Extremes* (London, Heinemann, 1970).

Wesley, J., *Primitive Physick: Or, an Easy and Natural Method of Curing Most Diseases* (London, T. Trye, 1747).

————, *The Desideratum; or Electricity Made Plain and Useful* (Bristol, W. Pine, 1771).

————, *Journal of John Wesley*, 4 vols (London, Dent, n.d).

White, H., *The Record of My Life: An Autobiography* (Cheltenham, the author, 1889).

Whitefield, G., *George Whitefield's Journal* (London, The Banner of Truth Trust, 1960).

Whittier, J. G. (ed.), *The Journal of John Woolman* (Glasgow, Robert Smeal, 1882).

Whorton, J. C., *Crusaders for Fitness: The History of American Health Reformers* (Princeton, Princeton University Press, 1982).

Whyte, L. L., *The Unconscious Before Freud* (New York, Doubleday, 1962).

Wilde, J., *The Hospital. A Poem in Three Books Written in the Devon and Exeter Hospital 1809* (Norwich, Stevenson, Matchett & Stevenson, 1810).

Williams, G., *The Age of Agony: the Art of Healing c.1700–1800* (London, Constable, 1975).

————, *The Age of Miracles: Medicine and Surgery in the Nineteenth Century* (London, Constable, 1981).

Williams, H. (ed.), *Jonathan Swift. Journal to Stella*, 2 vols (Oxford, Clarendon Press, 1948).

Williams, N., *Powder and Paint* (London, Longmans, 1957).

Williamson, G., *The Autobiography of George Williamson, 1782–1854* (London, n.p., 1891).

Williamson, G., 'Mutability, Decay and Seventeenth Century Melancholy', in *idem*, (ed.), *Seventeenth-Century Contexts* (London, Faber & Faber, 1961), 73–101.

Willich, A. F. M., *Lectures on Diet and Regimen* (London, Longman & Rees 1799).

Wilson, A., 'Participant or Patient?', in R. Porter (ed.), *Patients and Practitioners* (Cambridge, Cambridge University Press, 1985), 129–44.

————, 'William Hunter and the Varieties of Man-Midwifery', in W. F. Bynum and R. Porter (eds), *William Hunter and the Eighteenth-Century Medical World* (Cambridge, Cambridge University Press, 1985), 343–69.

Wintrobe, M. M., *Blood, Pure and Eloquent. A Story of Discovery, of People, and of Ideas* (New York, McGraw-Hill, 1980).

Withering, W., *An Account of the Foxglove and its Medical Uses* (Birmingham, Robinson, 1785).

Withers, T., *Observations on Chronic Weakness* (York, Ward & Cadell, 1777).

Woodall, J., *The Surgion's Mate . . .* (London, E. Griffin, 1655; 1st ed., 1617).

Woodforde, J., *The Strange Story of False Teeth* (London, Routledge & Kegan Paul, 1968).

Woods, R., and Woodward, J. (eds), *Urban Disease and Mortality in Nineteenth-Century England* (London, Batsford, 1984).

Woodward, J., *To Do The Sick No Harm. A Study of the British Voluntary Hospital System to 1875* (London and Boston, Routledge & Kegan Paul, 1974).

————, and Richards, D.(eds), *Health Care and Popular Medicine in*

Nineteenth-Century England: Essays in the Social History of Medicine (London, Croom Helm, 1977).

————, 'Towards a Social History of Medicine', in ibid., 15–55.

Woolf, V., 'On Being Ill', in *Collected Essays*, 4 vols, ed. by L. Woolf (London, Chatto & Windus, 1969), IV, 193–203.

Woolman, J., *The Journal and Essays of John Woolman*, ed. A. Gummere (London, Macmillan, 1922).

Wright, L., *Clean and Decent. The Fascinating History of the Bathroom and Water Closet* (London, Routledge & Kegan Paul, 1960).

Wright, P. G. W., 'The Radical Sociology of Medicine', *Social Studies of Science*, 10 (1980), 103–20.

Wrigley, E. A., 'No Death Without Birth: the Implications of English Mortality in the Early Modern Period', in R. Porter and A. Wear (eds), *Problems and Methods in the History of Medicine* (London, Croom Helm, 1987), 133–50.

————, and Schofield, R. S., *The Population History of England 1541–1971: A Reconstruction* (London, Edward Arnold, 1981).

Wyndham, M., *Chronicles of the Eighteenth Century* (London, Hodder and Stoughton, 1924).

Yearsley, M., *Le Roy Est Mort! An Account of the Deaths of the Rulers of England* (London, Unicorn Press, 1935).

Yolton, J., *John Locke and the Way of Ideas* (Oxford, Oxford University Press, 1956).

————, *Thinking Matter. Materialism in Eighteenth Century Britain* (Minneapolis, University of Minnesota Press, 1983).

Yorke, C. (ed.), *The Diary of John Baker, 1751–58* (London, Hutchinson, 1931).

Zuckerman, A., 'Dr Richard Mead (1673–1754): a Biographical Study' (University of Illinois, Ph.D. Thesis, 1965).

Zwanenberg, D. van, 'The Suttons and the Business of Inoculation', *Medical History*, 22 (1978), 71–82.

Index

Main references are in **bold** type